CW00644679

Cambridge English

OFFICIAL

CAMBRIDGE PREPARATION MATERIAL

IELTS 13

ACADEMIC

WITH ANSWERS

AUTHENTIC EXAMINATION PAPERS

Cambridge University Press
www.cambridge.org/elt

Cambridge Assessment English
www.cambridgeenglish.org

Information on this title: www.cambridge.org/9781108450492

© Cambridge University Press and UCLES 2018

It is normally necessary for written permission for copying to be obtained
in advance from a publisher. The sample answer sheets at the back of this
book are designed to be copied and distributed in class.
The normal requirements are waived here and it is not necessary to write to
Cambridge University Press for permission for an individual teacher to make copies
for use within his or her own classroom. Only those pages that carry the wording
'© UCLES 2018 Photocopiable ' may be copied.

First published 2018

20 19 18 17 16 15 14 13 12 11 10 9 8 7 6 5 4 3 2 1

Printed in Malaysia by Vivar Printing

A catalogue record for this publication is available from the British Library

ISBN 978-1-108-45049-2 Academic Student's Book with answers
ISBN 978-1-108-55309-4 Academic Student's Book with answers with Audio
ISBN 978-1-108-45055-3 General Training Student's Book with answers
ISBN 978-1-108-55319-3 General Training Student's Book with answers with Audio
ISBN 978-1-108-45067-6 Audio CDs (2)

The publishers have no responsibility for the persistence or accuracy of URLs
for external or third-party internet websites referred to in this publication, and
do not guarantee that any content on such websites is, or will remain, accurate
or appropriate. Information regarding prices, travel timetables, and other factual
information given in this work is correct at the time of first printing but the
publishers do not guarantee the accuracy of such information thereafter.

Contents

Introduction

The International English Language Testing System (IELTS) is widely recognised as a reliable means of assessing the language ability of candidates who need to study or work where English is the language of communication. These Practice Tests are designed to give future IELTS candidates an idea of whether their English is at the required level.

IELTS is owned by three partners: Cambridge English Language Assessment, part of the University of Cambridge; the British Council; IDP Education Pty Limited (through its subsidiary company, IELTS Australia Pty Limited). Further information on IELTS can be found on the IELTS website www.ielts.org.

WHAT IS THE TEST FORMAT?

IELTS consists of four components. All candidates take the same Listening and Speaking tests. There is a choice of Reading and Writing tests according to whether a candidate is taking the Academic or General Training module.

Academic	General Training
For candidates wishing to study at undergraduate or postgraduate levels, and for those seeking professional registration.	For candidates wishing to migrate to an English-speaking country (Australia, Canada, New Zealand, UK), and for those wishing to train or study at below degree level.

The test components are taken in the following order:

Listening 4 sections, 40 items, approximately 30 minutes		
Academic Reading 3 sections, 40 items 60 minutes	or	**General Training Reading** 3 sections, 40 items 60 minutes
Academic Writing 2 tasks 60 minutes	or	**General Training Writing** 2 tasks 60 minutes
Speaking 11 to 14 minutes		
Total Test Time 2 hours 44 minutes		

ACADEMIC TEST FORMAT

Listening

This test consists of four sections, each with ten questions. The first two sections are concerned with social needs. The first section is a conversation between two speakers and the second section is a monologue. The final two sections are concerned with situations related to educational or training contexts. The third section is a conversation between up to four people and the fourth section is a monologue.

A variety of question types is used, including: multiple choice, matching, plan/map/diagram labelling, form completion, note completion, table completion, flow-chart completion, summary completion, sentence completion and short-answer questions.

Candidates hear the recording once only and answer the questions as they listen. Ten minutes are allowed at the end for candidates to transfer their answers to the answer sheet.

Reading

This test consists of three sections with 40 questions. There are three texts, which are taken from journals, books, magazines and newspapers. The texts are on topics of general interest. At least one text contains detailed logical argument.

A variety of question types is used, including: multiple choice, identifying information (True/False/Not Given), identifying the writer's views/claims (Yes/No/Not Given), matching information, matching headings, matching features, matching sentence endings, sentence completion, summary completion, note completion, table completion, flow-chart completion, diagram label completion and short-answer questions.

Writing

This test consists of two tasks. It is suggested that candidates spend about 20 minutes on Task 1, which requires them to write at least 150 words, and 40 minutes on Task 2, which requires them to write at least 250 words. Task 2 contributes twice as much as Task 1 to the Writing score.

Task 1 requires candidates to look at a diagram or some data (in a graph, table or chart) and to present the information in their own words. They are assessed on their ability to organise, present and possibly compare data, and are required to describe the stages of a process, describe an object or event, or explain how something works.

In Task 2, candidates are presented with a point of view, argument or problem. They are assessed on their ability to present a solution to the problem, present and justify an opinion, compare and contrast evidence and opinions, and to evaluate and challenge ideas, evidence or arguments.

Candidates are also assessed on their ability to write in an appropriate style. More information on assessing the Writing test, including Writing assessment criteria (public version), is available on the IELTS website.

Speaking

This test takes between 11 and 14 minutes and is conducted by a trained examiner.
There are three parts:

Part 1

The candidate and the examiner introduce themselves. Candidates then answer general
questions about themselves, their home/family, their job/studies, their interests and a wide
range of similar familiar topic areas. This part lasts between four and five minutes.

Part 2

The candidate is given a task card with prompts and is asked to talk on a particular topic.
The candidate has one minute to prepare and they can make some notes if they wish,
before speaking for between one and two minutes. The examiner then asks one or two
questions on the same topic.

Part 3

The examiner and the candidate engage in a discussion of more abstract issues which are
thematically linked to the topic in Part 2. The discussion lasts between four and five minutes.

The Speaking test assesses whether candidates can communicate effectively in English.
The assessment takes into account Fluency and Coherence, Lexical Resource, Grammatical
Range and Accuracy, and Pronunciation. More information on assessing the Speaking test,
including Speaking assessment criteria (public version), is available on the IELTS website.

HOW IS IELTS SCORED?

IELTS results are reported on a nine-band scale. In addition to the score for overall language ability, IELTS provides a score in the form of a profile for each of the four skills (Listening, Reading, Writing and Speaking). These scores are also reported on a nine-band scale. All scores are recorded on the Test Report Form along with details of the candidate's nationality, first language and date of birth. Each Overall Band Score corresponds to a descriptive statement which gives a summary of the English language ability of a candidate classified at that level. The nine bands and their descriptive statements are as follows:

9 **Expert User** – *Has fully operational command of the language: appropriate, accurate and fluent with complete understanding.*

8 **Very Good User** – *Has fully operational command of the language with only occasional unsystematic inaccuracies and inappropriacies. Misunderstandings may occur in unfamiliar situations. Handles complex detailed argumentation well.*

7 **Good User** – *Has operational command of the language, though with occasional inaccuracies, inappropriacies and misunderstandings in some situations. Generally handles complex language well and understands detailed reasoning.*

6 **Competent User** – *Has generally effective command of the language despite some inaccuracies, inappropriacies and misunderstandings. Can use and understand fairly complex language, particularly in familiar situations.*

5 **Modest User** – *Has partial command of the language, coping with overall meaning in most situations, though is likely to make many mistakes. Should be able to handle basic communication in own field.*

4 **Limited User** – *Basic competence is limited to familiar situations. Has frequent problems in understanding and expression. Is not able to use complex language.*

3 **Extremely Limited User** – *Conveys and understands only general meaning in very familiar situations. Frequent breakdowns in communication occur.*

2 **Intermittent User** – *No real communication is possible except for the most basic information using isolated words or short formulae in familiar situations and to meet immediate needs. Has great difficulty understanding spoken and written English.*

1 **Non User** – *Essentially has no ability to use the language beyond possibly a few isolated words.*

0 **Did not attempt the test** – *No assessable information provided.*

MARKING THE PRACTICE TESTS

Listening and Reading

The Answer Keys are on pages 118–125.
Each question in the Listening and Reading tests is worth one mark.

Questions which require letter / Roman numeral answers

- For questions where the answers are letters or Roman numerals, you should write *only* the number of answers required. For example, if the answer is a single letter or numeral you should write only one answer. If you have written more letters or numerals than are required, the answer must be marked wrong.

Questions which require answers in the form of words or numbers

- Answers may be written in upper or lower case.
- Words in brackets are *optional* – they are correct, but not necessary.
- Alternative answers are separated by a slash (/).
- If you are asked to write an answer using a certain number of words and/or (a) number(s), you will be penalised if you exceed this. For example, if a question specifies an answer using NO MORE THAN THREE WORDS and the correct answer is 'black leather coat', the answer 'coat of black leather' is *incorrect*.
- In questions where you are expected to complete a gap, you should only transfer the necessary missing word(s) onto the answer sheet. For example, to complete 'in the …', where the correct answer is 'morning', the answer 'in the morning' would be *incorrect*.
- All answers require correct spelling (including words in brackets).
- Both US and UK spelling are acceptable and are included in the Answer Key.
- All standard alternatives for numbers, dates and currencies are acceptable.
- All standard abbreviations are acceptable.
- You will find additional notes about individual answers in the Answer Key.

Writing

The sample answers are on pages 126–135. It is not possible for you to give yourself a mark for the Writing tasks. We have provided sample answers (written by candidates), showing their score and the examiner's comments. These sample answers will give you an insight into what is required for the Writing test.

HOW SHOULD YOU INTERPRET YOUR SCORES?

At the end of each Listening and Reading Answer Key you will find a chart which will help you assess whether, on the basis of your Practice Test results, you are ready to take the IELTS test.

In interpreting your score, there are a number of points you should bear in mind. Your performance in the real IELTS test will be reported in two ways: there will be a Band Score from 1 to 9 for each of the components and an Overall Band Score from 1 to 9, which is the average of your scores in the four components. However, institutions considering your application are advised to look at both the Overall Band Score and the Bands for each component in order to determine whether you have the language skills needed for a particular course of study. For example, if your course involves a lot of reading and writing, but no lectures, listening skills might be less important and a score of 5 in Listening might be acceptable if the Overall Band Score was 7. However, for a course which has lots of lectures and spoken instructions, a score of 5 in Listening might be unacceptable even though the Overall Band Score was 7.

Once you have marked your tests, you should have some idea of whether your listening and reading skills are good enough for you to try the IELTS test. If you did well enough in one component, but not in others, you will have to decide for yourself whether you are ready to take the test.

The Practice Tests have been checked to ensure that they are of approximately the same level of difficulty as the real IELTS test. However, we cannot guarantee that your score in the Practice Tests will be reflected in the real IELTS test. The Practice Tests can only give you an idea of your possible future performance and it is ultimately up to you to make decisions based on your score.

Different institutions accept different IELTS scores for different types of courses. We have based our recommendations on the average scores which the majority of institutions accept. The institution to which you are applying may, of course, require a higher or lower score than most other institutions.

Further information

For more information about IELTS or any other Cambridge English Language Assessment examination, write to:

Cambridge English Language Assessment
1 Hills Road
Cambridge
CB1 2EU
United Kingdom

https://support.cambridgeenglish.org
http://www.ielts.org

Test 1

SECTION 1   *Questions 1–10*

Complete the table below.

Write **ONE WORD AND/OR A NUMBER** *for each answer.*

COOKERY CLASSES

Cookery Class	Focus	Other Information
Example The Food ......*Studio*......	how to **1** .... and cook with seasonal products	• small classes • also offers **2** .... classes • clients who return get a **3** .... discount
Bond's Cookery School	food that is **4**	• includes recipes to strengthen your **5** .... • they have a free **6** .... every Thursday
The **7** .... Centre	mainly **8** .... food	• located near the **9** .... • a special course in skills with a **10** .... is sometimes available

SECTION 2   *Questions 11–20*

Questions 11–13

*Choose the correct letter, **A**, **B** or **C**.*

Traffic Changes in Granford

11   Why are changes needed to traffic systems in Granford?

    A   The number of traffic accidents has risen.
    B   The amount of traffic on the roads has increased.
    C   The types of vehicles on the roads have changed.

12   In a survey, local residents particularly complained about

    A   dangerous driving by parents.
    B   pollution from trucks and lorries.
    C   inconvenience from parked cars.

13   According to the speaker, one problem with the new regulations will be

    A   raising money to pay for them.
    B   finding a way to make people follow them.
    C   getting the support of the police.

Questions 14–20

Label the map below.

*Write the correct letter, **A–I**, next to Questions 14–20.*

Proposed traffic changes in Granford

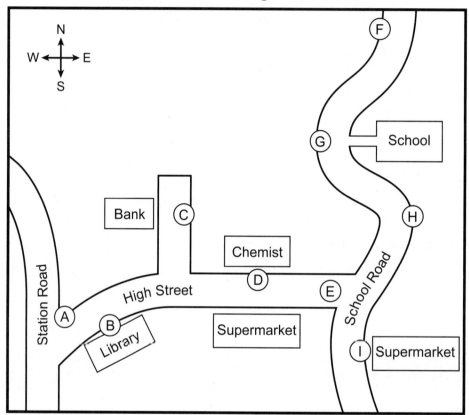

14	New traffic lights	....
15	Pedestrian crossing	....
16	Parking allowed	....
17	New 'No Parking' sign	....
18	New disabled parking spaces	....
19	Widened pavement	....
20	Lorry loading/unloading restrictions	....

SECTION 3   *Questions 21–30*

Questions 21–25

*Choose the correct letter, **A**, **B** or **C**.*

21 Why is Jack interested in investigating seed germination?

    A   He may do a module on a related topic later on.
    B   He wants to have a career in plant science.
    C   He is thinking of choosing this topic for his dissertation.

22 Jack and Emma agree the main advantage of their present experiment is that it can be

    A   described very easily.
    B   carried out inside the laboratory.
    C   completed in the time available.

23 What do they decide to check with their tutor?

    A   whether their aim is appropriate
    B   whether anyone else has chosen this topic
    C   whether the assignment contributes to their final grade

24 They agree that Graves' book on seed germination is disappointing because

    A   it fails to cover recent advances in seed science.
    B   the content is irrelevant for them.
    C   its focus is very theoretical.

25 What does Jack say about the article on seed germination by Lee Hall?

    A   The diagrams of plant development are useful.
    B   The analysis of seed germination statistics is thorough.
    C   The findings on seed germination after fires are surprising.

Test 1

Questions 26–30

Complete the flow-chart below.

Choose **FIVE** answers from the box and write the correct letter, **A–H**, next to Questions 26–30.

A	container	**B**	soil	**C**	weight	**D**	condition
E	height	**F**	colour	**G**	types	**H**	depths

Stages in the experiment

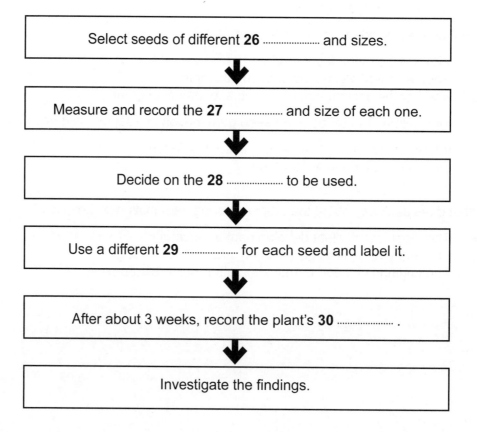

Select seeds of different **26** .... and sizes.

Measure and record the **27** .... and size of each one.

Decide on the **28** .... to be used.

Use a different **29** .... for each seed and label it.

After about 3 weeks, record the plant's **30** ....

Investigate the findings.

SECTION 4 *Questions 31–40*

Complete the notes below.

*Write **ONE WORD ONLY** for each answer.*

Effects of urban environments on animals

Introduction

Recent urban developments represent massive environmental changes. It was previously thought that only a few animals were suitable for city life, e.g.

- the **31** .... – because of its general adaptability

- the pigeon – because walls of city buildings are similar to **32** ....

In fact, many urban animals are adapting with unusual **33** ....

Recent research

- Emilie Snell-Rood studied small urbanised mammal specimens from museums in Minnesota.

  – She found the size of their **34** .... had increased.

  – She suggests this may be due to the need to locate new sources of **35** .... and to deal with new dangers.

- Catarina Miranda focused on the **36** .... of urban and rural blackbirds.

  – She found urban birds were often braver, but were afraid of situations that were **37** ....

- Jonathan Atwell studies how animals respond to urban environments.

  – He found that some animals respond to **38** .... by producing lower levels of hormones.

- Sarah Partan's team found urban squirrels use their **39** .... to help them communicate.

Long-term possibilities

Species of animals may develop which are unique to cities. However, some changes may not be **40** ....

READING PASSAGE 1

*You should spend about 20 minutes on **Questions 1–13**, which are based on Reading Passage 1 below.*

Case Study: *Tourism New Zealand* website

New Zealand is a small country of four million inhabitants, a long-haul flight from all the major tourist-generating markets of the world. Tourism currently makes up 9% of the country's gross domestic product, and is the country's largest export sector. Unlike other export sectors, which make products and then sell them overseas, tourism brings its customers to New Zealand. The product is the country itself – the people, the places and the experiences. In 1999, Tourism New Zealand launched a campaign to communicate a new brand position to the world. The campaign focused on New Zealand's scenic beauty, exhilarating outdoor activities and authentic Maori culture, and it made New Zealand one of the strongest national brands in the world.

A key feature of the campaign was the website www.newzealand.com, which provided potential visitors to New Zealand with a single gateway to everything the destination had to offer. The heart of the website was a database of tourism services operators, both those based in New Zealand and those based abroad which offered tourism services to the country. Any tourism-related business could be listed by filling in a simple form. This meant that even the smallest bed and breakfast address or specialist activity provider could gain a web presence with access to an audience of long-haul visitors. In addition, because participating businesses were able to update the details they gave on a regular basis, the information provided remained accurate. And to maintain and improve standards, Tourism New Zealand organised a scheme whereby organisations appearing on the website underwent an independent evaluation against a set of agreed national standards of quality. As part of this, the effect of each business on the environment was considered.

To communicate the New Zealand experience, the site also carried features relating to famous people and places. One of the most popular was an interview with former New Zealand All Blacks rugby captain Tana Umaga. Another feature that attracted a lot of attention was an interactive journey through a number of the locations chosen for blockbuster films which had made use of New Zealand's stunning scenery as a backdrop. As the site developed, additional features were added to help independent travellers devise their own customised itineraries. To make it easier to plan motoring holidays, the site catalogued the most popular driving routes in the country, highlighting different routes according to the season and indicating distances and times.

Later, a Travel Planner feature was added, which allowed visitors to click and 'bookmark' places or attractions they were interested in, and then view the results on a map. The Travel Planner offered suggested routes and public transport options between the chosen locations. There were also links to accommodation in the area. By registering with the website, users could save their Travel Plan and return to it later, or print it out to take on the visit. The website also had a 'Your Words' section where anyone could submit a blog of their New Zealand travels for possible inclusion on the website.

The Tourism New Zealand website won two Webby awards for online achievement and innovation. More importantly perhaps, the growth of tourism to New Zealand was impressive. Overall tourism expenditure increased by an average of 6.9% per year between 1999 and 2004. From Britain, visits to New Zealand grew at an average annual rate of 13% between 2002 and 2006, compared to a rate of 4% overall for British visits abroad.

The website was set up to allow both individuals and travel organisations to create itineraries and travel packages to suit their own needs and interests. On the website, visitors can search for activities not solely by geographical location, but also by the particular nature of the activity. This is important as research shows that activities are the key driver of visitor satisfaction, contributing 74% to visitor satisfaction, while transport and accommodation account for the remaining 26%. The more activities that visitors undertake, the more satisfied they will be. It has also been found that visitors enjoy cultural activities most when they are interactive, such as visiting a *marae* (meeting ground) to learn about traditional Maori life. Many long-haul travellers enjoy such learning experiences, which provide them with stories to take home to their friends and family. In addition, it appears that visitors to New Zealand don't want to be 'one of the crowd' and find activities that involve only a few people more special and meaningful.

It could be argued that New Zealand is not a typical destination. New Zealand is a small country with a visitor economy composed mainly of small businesses. It is generally perceived as a safe English-speaking country with a reliable transport infrastructure. Because of the long-haul flight, most visitors stay for longer (average 20 days) and want to see as much of the country as possible on what is often seen as a once-in-a-lifetime visit. However, the underlying lessons apply anywhere – the effectiveness of a strong brand, a strategy based on unique experiences and a comprehensive and user-friendly website.

Test 1

Complete the table below.

*Choose **ONE WORD ONLY** from the passage for each answer.*

Write your answers in boxes 1–7 on your answer sheet.

Section of website	Comments
Database of tourism services	• easy for tourism-related businesses to get on the list • allowed businesses to **1** .....update..... information regularly • provided a country-wide evaluation of businesses, including their impact on the **2** ....environment....
Special features on local topics	• e.g. an interview with a former sports **3** ....stars...... , and an interactive tour of various locations used in **4** ...films.........
Information on driving routes	• varied depending on the **5** ....season.......
Travel Planner	• included a map showing selected places, details of public transport and local **6** ....attractions....
'Your Words'	• travellers could send a link to their **7** ....blogs....

Questions 8–13

Do the following statements agree with the information given in Reading Passage 1?

In boxes 8–13 on your answer sheet, write

> **TRUE**   *if the statement agrees with the information*
> **FALSE**   *if the statement contradicts the information*
> **NOT GIVEN**   *if there is no information on this*

8   The website www.newzealand.com aimed to provide ready-made itineraries and packages for travel companies and individual tourists. FALSE ✓

9   It was found that most visitors started searching on the website by geographical location. NOT GIVEN ✓

10   According to research, 26% of visitor satisfaction is related to their accommodation. TRUE

11   Visitors to New Zealand like to become involved in the local culture. TRUE ✓

12   Visitors like staying in small hotels in New Zealand rather than in larger ones. NOT GIVEN ✓

13   Many visitors feel it is unlikely that they will return to New Zealand after their visit. TRUE ✓

5

READING PASSAGE 2

*You should spend about 20 minutes on **Questions 14–26**, which are based on Reading Passage 2 on pages 21 and 22.*

Questions 14–19

Reading Passage 2 has six paragraphs, **A–F**.

Choose the correct heading for each paragraph from the list of headings below.

*Write the correct number, **i–viii**, in boxes 14–19 on your answer sheet.*

List of Headings
i   The productive outcomes that may result from boredom
ii   What teachers can do to prevent boredom
iii   A new explanation and a new cure for boredom
iv   Problems with a scientific approach to boredom
v   A potential danger arising from boredom
vi   Creating a system of classification for feelings of boredom
vii   Age groups most affected by boredom
viii   Identifying those most affected by boredom

14 Paragraph **A**   iv ✓

15 Paragraph **B**   vi ✓

16 Paragraph **C**   i ✓

17 Paragraph **D**   v ✓

18 Paragraph **E**   viii

19 Paragraph **F**   iii

6 pkt

Why being bored is stimulating – and useful, too

This most common of emotions is turning out to be more interesting than we thought

A   We all know how it feels – it's impossible to keep your mind on anything, time stretches out, and all the things you could do seem equally unlikely to make you feel better. But defining boredom so that it can be studied in the lab has proved difficult. For a start, it can include a lot of other mental states, such as frustration, apathy, depression and indifference. There isn't even agreement over whether boredom is always a low-energy, flat kind of emotion or whether feeling agitated and restless counts as boredom, too. In his book, *Boredom: A Lively History*, Peter Toohey at the University of Calgary, Canada, compares it to disgust – an emotion that motivates us to stay away from certain situations. 'If disgust protects humans from infection, boredom may protect them from "infectious" social situations,' he suggests.

B   By asking people about their experiences of boredom, Thomas Goetz and his team at the University of Konstanz in Germany have recently identified five distinct types: indifferent, calibrating, searching, reactant and apathetic. These can be plotted on two axes – one running left to right, which measures low to high arousal, and the other from top to bottom, which measures how positive or negative the feeling is. Intriguingly, Goetz has found that while people experience all kinds of boredom, they tend to specialise in one. Of the five types, the most damaging is 'reactant' boredom with its explosive combination of high arousal and negative emotion. The most useful is what Goetz calls 'indifferent' boredom: someone isn't engaged in anything satisfying but still feels relaxed and calm. However, it remains to be seen whether there are any character traits that predict the kind of boredom each of us might be prone to.

C   Psychologist Sandi Mann at the University of Central Lancashire, UK, goes further. 'All emotions are there for a reason, including boredom,' she says. Mann has found that being bored makes us more creative. 'We're all afraid of being bored but in actual fact it can lead to all kinds of amazing things,' she says. In experiments published last year, Mann found that people who had been made to feel bored by copying numbers out of the phone book for 15 minutes came up with more creative ideas about how to use a polystyrene cup than a control group. Mann concluded that a passive, boring activity is best for creativity because it allows the mind to wander. In fact, she goes so far as to suggest that we should seek out more boredom in our lives.

D   Psychologist John Eastwood at York University in Toronto, Canada, isn't convinced. 'If you are in a state of mind-wandering you are not bored,' he says. 'In my view, by definition boredom is an undesirable state.' That doesn't necessarily mean that it isn't adaptive, he adds. 'Pain is adaptive – if we didn't have physical pain, bad things would happen to us. Does that mean that we should actively cause pain? No. But even if boredom has evolved to help us survive, it can still be toxic if allowed to fester.' For Eastwood, the central feature of boredom is a failure to put our 'attention system' into gear. This causes an inability to focus on anything, which makes time seem to go painfully slowly. What's more, your efforts to improve the situation can end up making you feel worse. 'People try to connect with the world and if they are not successful there's that frustration and irritability,' he says. Perhaps most worryingly, says Eastwood, repeatedly failing to engage attention can lead to a state where we don't know what to do any more, and no longer care.

E   Eastwood's team is now trying to explore why the attention system fails. It's early days but they think that at least some of it comes down to personality. Boredom proneness has been linked with a variety of traits. People who are motivated by pleasure seem to suffer particularly badly. Other personality traits, such as curiosity, are associated with a high boredom threshold. More evidence that boredom has detrimental effects comes from studies of people who are more or less prone to boredom. It seems those who bore easily face poorer prospects in education, their career and even life in general. But of course, boredom itself cannot kill – it's the things we do to deal with it that may put us in danger. What can we do to alleviate it before it comes to that? Goetz's group has one suggestion. Working with teenagers, they found that those who 'approach' a boring situation – in other words, see that it's boring and get stuck in anyway – report less boredom than those who try to avoid it by using snacks, TV or social media for distraction.

F   Psychologist Francoise Wemelsfelder speculates that our over-connected lifestyles might even be a new source of boredom. 'In modern human society there is a lot of overstimulation but still a lot of problems finding meaning,' she says. So instead of seeking yet more mental stimulation, perhaps we should leave our phones alone, and use boredom to motivate us to engage with the world in a more meaningful way.

Questions 20–23

Look at the following people (Questions 20–23) and the list of ideas below.

*Match each person with the correct idea, **A–E**.*

*Write the correct letter, **A–E**, in boxes 20–23 on your answer sheet.*

20   Peter Toohey

21   Thomas Goetz

22   John Eastwood

23   Francoise Wemelsfelder

List of Ideas

A   The way we live today may encourage boredom.

B   One sort of boredom is worse than all the others.

C   Levels of boredom may fall in the future.

D   Trying to cope with boredom can increase its negative effects.

E   Boredom may encourage us to avoid an unpleasant experience.

Questions 24–26

Complete the summary below.

*Choose **ONE WORD ONLY** from the passage for each answer.*

Write your answers in boxes 24–26 on your answer sheet.

Responses to boredom

For John Eastwood, the central feature of boredom is that people cannot
24 .... , due to a failure in what he calls the 'attention system', and as a
result they become frustrated and irritable. His team suggests that those for whom
25 .... is an important aim in life may have problems in coping with
boredom, whereas those who have the characteristic of **26** .... can
generally cope with it.

READING PASSAGE 3

*You should spend about 20 minutes on **Questions 27–40**, which are based on Reading Passage 3 below.*

Artificial artists

Can computers really create works of art?

The Painting Fool is one of a growing number of computer programs which, so their makers claim, possess creative talents. Classical music by an artificial composer has had audiences enraptured, and even tricked them into believing a human was behind the score. Artworks painted by a robot have sold for thousands of dollars and been hung in prestigious galleries. And software has been built which creates art that could not have been imagined by the programmer.

Human beings are the only species to perform sophisticated creative acts regularly. If we can break this process down into computer code, where does that leave human creativity? 'This is a question at the very core of humanity,' says Geraint Wiggins, a computational creativity researcher at Goldsmiths, University of London. 'It scares a lot of people. They are worried that it is taking something special away from what it means to be human.'

To some extent, we are all familiar with computerised art. The question is: where does the work of the artist stop and the creativity of the computer begin? Consider one of the oldest machine artists, Aaron, a robot that has had paintings exhibited in London's Tate Modern and the San Francisco Museum of Modern Art. Aaron can pick up a paintbrush and paint on canvas on its own. Impressive perhaps, but it is still little more than a tool to realise the programmer's own creative ideas.

Simon Colton, the designer of the Painting Fool, is keen to make sure his creation doesn't attract the same criticism. Unlike earlier 'artists' such as Aaron, the Painting Fool only needs minimal direction and can come up with its own concepts by going online for material. The software runs its own web searches and trawls through social media sites. It is now beginning to display a kind of imagination too, creating pictures from scratch. One of its original works is a series of fuzzy landscapes, depicting trees and sky. While some might say they have a mechanical look, Colton argues that such reactions arise from people's double standards towards software-produced and human-produced art. After all, he says, consider that the Painting Fool painted the landscapes without referring to a photo. 'If a child painted a new scene from its head, you'd say it has a certain level of imagination,' he points out. 'The same should be true of a machine.' Software bugs can also lead to unexpected results. Some of the Painting Fool's paintings of a chair came out in black and white, thanks to a technical glitch. This gives the work an eerie, ghostlike quality. Human artists like the renowned Ellsworth Kelly are lauded for limiting their colour palette – so why should computers be any different?

Researchers like Colton don't believe it is right to measure machine creativity directly to that of humans who 'have had millennia to develop our skills'. Others, though, are fascinated by the prospect that a computer might create something as original and subtle as our best artists. So far, only one has come close. Composer David Cope invented a program called Experiments in Musical Intelligence, or EMI. Not only did EMI create compositions in Cope's style, but also that of the most revered classical composers, including Bach, Chopin and Mozart. Audiences were moved to tears, and EMI even fooled classical music experts into thinking they were hearing genuine Bach. Not everyone was impressed however. Some, such as Wiggins, have blasted Cope's work as pseudoscience, and condemned him for his deliberately vague explanation of how the software worked. Meanwhile, Douglas Hofstadter of Indiana University said EMI created replicas which still rely completely on the original artist's creative impulses. When audiences found out the truth they were often outraged with Cope, and one music lover even tried to punch him. Amid such controversy, Cope destroyed EMI's vital databases.

But why did so many people love the music, yet recoil when they discovered how it was composed? A study by computer scientist David Moffat of Glasgow Caledonian University provides a clue. He asked both expert musicians and non-experts to assess six compositions. The participants weren't told beforehand whether the tunes were composed by humans or computers, but were asked to guess, and then rate how much they liked each one. People who thought the composer was a computer tended to dislike the piece more than those who believed it was human. This was true even among the experts, who might have been expected to be more objective in their analyses.

Where does this prejudice come from? Paul Bloom of Yale University has a suggestion: he reckons part of the pleasure we get from art stems from the creative process behind the work. This can give it an 'irresistible essence', says Bloom. Meanwhile, experiments by Justin Kruger of New York University have shown that people's enjoyment of an artwork increases if they think more time and effort was needed to create it. Similarly, Colton thinks that when people experience art, they wonder what the artist might have been thinking or what the artist is trying to tell them. It seems obvious, therefore, that with computers producing art, this speculation is cut short – there's nothing to explore. But as technology becomes increasingly complex, finding those greater depths in computer art could become possible. This is precisely why Colton asks the Painting Fool to tap into online social networks for its inspiration: hopefully this way it will choose themes that will already be meaningful to us.

Questions 27–31

*Choose the correct letter, **A**, **B**, **C** or **D**.*

Write the correct letter in boxes 27–31 on your answer sheet.

27 What is the writer suggesting about computer-produced works in the first paragraph?

    A People's acceptance of them can vary considerably.
    B A great deal of progress has already been attained in this field.
    C They have had more success in some artistic genres than in others.
    D The advances are not as significant as the public believes them to be.

28 According to Geraint Wiggins, why are many people worried by computer art?

    A It is aesthetically inferior to human art.
    B It may ultimately supersede human art.
    C It undermines a fundamental human quality.
    D It will lead to a deterioration in human ability.

29 What is a key difference between Aaron and the Painting Fool?

    A its programmer's background
    B public response to its work
    C the source of its subject matter
    D the technical standard of its output

30 What point does Simon Colton make in the fourth paragraph?

    A Software-produced art is often dismissed as childish and simplistic.
    B The same concepts of creativity should not be applied to all forms of art.
    C It is unreasonable to expect a machine to be as imaginative as a human being.
    D People tend to judge computer art and human art according to different criteria.

31 The writer refers to the paintings of a chair as an example of computer art which

    A achieves a particularly striking effect.
    B exhibits a certain level of genuine artistic skill.
    C closely resembles that of a well-known artist.
    D highlights the technical limitations of the software.

Questions 32–37

*Complete each sentence with the correct ending, **A–G** below.*

*Write the correct letter, **A–G**, in boxes 32–37 on your answer sheet.*

32 Simon Colton says it is important to consider the long-term view when D ? ✓

33 David Cope's EMI software surprised people by A ✓

34 Geraint Wiggins criticised Cope for not E ✓

35 Douglas Hofstadter claimed that EMI was C ✓

36 Audiences who had listened to EMI's music became angry after F ✓

37 The participants in David Moffat's study had to assess music without B ✓

List of Ideas

A   generating work that was virtually indistinguishable from that of humans.

B   knowing whether it was the work of humans or software.

C   producing work entirely dependent on the imagination of its creator.

D   comparing the artistic achievements of humans and computers.

E   revealing the technical details of his program.

F   persuading the public to appreciate computer art.

G   discovering that it was the product of a computer program.

---

6 pkt

Questions 38–40

Do the following statements agree with the claims of the writer in Reading Passage 3?

In boxes 38–40 on your answer sheet, write

> **YES**   *if the statement agrees with the claims of the writer*
> **NO**   *if the statement contradicts the claims of the writer*
> **NOT GIVEN**   *if it is impossible to say what the writer thinks about this*

38   Moffat's research may help explain people's reactions to EMI.   YES

39   The non-experts in Moffat's study all responded in a predictable way.   YES

40   Justin Kruger's findings cast doubt on Paul Bloom's theory about people's prejudice towards computer art.   NO

2 pkt

WRITING

WRITING TASK 1

You should spend about 20 minutes on this task.

> *The two maps below show road access to a city hospital in 2007 and in 2010.*
>
> *Summarise the information by selecting and reporting the main features, and make comparisons where relevant.*

Write at least 150 words.

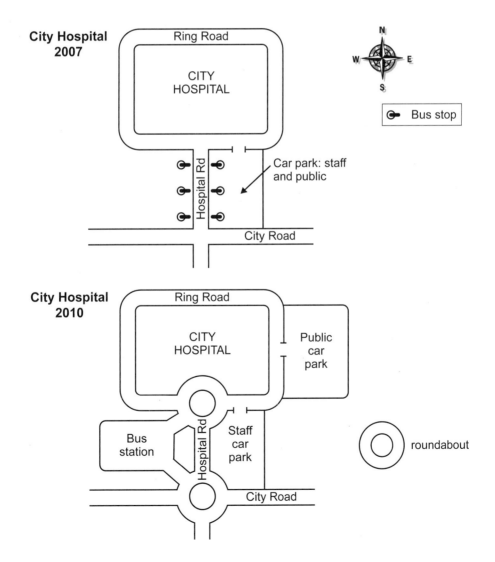

WRITING TASK 2

You should spend about 40 minutes on this task.

Write about the following topic:

> **Living in a country where you have to speak a foreign language can cause serious social problems, as well as practical problems.**
>
> **To what extent do you agree or disagree with this statement?**

Give reasons for your answer and include any relevant examples from your own knowledge or experience.

Write at least 250 words.

SPEAKING

PART 1

The examiner asks the candidate about him/herself, his/her home, work or studies and other familiar topics.

EXAMPLE

Television programmes

- Where do you usually watch TV programmes/shows? [Why?/Why not?]
- What's your favourite TV programme/show? [Why?]
- Are there any programmes/shows you don't like watching? [Why?/Why not?]
- Do you think you will watch more TV or fewer TV programmes/shows in the future? [Why?/Why not?]

PART 2

Describe someone you know who has started a business.

You should say:
    who this person is
    what work this person does
    why this person decided to start a business
and explain whether you would like to do the same kind of work as this person.

You will have to talk about the topic for one to two minutes. You have one minute to think about what you are going to say. You can make some notes to help you if you wish.

PART 3

Discussion topics:

Choosing work

Example questions:
What kinds of jobs do young people not want to do in your country?
Who is best at advising young people about choosing a job: teachers or parents?
Is money always the most important thing when choosing a job?

Work–Life balance

Example questions:
Do you agree that many people nowadays are under pressure to work longer hours and take less holiday?
What is the impact on society of people having a poor work–life balance?
Could you recommend some effective strategies for governments and employers to ensure people have a good work–life balance?

31

Test 2

SECTION 1   Questions 1–10

Complete the notes below.

Write **ONE WORD AND/OR A NUMBER** *for each answer.*

South City Cycling Club

Example
Name of club secretary: Jim ....*Hunter*..........

Membership

- Full membership costs $260; this covers cycling and **1** .... all over Australia

- Recreational membership costs $108

- Cost of membership includes the club fee and **2** ....

- The club kit is made by a company called **3** ....

Training rides

- Chance to improve cycling skills and fitness

- Level B: speed about **4** .... kph

- Weekly sessions

  – Tuesdays at 5.30 am, meet at the **5** ....

  – Thursdays at 5.30 am, meet at the entrance to the **6** ....

Further information

- Rides are about an hour and a half

- Members often have **7** .... together afterwards

- There is not always a **8** .... with the group on these rides

- Check and print the **9** .... on the website beforehand

- Bikes must have **10** ....

SECTION 2   *Questions 11–20*

Questions 11–16

*Choose the correct letter, **A**, **B** or **C**.*

Information on company volunteering projects

11 How much time for volunteering does the company allow per employee?

    A   two hours per week
    B   one day per month
    C   8 hours per year

12 In feedback almost all employees said that volunteering improved their

    A   chances of promotion.
    B   job satisfaction.
    C   relationships with colleagues.

13 Last year some staff helped unemployed people with their

    A   literacy skills.
    B   job applications.
    C   communication skills.

14 This year the company will start a new volunteering project with a local

    A   school.
    B   park.
    C   charity.

15 Where will the Digital Inclusion Day be held?

    A   at the company's training facility
    B   at a college
    C   in a community centre

16 What should staff do if they want to take part in the Digital Inclusion Day?

    A   fill in a form
    B   attend a training workshop
    C   get permission from their manager

Questions 17 and 18

*Choose **TWO** letters, **A–E**.*

What **TWO** things are mentioned about the participants on the last Digital Inclusion Day?

    A   They were all over 70.
    B   They never used their computer.
    C   Their phones were mostly old-fashioned.
    D   They only used their phones for making calls.
    E   They initially showed little interest.

Questions 19 and 20

*Choose **TWO** letters, **A–E**.*

What **TWO** activities on the last Digital Inclusion Day did participants describe as useful?

    A   learning to use tablets
    B   communicating with family
    C   shopping online
    D   playing online games
    E   sending emails

SECTION 3   *Questions 21–30*

Questions 21–25

*Choose the correct letter, **A**, **B** or **C**.*

Planning a presentation on nanotechnology

21 Russ says that his difficulty in planning the presentation is due to

    A   his lack of knowledge about the topic.
    B   his uncertainty about what he should try to achieve.
    C   the short time that he has for preparation.

22 Russ and his tutor agree that his approach in the presentation will be

    A   to concentrate on how nanotechnology is used in one field.
    B   to follow the chronological development of nanotechnology.
    C   to show the range of applications of nanotechnology.

23 In connection with slides, the tutor advises Russ to

    A   talk about things that he can find slides to illustrate.
    B   look for slides to illustrate the points he makes.
    C   consider omitting slides altogether.

24 They both agree that the best way for Russ to start his presentation is

    A   to encourage the audience to talk.
    B   to explain what Russ intends to do.
    C   to provide an example.

25 What does the tutor advise Russ to do next while preparing his presentation?

    A   summarise the main point he wants to make
    B   read the notes he has already made
    C   list the topics he wants to cover

Questions 26–30

What comments do the speakers make about each of the following aspects of Russ's previous presentation?

*Choose **FIVE** answers from the box and write the correct letter, **A–G**, next to Questions 26–30.*

Comments
A lacked a conclusion
B useful in the future
C not enough
D sometimes distracting
E showed originality
F covered a wide range
G not too technical

Aspects of Russ's previous presentation

26 structure   ....

27 eye contact   ....

28 body language   ....

29 choice of words   ....

30 handouts   ....

SECTION 4   *Questions 31–40*

Complete the notes below.

*Write **ONE WORD ONLY** for each answer.*

Episodic memory

- the ability to recall details, e.g. the time and **31** .... of past events

- different to semantic memory – the ability to remember general information about the **32** .... , which does not involve recalling **33** .... information

Forming episodic memories involves three steps:

Encoding

- involves receiving and processing information

- the more **34** .... given to an event, the more successfully it can be encoded

- to remember a **35** .... , it is useful to have a strategy for encoding such information

Consolidation

- how memories are strengthened and stored

- most effective when memories can be added to a **36** .... of related information

- the **37** .... of retrieval affects the strength of memories

Retrieval

- memory retrieval often depends on using a prompt, e.g. the **38** .... of an object near to the place where you left your car

Episodic memory impairments

- these affect people with a wide range of medical conditions

- games which stimulate the **39** .... have been found to help people with schizophrenia

- children with autism may have difficulty forming episodic memories – possibly because their concept of the **40** .... may be absent

- memory training may help autistic children develop social skills

---

READING

READING PASSAGE 1

*You should spend about 20 minutes on **Questions 1–13**, which are based on Reading Passage 1 below.*

Bringing cinnamon to Europe

Cinnamon is a sweet, fragrant spice produced from the inner bark of trees of the genus Cinnamomum, which is native to the Indian sub-continent. It was known in biblical times, and is mentioned in several books of the Bible, both as an ingredient that was mixed with oils for anointing people's bodies, and also as a token indicating friendship among lovers and friends. In ancient Rome, mourners attending funerals burnt cinnamon to create a pleasant scent. Most often, however, the spice found its primary use as an additive to food and drink. In the Middle Ages, Europeans who could afford the spice used it to flavour food, particularly meat, and to impress those around them with their ability to purchase an expensive condiment from the 'exotic' East. At a banquet, a host would offer guests a plate with various spices piled upon it as a sign of the wealth at his or her disposal. Cinnamon was also reported to have health benefits, and was thought to cure various ailments, such as indigestion.

Toward the end of the Middle Ages, the European middle classes began to desire the lifestyle of the elite, including their consumption of spices. This led to a growth in demand for cinnamon and other spices. At that time, cinnamon was transported by Arab merchants, who closely guarded the secret of the source of the spice from potential rivals. They took it from India, where it was grown, on camels via an overland route to the Mediterranean. Their journey ended when they reached Alexandria. European traders sailed there to purchase their supply of cinnamon, then brought it back to Venice. The spice then travelled from that great trading city to markets all around Europe. Because the overland trade route allowed for only small quantities of the spice to reach Europe, and because Venice had a virtual monopoly of the trade, the Venetians could set the price of cinnamon exorbitantly high. These prices, coupled with the increasing demand, spurred the search for new routes to Asia by Europeans eager to take part in the spice trade.

Seeking the high profits promised by the cinnamon market, Portuguese traders arrived on the island of Ceylon in the Indian Ocean toward the end of the 15th century. Before Europeans arrived on the island, the state had organized the cultivation of cinnamon. People belonging to the ethnic group called the Salagama would peel the bark off young shoots of the cinnamon plant in the rainy season, when the wet bark was more pliable. During the peeling process, they curled the bark into the 'stick' shape still associated with the spice today. The Salagama then gave the finished product to the king as a form of tribute. When the Portuguese arrived, they needed to increase production significantly, and so enslaved many other members of the Ceylonese native population, forcing them to work in cinnamon harvesting. In 1518, the Portuguese built a fort on Ceylon, which enabled them to protect the island, so helping them to develop a monopoly in the cinnamon trade and generate very high profits. In the late 16th century, for example, they enjoyed a tenfold profit when shipping cinnamon over a journey of eight days from Ceylon to India.

When the Dutch arrived off the coast of southern Asia at the very beginning of the 17th century, they set their sights on displacing the Portuguese as kings of cinnamon. The Dutch allied themselves with Kandy, an inland kingdom on Ceylon. In return for payments of elephants and cinnamon, they protected the native king from the Portuguese. By 1640, the Dutch broke the 150-year Portuguese monopoly when they overran and occupied their factories. By 1658, they had permanently expelled the Portuguese from the island, thereby gaining control of the lucrative cinnamon trade.

In order to protect their hold on the market, the Dutch, like the Portuguese before them, treated the native inhabitants harshly. Because of the need to boost production and satisfy Europe's ever-increasing appetite for cinnamon, the Dutch began to alter the harvesting practices of the Ceylonese. Over time, the supply of cinnamon trees on the island became nearly exhausted, due to systematic stripping of the bark. Eventually, the Dutch began cultivating their own cinnamon trees to supplement the diminishing number of wild trees available for use.

Then, in 1796, the English arrived on Ceylon, thereby displacing the Dutch from their control of the cinnamon monopoly. By the middle of the 19th century, production of cinnamon reached 1,000 tons a year, after a lower grade quality of the spice became acceptable to European tastes. By that time, cinnamon was being grown in other parts of the Indian Ocean region and in the West Indies, Brazil, and Guyana. Not only was a monopoly of cinnamon becoming impossible, but the spice trade overall was diminishing in economic potential, and was eventually superseded by the rise of trade in coffee, tea, chocolate, and sugar.

Questions 1–9

Complete the notes below.

Choose ONE WORD ONLY from the passage for each answer.

Write your answers in boxes 1–9 on your answer sheet.

The Early History of Cinnamon

Biblical times: added to **1** ....

     used to show **2** .... between people

Ancient Rome: used for its sweet smell at **3** ....

Middle Ages: added to food, especially meat

     was an indication of a person's **4** ....

     known as a treatment for **5** .... and other health problems

     grown in **6** ....

     merchants used **7** .... to bring it to the Mediterranean

     arrived in the Mediterranean at **8** ....

     traders took it to **9** .... and sold it to destinations around Europe

Questions 10–13

Do the following statements agree with the information given in Reading Passage 1?

In boxes 10–13 on your answer sheet, write

TRUE	*if the statement agrees with the information*
FALSE	*if the statement contradicts the information*
NOT GIVEN	*if there is no information on this*

10 The Portuguese had control over the cinnamon trade in Ceylon throughout the 16th century.

11 The Dutch took over the cinnamon trade from the Portuguese as soon as they arrived in Ceylon.

12 The trees planted by the Dutch produced larger quantities of cinnamon than the wild trees.

13 The spice trade maintained its economic importance during the 19th century.

READING PASSAGE 2

*You should spend about 20 minutes on **Questions 14–26**, which are based on Reading Passage 2 below.*

Oxytocin

The positive and negative effects of the chemical known as the 'love hormone'

A   Oxytocin is a chemical, a hormone produced in the pituitary gland in the brain. It was through various studies focusing on animals that scientists first became aware of the influence of oxytocin. They discovered that it helps reinforce the bonds between prairie voles, which mate for life, and triggers the motherly behaviour that sheep show towards their newborn lambs. It is also released by women in childbirth, strengthening the attachment between mother and baby. Few chemicals have as positive a reputation as oxytocin, which is sometimes referred to as the 'love hormone'. One sniff of it can, it is claimed, make a person more trusting, empathetic, generous and cooperative. It is time, however, to revise this wholly optimistic view. A new wave of studies has shown that its effects vary greatly depending on the person and the circumstances, and it can impact on our social interactions for worse as well as for better.

B   Oxytocin's role in human behaviour first emerged in 2005. In a groundbreaking experiment, Markus Heinrichs and his colleagues at the University of Freiburg, Germany, asked volunteers to do an activity in which they could invest money with an anonymous person who was not guaranteed to be honest. The team found that participants who had sniffed oxytocin via a nasal spray beforehand invested more money than those who received a placebo instead. The study was the start of research into the effects of oxytocin on human interactions. 'For eight years, it was quite a lonesome field,' Heinrichs recalls. 'Now, everyone is interested.' These follow-up studies have shown that after a sniff of the hormone, people become more charitable, better at reading emotions on others' faces and at communicating constructively in arguments. Together, the results fuelled the view that oxytocin universally enhanced the positive aspects of our social nature.

C   Then, after a few years, contrasting findings began to emerge. Simone Shamay-Tsoory at the University of Haifa, Israel, found that when volunteers played a competitive game, those who inhaled the hormone showed more pleasure when they beat other players, and felt more envy when others won. What's more, administering oxytocin also has sharply contrasting outcomes depending on a person's disposition. Jennifer Bartz from Mount Sinai School of Medicine, New York, found that it improves people's ability to read emotions, but only if they are not very socially adept to begin with. Her research also shows that oxytocin in fact reduces cooperation in subjects who are particularly anxious or sensitive to rejection.

D   Another discovery is that oxytocin's effects vary depending on who we are interacting with. Studies conducted by Carolyn DeClerck of the University of Antwerp, Belgium, revealed that people who had received a dose of oxytocin actually became less cooperative when dealing with complete strangers. Meanwhile, Carsten De Dreu at the University of Amsterdam in the Netherlands discovered that volunteers given oxytocin showed favouritism: Dutch men became quicker to associate positive words with Dutch names than with foreign ones, for example. According to De Dreu, oxytocin drives people to care for those in their social circles and defend them from outside dangers. So, it appears that oxytocin strengthens biases, rather than promoting general goodwill, as was previously thought.

E   There were signs of these subtleties from the start. Bartz has recently shown that in almost half of the existing research results, oxytocin influenced only certain individuals or in certain circumstances. Where once researchers took no notice of such findings, now a more nuanced understanding of oxytocin's effects is propelling investigations down new lines. To Bartz, the key to understanding what the hormone does lies in pinpointing its core function rather than in cataloguing its seemingly endless effects. There are several hypotheses which are not mutually exclusive. Oxytocin could help to reduce anxiety and fear. Or it could simply motivate people to seek out social connections. She believes that oxytocin acts as a chemical spotlight that shines on social clues – a shift in posture, a flicker of the eyes, a dip in the voice – making people more attuned to their social environment. This would explain why it makes us more likely to look others in the eye and improves our ability to identify emotions. But it could also make things worse for people who are overly sensitive or prone to interpreting social cues in the worst light.

F   Perhaps we should not be surprised that the oxytocin story has become more perplexing. The hormone is found in everything from octopuses to sheep, and its evolutionary roots stretch back half a billion years. 'It's a very simple and ancient molecule that has been co-opted for many different functions,' says Sue Carter at the University of Illinois, Chicago, USA. 'It affects primitive parts of the brain like the amygdala, so it's going to have many effects on just about everything.' Bartz agrees. 'Oxytocin probably does some very basic things, but once you add our higher-order thinking and social situations, these basic processes could manifest in different ways depending on individual differences and context.'

Questions 14–17

Reading Passage 2 has six paragraphs, **A–F**.

Which paragraph contains the following information?

Write the correct letter, **A–F**, in boxes 14–17 on your answer sheet.

NB You may use any letter more than once.

14 reference to research showing the beneficial effects of oxytocin on people

15 reasons why the effects of oxytocin are complex

16 mention of a period in which oxytocin attracted little scientific attention

17 reference to people ignoring certain aspects of their research data

Questions 18–20

Look at the following research findings (Questions 18–20) and the list of researchers below.

Match each research finding with the correct researcher, **A–F**.

Write the correct letter, **A–F**, in boxes 18–20 on your answer sheet.

18 People are more trusting when affected by oxytocin.

19 Oxytocin increases people's feelings of jealousy.

20 The effect of oxytocin varies from one type of person to another.

List of Researchers
A Markus Heinrichs
B Simone Shamay-Tsoory
C Jennifer Bartz
D Carolyn DeClerck
E Carsten De Dreu
F Sue Carter

Questions 21–26

Complete the summary below.

*Choose **ONE WORD ONLY** from the passage for each answer.*

Write your answers in boxes 21–26 on your answer sheet.

Oxytocin research

The earliest findings about oxytocin and bonding came from research involving
21 ~~Animals~~ . It was also discovered that humans produce oxytocin during
22 ~~Childbirth~~ . An experiment in 2005, in which participants were given either
oxytocin or a 23 ~~Placebo~~ , reinforced the belief that the hormone had a
positive effect.

However, later research suggests that this is not always the case. A study at the
University of Haifa where participants took part in a 24 ~~game~~ revealed
the negative emotions which oxytocin can trigger. A study at the University of Antwerp
showed people's lack of willingness to help 25 ~~strangers~~ while under the
influence of oxytocin. Meanwhile, research at the University of Amsterdam revealed that
people who have been given oxytocin consider 26 ~~Names~~ that are familiar
to them in their own country to have more positive associations than those from other
cultures.

READING PASSAGE 3

*You should spend about 20 minutes on **Questions 27–40**, which are based on Reading Passage 3 below.*

MAKING THE MOST OF TRENDS

Experts from Harvard Business School give advice to managers

Most managers can identify the major trends of the day. But in the course of conducting research in a number of industries and working directly with companies, we have discovered that managers often fail to recognize the less obvious but profound ways these trends are influencing consumers' aspirations, attitudes, and behaviors. This is especially true of trends that managers view as peripheral to their core markets.

Many ignore trends in their innovation strategies or adopt a wait-and-see approach and let competitors take the lead. At a minimum, such responses mean missed profit opportunities. At the extreme, they can jeopardize a company by ceding to rivals the opportunity to transform the industry. The purpose of this article is twofold: to spur managers to think more expansively about how trends could engender new value propositions in their core markets, and to provide some high-level advice on how to make market research and product development personnel more adept at analyzing and exploiting trends.

One strategy, known as 'infuse and augment', is to design a product or service that retains most of the attributes and functions of existing products in the category but adds others that address the needs and desires unleashed by a major trend. A case in point is the Poppy range of handbags, which the firm Coach created in response to the economic downturn of 2008. The Coach brand had been a symbol of opulence and luxury for nearly 70 years, and the most obvious reaction to the downturn would have been to lower prices. However, that would have risked cheapening the brand's image. Instead, they initiated a consumer-research project which revealed that customers were eager to lift themselves and the country out of tough times. Using these insights, Coach launched the lower-priced Poppy handbags, which were in vibrant colors, and looked more youthful and playful than conventional Coach products. Creating the sub-brand allowed Coach to avert an across-the-board price cut. In contrast to the many companies that responded to the recession by cutting prices, Coach saw the new consumer mindset as an opportunity for innovation and renewal.

A further example of this strategy was supermarket Tesco's response to consumers' growing concerns about the environment. With that in mind, Tesco, one of the world's top five retailers, introduced its Greener Living program, which demonstrates the company's commitment to protecting the environment by involving consumers in ways that produce tangible results. For example, Tesco customers can accumulate points for such activities as reusing bags, recycling cans and printer cartridges, and buying home-insulation materials. Like points earned on regular purchases, these green points can be redeemed for cash. Tesco has not abandoned its traditional retail offerings but augmented its business with these innovations, thereby infusing its value proposition with a green streak.

A more radical strategy is 'combine and transcend'. This entails combining aspects of the product's existing value proposition with attributes addressing changes arising from a trend, to create a novel experience – one that may land the company in an entirely new market space. At first glance, spending resources to incorporate elements of a seemingly irrelevant trend into one's core offerings sounds like it's hardly worthwhile. But consider Nike's move to integrate the digital revolution into its reputation for high-performance athletic footwear. In 2006, they teamed up with technology company Apple to launch Nike+, a digital sports kit comprising a sensor that attaches to the running shoe and a wireless receiver that connects to the user's iPod. By combining Nike's original value proposition for amateur athletes with one for digital consumers, the Nike+ sports kit and web interface moved the company from a focus on athletic apparel to a new plane of engagement with its customers.

A third approach, known as 'counteract and reaffirm', involves developing products or services that stress the values traditionally associated with the category in ways that allow consumers to oppose – or at least temporarily escape from – the aspects of trends they view as undesirable. A product that accomplished this is the ME2, a video game created by Canada's iToys. By reaffirming the toy category's association with physical play, the ME2 counteracted some of the widely perceived negative impacts of digital gaming devices. Like other handheld games, the device featured a host of exciting interactive games, a full-color LCD screen, and advanced 3D graphics. What set it apart was that it incorporated the traditional physical component of children's play: it contained a pedometer, which tracked and awarded points for physical activity (walking, running, biking, skateboarding, climbing stairs). The child could use the points to enhance various virtual skills needed for the video game. The ME2, introduced in mid-2008, catered to kids' huge desire to play video games while countering the negatives, such as associations with lack of exercise and obesity.

Once you have gained perspective on how trend-related changes in consumer opinions and behaviors impact on your category, you can determine which of our three innovation strategies to pursue. When your category's basic value proposition continues to be meaningful for consumers influenced by the trend, the infuse-and-augment strategy will allow you to reinvigorate the category. If analysis reveals an increasing disparity between your category and consumers' new focus, your innovations need to transcend the category to integrate the two worlds. Finally, if aspects of the category clash with undesired outcomes of a trend, such as associations with unhealthy lifestyles, there is an opportunity to counteract those changes by reaffirming the core values of your category.

Trends – technological, economic, environmental, social, or political – that affect how people perceive the world around them and shape what they expect from products and services present firms with unique opportunities for growth.

Questions 27–31

*Choose the correct letter, **A**, **B**, **C** or **D**.*

Write the correct letter in boxes 27–31 on your answer sheet.

27 In the first paragraph, the writer says that most managers

    A   fail to spot the key consumer trends of the moment.
    B   make the mistake of focusing only on the principal consumer trends.
    C   misinterpret market research data relating to current consumer trends.
    D   are unaware of the significant impact that trends have on consumers' lives.

28 According to the third paragraph, Coach was anxious to

    A   follow what some of its competitors were doing.
    B   maintain its prices throughout its range.
    C   safeguard its reputation as a manufacturer of luxury goods.
    D   modify the entire look of its brand to suit the economic climate.

29 What point is made about Tesco's Greener Living programme?

    A   It did not require Tesco to modify its core business activities.
    B   It succeeded in attracting a more eco-conscious clientele.
    C   Its main aim was to raise consumers' awareness of environmental issues.
    D   It was not the first time that Tesco had implemented such an initiative.

30 What does the writer suggest about Nike's strategy?

    A   It was an extremely risky strategy at the time.
    B   It was a strategy that only a major company could afford to follow.
    C   It was the type of strategy that would not have been possible in the past.
    D   It was the kind of strategy which might appear to have few obvious benefits.

31 What was original about the ME2?

    A   It contained technology that had been developed for the sports industry.
    B   It appealed to young people who were keen to improve their physical fitness.
    C   It took advantage of a current trend for video games with colourful 3D graphics.
    D   It was a handheld game that addressed people's concerns about unhealthy lifestyles.

Questions 32–37

Look at the following statements (Questions 32–37) and the list of companies below.

*Match each statement with the correct company, **A, B, C** or **D**.*

*Write the correct letter, **A, B, C** or **D**, in boxes 32–37 on your answer sheet.*

NB   *You may use any letter more than once.*

32   It turned the notion that its products could have harmful effects to its own advantage.

33   It extended its offering by collaborating with another manufacturer.

34   It implemented an incentive scheme to demonstrate its corporate social responsibility.

35   It discovered that customers had a positive attitude towards dealing with difficult circumstances.

36   It responded to a growing lifestyle trend in an unrelated product sector.

37   It successfully avoided having to charge its customers less for its core products.

List of companies	
A	Coach
B	Tesco
C	Nike
D	iToys

Questions 38–40

*Complete each sentence with the correct ending, **A**, **B**, **C** or **D** below.*

*Write the correct letter, **A**, **B**, **C** or **D**, in boxes 38–40 on your answer sheet.*

38   If there are any trend-related changes impacting on your category, you should

39   If a current trend highlights a negative aspect of your category, you should

40   If the consumers' new focus has an increasing lack of connection with your offering, you should

---

    A   employ a combination of strategies to maintain your consumer base.

    B   identify the most appropriate innovation strategy to use.

    C   emphasise your brand's traditional values with the counteract-and-affirm strategy.

    D   use the combine-and-transcend strategy to integrate the two worlds.

WRITING

WRITING TASK 1

You should spend about 20 minutes on this task.

> *The chart below shows the percentage of households in owned and rented accommodation in England and Wales between 1918 and 2011.*
>
> *Summarise the information by selecting and reporting the main features, and make comparisons where relevant.*

Write at least 150 words.

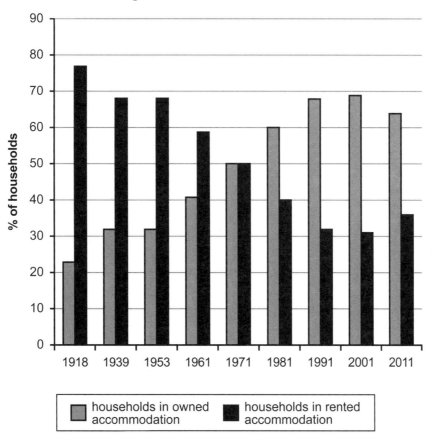

Households owning and renting accommodation in England and Wales 1918 to 2011

WRITING TASK 2

You should spend about 40 minutes on this task.

Write about the following topic:

> **Some people believe that nowadays we have too many choices.**
>
> **To what extent do you agree or disagree with this statement?**

Give reasons for your answer and include any relevant examples from your own knowledge or experience.

Write at least 250 words.

SPEAKING

PART 1

The examiner asks the candidate about him/herself, his/her home, work or studies and other familiar topics.

EXAMPLE

Age

- Are you happy to be the age you are now? [Why/Why not?]
- When you were a child, did you think a lot about your future? [Why/Why not?]
- Do you think you have changed as you have got older? [Why/Why not?]
- What will be different about your life in the future? [Why]

PART 2

> **Describe a time when you started using a new technological device (e.g. a new computer or phone).**
>
> **You should say:**
> **what device you started using**
> **why you started using this device**
> **how easy or difficult it was to use**
> **and explain how helpful this device was to you.**

You will have to talk about the topic for one to two minutes. You have one minute to think about what you are going to say. You can make some notes to help you if you wish.

PART 3

Discussion topics:

Technology and education

Example questions:
What is the best age for children to start computer lessons?
Do you think that schools should use more technology to help children learn?
Do you agree or disagree that computers will replace teachers one day?

Technology and society

Example questions:
How much has technology improved how we communicate with each other?
Do you agree that there are still many more major technological innovations to be made?
Could you suggest some reasons why some people are deciding to reduce their use of technology?

Test 3

SECTION 1   Questions 1–10

Complete the notes below.

*Write **ONE WORD AND/OR A NUMBER** for each answer.*

Moving to Banford City

Example

Linda recommends living in suburb of: ....*Dalton*............

Accommodation

* Average rent: **1** £ .... a month

Transport

* Linda travels to work by **2** ....
* Limited **3** .... in city centre
* Trains to London every **4** .... minutes
* Poor train service at **5** ....

Advantages of living in Banford

* New **6** .... opened recently
* **7** .... has excellent reputation
* Good **8** .... on Bridge Street

Meet Linda

* Meet Linda on **9** .... after 5.30 pm
* In the **10** .... opposite the station

SECTION 2   *Questions 11–20*

Questions 11–16

What advantage does the speaker mention for each of the following physical activities?

*Choose **SIX** answers from the box and write the correct letter, **A–G**, next to Questions 11–16.*

Advantages
A   not dependent on season
B   enjoyable
C   low risk of injury
D   fitness level unimportant
E   sociable
F   fast results
G   motivating

Physical activities

11   using a gym   ....

12   running   ....

13   swimming   ....

14   cycling   ....

15   doing yoga   ....

16   training with a personal trainer ....

Questions 17 and 18

*Choose **TWO** letters, **A–E**.*

For which **TWO** reasons does the speaker say people give up going to the gym?

    A   lack of time
    B   loss of confidence
    C   too much effort required
    D   high costs
    E   feeling less successful than others

Questions 19 and 20

*Choose **TWO** letters, **A–E**.*

Which **TWO** pieces of advice does the speaker give for setting goals?

    A   write goals down
    B   have achievable aims
    C   set a time limit
    D   give yourself rewards
    E   challenge yourself

SECTION 3   *Questions 21–30*

Questions 21–24

Choose the correct letter, A, B or C.

Project on using natural dyes to colour fabrics

21 What first inspired Jim to choose this project?

    A   textiles displayed in an exhibition
    B   a book about a botanic garden
    C   carpets he saw on holiday

22 Jim eventually decided to do a practical investigation which involved

    A   using a range of dyes with different fibres.
    B   applying different dyes to one type of fibre.
    C   testing one dye and a range of fibres.

23 When doing his experiments, Jim was surprised by

    A   how much natural material was needed to make the dye.
    B   the fact that dyes were widely available on the internet.
    C   the time that he had to leave the fabric in the dye.

24 What problem did Jim have with using tartrazine as a fabric dye?

    A   It caused a slight allergic reaction.
    B   It was not a permanent dye on cotton.
    C   It was ineffective when used on nylon.

Questions 25–30

What problem is identified with each of the following natural dyes?

*Choose **SIX** answers from the box and write the correct letter, **A–H**, next to Questions 25–30.*

	Problems
A	It is expensive.
B	The colour is too strong.
C	The colour is not long-lasting.
D	It is very poisonous.
E	It can damage the fabric.
F	The colour may be unexpected.
G	It is unsuitable for some fabrics.
H	It is not generally available.

Natural dyes

25 turmeric ....

26 beetroot ....

27 Tyrian purple ....

28 logwood ....

29 cochineal ....

30 metal oxide ....

SECTION 4   *Questions 31–40*

Complete the notes below.

*Write **ONE WORD ONLY** for each answer.*

The sleepy lizard (*tiliqua rugosa*)

Description

- They are common in Western and South Australia

- They are brown, but recognisable by their blue **31** ....

- They are relatively large

- Their diet consists mainly of **32** ....

- Their main predators are large birds and **33** ....

Navigation study

- One study found that lizards can use the **34** .... to help them navigate

Observations in the wild

- Observations show that these lizards keep the same **35** .... for several years

What people want

- Possible reasons:

    - to improve the survival of their young
      (but little **36** .... has been noted between parents and children)

    - to provide **37** .... for female lizards

Tracking study

- A study was carried out using GPS systems attached to the **38** .... of the lizards

- This provided information on the lizards' location and even the number of **39** .... taken

- It appeared that the lizards were trying to avoid one another

- This may be in order to reduce chances of **40** ....

READING

READING PASSAGE 1

*You should spend about 20 minutes on **Questions 1–13**, which are based on Reading Passage 1 below.*

The coconut palm

For millennia, the coconut has been central to the lives of Polynesian and Asian peoples. In the western world, on the other hand, coconuts have always been exotic and unusual, sometimes rare. The Italian merchant traveller Marco Polo apparently saw coconuts in South Asia in the late 13th century, and among the mid-14th-century travel writings of Sir John Mandeville there is mention of 'great Notes of Ynde' (great Nuts of India). Today, images of palm-fringed tropical beaches are clichés in the west to sell holidays, chocolate bars, fizzy drinks and even romance.

Typically, we envisage coconuts as brown cannonballs that, when opened, provide sweet white flesh. But we see only part of the fruit and none of the plant from which they come. The coconut palm has a smooth, slender, grey trunk, up to 30 metres tall. This is an important source of timber for building houses, and is increasingly being used as a replacement for endangered hardwoods in the furniture construction industry. The trunk is surmounted by a rosette of leaves, each of which may be up to six metres long. The leaves have hard veins in their centres which, in many parts of the world, are used as brushes after the green part of the leaf has been stripped away. Immature coconut flowers are tightly clustered together among the leaves at the top of the trunk. The flower stems may be tapped for their sap to produce a drink, and the sap can also be reduced by boiling to produce a type of sugar used for cooking.

Coconut palms produce as many as seventy fruits per year, weighing more than a kilogram each. The wall of the fruit has three layers: a waterproof outer layer, a fibrous middle layer and a hard, inner layer. The thick fibrous middle layer produces coconut fibre, 'coir', which has numerous uses and is particularly important in manufacturing ropes. The woody innermost layer, the shell, with its three prominent 'eyes', surrounds the seed. An important product obtained from the shell is charcoal, which is widely used in various industries as well as in the home as a cooking fuel. When broken in half, the shells are also used as bowls in many parts of Asia.

Inside the shell are the nutrients (endosperm) needed by the developing seed. Initially, the endosperm is a sweetish liquid, coconut water, which is enjoyed as a drink, but also provides the hormones which encourage other plants to grow more rapidly and produce higher yields. As the fruit matures, the coconut water gradually solidifies to form the brilliant white, fat-rich, edible flesh or meat. Dried coconut flesh, 'copra', is made into coconut oil and coconut milk, which are widely used in cooking in different parts of the world, as well as in cosmetics. A derivative of coconut fat, glycerine, acquired strategic importance in a quite different sphere, as Alfred Nobel introduced the world to his nitroglycerine-based invention: dynamite.

Their biology would appear to make coconuts the great maritime voyagers and coastal colonizers of the plant world. The large, energy-rich fruits are able to float in water and tolerate salt, but cannot remain viable indefinitely; studies suggest after about 110 days at sea they are no longer able to germinate. Literally cast onto desert island shores, with little more than sand to grow in and exposed to the full glare of the tropical sun, coconut seeds are able to germinate and root. The air pocket in the seed, created as the endosperm solidifies, protects the embryo. In addition, the fibrous fruit wall that helped it to float during the voyage stores moisture that can be taken up by the roots of the coconut seedling as it starts to grow.

There have been centuries of academic debate over the origins of the coconut. There were no coconut palms in West Africa, the Caribbean or the east coast of the Americas before the voyages of the European explorers Vasco da Gama and Columbus in the late 15th and early 16th centuries. 16th century trade and human migration patterns reveal that Arab traders and European sailors are likely to have moved coconuts from South and Southeast Asia to Africa and then across the Atlantic to the east coast of America. But the origin of coconuts discovered along the west coast of America by 16th century sailors has been the subject of centuries of discussion. Two diametrically opposed origins have been proposed: that they came from Asia, or that they were native to America. Both suggestions have problems. In Asia, there is a large degree of coconut diversity and evidence of millennia of human use – but there are no relatives growing in the wild. In America, there are close coconut relatives, but no evidence that coconuts are indigenous. These problems have led to the intriguing suggestion that coconuts originated on coral islands in the Pacific and were dispersed from there.

Test 3

Questions 1–8

Complete the table below.

Choose ONE WORD ONLY from the passage for each answer.

Write your answers in boxes 1–8 on your answer sheet.

THE COCONUT PALM		
Part	**Description**	**Uses**
trunk	up to 30 metres	timber for houses and the making of 1 ...furniture...... ✓
leaves	up to 6 metres long	to make brushes
flowers	at the top of the trunk	stems provide sap, used as a drink or a source of 2 ...sugar...... ✓
fruits	outer layer	
	middle layer (coir fibres)	used for 3 ...ropes........ , etc. ✓
	inner layer (shell)	a source of 4 ...charcoal..... ✓ (when halved) for 5 ...bowls...... ✓
	coconut water	a drink a source of 6 ...hormones...... for other plants ✓
	coconut flesh	oil and milk for cooking and 7 ...cosmetics...... ✓ glycerine (an ingredient in 8 ...dynamite...) ✓

62

Questions 9–13

Do the following statements agree with the information given in Reading Passage 1?

In boxes 9–13 on your answer sheet, write

> **TRUE**　　　*if the statement agrees with the information*
> **FALSE**　　*if the statement contradicts the information*
> **NOT GIVEN**　*if there is no information on this*

9 Coconut seeds need shade in order to germinate.　FALSE　✓

10 Coconuts were probably transported to Asia from America in the 16th century.　FALSE　✓

11 Coconuts found on the west coast of America were a different type from those found on the east coast.　TRUE　—

12 All the coconuts found in Asia are cultivated varieties.　TRUE　✓

13 Coconuts are cultivated in different ways in America and the Pacific.　NOT GIVEN　✓

4

READING PASSAGE 2

You should spend about 20 minutes on **Questions 14–26**, which are based on Reading Passage 2 below.

How baby talk gives infant brains a boost

A   The typical way of talking to a baby – high-pitched, exaggerated and repetitious – is a source of fascination for linguists who hope to understand how 'baby talk' impacts on learning. Most babies start developing their hearing while still in the womb, prompting some hopeful parents to play classical music to their pregnant bellies. Some research even suggests that infants are listening to adult speech as early as 10 weeks before being born, gathering the basic building blocks of their family's native tongue.

B   Early language exposure seems to have benefits to the brain – for instance, studies suggest that babies raised in bilingual homes are better at learning how to mentally prioritize information. So how does the sweet if sometimes absurd sound of infant-directed speech influence a baby's development? Here are some recent studies that explore the science behind baby talk.

C   Fathers don't use baby talk as often or in the same ways as mothers – and that's perfectly OK, according to a new study. Mark VanDam of Washington State University at Spokane and colleagues equipped parents with recording devices and speech-recognition software to study the way they interacted with their youngsters during a normal day. 'We found that moms do exactly what you'd expect and what's been described many times over,' VanDam explains. 'But we found that dads aren't doing the same thing. Dads didn't raise their pitch or fundamental frequency when they talked to kids.' Their role may be rooted in what is called the bridge hypothesis, which dates back to 1975. It suggests that fathers use less familial language to provide their children with a bridge to the kind of speech they'll hear in public. 'The idea is that a kid gets to practice a certain kind of speech with mom and another kind of speech with dad, so the kid then has a wider repertoire of kinds of speech to practice,' says VanDam.

D   Scientists from the University of Washington and the University of Connecticut collected thousands of 30-second conversations between parents and their babies, fitting 26 children with audio-recording vests that captured language and sound during a typical eight-hour day. The study found that the more baby talk parents used, the more their youngsters began to babble. And when researchers saw the same babies at age two, they found that frequent baby talk had dramatically boosted vocabulary, regardless of socioeconomic status. 'Those children who listened to a lot of baby talk were talking more than the babies that listened to more adult talk or standard speech,' says Nairán Ramírez-Esparza of the University of Connecticut. 'We also found that it really matters whether you use baby talk in a one-on-one context,' she adds. 'The more parents use baby talk one-on-one, the more babies babble, and the more they babble, the more words they produce later in life.'

E   Another study suggests that parents might want to pair their youngsters up so they can babble more with their own kind. Researchers from McGill University and Université du Québec à Montréal found that babies seem to like listening to each other rather than to adults – which may be why baby talk is such a universal tool among parents. They played repeating vowel sounds made by a special synthesizing device that mimicked sounds made by either an adult woman or another baby. This way, only the impact of the auditory cues was observed. The team then measured how long each type of sound held the infants' attention. They found that the 'infant' sounds held babies' attention nearly 40 percent longer. The baby noises also induced more reactions in the listening infants, like smiling or lip moving, which approximates sound making. The team theorizes that this attraction to other infant sounds could help launch the learning process that leads to speech. 'It may be some property of the sound that is just drawing their attention,' says study co-author Linda Polka. 'Or maybe they are really interested in that particular type of sound because they are starting to focus on their own ability to make sounds. We are speculating here but it might catch their attention because they recognize it as a sound they could possibly make.'

F   In a study published in *Proceedings of the National Academy of Sciences*, a total of 57 babies from two slightly different age groups – seven months and eleven and a half months – were played a number of syllables from both their native language (English) and a non-native tongue (Spanish). The infants were placed in a brain-activation scanner that recorded activity in a brain region known to guide the motor movements that produce speech. The results suggest that listening to baby talk prompts infant brains to start practicing their language skills. 'Finding activation in motor areas of the brain when infants are simply listening is significant, because it means the baby brain is engaged in trying to talk back right from the start, and suggests that seven-month-olds' brains are already trying to figure out how to make the right movements that will produce words,' says co-author Patricia Kuhl. Another interesting finding was that while the seven-month-olds responded to all speech sounds regardless of language, the brains of the older infants worked harder at the motor activations of non-native sounds compared to native sounds. The study may have also uncovered a process by which babies recognize differences between their native language and other tongues.

Questions 14–17

Look at the following ideas (Questions 14–17) and the list of researchers below.

*Match each idea with the correct researcher, **A**, **B** or **C**.*

*Write the correct letter, **A**, **B** or **C**, in boxes 14–17 on your answer sheet.*

NB *You may use any letter more than once.*

14   the importance of adults giving babies individual attention when talking to them

15   the connection between what babies hear and their own efforts to create speech

16   the advantage for the baby of having two parents each speaking in a different way

17   the connection between the amount of baby talk babies hear and how much vocalising they do themselves

List of Researchers		
A	Mark VanDam	
B	Nairán Ramirez-Esparza	
C	Patricia Kuhl	

Questions 18–23

Complete the summary below.

Choose **NO MORE THAN TWO WORDS** *from the passage for each answer.*

Write your answers in boxes 18–23 on your answer sheet.

Research into how parents talk to babies

Researchers at Washington State University used **18** ...recording devices... , together with specialised computer programs, to analyse how parents interacted with their babies during a normal day. The study revealed that **19** ...fathers... tended not to modify their ordinary speech patterns when interacting with their babies. According to an idea known as the **20** ...bridge hypothesis..., they may use a more adult type of speech to prepare infants for the language they will hear outside the family home. According to the researchers, hearing baby talk from one parent and 'normal' language from the other expands the baby's **21** ...repertoire... of types of speech which they can practise.

Meanwhile, another study carried out by scientists from the University of Washington and the University of Connecticut recorded speech and sound using special **22** ...audio-recording vests... that the babies were equipped with. When they studied the babies again at age two, they found that those who had heard a lot of baby talk in infancy had a much larger **23** ...vocabulary... than those who had not.

6

Questions 24–26

Reading Passage 2 has six paragraphs, **A–F**.

Which paragraph contains the following information?

Write the correct letter, **A–F**, *in boxes 24–26 on your answer sheet.*

24 a reference to a change which occurs in babies' brain activity before the end of their first year   F

25 an example of what some parents do for their baby's benefit before birth   A

26 a mention of babies' preference for the sounds that other babies make   E

3

READING PASSAGE 3

*You should spend about 20 minutes on **Questions 27–40**, which are based on Reading Passage 3 below.*

Whatever happened to the Harappan Civilisation?

New research sheds light on the disappearance of an ancient society

A   The Harappan Civilisation of ancient Pakistan and India flourished 5,000 years ago, but a thousand years later their cities were abandoned. The Harappan Civilisation was a sophisticated Bronze Age society who built 'megacities' and traded internationally in luxury craft products, and yet seemed to have left almost no depictions of themselves. But their lack of self-imagery – at a time when the Egyptians were carving and painting representations of themselves all over their temples – is only part of the mystery.

B   'There is plenty of archaeological evidence to tell us about the rise of the Harappan Civilisation, but relatively little about its fall,' explains archaeologist Dr Cameron Petrie of the University of Cambridge. 'As populations increased, cities were built that had great baths, craft workshops, palaces and halls laid out in distinct sectors. Houses were arranged in blocks, with wide main streets and narrow alleyways, and many had their own wells and drainage systems. It was very much a "thriving" civilisation.' Then around 2100 BC, a transformation began. Streets went uncleaned, buildings started to be abandoned, and ritual structures fell out of use. After their final demise, a millennium passed before really large-scale cities appeared once more in South Asia.

C   Some have claimed that major glacier-fed rivers changed their course, dramatically affecting the water supply and agriculture; or that the cities could not cope with an increasing population, they exhausted their resource base, the trading economy broke down or they succumbed to invasion and conflict; and yet others that climate change caused an environmental change that affected food and water provision. 'It is unlikely that there was a single cause for the decline of the civilisation. But the fact is, until now, we have had little solid evidence from the area for most of the key elements,' said Petrie. 'A lot of the archaeological debate has really only been well-argued speculation.'

D   A research team led by Petrie, together with Dr Ravindanath Singh of Banaras Hindu University in India, found early in their investigations that many of the archaeological sites were not where they were supposed to be, completely altering understanding of the way that this region was inhabited in the past. When they carried out a survey of how the larger area was settled in relation to sources of water, they found inaccuracies in the published geographic locations of ancient settlements ranging from several hundred metres to many kilometres. They realised that any attempts to use the existing data were likely to be fundamentally flawed. Over the course of several seasons of fieldwork they carried out new surveys, finding an astonishing 198 settlement sites that were previously unknown.

E   Now, research published by Dr Yama Dixit and Professor David Hodell, both from Cambridge's Department of Earth Sciences, has provided the first definitive evidence for climate change affecting the plains of north-western India, where hundreds of Harappan sites are known to have been situated. The researchers gathered shells of *Melanoides tuberculata* snails from the sediments of an ancient lake and used geochemical analysis as a means of tracing the climate history of the region. 'As today, the major source of water into the lake is likely to have been the summer monsoon,' says Dixit. 'But we have observed that there was an abrupt change about 4,100 years ago, when the amount of evaporation from the lake exceeded the rainfall – indicative of a drought.' Hodell adds: 'We estimate that the weakening of the Indian summer monsoon climate lasted about 200 years before recovering to the previous conditions, which we still see today.'

F   It has long been thought that other great Bronze Age civilisations also declined at a similar time, with a global-scale climate event being seen as the cause. While it is possible that these local-scale processes were linked, the real archaeological interest lies in understanding the impact of these larger-scale events on different environments and different populations. 'Considering the vast area of the Harappan Civilisation with its variable weather systems,' explains Singh, 'it is essential that we obtain more climate data from areas close to the two great cities at Mohenjodaro and Harappa and also from the Indian Punjab.'

G   Petrie and Singh's team is now examining archaeological records and trying to understand details of how people led their lives in the region five millennia ago. They are analysing grains cultivated at the time, and trying to work out whether they were grown under extreme conditions of water stress, and whether they were adjusting the combinations of crops they were growing for different weather systems. They are also looking at whether the types of pottery used, and other aspects of their material culture, were distinctive to specific regions or were more similar across larger areas. This gives us insight into the types of interactive networks that the population was involved in, and whether those changed.

H   Petrie believes that archaeologists are in a unique position to investigate how past societies responded to environmental and climatic change. 'By investigating responses to environmental pressures and threats, we can learn from the past to engage with the public, and the relevant governmental and administrative bodies, to be more proactive in issues such as the management and administration of water supply, the balance of urban and rural development, and the importance of preserving cultural heritage in the future.'

Questions 27–31

Reading Passage 3 has eight paragraphs, **A–H**.

Which paragraph contains the following information?

*Write the correct letter, **A–H**, in boxes 27–31 on your answer sheet.*

NB *You may use any letter more than once.*

27 proposed explanations for the decline of the Harappan Civilisation

28 reference to a present-day application of some archaeological research findings

29 a difference between the Harappan Civilisation and another culture of the same period

30 a description of some features of Harappan urban design

31 reference to the discovery of errors made by previous archaeologists

Questions 32–36

Complete the summary below.

*Choose **ONE WORD ONLY** from the passage for each answer.*

Write your answers in boxes 32–36 on your answer sheet.

Looking at evidence of climate change

Yama Dixit and David Hodell have found the first definitive evidence of climate change affecting the plains of north-western India thousands of years ago. By collecting the 32 ......Shells...... of snails and analysing them, they discovered evidence of a change in water levels in a 33 ......lake...... in the region. This occurred when there was less 34 ......rain fall...... than evaporation, and suggests that there was an extended period of drought.

Petrie and Singh's team are using archaeological records to look at 35 ......grains...... from five millennia ago, in order to know whether people had adapted their agricultural practices to changing climatic conditions. They are also examining objects including 36 ......pottery......, so as to find out about links between inhabitants of different parts of the region and whether these changed over time.

5

Questions 37–40

Look at the following statements (Questions 37–40) and the list of researchers below.

*Match each statement with the correct researcher, **A**, **B**, **C** or **D**.*

*Write the correct letter, **A**, **B**, **C** or **D**, in boxes 37–40 on your answer sheet.*

NB *You may use any letter more than once.*

37 Finding further information about changes to environmental conditions in the region is vital.

38 Examining previous patterns of behaviour may have long-term benefits.

39 Rough calculations indicate the approximate length of a period of water shortage.

40 Information about the decline of the Harappan Civilisation has been lacking.

List of Researchers	
A	Cameron Petrie
B	Ravindanath Singh
C	Yama Dixit
D	David Hodell

WRITING

WRITING TASK 1

You should spend about 20 minutes on this task.

> **The bar chart below shows the top ten countries for the production and consumption of electricity in 2014.**
>
> **Summarise the information by selecting and reporting the main features, and make comparisons where relevant.**

Write at least 150 words.

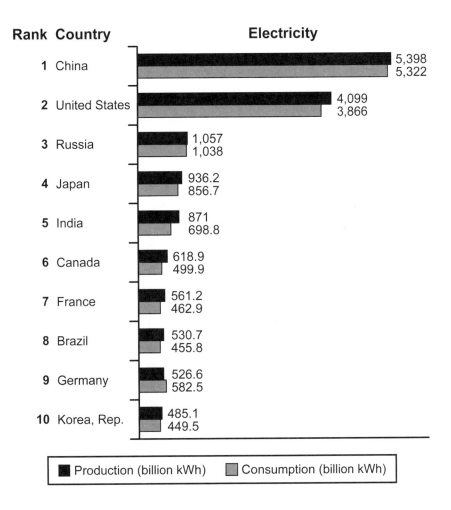

WRITING TASK 2

You should spend about 40 minutes on this task.

Write about the following topic:

> **Some people say History is one of the most important school subjects. Other people think that, in today's world, subjects like Science and Technology are more important than History.**
>
> **Discuss both these views and give your own opinion.**

Give reasons for your answer and include any relevant examples from your own knowledge or experience.

Write at least 250 words.

SPEAKING

PART 1

The examiner asks the candidate about him/herself, his/her home, work or studies and other familiar topics.

EXAMPLE

Money

- When you go shopping, do you prefer to pay for things in cash or by card? [Why?]
- Do you ever save money to buy special things? [Why/Why not?]
- Would you ever take a job which had low pay? [Why/Why not?]
- Would winning a lot of money make a big difference to your life? [Why/Why not?]

PART 2

Describe an interesting discussion you had as part of your work or studies. **You should say:** 　　**what the subject of the discussion was** 　　**who you discussed the subject with** 　　**what opinions were expressed** **and explain why you found the discussion interesting.**

You will have to talk about the topic for one to two minutes. You have one minute to think about what you are going to say. You can make some notes to help you if you wish.

PART 3

Discussion topics:

Discussing problems with others

Example questions:
Why is it good to discuss problems with other people?
Do you think that it's better to talk to friends and not family about problems?
Is it always a good idea to tell lots of people about a problem?

Communication skills at work

Example questions:
Which communication skills are most important when taking part in meetings with colleagues?
What are the possible effects of poor written communication skills at work?
What do you think will be the future impact of technology on communication in the workplace?

Test 4

LISTENING

SECTION 1   Questions 1–10

Complete the notes below.

Write ONE WORD AND/OR A NUMBER for each answer.

Alex's Training

Example

Alex completed his training in ....*2014*..........

About the applicant:

- At first, Alex did his training in the **1** .... department.
- Alex didn't have a qualification from school in **2** ....
- Alex thinks he should have done the diploma in **3** .... skills.
- Age of other trainees: the youngest was **4** ....

Benefits of doing training at JPNW:

- Lots of opportunities because of the size of the organisation.
- Trainees receive the same amount of **5** .... as permanent staff.
- The training experience increases people's confidence a lot.
- Trainees go to **6** .... one day per month.
- The company is in a convenient **7** ....

Advice for interview:

- Don't wear **8** ....
- Don't be **9** ....
- Make sure you **10** ....

SECTION 2   *Questions 11–20*

Questions 11–16

*Choose the correct letter, **A**, **B** or **C**.*

The Snow Centre

11 Annie recommends that when cross-country skiing, the visitors should

    A   get away from the regular trails.
    B   stop to enjoy views of the scenery.
    C   go at a slow speed at the beginning.

12 What does Annie tell the group about this afternoon's dog-sled trip?

    A   Those who want to can take part in a race.
    B   Anyone has the chance to drive a team of dogs.
    C   One group member will be chosen to lead the trail.

13 What does Annie say about the team relay event?

    A   All participants receive a medal.
    B   The course is 4 km long.
    C   Each team is led by a teacher.

14 On the snow-shoe trip, the visitors will

    A   visit an old gold mine.
    B   learn about unusual flowers.
    C   climb to the top of a mountain.

15 The cost of accommodation in the mountain hut includes

    A   a supply of drinking water.
    B   transport of visitors' luggage.
    C   cooked meals.

16 If there is a storm while the visitors are in the hut, they should

    A   contact the bus driver.
    B   wait until the weather improves.
    C   use the emergency locator beacon.

Questions 17–20

What information does Annie give about skiing on each of the following mountain trails?

*Choose **FOUR** answers from the box and write the correct letter, **A–F**, next to Questions 17–20.*

Information
A   It has a good place to stop and rest.
B   It is suitable for all abilities.
C   It involves crossing a river.
D   It demands a lot of skill.
E   It may be closed in bad weather.
F   It has some very narrow sections.

Mountain trails

17   Highland Trail   ....

18   Pine Trail   ....

19   Stony Trail   ....

20   Loser's Trail   ....

SECTION 3   *Questions 21–30*

Questions 21–26

Choose the correct letter, A, B or C.

Labels giving nutritional information on food packaging

21 What was Jack's attitude to nutritional food labels before this project?

  A   He didn't read everything on them.
  B   He didn't think they were important.
  C   He thought they were too complicated.

22 Alice says that before doing this project,

  A   she was unaware of what certain foods contained.
  B   she was too lazy to read food labels.
  C   she was only interested in the number of calories.

23 When discussing supermarket brands of pizza, Jack agrees with Alice that

  A   the list of ingredients is shocking.
  B   he will hesitate before buying pizza again.
  C   the nutritional label is misleading.

24 Jack prefers the daily value system to other labelling systems because it is

  A   more accessible.
  B   more logical.
  C   more comprehensive.

25 What surprised both students about one flavour of crisps?

  A   The percentage of artificial additives given was incorrect.
  B   The products did not contain any meat.
  C   The labels did not list all the ingredients.

26 What do the students think about research into the impact of nutritional food labelling?

  A   It did not produce clear results.
  B   It focused on the wrong people.
  C   It made unrealistic recommendations.

Questions 27 and 28

*Choose **TWO** letters, **A–E**.*

Which **TWO** things surprised the students about the traffic-light system for nutritional labels?

    A   its widespread use
    B   the fact that it is voluntary for supermarkets
    C   how little research was done before its introduction
    D   its unpopularity with food manufacturers
    E   the way that certain colours are used

Questions 29 and 30

*Choose **TWO** letters, **A–E**.*

Which **TWO** things are true about the participants in the study on the traffic-light system?

    A   They had low literacy levels.
    B   They were regular consumers of packaged food.
    C   They were selected randomly.
    D   They were from all socio-economic groups.
    E   They were interviewed face-to-face.

SECTION 4   *Questions 31–40*

Complete the notes below.

Write **ONE WORD ONLY** *for each answer.*

The history of coffee

Coffee in the Arab world

- There was small-scale trade in wild coffee from Ethiopia.

- 1522: Coffee was approved in the Ottoman court as a type of medicine.

- 1623: In Constantinople, the ruler ordered the **31** .... of every coffee house.

Coffee arrives in Europe (17th century)

- Coffee shops were compared to **32** ....

- They played an important part in social and **33** .... changes.

Coffee and European colonisation

- European powers established coffee plantations in their colonies.

- Types of coffee were often named according to the **34** .... they came from.

- In Brazil and the Caribbean, most cultivation depended on **35** ....

- In Java, coffee was used as a form of **36** ....

- Coffee became almost as important as **37** ....

- The move towards the consumption of **38** .... in Britain did not also take place in the USA.

Coffee in the 19th century

- Prices dropped because of improvements in **39** ....

- Industrial workers found coffee helped them to work at **40** ....

READING

READING PASSAGE 1

*You should spend about 20 minutes on **Questions 1–13**, which are based on Reading Passage 1 below.*

Cutty Sark: the fastest sailing ship of all time

The nineteenth century was a period of great technological development in Britain, and for shipping the major changes were from wind to steam power, and from wood to iron and steel.

The fastest commercial sailing vessels of all time were clippers, three-masted ships built to transport goods around the world, although some also took passengers. From the 1840s until 1869, when the Suez Canal opened and steam propulsion was replacing sail, clippers dominated world trade. Although many were built, only one has survived more or less intact: *Cutty Sark*, now on display in Greenwich, southeast London.

Cutty Sark's unusual name comes from the poem *Tam O'Shanter* by the Scottish poet Robert Burns. Tam, a farmer, is chased by a witch called Nannie, who is wearing a '*cutty sark*' – an old Scottish name for a short nightdress. The witch is depicted in *Cutty Sark*'s figurehead – the carving of a woman typically at the front of old sailing ships. In legend, and in Burns's poem, witches cannot cross water, so this was a rather strange choice of name for a ship.

Cutty Sark was built in Dumbarton, Scotland, in 1869, for a shipping company owned by John Willis. To carry out construction, Willis chose a new shipbuilding firm, Scott & Linton, and ensured that the contract with them put him in a very strong position. In the end, the firm was forced out of business, and the ship was finished by a competitor.

Willis's company was active in the tea trade between China and Britain, where speed could bring shipowners both profits and prestige, so *Cutty Sark* was designed to make the journey more quickly than any other ship. On her maiden voyage, in 1870, she set sail from London, carrying large amounts of goods to China. She returned laden with tea, making the journey back to London in four months. However, *Cutty Sark* never lived up to the high expectations of her owner, as a result of bad winds and various misfortunes. On one occasion, in 1872, the ship and a rival clipper, *Thermopylae*, left port in China on the same day. Crossing the Indian Ocean, *Cutty Sark* gained a lead of over 400 miles, but then her rudder was severely damaged in stormy seas, making her impossible to steer. The ship's crew had the daunting task of repairing the rudder at sea, and only succeeded at the second attempt. *Cutty Sark* reached London a week after *Thermopylae*.

Steam ships posed a growing threat to clippers, as their speed and cargo capacity increased. In addition, the opening of the Suez Canal in 1869, the same year that *Cutty Sark* was launched, had a serious impact. While steam ships could make use of the quick, direct route between the Mediterranean and the Red Sea, the canal was of no use to sailing ships, which needed the much stronger winds of the oceans, and so had to sail a far greater distance. Steam ships reduced the journey time between Britain and China by approximately two months.

By 1878, tea traders weren't interested in *Cutty Sark*, and instead, she took on the much less prestigious work of carrying any cargo between any two ports in the world. In 1880, violence aboard the ship led ultimately to the replacement of the captain with an incompetent drunkard who stole the crew's wages. He was suspended from service, and a new captain appointed. This marked a turnaround and the beginning of the most successful period in *Cutty Sark*'s working life, transporting wool from Australia to Britain. One such journey took just under 12 weeks, beating every other ship sailing that year by around a month.

The ship's next captain, Richard Woodget, was an excellent navigator, who got the best out of both his ship and his crew. As a sailing ship, *Cutty Sark* depended on the strong trade winds of the southern hemisphere, and Woodget took her further south than any previous captain, bringing her dangerously close to icebergs off the southern tip of South America. His gamble paid off, though, and the ship was the fastest vessel in the wool trade for ten years.

As competition from steam ships increased in the 1890s, and *Cutty Sark* approached the end of her life expectancy, she became less profitable. She was sold to a Portuguese firm, which renamed her *Ferreira*. For the next 25 years, she again carried miscellaneous cargoes around the world.

Badly damaged in a gale in 1922, she was put into Falmouth harbour in southwest England, for repairs. Wilfred Dowman, a retired sea captain who owned a training vessel, recognised her and tried to buy her, but without success. She returned to Portugal and was sold to another Portuguese company. Dowman was determined, however, and offered a high price: this was accepted, and the ship returned to Falmouth the following year and had her original name restored.

Dowman used *Cutty Sark* as a training ship, and she continued in this role after his death. When she was no longer required, in 1954, she was transferred to dry dock at Greenwich to go on public display. The ship suffered from fire in 2007, and again, less seriously, in 2014, but now *Cutty Sark* attracts a quarter of a million visitors a year.

Questions 1–8

Do the following statements agree with the information given in Reading Passage 1?

In boxes 1–8 on your answer sheet, write

> **TRUE**   *if the statement agrees with the information*
> **FALSE**   *if the statement contradicts the information*
> **NOT GIVEN** *if there is no information on this*

1   Clippers were originally intended to be used as passenger ships.

2   *Cutty Sark* was given the name of a character in a poem.

3   The contract between John Willis and Scott & Linton favoured Willis.

4   John Willis wanted *Cutty Sark* to be the fastest tea clipper travelling between the UK and China.

5   Despite storm damage, *Cutty Sark* beat *Thermopylae* back to London.

6   The opening of the Suez Canal meant that steam ships could travel between Britain and China faster than clippers.

7   Steam ships sometimes used the ocean route to travel between London and China.

8   Captain Woodget put *Cutty Sark* at risk of hitting an iceberg.

Questions 9–13

Complete the sentences below.

Choose **ONE WORD ONLY** from the passage for each answer.

Write your answers in boxes 9–13 on your answer sheet.

9   After 1880, *Cutty Sark* carried .... as its main cargo during its most successful time.

10   As a captain and .... , Woodget was very skilled.

11   *Ferreira* went to Falmouth to repair damage that a .... had caused.

12   Between 1923 and 1954, *Cutty Sark* was used for ....

13   *Cutty Sark* has twice been damaged by .... in the 21st century.

READING PASSAGE 2

*You should spend about 20 minutes on **Questions 14–26**, which are based on Reading Passage 2 below.*

SAVING THE SOIL

More than a third of the Earth's top layer is at risk. Is there hope for our planet's most precious resource?

A   More than a third of the world's soil is endangered, according to a recent UN report. If we don't slow the decline, all farmable soil could be gone in 60 years. Since soil grows 95% of our food, and sustains human life in other more surprising ways, that is a huge problem.

B   Peter Groffman, from the Cary Institute of Ecosystem Studies in New York, points out that soil scientists have been warning about the degradation of the world's soil for decades. At the same time, our understanding of its importance to humans has grown. A single gram of healthy soil might contain 100 million bacteria, as well as other microorganisms such as viruses and fungi, living amid decomposing plants and various minerals.

That means soils do not just grow our food, but are the source of nearly all our existing antibiotics, and could be our best hope in the fight against antibiotic-resistant bacteria. Soil is also an ally against climate change: as microorganisms within soil digest dead animals and plants, they lock in their carbon content, holding three times the amount of carbon as does the entire atmosphere. Soils also store water, preventing flood damage: in the UK, damage to buildings, roads and bridges from floods caused by soil degradation costs £233 million every year.

C   If the soil loses its ability to perform these functions, the human race could be in big trouble. The danger is not that the soil will disappear completely, but that the microorganisms that give it its special properties will be lost. And once this has happened, it may take the soil thousands of years to recover.

Agriculture is by far the biggest problem. In the wild, when plants grow they remove nutrients from the soil, but then when the plants die and decay these nutrients are returned directly to the soil. Humans tend not to return unused parts of harvested crops directly to the soil to enrich it, meaning that the soil gradually becomes less fertile. In the past we developed strategies to get around the problem, such as regularly varying the types of crops grown, or leaving fields uncultivated for a season.

D   But these practices became inconvenient as populations grew and agriculture had to be run on more commercial lines. A solution came in the early 20th century with the Haber-Bosch process for manufacturing ammonium nitrate. Farmers have been putting this synthetic fertiliser on their fields ever since.

But over the past few decades, it has become clear this wasn't such a bright idea. Chemical fertilisers can release polluting nitrous oxide into the atmosphere and excess is often washed away with the rain, releasing nitrogen into rivers. More recently, we have found that indiscriminate use of fertilisers hurts the soil itself, turning it acidic and salty, and degrading the soil they are supposed to nourish.

E   One of the people looking for a solution to this problem is Pius Floris, who started out running a tree-care business in the Netherlands, and now advises some of the world's top soil scientists. He came to realise that the best way to ensure his trees flourished was to take care of the soil, and has developed a cocktail of beneficial bacteria, fungi and humus* to do this. Researchers at the University of Valladolid in Spain recently used this cocktail on soils destroyed by years of fertiliser overuse. When they applied Floris's mix to the desert-like test plots, a good crop of plants emerged that were not just healthy at the surface, but had roots strong enough to pierce dirt as hard as rock. The few plants that grew in the control plots, fed with traditional fertilisers, were small and weak.

F   However, measures like this are not enough to solve the global soil degradation problem. To assess our options on a global scale we first need an accurate picture of what types of soil are out there, and the problems they face. That's not easy. For one thing, there is no agreed international system for classifying soil. In an attempt to unify the different approaches, the UN has created the Global Soil Map project. Researchers from nine countries are working together to create a map linked to a database that can be fed measurements from field surveys, drone surveys, satellite imagery, lab analyses and so on to provide real-time data on the state of the soil. Within the next four years, they aim to have mapped soils worldwide to a depth of 100 metres, with the results freely accessible to all.

G   But this is only a first step. We need ways of presenting the problem that bring it home to governments and the wider public, says Pamela Chasek at the International Institute for Sustainable Development, in Winnipeg, Canada. 'Most scientists don't speak language that policy-makers can understand, and vice versa.' Chasek and her colleagues have proposed a goal of 'zero net land degradation'. Like the idea of carbon neutrality, it is an easily understood target that can help shape expectations and encourage action.

For soils on the brink, that may be too late. Several researchers are agitating for the immediate creation of protected zones for endangered soils. One difficulty here is defining what these areas should conserve: areas where the greatest soil diversity is present? Or areas of unspoilt soils that could act as a future benchmark of quality?

Whatever we do, if we want our soils to survive, we need to take action now.

* Humus: the part of the soil formed from dead plant material

Questions 14–17

Complete the summary below.

Write ONE WORD ONLY from the passage for each answer.

Write your answers in boxes 14–17 on your answer sheet.

Why soil degradation could be a disaster for humans

Healthy soil contains a large variety of bacteria and other microorganisms, as well as plant remains and **14** .... It provides us with food and also with antibiotics, and its function in storing **15** .... has a significant effect on the climate. In addition, it prevents damage to property and infrastructure because it holds **16** ....

If these microorganisms are lost, soil may lose its special properties. The main factor contributing to soil degradation is the **17** .... carried out by humans.

Questions 18–21

Complete each sentence with the correct ending, A–F, below.

Write the correct letter, A–F, in boxes 18–21 on your answer sheet.

18 Nutrients contained in the unused parts of harvested crops

19 Synthetic fertilisers produced with the Haber-Bosch process

20 Addition of a mixture developed by Pius Floris to the soil

21 The idea of zero net soil degradation

A	may improve the number and quality of plants growing there.
B	may contain data from up to nine countries.
C	may not be put back into the soil.
D	may help governments to be more aware of soil-related issues.
E	may cause damage to different aspects of the environment.
F	may be better for use at a global level.

Questions 22–26

*Reading Passage 2 has seven paragraphs, **A–G**.*

Which section contains the following information?

*Write the correct letter, **A–G**, in boxes 22–26 on your answer sheet.*

NB *You may use any letter more than once.*

22 a reference to one person's motivation for a soil-improvement project

23 an explanation of how soil stayed healthy before the development of farming

24 examples of different ways of collecting information on soil degradation

25 a suggestion for a way of keeping some types of soil safe in the near future

26 a reason why it is difficult to provide an overview of soil degradation

READING PASSAGE 3

*You should spend about 20 minutes on **Questions 27–40**, which are based on Reading Passage 3 below.*

Book Review

The Happiness Industry: How the Government and Big Business
Sold Us Well-Being

By William Davies

'Happiness is the ultimate goal because it is self-evidently good. If we are asked why happiness matters we can give no further external reason. It just obviously does matter.' This pronouncement by Richard Layard, an economist and advocate of 'positive psychology', summarises the beliefs of many people today. For Layard and others like him, it is obvious that the purpose of government is to promote a state of collective well-being. The only question is how to achieve it, and here positive psychology – a supposed science that not only identifies what makes people happy but also allows their happiness to be measured – can show the way. Equipped with this science, they say, governments can secure happiness in society in a way they never could in the past.

It is an astonishingly crude and simple-minded way of thinking, and for that very reason increasingly popular. Those who think in this way are oblivious to the vast philosophical literature in which the meaning and value of happiness have been explored and questioned, and write as if nothing of any importance had been thought on the subject until it came to their attention. It was the philosopher Jeremy Bentham (1748–1832) who was more than anyone else responsible for the development of this way of thinking. For Bentham it was obvious that the human good consists of pleasure and the absence of pain. The Greek philosopher Aristotle may have identified happiness with self-realisation in the 4th century BC, and thinkers throughout the ages may have struggled to reconcile the pursuit of happiness with other human values, but for Bentham all this was mere metaphysics or fiction. Without knowing anything much of him or the school of moral theory he established – since they are by education and intellectual conviction illiterate in the history of ideas – our advocates of positive psychology follow in his tracks in rejecting as outmoded and irrelevant pretty much the entirety of ethical reflection on human happiness to date.

But as William Davies notes in his recent book *The Happiness Industry*, the view that happiness is the only self-evident good is actually a way of limiting moral inquiry. One of the virtues of this rich, lucid and arresting book is that it places the current cult of happiness in a well-defined historical framework. Rightly, Davies begins his story with Bentham, noting that he was far more than a philosopher. Davies writes, 'Bentham's activities were those which we might now associate with a public sector management consultant'. In the 1790s, he wrote to the Home Office suggesting that the departments of government be linked together through a set of 'conversation tubes', and to the Bank of England with a design for a printing device that could produce unforgeable banknotes. He drew up plans for a 'frigidarium' to keep provisions such as meat, fish, fruit and vegetables fresh. His celebrated design for a prison to be known as a 'Panopticon', in which prisoners would be kept in solitary confinement while being visible at all times to the guards, was very nearly adopted. (Surprisingly, Davies does not discuss the fact that Bentham meant his Panopticon not just as a model prison but also as an instrument of control that could be applied to schools and factories.)

Bentham was also a pioneer of the 'science of happiness'. If happiness is to be regarded as a science, it has to be measured, and Bentham suggested two ways in which this might be done. Viewing happiness as a complex of pleasurable sensations, he suggested that it might be quantified by measuring the human pulse rate. Alternatively, money could be used as the standard for quantification: if two different goods have the same price, it can be claimed that they produce the same quantity of pleasure in the consumer. Bentham was more attracted by the latter measure. By associating money so closely to inner experience, Davies writes, Bentham 'set the stage for the entangling of psychological research and capitalism that would shape the business practices of the twentieth century'.

The Happiness Industry describes how the project of a science of happiness has become integral to capitalism. We learn much that is interesting about how economic problems are being redefined and treated as psychological maladies. In addition, Davies shows how the belief that inner states of pleasure and displeasure can be objectively measured has informed management studies and advertising. The tendency of thinkers such as J B Watson, the founder of behaviourism*, was that human beings could be shaped, or manipulated, by policymakers and managers. Watson had no factual basis for his view of human action. When he became president of the American Psychological Association in 1915, he 'had never even studied a single human being': his research had been confined to experiments on white rats. Yet Watson's reductive model is now widely applied, with 'behaviour change' becoming the goal of governments: in Britain, a 'Behaviour Insights Team' has been established by the government to study how people can be encouraged, at minimum cost to the public purse, to live in what are considered to be socially desirable ways.

Modern industrial societies appear to need the possibility of ever-increasing happiness to motivate them in their labours. But whatever its intellectual pedigree, the idea that governments should be responsible for promoting happiness is always a threat to human freedom.

* 'behaviourism': a branch of psychology which is concerned with observable behaviour

Questions 27–29

*Choose the correct letter, **A**, **B**, **C** or **D**.*

Write the correct letter in boxes 27–29 on your answer sheet.

27   What is the reviewer's attitude to advocates of positive psychology?

    A   They are wrong to reject the ideas of Bentham.
    B   They are over-influenced by their study of Bentham's theories.
    C   They have a fresh new approach to ideas on human happiness.
    D   They are ignorant about the ideas they should be considering.

28   The reviewer refers to the Greek philosopher Aristotle in order to suggest that happiness

    A   may not be just pleasure and the absence of pain.
    B   should not be the main goal of humans.
    C   is not something that should be fought for.
    D   is not just an abstract concept.

29   According to Davies, Bentham's suggestion for linking the price of goods to happiness was significant because

    A   it was the first successful way of assessing happiness.
    B   it established a connection between work and psychology.
    C   it was the first successful example of psychological research.
    D   it involved consideration of the rights of consumers.

Questions 30–34

*Complete the summary using the list of words **A–G** below.*

*Write the correct letter, **A–G**, in boxes 30–34 on your answer sheet.*

Jeremy Bentham

Jeremy Bentham was active in other areas besides philosophy. In the 1790s he suggested a type of technology to improve **30** .... for different Government departments. He developed a new way of printing banknotes to increase **31** .... and also designed a method for the **32** .... of food. He also drew up plans for a prison which allowed the **33** .... of prisoners at all times, and believed the same design could be used for other institutions as well. When researching happiness, he investigated possibilities for its **34** .... , and suggested some methods of doing this.

A measurement	**B** security	**C** implementation
D profits	**E** observation	**F** communication
G preservation		

Questions 35–40

Do the following statements agree with the claims of the writer in Reading Passage 3?

In boxes 35–40 on your answer sheet, write

> **YES** if the statement agrees with the claims of the writer
> **NO** if the statement contradicts the claims of the writer
> **NOT GIVEN** if it is impossible to say what the writer thinks about this

35 One strength of *The Happiness Industry* is its discussion of the relationship between psychology and economics.

36 It is more difficult to measure some emotions than others.

37 Watson's ideas on behaviourism were supported by research on humans he carried out before 1915.

38 Watson's ideas have been most influential on governments outside America.

39 The need for happiness is linked to industrialisation.

40 A main aim of government should be to increase the happiness of the population.

WRITING

WRITING TASK 1

You should spend about 20 minutes on this task.

The plans below show the layout of a university's sports centre now, and how it will look after redevelopment.

Summarise the information by selecting and reporting the main features, and make comparisons where relevant.

Write at least 150 words.

UNIVERSITY SPORTS CENTRE (present)

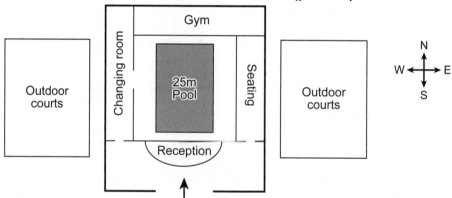

UNIVERSITY SPORTS CENTRE (future plans)

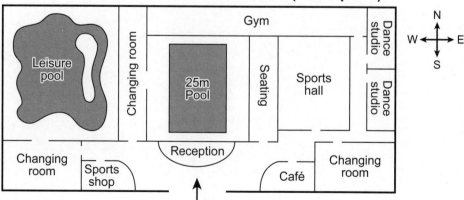

WRITING TASK 2

You should spend about 40 minutes on this task.

Write about the following topic:

> **In spite of the advances made in agriculture, many people around the world still go hungry.**
>
> **Why is this the case?**
>
> **What can be done about this problem?**

Give reasons for your answer and include any relevant examples from your own knowledge or experience.

Write at least 250 words.

SPEAKING

PART 1

The examiner asks the candidate about him/herself, his/her home, work or studies and other familiar topics.

EXAMPLE

Animals

- Are there many animals or birds where you live? [Why/Why not?]
- How often do you watch programmes or read articles about wild animals? [Why?]
- Have you ever been to a zoo or a wildlife park? [Why/Why not?]
- Would you like to have a job working with animals? [Why/Why not?]

PART 2

Describe a website you use that helps you a lot in your work or studies.
 	
 You should say:
    what the website is
    how often you use the website
    what information the website gives you
 and explain how your work or studies would change if this website didn't exist.

You will have to talk about the topic for one to two minutes. You have one minute to think about what you are going to say. You can make some notes to help you if you wish.

PART 3

Discussion topics:

The internet

Example questions:
Why do some people find the internet addictive?
What would the world be like without the internet?
Do you think that the way people use the internet may change in the future?

Social media websites

Example questions:
What are the ways that social media can be used for positive purposes?
Why do some individuals post highly negative comments about other people on social media?
Do you think that companies' main form of advertising will be via social media in the future?

Audioscripts

TEST 1

SECTION 1

OFFICIAL:	Hello, Tourist Information Centre, Mike speaking, how can I help you?
WOMAN:	Oh, hi. I wanted to find out about cookery classes. I believe there are some one-day classes for tourists?
OFFICIAL:	Well, they're open to everyone, but tourists are always welcome. OK, let me give you some details of what's available. There are several classes. One very popular one is at the <u>Food Studio</u>.
WOMAN:	OK.
OFFICIAL:	They focus on seasonal products, and as well as teaching you how to cook them, they also show you how to <u>choose</u> them.
WOMAN:	Right, that sounds good. How big are the classes?
OFFICIAL:	I'm not sure exactly, but they'll be quite small.
WOMAN:	And could I get a <u>private</u> lesson there?
OFFICIAL:	I think so ... let me check, yes, they do offer those. Though in fact most of the people who attend the classes find it's a nice way of getting to know one another.
WOMAN:	I suppose it must be, yes.
OFFICIAL:	And this company has a special deal for clients where they offer a discount of <u>20 percent</u> if you return for a further class.
WOMAN:	OK. But you said there were several classes?
OFFICIAL:	That's right. Another one you might be interested in is Bond's Cookery School. They're quite new, they just opened six months ago, but I've heard good things about them. They concentrate on teaching you to prepare <u>healthy</u> food, and they have quite a lot of specialist staff.
WOMAN:	So is that food for people on a diet and things like that? I don't know if I'd be interested in that.
OFFICIAL:	Well, I don't think they particularly focus on low calorie diets or weight loss. It's more to do with recipes that look at specific needs, like including ingredients that will help build up your <u>bones</u> and make them stronger, that sort of thing.
WOMAN:	I see. Well, I might be interested, I'm not sure. Do they have a website I could check?
OFFICIAL:	Yes, just key in the name of the school – it'll come up. And if you want to know more about them, every Thursday evening they have a <u>lecture</u> at the school. It's free and you don't need to book or anything, just turn up at 7.30. And that might give you an idea of whether you want to go to an actual class.

Example

Q1

Q2

Q3

Q4

Q5

Q6

OFFICIAL:	OK, there's one more place you might be interested in. That's got a rather strange name, it's called The <u>Arretsa</u> Centre – that's spelled A-R-R-E-T-S-A.
WOMAN:	OK.
OFFICIAL:	They've got a very good reputation. They do a bit of meat and fish cookery but they mostly specialise in <u>vegetarian</u> dishes.
WOMAN:	Right. That's certainly an area I'd like to learn more about. I've got lots of friends who don't eat meat. In fact, I think I might have seen that school today. Is it just by the <u>market</u>?

Q7

Q8

Q9

OFFICIAL: That's right. So they don't have any problem getting their ingredients. They're right next door. And they also offer a special two-hour course in how to use a <u>knife</u>. They cover all the different skills – buying them, sharpening, chopping techniques. It gets booked up quickly though so you'd need to check it was available.   *Q10*

WOMAN: Right, well thank you very much. I'll go and …

SECTION 2

Good evening everyone. My name's Phil Sutton, and I'm chairman of the Highways Committee. We've called this meeting to inform members of the public about the new regulations for traffic and parking we're proposing for Granford. I'll start by summarising these changes before we open the meeting to questions.

So, why do we need to make these changes to traffic systems in Granford? Well, we're very aware that traffic is becoming an increasing problem. It's been especially noticeable with the increase in heavy traffic while they've been building the new hospital. <u>But it's the overall rise in the volume of traffic of all kinds that's concerning us</u>. To date there's not been any increase in traffic accidents, but that's not something we want to see happen, obviously.   *Q11*

We recently carried out a survey of local residents, and their responses were interesting. <u>People were very concerned about the lack of visibility on some roads due to cars parked along the sides of the roads</u>. We'd expected complaints about the congestion near the school when parents are dropping off their children or picking them up, but this wasn't top of the list, and nor were noise and fumes from trucks and lorries, though they were mentioned by some people.   *Q12*

We think these new traffic regulations would make a lot of difference. But we still have a long way to go. We've managed to keep our proposals within budget, just, so they can be covered by the Council. <u>But, of course, it's no good introducing new regulations if we don't have a way of making sure that everyone obeys them</u>, and that's an area we're still working on with the help of representatives from the police force.   *Q13*

OK, so this slide shows a map of the central area of Granford, with the High Street in the middle and School Road on the right. Now, <u>we already have a set of traffic lights in the High Street at the junction with Station Road, but we're planning to have another set at the other end, at the School Road junction</u>, to regulate the flow of traffic along the High Street.   *Q14*

We've decided we definitely need a pedestrian crossing. We considered putting this on School Road, just outside the school, but in the end we decided that could lead to a lot of traffic congestion so <u>we decided to locate it on the High Street, crossing the road in front of the supermarket</u>. That's a very busy area, so it should help things there.   *Q15*

We're proposing some changes to parking. <u>At present, parking isn't allowed on the High Street outside the library, but we're going to change that, and allow parking there</u>, but not at the other end of the High Street near School Road.   *Q16*

<u>There'll be a new 'No Parking' sign on School Road, just by the entrance to the school</u>, forbidding parking for 25 metres. This should improve visibility for drivers and pedestrians, especially on the bend just to the north of the school.   *Q17*

As far as disabled drivers are concerned, at present they have parking outside the supermarket, but lorries also use those spaces, so <u>we've got two new disabled parking spaces on the side road up towards the bank</u>. It's not ideal, but probably better than the present arrangement.

Q18

<u>We also plan to widen the pavement on School Road. We think we can manage to get an extra half-metre on the bend just before you get to the school, on the same side of the road.</u>

Q19

Finally, <u>we've introduced new restrictions on loading and unloading for the supermarket, so lorries will only be allowed to stop there before 8 am. That's the supermarket on School Road</u> – we kept to the existing arrangements with the High Street supermarket.

Q20

OK. So that's about it. Now, would anyone …

SECTION 3

EMMA: We've got to choose a topic for our experiment, haven't we, Jack? Were you thinking of something to do with seeds?

JACK: That's right. I thought we could look at seed germination – how a seed begins to grow.

EMMA: OK. Any particular reason? I know you're hoping to work in plant science eventually …

JACK: Yeah, but practically everything we do is going to feed into that. No, <u>there's an optional module on seed structure and function in the third year that I might do, so I thought it might be useful for that.</u> If I choose that option, I don't have to do a dissertation module.

Q21

EMMA: Good idea.

JACK: Well, I thought for this experiment we could look at the relationship between seed size and the way the seeds are planted. So, we could plant different sized seeds in different ways, and see which grow best.

EMMA: OK. <u>We'd need to allow time for the seeds to come up.</u>

Q22

JACK: <u>That should be fine if we start now. A lot of the other possible experiments need quite a bit longer.</u>

EMMA: <u>So that'd make it a good one to choose.</u> And I don't suppose it'd need much equipment; we're not doing chemical analysis or anything. Though that's not really an issue, we've got plenty of equipment in the laboratory.

JACK: Yeah. We need to have a word with the tutor if we're going to go ahead with it though. I'm sure our aim's OK. It's not very ambitious but the assignment's only ten percent of our final mark, isn't it? But <u>we need to be sure we're the only ones doing it.</u>

Q23

EMMA: Yeah, it's only five percent actually, but it'd be a bit boring if everyone was doing it.

JACK: Did you read that book on seed germination on our reading list?

EMMA: The one by Graves? I looked through it for my last experiment, though it wasn't all that relevant there. It would be for this experiment, though. <u>I found it quite hard to follow – lots about the theory, which I hadn't expected.</u>

Q24

JACK: Yes, I'd been hoping for something more practical. It does include references to the recent findings on genetically-modified seeds, though.

EMMA: Yes, that was interesting.

JACK: I read an article about seed germination by Lee Hall.

EMMA: About seeds that lie in the ground for ages and only germinate after a fire?

JACK: That's the one. I knew a bit about it already, but not about this research. <u>His</u>   *Q25*
<u>analysis of figures comparing the times of the fires and the proportion of seeds that</u>
<u>germinated was done in a lot of detail – very impressive.</u>

EMMA: Was that the article with the illustrations of early stages of plant development?
They were very clear.

JACK: I think those diagrams were in another article.

EMMA: Anyway, shall we have a look at the procedure for our experiment? We'll need to
get going with it quite soon.

JACK: Right. So the first thing we have to do is find our seeds. I think vegetable seeds
would be best. And obviously they mustn't all be the same size. <u>So, how many</u>   *Q26*
<u>sorts do we need? About four different ones</u>?

EMMA: I think that would be enough. There'll be quite a large number of seeds for each
one.

JACK: <u>Then, for each seed we need to find out how much it weighs,</u> and also measure its *Q27*
dimensions, and we need to keep a careful record of all that.

EMMA: That'll be quite time-consuming. <u>And we also need to decide how deep we're</u>   *Q28*
<u>going to plant the seeds</u> – right on the surface, a few millimetres down, or several
centimetres.

JACK: OK. So then we get planting. <u>Do you think we can plant several seeds together in</u> *Q29*
<u>the same plant pot</u>?

EMMA: <u>No, I think we need a different one for each seed.</u>

JACK: Right. And we'll need to label them – we can use different coloured labels. Then we
wait for the seeds to germinate – I reckon that'll be about three weeks, depending
on what the weather's like. <u>Then we see if our plants have come up, and write</u>   *Q30*
<u>down how tall they've grown.</u>

EMMA: Then all we have to do is look at our numbers, and see if there's any relation
between them.

JACK: That's right. So …

SECTION 4

Hi. Today we're going to be looking at animals in urban environments and I'm going to be
telling you about some research on how they're affected by these environments.

Now, in evolutionary terms, urban environments represent huge upheavals, the sorts of
massive changes that usually happen over millions of years. And we used to think that only a
few species could adapt to this new environment. <u>One species which is well known as being</u> *Q31*
<u>highly adaptable is the crow, and there've been various studies about how they manage to</u>
<u>learn new skills.</u> Another successful species is <u>the pigeon, because they're able to perch on</u> *Q32*
<u>ledges on the walls of city buildings, just like they once perched on cliffs by the sea.</u>

But in fact, we're now finding that these early immigrants were just the start of a more general
movement of animals into cities, and of adaptation by these animals to city life. And <u>one thing</u> *Q33*
<u>that researchers are finding especially interesting is the speed with which they're doing this –</u>
<u>we're not talking about gradual evolution here – these animals are changing fast.</u>

Let me tell you about some of the studies that have been carried out in this area. So, in the
University of Minnesota, a biologist called Emilie Snell-Rood and her colleagues looked at
specimens of urbanised small mammals such as mice and gophers that had been collected
in Minnesota, and that are now kept in museums there. And she looked at specimens that

had been collected over the last hundred years, which is a very short time in evolutionary terms. And she found that during that time, these small mammals had experienced a jump in brain size when compared to rural mammals. Now, we can't be sure this means they're more intelligent, but since the sizes of other parts of the body didn't change, it does suggest that something cognitive was going on. And Snell-Rood thinks that this change might reflect the cognitive demands of adjusting to city life – having to look in different places to find food, for example, and coping with a whole new set of dangers.

Q34

Q35

Then over in Germany at the Max Planck Institute, there's another biologist called Catarina Miranda who's done some experiments with blackbirds living in urban and rural areas. And she's been looking not at their anatomy but at their behaviour. So as you might expect, she's found that the urban blackbirds tend to be quite bold – they're prepared to face up to a lot of threats that would frighten away their country counterparts. But there's one type of situation that does seem to frighten the urban blackbirds, and that's anything new – anything they haven't experienced before. And if you think about it, that's quite sensible for a bird living in the city.

Q36

Q37

Jonathan Atwell, in Indiana University, is looking at how a range of animals respond to urban environments. He's found that when they're under stress, their endocrine systems react by reducing the amount of hormones such as corticosterone into their blood. It's a sensible-seeming adaptation. A rat that gets scared every time a subway train rolls past won't be very successful.

Q38

There's just one more study I'd like to mention which is by Sarah Partan and her team, and they've been looking at how squirrels communicate in an urban environment, and they've found that a routine part of their communication is carried out by waving their tails. You do also see this in the country, but it's much more prevalent in cities, possibly because it's effective in a noisy environment.

Q39

So what are the long-term implications of this? One possibility is that we may see completely new species developing in cities. But on the other hand, it's possible that not all of these adaptations will be permanent. Once the animal's got accustomed to its new environment, it may no longer need the features it's developed.

Q40

So, now we've had a look ...

TEST 2

SECTION 1

JIM:	Hello, South City Cycling Club.
WOMAN:	Oh, hi. Er … I want to find out about joining the club.
JIM:	Right. I can help you there. I'm the club secretary and my name's <u>Jim Hunter</u>.

Example (right-aligned, next to Jim Hunter line)

WOMAN:	Oh, hi Jim.
JIM:	So, are you interested in membership for yourself?
WOMAN:	That's right.
JIM:	OK. Well there are basically two types of adult membership. If you're pretty serious about cycling, there's the Full membership. That costs 260 dollars and <u>that covers you not just for ordinary cycling but also for races both here in the city and also in other parts of Australia</u>.

Q1

WOMAN:	Right. Well, I'm not really up to that standard. I was more interested in just joining a group to do some cycling in my free time.
JIM:	Sure. That's why most people join. So, in that case you'd be better with the Recreational membership. That's 108 dollars if you're over 19, and 95 dollars if you're under.
WOMAN:	I'm 25.
JIM:	OK. It's paid quarterly, and you can upgrade it later to the Full membership if you want to, of course. Now <u>both types of membership include the club fee of 20 dollars. They also provide insurance in case you have an accident</u>, though we hope you won't need that, of course.

Q2

WOMAN:	No. OK, well, I'll go with the Recreational membership, I think. And that allows me to join in the club activities, and so on?
JIM:	That's right. And once you're a member of the club, you're also permitted to wear our kit when you're out cycling. It's green and white.
WOMAN:	Yes, I've seen cyclists wearing it. So, can I buy that at the club?
JIM:	No, it's made to order by a company in Brisbane. <u>You can find them online; they're called Jerriz</u>. That's J-E-R-R-I-Z. You can use your membership number to put in an order on their website.

Q3

WOMAN:	OK. Now, can you tell me a bit about the rides I can do?
JIM:	Sure. So we have training rides pretty well every morning, and they're a really good way of improving your cycling skills as well as your general level of fitness, but they're different levels. Level A is pretty fast – you're looking at about 30 or 35 kilometres an hour. <u>If you can do about 25 kilometres an hour, you'd probably be level B</u>, and then level C are the novices, who stay at about 15 kilometres per hour.

Q4

WOMAN:	Right. Well I reckon I'd be level B. So, when are the sessions for that level?
JIM:	There are a couple each week. They're both early morning sessions. <u>There's one on Tuesdays, and for that one you meet at 5.30 am, and the meeting point's the stadium</u> – do you know where that is?

Q5

WOMAN:	Yes, it's quite near my home, in fact. OK, and how about the other one?
JIM:	<u>That's on Thursdays. It starts at the same time, but they meet at the main gate to the park</u>.

Q6

WOMAN:	Is that the one just past the shopping mall?
JIM:	That's it.

WOMAN:	So how long are the rides?	
JIM:	They're about an hour and a half. So, if you have a job it's easy to fit in before you go to work. <u>And the members often go somewhere for coffee afterwards</u>, so it's quite a social event.	*Q7*
WOMAN:	OK. That sounds good. I've only just moved to the city so I don't actually know many people yet.	
JIM:	Well, it's a great way to meet people.	
WOMAN:	<u>And does each ride have a leader</u>?	*Q8*
JIM:	<u>Sometimes, but not always</u>. But you don't really need one; the group members on the ride support one another, anyway.	
WOMAN:	How would we know where to go?	
JIM:	<u>If you check the club website, you'll see that the route for each ride is clearly marked. So you can just print that out</u> and take it along with you. It's similar from one week to another, but it's not always exactly the same.	*Q9*
WOMAN:	And what do I need to bring?	
JIM:	Well, bring a bottle of water, and your phone. You shouldn't use it while you're cycling, but have it with you.	
WOMAN:	Right.	
JIM:	And in winter, it's well before sunrise when we set out, <u>so you need to make sure your bike's got lights</u>.	*Q10*
WOMAN:	That's OK. Well, thanks Jim. I'd definitely like to join. So what's the best way of going about it?	
JIM:	You can …	

SECTION 2

Thanks for coming everyone. OK, so this meeting is for new staff and staff who haven't been involved with our volunteering projects yet. So basically, the idea is that we allow staff to give up some of their work time to help on various charity projects to benefit the local community. We've been doing this for the last five years and it's been very successful.

Participating doesn't necessarily involve a huge time commitment. <u>The company will pay for eight hours of your time. That can be used over one or two days all at once, or spread over several months throughout the year</u>. There are some staff who enjoy volunteering so much they also give up their own free time for a couple of hours every week. It's completely up to you. Obviously, many people will have family commitments and aren't as available as other members of staff.   *Q11*

Feedback from staff has been overwhelmingly positive. <u>Because they felt they were doing something really useful, nearly everyone agreed that volunteering made them feel more motivated at work</u>. They also liked building relationships with the people in the local community and felt valued by them. One or two people also said it was a good thing to have on their CVs.   *Q12*

One particularly successful project last year was the Get Working Project. This was aimed at helping unemployed people in the area get back to work. <u>Our staff were able to help them improve their telephone skills, such as writing down messages and speaking with confidence to potential customers, which they had found quite difficult</u>. This is something many employers look for in job applicants – and something we all do without even thinking about, every day at work.   *Q13*

We've got an exciting new project starting this year. Up until now, we've mainly focused on projects to do with education and training. And we'll continue with our reading project in schools and our work with local charities. But we've also agreed to help out on a conservation   *Q14* project in Redfern Park. So if any of you fancy being outside and getting your hands dirty, this is the project for you.

I also want to mention the annual Digital Inclusion Day, which is coming up next month. The   *Q15* aim of this is to help older people keep up with technology. And this year, instead of hosting the event in our own training facility, we're using the ICT suite at Hill College, as it can hold far more people.

We've invited over 60 people from the Silver Age Community Centre to take part, so we'll need a lot of volunteers to help with this event.

If you're interested in taking part, please go to the volunteering section of our website and   *Q16* complete the relevant form. We won't be providing any training for this but you'll be paired with an experienced volunteer if you've never done it before. By the way, don't forget to tell your manager about any volunteering activities you decide to do.

The participants on the Digital Inclusion Day really benefited. The majority were in their seventies, though some were younger and a few were even in their nineties! Quite a few owned both a computer and a mobile phone, but these tended to be outdated models.   *Q17* They generally knew how to do simple things, like send texts, but weren't aware of recent developments in mobile phone technology. A few were keen to learn but most were quite   *Q18* dismissive at first – they couldn't see the point of updating their skills. But that soon changed.

The feedback was very positive. The really encouraging thing was that participants all   *Q19* said they felt much more confident about using social media to keep in touch with their grandchildren, who prefer this form of communication to phoning or sending emails. A lot   *Q20* of them also said playing online games would help them make new friends and keep their brains active. They weren't that impressed with being able to order their groceries online, as they liked going out to the shops, but some said it would come in handy if they were ill or the weather was really bad. One thing they asked about was using tablets for things like reading newspapers – some people had been given tablets as presents but had never used them, so that's something we'll make sure we include this time …

SECTION 3

TUTOR: Ah … come in, Russ.

RUSS: Thank you.

TUTOR: Now you wanted to consult me about your class presentation on nanotechnology – you're due to give it in next week, aren't you?

RUSS: That's right. And I'm really struggling. I chose the topic because I didn't know much about it and wanted to learn more, but now I've read so much about it, in a way there's too much to say – I could talk for much longer than the twenty minutes I've been allocated. Should I assume the other students don't know much, and give them   *Q21* a kind of general introduction, or should I try and make them share my fascination with a particular aspect?

TUTOR: You could do either, but you'll need to have it clear in your own mind.

RUSS: Then I think I'll give an overview.

TUTOR: OK. Now, one way of approaching this is to work through developments in chronological order.

RUSS: Uh-huh.

TUTOR:	On the other hand, you could talk about the numerous ways that nanotechnology is being applied.	
RUSS:	You mean things like thin films on camera displays to make them water-repellent, and additives to make motorcycle helmets stronger and lighter.	
TUTOR:	Exactly. Or another way would be to focus on its impact in one particular area, say medicine, or space exploration.	*Q22*
RUSS:	That would make it easier to focus. Perhaps I should do that.	
TUTOR:	I think that would be a good idea.	
RUSS:	Right. How important is it to include slides in the presentation?	
TUTOR:	They aren't essential, by any means. And there's a danger of tailoring what you say to fit whatever slides you can find. While it can be good to include slides, you could end up spending too long looking for suitable ones. You might find it better to leave them out.	*Q23*
RUSS:	I see. Another thing I was wondering about was how to start. I know presentations often begin with 'First I'm going to talk about this, and then I'll talk about that', but I thought about asking the audience what they know about nanotechnology.	
TUTOR:	That would be fine if you had an hour or two for the presentation, but you might find that you can't do anything with the answers you get, and it simply eats into the short time that's available.	
RUSS:	So, maybe I should mention a particular way that nanotechnology is used, to focus people's attention.	*Q24*
TUTOR:	That sounds sensible.	
RUSS:	What do you think I should do next? I really have to plan the presentation today and tomorrow.	
TUTOR:	Well, initially I think you should ignore all the notes you've made, take a small piece of paper, and write a single short sentence that ties together the whole presentation: it can be something as simple as 'Nanotechnology is already improving our lives'. Then start planning the content around that. You can always modify that sentence later, if you need to.	*Q25*
RUSS:	OK.	

TUTOR:	OK, now let's think about actually giving the presentation. You've only given one before, if I remember correctly, about an experiment you'd been involved in.	
RUSS:	That's right. It was pretty rubbish!	
TUTOR:	Let's say it was better in some respects than in others. With regard to the structure, I felt that you ended rather abruptly, without rounding it off. Be careful not to do that in next week's presentation.	*Q26*
RUSS:	OK.	
TUTOR:	And you made very little eye contact with the audience, because you were looking down at your notes most of the time. You need to be looking at the audience and only occasionally glancing at your notes.	*Q27*
RUSS:	Mmm.	
TUTOR:	Your body language was a little odd. Every time you showed a slide, you turned your back on the audience so you could look at it – you should have been looking at your laptop. And you kept scratching your head, so I found myself wondering when you were next going to do that, instead of listening to what you were saying!	*Q28*
RUSS:	Oh dear. What did you think of the language? I knew that not everyone was familiar with the subject, so I tried to make it as simple as I could.	
TUTOR:	Yes, that came across. You used a few words that are specific to the field, but you always explained what they meant, so the audience wouldn't have had any difficulty understanding.	*Q29*

RUSS: Uh-huh.

TUTOR: I must say <u>the handouts you prepared were well thought out. They were a good summary of your presentation, which people would be able to refer to later on</u>. So well done on that.   *Q30*

RUSS: Thank you.

TUTOR: Well, I hope that helps you with next week's presentation.

RUSS: Yes, it will. Thanks a lot.

TUTOR: I'll look forward to seeing a big improvement, then.

SECTION 4

Today, we'll be continuing the series of lectures on memory by focusing on what is called episodic memory and what can happen if this is not working properly.

Episodic memory refers to the memory of an event or 'episode'. Episodic memories allow us to mentally travel back in time to an event from the past. <u>Episodic memories include various details about these events, for example, when an event happened and other information such as the location</u>. To help understand this concept, try to remember the last time you ate dinner at a restaurant. The ability to remember where you ate, who you were with and the items you ordered are all features of an episodic memory.   *Q31*

Episodic memory is distinct from another type of memory called semantic memory. <u>This is the type of factual memory that we have in common with everyone else – that is your general knowledge of the world</u>. To build upon a previous example, remembering where you parked your car is an example of episodic memory, but your understanding of what a car is and how an engine works are examples of semantic memory. <u>Unlike episodic memory, semantic memory isn't dependent on recalling personal experiences</u>.   *Q32*   *Q33*

Episodic memory can be thought of as a process with several different steps of memory processing: encoding, consolidation and retrieval.

The initial step is called encoding. This involves the process of receiving and registering information, which is necessary for creating memories of information or events that you experience. <u>The degree to which you can successfully encode information depends on the level of attention you give to an event while it's actually happening</u>. Being distracted can make effective encoding very difficult. Encoding of episodic memories is also influenced by how you process the event. For example, <u>if you were introduced to someone called Charlie, you might make the connection that your uncle has the same name. Future recollection of Charlie's name is much easier if you have a strategy to help you encode it</u>.   *Q34*   *Q35*

Memory consolidation, the next step in forming an episodic memory, is the process by which memories of encoded information are strengthened, stabilised and stored to facilitate later retrieval. <u>Consolidation is most effective when the information being stored can be linked to an existing network of information</u>. Consolidation makes it possible for you to store memories for later retrieval indefinitely. <u>Forming strong memories depends on the frequency with which you try to retrieve them</u>. Memories can fade or become harder to retrieve if they aren't used very often.   *Q36*   *Q37*

The last step in forming episodic memories is called retrieval, which is the conscious recollection of encoded information. Retrieving information from episodic memory depends upon semantic, olfactory, auditory and visual factors. <u>These help episodic memory retrieval by acting as a prompt. For example, when recalling where you parked your car you may use the colour of a sign close to where you parked</u>. You actually have to mentally travel back to the moment you parked.   *Q38*

There are a wide range of neurological diseases and conditions that can affect episodic memory. These range from Alzheimer's to schizophrenia to autism. An impairment of episodic memory can have a profound effect on individuals' lives. For example, the symptoms of schizophrenia can be reasonably well controlled by medication; however, patients' episodic memory may still be impaired and so they are often unable to return to university or work. Recent studies have shown that computer-assisted games designed to keep the brain active can help improve their episodic memory.   Q39

Episodic memories can help people connect with others, for instance by sharing intimate details about their past; something individuals with autism often have problems with. This may be caused by an absence of a sense of self. This is essential for the storage of episodic memory, and has been found to be impaired in children with autism. Research has shown that treatments that improve memory may also have a positive impact on children's social development.   Q40

One study looked at a …

TEST 3

SECTION 1

LINDA:	Hello, Linda speaking.
MATT:	Oh hi, Linda. This is Matt Brooks. Alex White gave me your number. He said you'd be able to give me some advice about moving to Banford.
LINDA:	Yes, Alex did mention you. How can I help?
MATT:	Well, first of all – which area to live in?
LINDA:	Well, I live in <u>Dalton</u>, which is a really nice suburb – not too expensive, and there's a nice park. *Example*
MATT:	Sounds good. Do you know how much it would be to rent a two bedroom flat there?
LINDA:	Yeah, you should be able to get something reasonable for <u>850</u> pounds per month. *Q1* That's what people typically pay. You certainly wouldn't want to pay more than 900 pounds. That doesn't include bills or anything.
MATT:	No. That sounds alright. I'll definitely have a look there. Are the transport links easy from where you live?
LINDA:	Well, I'm very lucky. I work in the city centre so I don't have to use public transport. <u>I go by bike</u>. *Q2*
MATT:	Oh, I wish I could do that. Is it safe to cycle around the city?
LINDA:	Yes, it's fine. And it keeps me fit. Anyway, driving to work in the city centre would be a nightmare because <u>there's hardly any parking</u>. And the traffic during the rush *Q3* hour can be bad.
MATT:	I'd be working from home but I'd have to go to London one or two days a week.
LINDA:	Oh, that's perfect. Getting to London is no problem. There's a fast train every <u>30 minutes</u> which only takes 45 minutes. *Q4*
MATT:	That's good.
LINDA:	Yeah, the train service isn't bad during the week. And they run quite late at night. <u>It's weekends that are a problem</u>. They're always doing engineering work and you *Q5* have to take a bus to Hadham and pick up the train there, which is really slow. But other than that, Banford's a great place to live. I've never been happier.

LINDA:	There are some nice restaurants in the city centre and a brand new <u>cinema which</u> *Q6* <u>has only been open a couple of months</u>. There's a good arts centre too.
MATT:	Sounds like Banford's got it all.
LINDA:	Yes! We're really lucky. There are lots of really good aspects to living here. The schools are good and the <u>hospital here is one of the best in the country</u>. Everyone I *Q7* know who's been there's had a positive experience. Oh, I can give you the name of my <u>dentist too in Bridge Street</u>, if you're interested. I've been going to him for years *Q8* and I've never had any problems.
MATT:	Oh, OK. Thanks!
LINDA:	I'll find his number and send it to you.
MATT:	Thanks, that would be really helpful.
LINDA:	Are you planning to visit Banford soon?
MATT:	Yes. My wife and I are both coming next week. We want to make some appointments with estate agents.
LINDA:	I could meet you if you like and show you around.
MATT:	Are you sure? We'd really appreciate that.
LINDA:	Either a Tuesday or <u>Thursday is good for me, after 5.30</u>. *Q9*
MATT:	Thursday's preferable – Tuesday I need to get home before 6 pm.

LINDA: OK. Great. Let me know which train you're catching and <u>I'll meet you in the café</u>   *Q10*
<u>outside. You can't miss it. It's opposite the station</u> and next to the museum.

MATT: Brilliant. I'll text you next week then. Thanks so much for all the advice.

LINDA: No problem. I'll see you next week.

SECTION 2

So if you're one of those people who hasn't found the perfect physical activity yet – here are some things to think about which might help you make the right decision for you.

The first question to ask yourself is whether you would enjoy training in a gym. Many people are put off by the idea of having to fit a visit to the gym into their busy day – you often have to go very early or late as some gyms can get very crowded. But with regular training <u>you'll see a big</u>   *Q11*
<u>difference in a relatively short space of time.</u>

Running has become incredibly popular in recent years. That's probably got a lot to do with the fact that <u>it's a very accessible form of exercise – anyone can run – even if you can only run a</u>   *Q12*
<u>few metres to begin with.</u> But make sure you get the right shoes – it's worth investing in a high quality pair and they don't come cheap. Another great thing about running is that you can do it at any time of day or night – the only thing that may stop you is snow and ice.

Swimming is another really good way to build fitness. What attracts many people is that <u>you</u>   *Q13*
<u>can swim in an indoor pool at any time of year.</u> On the other hand, it can be quite boring or solitary – it's hard to chat to people while you're swimming lengths.

Cycling has become almost as popular as running in recent years. That's probably because as well as improving their fitness, <u>many people say being out in the fresh air in a park or in the</u>   *Q14*
<u>countryside can be fun,</u> provided the conditions are right, of course – only fanatics go out in the wind and rain!

Yoga is a good choice for those of you looking for exercise which focuses on developing both a healthy mind and body. It's a good way of building strength and with the right instructor, <u>there's</u>   *Q15*
<u>less chance of hurting yourself than with other more active sports.</u> But don't expect to find it easy – it can be surprisingly challenging, especially for people who aren't very flexible.

Getting a personal trainer is a good way to start your fitness programme. Obviously there can be significant costs involved. <u>But if you've got someone there to encourage you and help you</u>   *Q16*
<u>achieve your goals, you're less likely to give up.</u> Make sure you get someone with a recognised qualification, though, or you could do yourself permanent damage.

Whatever you do, don't join a gym unless you're sure you'll make good use of it. So many people waste lots of money by signing up for membership and then hardly ever go. What happens to their good intentions? I don't think people suddenly stop caring about improving their fitness, or decide they have more important things to do. I think people lose interest when they don't think they're making enough progress. <u>That's when they give up hope and</u>   *Q17 & Q18*
<u>stop believing they'll ever achieve their goals. Also, what people sometimes don't realise</u>
<u>when they start is that it takes a lot of determination and hard work to keep training week</u>
<u>after week</u> and lots of people don't have that kind of commitment.

One thing you can do to help yourself is to <u>set manageable goals – be realistic and don't</u>   *Q19 & Q20*
<u>push yourself too far.</u> Some people advise writing goals down, but I think it's better to have a flexible approach. <u>Give yourself a really nice treat every time you reach one of your goals.</u> And don't get too upset if you experience setbacks – it's a journey – there are bound to be difficulties along the way.

SECTION 3

TUTOR: OK, Jim. You wanted to see me about your textile design project.

JIM: That's right. I've been looking at how a range of natural dyes can be used to colour fabrics like cotton and wool.

TUTOR: Why did you choose that topic?

JIM: Well, I got a lot of useful ideas from the museum, you know, at that exhibition of textiles. But I've always been interested in anything to do with colour. Years ago, I went to a carpet shop with my parents when we were on holiday in Turkey, and I remember all the amazing colours.   *Q21*

TUTOR: They might not all have been natural dyes.

JIM: Maybe not, but for the project I decided to follow it up. And I found a great book about a botanic garden in California that specialises in plants used for dyes.

TUTOR: OK. So, in your project, you had to include a practical investigation.

JIM: Yeah. At first I couldn't decide on my variables. I was going to just look at one type of fibre for example, like cotton ...

TUTOR: ... and see how different types of dyes affected it?

JIM: Yes. Then I decided to include others as well, so I looked at cotton and wool and nylon.   *Q22*

TUTOR: With just one type of dye?

JIM: Various types, including some that weren't natural, for comparison.

TUTOR: OK.

JIM: So, I did the experiments last week. I used some ready-made natural dyes, I found a website which supplied them, they came in just a few days, but I also made some of my own.

TUTOR: That must have taken quite a bit of time.

JIM: Yes, I'd thought it'd just be a matter of a teaspoon or so of dye, and actually that wasn't the case at all. Like I was using one vegetable, beetroot, for a red dye, and I had to chop up a whole pile of it. So it all took longer than I'd expected.   *Q23*

TUTOR: One possibility is to use food colourings.

JIM: I did use one. That was a yellow dye, an artificial one.

TUTOR: Tartrazine?

JIM: Yeah. I used it on cotton first. It came out a great colour, but when I rinsed the material, the colour just washed away. I'd been going to try it out on nylon, but I abandoned that idea.   *Q24*

TUTOR: Were you worried about health issues?

JIM: I'd thought if it's a legal food colouring, it must be safe.

TUTOR: Well, it can occasionally cause allergic reactions, I believe.

TUTOR: So what natural dyes did you look at?

JIM: Well, one was turmeric. The colour's great, it's a really strong yellow. It's generally used in dishes like curry.

TUTOR: It's meant to be quite good for your health when eaten, but you might find it's not permanent when it's used as a dye – a few washes, and it's gone.   *Q25*

JIM: Right. I used beetroot as a dye for wool. When I chop up beetroot to eat I always end up with bright red hands, but the wool ended up just a sort of watery cream shade. Disappointing.   *Q26*

TUTOR: There's a natural dye called Tyrian purple. Have you heard of that?

JIM: Yes. It comes from a shellfish, and it was worn in ancient times but only by important people as it was so rare. I didn't use it.   *Q27*

TUTOR: It fell out of use centuries ago, though one researcher managed to get hold of some recently. But that shade of purple can be produced by chemical dyes nowadays. Did you use any black dyes?

JIM:	Logwood. That was quite complicated. I had to prepare the fabric so the dye would take.	
TUTOR:	I hope you were careful to wear gloves.	
JIM:	Yes. I know the danger with that dye.	
TUTOR:	Good. <u>It can be extremely dangerous if it's ingested</u>. Now, presumably you had a look at an insect-based dye? Like cochineal, for example?	*Q28*
JIM:	Yes. I didn't actually make that, I didn't have time to start crushing up insects to get the red colour and anyway they're not available here, but I managed to get the dye quite easily from a website. <u>But it cost a fortune</u>. I can see why it's generally just used in cooking, and in small quantities.	*Q29*
TUTOR:	Yes, it's very effective, but that's precisely why it's not used as a dye.	
JIM:	I also read about using metal oxide. Apparently you can allow iron to rust while it's in contact with the fabric, and that colours it.	
TUTOR:	Yes, that works well for dying cotton. But you have to be careful as <u>the metal can actually affect the fabric</u> and so you can't expect to get a lot of wear out of fabrics treated in this way. And the colours are quite subtle, not everyone likes them. Anyway, it looks as if you've done a lot of work …	*Q30*

SECTION 4

Last week, we started looking at reptiles, including crocodiles and snakes. Today, I'd like us to have a look at another reptile – the lizard – and in particular, at some studies that have been done on a particular type of lizard whose Latin name is *tiliqua rugosa*. This is commonly known as the sleepy lizard, because it's quite slow in its movements and spends quite a lot of its time dozing under rocks or lying in the sun.

I'll start with a general description. Sleepy lizards live in Western and South Australia, where they're quite common. Unlike European lizards, which are mostly small, green and fast-moving, sleepy lizards are brown, but what's particularly distinctive about them is <u>the colour of their tongue, which is dark blue</u>, in contrast with the lining of their mouth which is bright pink. And they're much bigger than most European lizards. <u>They have quite a varied diet, including insects and even small animals, but they mostly eat plants of varying kinds.</u> *Q31* *Q32*

Even though they're quite large and powerful, with strong jaws that can crush beetles and snail shells, they still have quite a few predators. Large birds like cassowaries were one of the main ones in the past, but nowadays <u>they're more likely to be caught and killed by snakes</u>. Actually, another threat to their survival isn't a predator at all, but is man-made – quite a large number of sleepy lizards are killed by cars when they're trying to cross highways. *Q33*

One study carried out by Michael Freake at Flinders University investigated the methods of navigation of these lizards. Though they move slowly, they can travel quite long distances. And he found that even if they were taken some distance away from their home territory, <u>they could usually find their way back home as long as they could see the sky – they didn't need any other landmarks on the ground.</u> *Q34*

Observations of these lizards in the wild have also revealed that their mating habits are quite unusual. Unlike most animals, <u>it seems that they're relatively monogamous, returning to the same partner year after year</u>. And the male and female also stay together for a long time, both before and after the birth of their young. *Q35*

It's quite interesting to think about the possible reasons for this. It could be that it's to do with protecting their young – you'd expect them to have a much better chance of survival if they have both parents around. But in fact observers have noted that once the babies have

hatched out of their eggs, <u>they have hardly any contact with their parents</u>. So, there's not   *Q36*
really any evidence to support that idea.

Another suggestion's based on the observation that male lizards in monogamous
relationships tend to be bigger and stronger than other males. So maybe the male lizards
stay around so <u>they can give the female lizards protection from other males</u>. But again, we're   *Q37*
not really sure.

Finally, I'd like to mention another study that involved collecting data by tracking the lizards. I
was actually involved in this myself. So we caught some lizards in the wild and <u>we developed</u>   *Q38*
<u>a tiny GPS system that would allow us to track them, and we fixed this onto their tails</u>. Then
we set the lizards free again, and we were able to track them for twelve days and gather data,
not just about their location, <u>but even about how many steps they took during this period</u>.   *Q39*

One surprising thing we discovered from this is that there were far fewer meetings between
lizards than we expected – it seems that they were actually trying to avoid one another. So
why would that be? Well, again we have no clear evidence, but <u>one hypothesis is that male</u>   *Q40*
<u>lizards can cause quite serious injuries to one another, so maybe this avoidance is a way of</u>
<u>preventing this</u> – of self-preservation, if you like. But we need to collect a lot more data before
we can be sure of any of this.

TEST 4

SECTION 1

MARTHA:	Hi Alex. It's Martha Clines here. James White gave me your number. I hope you don't mind me calling you.
ALEX:	Of course not. How are you, Martha?
MARTHA:	Good thanks. I'm ringing because I need a bit of advice.
ALEX:	Oh yeah. What about?
MARTHA:	The training you did at JPNW a few years ago. I'm applying for the same thing.
ALEX:	Oh right. Yes, I did mine in <u>2014</u>. Best thing I ever did. I'm still working there. *Example*
MARTHA:	Really? What are you doing?
ALEX:	Well, now I work in the customer services department but <u>I did my initial training Q1 in Finance</u>. I stayed there for the first two years and then moved to where I am now.
MARTHA:	That's the same department I'm applying for. Did you enjoy it?
ALEX:	I was pretty nervous to begin with. I didn't do well in my exams at school and I was really worried because <u>I failed Maths</u>. But it didn't actually matter because I Q2 did lots of courses on the job.
MARTHA:	Did you get a diploma at the end of your trainee period? I'm hoping to do the one in business skills.
ALEX:	Yes. That sounds good. <u>I took the one on IT skills but I wish I'd done that Q3 one instead</u>.
MARTHA:	OK, that's good to know. What about the other trainees? How did you get on with them?
ALEX:	There were about 20 of us who started at the same time and we were all around the same age – I was 18 and <u>there was only one person younger than me, who Q4 was 17</u>. The rest were between 18 and 20. I made some good friends.
MARTHA:	I've heard lots of good things about the training at JPNW. It seems like there are a lot of opportunities there.
ALEX:	Yeah, definitely. Because of its size you can work in loads of different areas within the organisation.
MARTHA:	What about pay? I know you get a lower minimum wage than regular employees.
ALEX:	That's right – which isn't great. But <u>you get the same number of days' holiday as Q5 everyone else</u>. And the pay goes up massively if they offer you a job at the end of the training period.
MARTHA:	Yeah, but I'm not doing it for the money – it's the experience I think will be really useful. Everyone says by the end of the year you gain so much confidence.
ALEX:	You're right. That's the most useful part about it. There's a lot of variety too. You're given lots of different things to do. I enjoyed it all – I didn't even mind the studying.
MARTHA:	Do you have to spend any time in college?
ALEX:	Yes, <u>one day each month</u>. So you get lots of support from both your tutor and Q6 your manager.
MARTHA:	That's good. And the company is easy to get to, isn't it?
ALEX:	Yes, it's very close to the train station so the <u>location's a real advantage</u>. Q7

ALEX:	Have you got a date for your interview yet?
MARTHA:	Yes, it's on the 23rd of this month.
ALEX:	So long as you're well prepared there's nothing to worry about. Everyone's very friendly.

MARTHA:	I am not sure what I should wear. What do you think?	
ALEX:	<u>Nothing too casual – like jeans</u>, for example. If you've got a nice jacket, wear that with a skirt or trousers.	Q8
MARTHA:	OK. Thanks. Any other tips?	
ALEX:	Erm, well I know it's really obvious but <u>arrive in plenty of time</u>. They hate people who are late. So make sure you know exactly where you have to get to. <u>And one other useful piece of advice my manager told me before I had the interview for this job – is to smile</u>. Even if you feel terrified. It makes people respond better to you.	Q9 Q10
MARTHA:	I'll have to practise doing that in the mirror!	
ALEX:	Yeah – well, good luck. Let me know if you need any more information.	
MARTHA:	Thanks very much.	

SECTION 2

Hi everyone, welcome to the Snow Centre. My name's Annie. I hope you enjoyed the bus trip from the airport – we've certainly got plenty of snow today! Well, you've come to New Zealand's premier snow and ski centre, and we've a whole load of activities for you during your week here.

Most visitors come here for the cross-country skiing, where you're on fairly flat ground for most of the time, rather than going down steep mountainsides. <u>There are marked trails, but you can also leave these and go off on your own and that's an experience not to be missed</u>. You can go at your own speed – it's great aerobic exercise if you really push yourself, or if you prefer you can just glide gently along and enjoy the beautiful scenery. Q11

This afternoon, you'll be going on a dog-sled trip. You may have seen our dogs on TV recently racing in the winter sled festival. <u>If you want, you can have your own team for the afternoon and learn how to drive them</u>, following behind our leader on the trail. Or if you'd prefer, you can just sit back in the sled and enjoy the ride as a passenger. Q12

At the weekend, we have the team relay event, and you're all welcome to join in. We have a local school coming along, and a lot of the teachers are taking part too. Participation rather than winning is the main focus, and <u>there's a medal for everyone who takes part</u>. Participants are in teams of two to four, and each team must complete four laps of the course. Q13

For your final expedition, you'll head off to Mount Frenner wearing a pair of special snow shoes which allow you to walk on top of the snow. This is an area where miners once searched for gold, though there are very few traces of their work left now. When the snow melts in summer, the mountain slopes are carpeted in flowers and plants. <u>It's a long ascent, though not too steep, and walkers generally take a couple of days to get to the summit</u> and return. Q14

You'll spend the night in our hut half-way up the mountain. That's included in your package for the stay. <u>It's got cooking facilities, firewood and water for drinking</u>. For washing, we recommend you use melted snow, though, to conserve supplies. We can take your luggage up on our snowmobile for you for just ten dollars a person. The hut has cooking facilities so you can make a hot meal in the evening and morning, but you need to take your own food. Q15

The weather on Mount Frenner can be very stormy. <u>In that case, stay in the hut – generally the storms don't last long</u>. Don't stress about getting back here to the centre in time to catch the airport bus – they'll probably not be running anyway. We do have an emergency locator beacon in the hut but only use that if it's a real emergency, like if someone's ill or injured. Q16

Now, let me tell you something about the different ski trails you can follow during your stay here.

Highland Trail's directly accessible from where we are now. <u>This trail's been designed to give first-timers an experience they'll enjoy regardless of their age or skill, but it's also ideal for experts to practise their technique.</u>   Q17

Then there's Pine Trail … if you're nervous about skiing, leave this one to the experts! You follow a steep valley looking right down on the river below – scary! <u>But if you've fully mastered the techniques needed for hills, it's great fun.</u>   Q18

Stony Trail's a good choice once you've got a general idea of the basics. There are one or two tricky sections, but nothing too challenging. <u>There's a shelter half-way where you can sit and take a break and enjoy the afternoon sunshine.</u>   Q19

And finally, Loser's Trail. This starts off following a gentle river valley but the last part is quite exposed so the snow conditions can be challenging – if it's snowing or windy, <u>check with us before you set out to make sure the trail's open that day.</u>   Q20

Right, so now if you'd like to follow me, we'll get started …

SECTION 3

JACK: I've still got loads to do for our report on nutritional food labels.

ALICE: Me too. What did you learn from doing the project about your own shopping habits?

JACK: Well, I've always had to check labels for traces of peanuts in everything I eat because of my allergy. But beyond that <u>I've never really been concerned enough to check how healthy a product is.</u>   Q21

ALICE: This project has actually taught me to read the labels much more carefully. <u>I tended to believe claims on packaging like 'low in fat'. But I now realise that the 'healthy' yoghurt I've bought for years is full of sugar and that it's actually quite high in calories.</u>   Q22

JACK: Ready meals are the worst … comparing the labels on supermarket pizzas was a real eye-opener. Did you have any idea how many calories they contain? I was amazed.

ALICE: Yes, because <u>unless you read the label really carefully, you wouldn't know that the nutritional values given are for half a pizza.</u>   Q23

JACK: When most people eat the whole pizza. <u>Not exactly transparent is it?</u>

ALICE: Not at all. But I expect it won't stop you from buying pizza?

JACK: Probably not, no! I thought comparing the different labelling systems used by food manufacturers was interesting. I think the kind of labelling system used makes a big difference.

ALICE: Which one did you prefer?

JACK: I liked the traditional daily value system best – the one which tells you what proportion of your required daily intake of each ingredient the product contains. <u>I'm not sure it's the easiest for people to use but at least you get the full story.</u> I like to know all the ingredients in a product – not just how much fat, salt and sugar they contain.   Q24

ALICE: But it's good supermarkets have been making an effort to provide reliable information for customers.

JACK: Yes. There just needs to be more consistency between labelling systems used by different supermarkets, in terms of portion sizes, etc.

ALICE: Mmm. The labels on the different brands of chicken flavour crisps were quite revealing too, weren't they?

JACK: Yeah. <u>I don't understand how they can get away with calling them chicken flavour when they only contain artificial additives.</u>   Q25

ALICE: I know. <u>I'd at least have expected them to contain a small percentage of real chicken</u>.

JACK: Absolutely.

ALICE: I think having nutritional food labeling has been a good idea, don't you? I think it will change people's behaviour and stop mothers, in particular, buying the wrong things.

JACK: But didn't that study kind of prove the opposite? People didn't necessarily stop buying unhealthy products.

ALICE: They only said that might be the case. <u>Those findings weren't that conclusive</u> and it   *Q26* was quite a small-scale study. I think more research has to be done.

JACK: Yes, I think you're probably right.

JACK: What do you think of the traffic-light system?

ALICE: I think supermarkets like the idea of having a colour-coded system – red, orange or green – for levels of fat, sugar and salt in a product.

JACK: But <u>it's not been adopted universally</u>. And not on all products. Why do you suppose   *Q27 & Q28* that is?

ALICE: Pressure from the food manufacturers. Hardly surprising that some of them are opposed to flagging up how unhealthy their products are.

JACK: I'd have thought it would have been compulsory. It seems ridiculous it isn't.

ALICE: I know. And <u>what I couldn't get over is the fact that it was brought in without enough consultation</u> – a lot of experts had deep reservations about it.

JACK: That is a bit weird. I suppose there's an argument for doing the research now when consumers are familiar with this system.

ALICE: Yeah, maybe.

JACK: The participants in the survey were quite positive about the traffic-light system.

ALICE: Mmm. But I don't think they targeted the right people. They should have focused on people with low literacy levels because these labels are designed to be accessible to them.

JACK: <u>Yeah. But it's good to get feedback from all socio-economic groups</u>. And there wasn't   *Q29 & Q30* much variation in their responses.

ALICE: No. But <u>if they hadn't interviewed participants face-to-face, they could have used a much bigger sample size</u>. I wonder why they chose that method?

JACK: Dunno. How were they selected? Did they volunteer or were they approached?

ALICE: I think they volunteered. The thing that wasn't stated was how often they bought packaged food – all we know is how frequently they used the supermarket.

SECTION 4

In my presentation, I'm going to talk about coffee, and its importance both in economic and social terms. We think it was first drunk in the Arab world, but there's hardly any documentary evidence of it before the 1500s, although of course that doesn't mean that people didn't know about it before then.

However, there is evidence that coffee was originally gathered from bushes growing wild in Ethiopia, in the northeast of Africa. In the early sixteenth century, it was being bought by traders, and gradually its use as a drink spread throughout the Middle East. It's also known that in 1522, in the Turkish city of Constantinople, which was the centre of the Ottoman Empire, the court physician approved its use as a medicine.

By the mid-1500s, coffee bushes were being cultivated in the Yemen and for the next hundred years this region produced most of the coffee drunk in Africa and the Arab world. What's particularly interesting about coffee is its effect on social life. It was rarely drunk at home, but instead people went to coffee houses to drink it. These people, usually men, would meet to drink coffee and chat about issues of the day. But at the time, this chance to share ideas and opinions was seen as something that was potentially dangerous, and <u>in 1623 the ruler of Constantinople demanded the destruction of all the coffee houses in the city</u>, *Q31* although after his death many new ones opened, and coffee consumption continued. In the seventeenth century, coffee drinking spread to Europe, and here too <u>coffee shops became</u> *Q32* <u>places where ordinary people, nearly always men, could meet to exchange ideas. Because of this, some people said that these places performed a similar function to universities.</u> The opportunity they provided for people to meet together outside their own homes and to discuss the topics of the day had an enormous impact on social life, and <u>many social movements and</u> *Q33* <u>political developments had their origins in coffee house discussions</u>.

In the late 1600s, the Yemeni monopoly on coffee production broke down and coffee production started to spread around the world, helped by European colonisation. Europeans set up coffee plantations in Indonesia and the Caribbean and production of coffee in the colonies skyrocketed. Different types of coffee were produced in different areas, and <u>it's</u> *Q34* <u>interesting that the names given to these different types, like Mocha or Java coffee, were often taken from the port they were shipped to Europe from</u>. But if you look at the labour system in the different colonies, there were some significant differences.

<u>In Brazil and the various Caribbean colonies, coffee was grown in huge plantations and the</u> *Q35* <u>workers there were almost all slaves.</u> But this wasn't the same in all colonies; for example <u>in Java, which had been colonised by the Dutch, the peasants grew coffee and passed</u> *Q36* <u>a proportion of this on to the Dutch, so it was used as a means of taxation</u>. But whatever system was used, under the European powers of the eighteenth century, coffee production was very closely linked to colonisation. <u>Coffee was grown in ever-increasing quantities</u> *Q37* <u>to satisfy the growing demand from Europe, and it became nearly as important as sugar production</u>, which was grown under very similar conditions. However, coffee prices were not yet low enough for people to drink it regularly at home, so most coffee consumption still took place in public coffee houses and it still remained something of a luxury item. In Britain, however, a new drink was introduced from China, and started to become popular, gradually taking over from coffee, although at first it was so expensive that only the upper classes could afford it. This was tea, and by the late 1700s it was being widely drunk. However, <u>when the</u> *Q38* <u>USA gained independence from Britain in 1776, they identified this drink with Britain, and coffee remained the preferred drink in the USA</u>, as it still is today.

So, by the early nineteenth century, coffee was already being widely produced and consumed. But during this century, production boomed and coffee prices started to fall. <u>This</u> *Q39* <u>was partly because new types of transportation had been developed which were cheaper and more efficient</u>. So now, working people could afford to buy coffee – it wasn't just a drink for the middle classes. And this was at a time when large parts of Europe were starting to work in industries. And <u>sometimes this meant their work didn't stop when it got dark; they might have</u> *Q40* <u>to continue throughout the night</u>. So, the use of coffee as a stimulant became important – it wasn't just a drink people drank in the morning, for breakfast.

There were also changes in cultivation …

Listening and Reading Answer Keys

TEST 1

LISTENING

Section 1, Questions 1–10

1	choose
2	private
3	20 / twenty percent
4	healthy
5	bones
6	lecture
7	Arretsa
8	vegetarian
9	market
10	knife

Section 2, Questions 11–20

11	B
12	C
13	B
14	E
15	D
16	B
17	G
18	C
19	H
20	I

Section 3, Questions 21–30

21	A
22	C
23	B
24	C
25	B
26	G
27	C
28	H
29	A
30	E

Section 4, Questions 31–40

31	crow
32	cliffs
33	speed
34	brain(s)
35	food
36	behaviour(s) / behavior(s)
37	new
38	stress
39	tail(s)
40	permanent

If you score …

0–16	17–25	26–40
you are unlikely to get an acceptable score under examination conditions and we recommend that you spend a lot of time improving your English before you take IELTS.	you may get an acceptable score under examination conditions but we recommend that you think about having more practice or lessons before you take IELTS.	you are likely to get an acceptable score under examination conditions but remember that different institutions will find different scores acceptable.

TEST 1

READING

Reading Passage 1, Questions 1–13

1	update
2	environment
3	captain
4	films
5	season
6	accommodation
7	blog
8	FALSE
9	NOT GIVEN
10	FALSE *?*
11	TRUE
12	NOT GIVEN
13	TRUE

Reading Passage 2, Questions 14–26

14	iv
15	vi
16	i
17	v
18	viii
19	iii
20	E
21	B
22	D
23	A
24	focus
25	pleasure
26	curiosity

Reading Passage 3, Questions 27–40

27	B
28	C
29	C
30	D
31	A
32	D
33	A
34	E
35	C
36	G
37	B
38	YES
39	NOT GIVEN
40	NO

If you score …

0–16	17–25	26–40
you are unlikely to get an acceptable score under examination conditions and we recommend that you spend a lot of time improving your English before you take IELTS.	you may get an acceptable score under examination conditions but we recommend that you think about having more practice or lessons before you take IELTS.	you are likely to get an acceptable score under examination conditions but remember that different institutions will find different scores acceptable.

2 + 6 + 3 + 3 + 1 + 6 + 5 + 4 = 30

TEST 2

LISTENING

Section 1, Questions 1–10

1	races
2	insurance
3	Jerriz
4	25 / twenty-five
5	stadium
6	park
7	coffee
8	leader
9	route
10	lights

Section 2, Questions 11–20

11	C
12	B
13	C
14	B
15	B
16	A
17&18	*IN EITHER ORDER*
	C
	E
19&20	*IN EITHER ORDER*
	B
	D

Section 3, Questions 21–30

21	B
22	A
23	C
24	C
25	A
26	A
27	C
28	D
29	G
30	B

Section 4, Questions 31–40

31	location
32	world
33	personal
34	attention
35	name
36	network
37	frequency
38	colour / color
39	brain
40	self

If you score …

0–17	18–26	27–40
you are unlikely to get an acceptable score under examination conditions and we recommend that you spend a lot of time improving your English before you take IELTS.	you may get an acceptable score under examination conditions but we recommend that you think about having more practice or lessons before you take IELTS.	you are likely to get an acceptable score under examination conditions but remember that different institutions will find different scores acceptable.

TEST 2

READING

Reading Passage 1, Questions 1–13

1 oils
2 friendship
3 funerals
4 wealth
5 indigestion
6 India
7 camels
8 Alexandria
9 Venice
10 TRUE
11 FALSE
12 NOT GIVEN
13 FALSE

Reading Passage 2, Questions 14–26

14 B
15 F
16 B
17 E
18 A
19 B
20 C
21 animals
22 childbirth
23 placebo
24 game
25 strangers
26 names

Reading Passage 3, Questions 27–40

27 D
28 C
29 A
30 D
31 D
32 D
33 C
34 B
35 A
36 C
37 A
38 B
39 C
40 D

If you score …

0–15	16–23	24–40
you are unlikely to get an acceptable score under examination conditions and we recommend that you spend a lot of time improving your English before you take IELTS.	you may get an acceptable score under examination conditions but we recommend that you think about having more practice or lessons before you take IELTS.	you are likely to get an acceptable score under examination conditions but remember that different institutions will find different scores acceptable.

8 + 3 + 2 + 3 + 6 + 3 + 6 + 3 = 34

TEST 3

LISTENING

Section 1, Questions 1–10

1	850
2	bike / bicycle
3	parking
4	30 / thirty
5	weekend(s)
6	cinema
7	hospital
8	dentist
9	Thursday
10	café

Section 2, Questions 11–20

11	F
12	D
13	A
14	B
15	C
16	G
17&18	*IN EITHER ORDER*
	B
	C
19&20	*IN EITHER ORDER*
	B
	D

Section 3, Questions 21–30

21	C
22	A
23	A
24	B
25	C
26	F
27	H
28	D
29	A
30	E

Section 4, Questions 31–40

31	tongue(s)
32	plants
33	snakes
34	sky
35	partner(s)
36	contact
37	protection
38	tail(s)
39	steps
40	injury / injuries

If you score ...

0–17	18–26	27–40
you are unlikely to get an acceptable score under examination conditions and we recommend that you spend a lot of time improving your English before you take IELTS.	you may get an acceptable score under examination conditions but we recommend that you think about having more practice or lessons before you take IELTS.	you are likely to get an acceptable score under examination conditions but remember that different institutions will find different scores acceptable.

TEST 3

READING

Reading Passage 1,
Questions 1–13

1 furniture
2 sugar
3 ropes
4 charcoal
5 bowls
6 hormones
7 cosmetics
8 dynamite
9 FALSE
10 FALSE
11 NOT GIVEN
12 TRUE
13 NOT GIVEN

Reading Passage 2,
Questions 14–26

14 B
15 C
16 A
17 B
18 recording devices
19 fathers / dads
20 bridge hypothesis
21 repertoire
22 (audio-recording) vests
23 vocabulary
24 F
25 A
26 E

Reading Passage 3,
Questions 27–40

27 C
28 H
29 A
30 B
31 D
32 shells
33 lake
34 rainfall
35 grains
36 pottery
37 B
38 A
39 D
40 A

If you score …

0–16	17–24	25–40
you are unlikely to get an acceptable score under examination conditions and we recommend that you spend a lot of time improving your English before you take IELTS.	you may get an acceptable score under examination conditions but we recommend that you think about having more practice or lessons before you take IELTS.	you are likely to get an acceptable score under examination conditions but remember that different institutions will find different scores acceptable.

4 + 5 + 4 + 3 + 6 + 4 + 4 + 8 = 38

TEST 4

LISTENING

Section 1, Questions 1–10

1	Finance
2	Maths / Math / Mathematics
3	business
4	17 / seventeen
5	holiday(s) / vacation(s)
6	college
7	location
8	jeans
9	late
10	smile

Section 2, Questions 11–20

11	A
12	B
13	A
14	C
15	A
16	B
17	B
18	D
19	A
20	E

Section 3, Questions 21–30

21	A
22	A
23	C
24	C
25	B
26	A
27&28	*IN EITHER ORDER*
	B
	C
29&30	*IN EITHER ORDER*
	D
	E

Section 4, Questions 31–40

31	destruction
32	universities / university
33	political
34	port(s)
35	slaves / slavery
36	taxation
37	sugar
38	tea
39	transportation
40	night

If you score ...

0–17	18–26	27–40
you are unlikely to get an acceptable score under examination conditions and we recommend that you spend a lot of time improving your English before you take IELTS.	you may get an acceptable score under examination conditions but we recommend that you think about having more practice or lessons before you take IELTS.	you are likely to get an acceptable score under examination conditions but remember that different institutions will find different scores acceptable.

TEST 4

READING

Reading Passage 1,
Questions 1–13

1   FALSE
2   FALSE
3   TRUE
4   TRUE
5   FALSE
6   TRUE
7   NOT GIVEN
8   TRUE
9   wool
10 navigator
11 gale
12 training
13 fire

Reading Passage 2,
Questions 14–26

14 minerals
15 carbon
16 water
17 agriculture
18 C
19 E
20 A
21 D
22 E
23 C
24 F
25 G
26 F

Reading Passage 3,
Questions 27–40

27 D
28 A
29 B
30 F
31 B
32 G
33 E
34 A
35 YES
36 NOT GIVEN
37 NO
38 NOT GIVEN
39 YES
40 NO

If you score …

0–16	17–25	26–40
you are unlikely to get an acceptable score under examination conditions and we recommend that you spend a lot of time improving your English before you take IELTS.	you may get an acceptable score under examination conditions but we recommend that you think about having more practice or lessons before you take IELTS.	you are likely to get an acceptable score under examination conditions but remember that different institutions will find different scores acceptable.

Sample answers for Writing tasks

TEST 1, WRITING TASK 1

SAMPLE ANSWER

This is an answer written by a candidate who achieved a **Band 5.5** score. Here is the examiner's comment:

> The candidate has identified all the key features (hospital, ring road, new public car park, staff car park and bus station in 2010) but the descriptions are not always accurate e.g. [*two features that still remained. This two features are City Hospital and staff car park*] whereas the staff car park was formerly a car park for both staff and public, while the mention of the bus station is not developed. Organisation is clear, however, with some good use of cohesive devices [*According to | Apart from | The further additional features*], although there is an error in the use of reference pronouns [*This/These two features*]. The range of vocabulary is sufficient for the task [*two different years | features | remained | additional*], though [*features*] is over-used. A spelling error is noted in the second line [*sourrounded*] but this does not cause any difficulty for the reader; similarly, the use of [*around-turn*] can be easily understood as 'roundabout'. There is a mix of simple and complex sentences, mainly used accurately.

Two maps illustrate the way to get to a city hospital of two different years (2007 and 2010).

According to both maps, the main features which is city hospital is sourrounded by Ring Road. In these two maps, there have been two features that still remained. This two features are City Hospital and staff car park. Apart from these two features there are some features that shows on 2010 map but haven't shown on 2007 map. The additional features that appear on the map of 2010 are public car park which located on the east-side of the city hospital. The further additional features are two around-turn on the hospital Rd. which can lead to the bus station.

Overall, there are two major features that never change on both 2007 and 2010 map. These features are city hospital and staff car park. However, there are some additional features that appear on the map of 2010 but not on 2007. These features are public car park, bus station and two around-turns.

TEST 1, WRITING TASK 2

SAMPLE ANSWER

This is an answer written by a candidate who achieved a **Band 6.5** score. Here is the examiner's comment:

> The candidate deals with both parts of the prompt and addresses some social and practical problems that might be experienced in a foreign language environment. Ideas are supported by examples, though there is room for further development here. Organisation is logical and there is clear progression throughout the response. Cohesive devices are used appropriately [*Another problem* | *For example* | *Therefore* | *That means …* | *The second … problem* | *To summarize*]. There is a sufficient range of vocabulary to allow some flexibility and precision and to demonstrate awareness of style and collocation [*language barrier* | *linked to* | *influence the behaviour* | *offend* | *misunderstanding* | *misconceptions*]. There is a mix of simple and complex sentence forms including subordinate clauses [*which means that* | *a person who*], modal verbs [*should* | *might* | *would*] and gerunds [*finding a job*]. Grammatical control is generally good as is the use of punctuation, although the first sentence in the second paragraph is incomplete.

It is clear that living in a foreign country has its own benefits and drawbacks to consider. I agre with this statement, however I think that anybody coming in another country should respect national culture. In this essay, I would like to outline the social and practical problems.

The social problems would be language barrier, which means that a person coming from another country might not be able to speak and understand the language which might be a problem as far a person who is living in a country, and a person who came in the country. Another problem is linked to the language barrier, but it might influence the behaviour of others. An individual who come into the country might offend others with their behaviour or language. For example; some cultures like English people prefer to be very polite and say things differently from other cultures. Therefore a person who doesn't know how to behave in a particular culture might offend others around him.

The practical problems would be misunderstanding of culture. That means that a person who visits other countries does not understand other culture and he behaves as he wants to.

The second practical problem is finding a job. An individual who works in foreign country might not be appropriate for people who he serves. For example if an individual works in a restaurant, the people who live in a country and they were born in that country might not respect and not like the behaviour of a person who works in a restaurant, it might be because, the cultures are different.

To summarize, it can be said that there are a lot of misconceptions which people have when they come in a foreign country, and in my opinion and from my personal experience people should educate themselves in order to know how to behave in different situations with different cultures.

TEST 2, WRITING TASK 1

SAMPLE ANSWER

This is an answer written by a candidate who achieved a **Band 6.0** score. Here is the examiner's comment:

> The candidate has identified all the main features and trends, including the fact that in 1971 the number of households in owned and rented households was the same. Comments are supported by dates and percentages of households and there is a short overview at the end of the script. Organisation is clear as the writer deals with each category in turn. The range of vocabulary is adequate but there are frequent spelling errors [*comprssion* / comparison | *dramaticly droped* / dramatically dropped | *stated* / stayed | *yeas* / year | *leveled* / levelled | *Genarally* / Generally | *prectarge* / percentage]. These do not noticeably impede communication, however. There is a mix of grammatical structures and some complex sentence forms, though these are not always accurate: the meaning is still clear, however.

The provided bar chart depicts the comprssion of buying or renting houses in England and Wales from 1918 to 2011.

1918 the rented households was raised about 78 percentage. Then it leveled of between 1939 to 1953. From 1961 to 1981 it dramaticly droped to 35 percentage. This accommodation stated the same until 2001. In 2011 there was a slight increase in rented households and it was up to 38%.

The same yeas the owned ones has raise from 21% to 32% in 1918 to1953. In 1939 to 1953 the was a graduate stade in the percentage. Then it starts to leveled up to 69% In 1991. At 2001 to 2011 there was a decline in the owned accommodation and it was 62%.

Genarally , both of the rented and owned households has raised and droped throug the years from 1918 to 2011. The was a year that the were the same prectarge and it was 1971 which 50%

TEST 2, WRITING TASK 2

SAMPLE ANSWER

This is an answer written by a candidate who achieved a **Band 7.0** score. Here is the examiner's comment:

> The candidate explains why s/he both agrees and disagrees with the statement, meeting the requirements of 'To what extent do you agree or disagree with this statement?' S/he singles out two areas of disagreement (food and jobs) and provides clear examples to support these opinions, then goes on to identify an area of agreement (TV channels), again providing support and then some development of the example. Organisation is logical and there is clear progression throughout the writing. There is a range of cohesive devices, used appropriately [*Take for example | Actually | Therefore | Naturally | However | This specific area | From this point of view | In conclusion*]. The range of vocabulary is sufficient to show some flexibility and precision, as well as less common items and an awareness of style and collocation [*Complex | list of favourites | fits … my abilities | specific area | many available channels*]. There is only one spelling error [*beome*], probably a slip of the pen. Control over grammar and punctuation is generally good and there is a variety of complex structures with frequent error-free sentences.

The answer is complex since there are a lot of choices in our life and all of them are different kinds. In some cases I would say that it is a good thing to have the ability to choose from a wide variety. Take for example gastronomy. Every single person has different meals on their list of favourites. Actually if you have a bigger family it is almost impossible to cook something that everyone would like. Therefore I would say that it is great that you can go to a shopping center and choose from a dozen different food types. I can always find something that looks delicious.

Naturally, there are some people who say that it is against evolution. They claim to say that back in the old days we had a perfect life when technically everybody was farming. I personally disagree with that. I am happy that I could choose a job that fits best to my abilities. I mean no one is the same, why would we want to do the same? Different kinds of universities give us the opportunity to beome who we are meant to be. We have the right to choose.

However there is one topic where, according to my opinion, we have too many choices. This specific area is television. There are hundreds of channels, therefore you can always find something that is worth watching. Literally you could sit in your sofa the whole day and watch films. I think that people doing less outdoor activities are the results of the many available channels. From this point of view I would agree that we have too many choices.

In conclusion I would say that we can't generally talk about choices since they could be different. In some cases it is good to have many of them while in other areas they could have a negative effect.

TEST 3, WRITING TASK 1

SAMPLE ANSWER

This is an answer written by a candidate who achieved a **Band 5.0** score. Here is the examiner's comment:

> This response is rather mechanical as it lists the countries in order of production and consumption of electricity, identifies the countries that produce and consume most and least and notes the fact that all the countries except Germany produce more than they consume. However, the writing is supported by data, although there are some errors in the figures (the figures for production in Russia, India and Brazil are inaccurate as is the figure for consumption in Japan). Organisation is limited and there are few examples of cohesive devices; similarly the range of vocabulary is limited although just adequate for the task. There is a mix of simple and complex sentence structures, but complex forms are mainly inaccurate [*that have /* has | *Almost all the country have /* Almost all the countries have].

From the bar chart that show the top ten countries for the production and consumption of electricity in 2014. For the production of electricity, the 1st rank is China that have 5,398 billion kwh, the 2nd rank is United States that have 4,099 billion kwh, the 3rd rank is Russia that have 1,059 billion kwh, the 4th rank is Japan that have 936.2 billion kwh, the 5th rank is India that have 891 billion kwh, the 6th rank is Canada that have 618.9 billion kwh, the 7th rank is France that have 561.2 billion kwh, the 8th rank is Brazil that have 530.9 billion kwh, the 9th rank is Germany that have 526.6 billion kwh and the 10th rank is Republic of Korea that have 485.1 billion kwh. For the comsumption of electricity, the 1st rank is China that have 5,322 billion kwh, the 2nd rank is United States that have 3,866 billion kwh, the 3rd is Russia that have 1,038 billion kwh, the 4th rank is Japan that have 856.9 billion kwh, the 5th rank is India that have 698.8 billion kwh, the 6th rank is Germany that have 582.5 billion kwh, the 7th rank is Canada that have 499.9 kwh, the 8th rank is France that have 462.9 billion kwh, the 9th rank is Brazil that have 455.8 kwh and the 10th is Republic of Korea that have 449.5 billion kwh.

From the information. The country that have the most in production and consumption is China. The country that have the least in production and consumption is Republic of Korea.

Almost all the country have production more than consumption, exept Germany that have consumption more than production.

TEST 3, WRITING TASK 2

SAMPLE ANSWER

This is an answer written by a candidate who achieved a **Band 6.0** score. Here is the examiner's comment:

> The writer addresses all parts of the prompt and outlines why the various subjects are all important, supporting these ideas with relevant examples. Although the organisation is sometimes confused, there is a sense of progression and a definite conclusion is reached. Cohesive devices are used effectively [*In my opinion | Of course | especially*]. Referencing is generally accurate [*we wouldn't know that without them | these things | that hope | that is a reason why*], but there is one error [*With this / these two things*]. The range of vocabulary is quite varied [*go along with today's world | to move forward | daily life | transportation, communication, collaboration etc. | political standing, culture and traditions*], though errors occur [*every subjects /* subject | *normally /* normal *human beings | a bright chances /* chance], while a reference to [*stuff and things*] suggests the writer struggled to find more precise terms. There is a mix of simple and complex sentence forms, including different types of subordinate clauses [*Some people say that … | … which is science and technology | … people who pushes /* push *us to | The / They taught us how to*] and although errors occur, these do not usually cause misunderstanding or difficulty for the reader. Punctuation is sometimes faulty, particularly omission of full stops.

In my opinion I think every subjects is important for us. We have to learn everything through our past, present and future. Some people say that History is one of the most important school subjects it's true but it has to go along with today's world which is science and Technology. How can we move without our history, the people behind us "The ancient people" is the most powerful people who pushes us to move forward. The taught us how to fire a light, How to find a food, How to lives with other and animals, How to survive and others. Of course we wouldn't know that without them. Science and Technology are important too. They give us a chance to move forward with them. Without Science and Technology we're just a normally humans being. We spend our daily life with no useful. Without them we have no light we have no food, we have no comfortable stuff and things. Old people can survived without these things. Humans creates lots of invention to give an unlimited wants of people based on a limited government.

May I gives one example of the development of science and Technology. With this two things it give us a chance to be a member of ASEAN "Association of South East Asia Nation" we can be able to communicate with the other 9 countries with the high technology. it help us to be a TEAMWORK with the 9 other countries to develop our country. help us in terms of transportation, communication, collaboration etc. it can definitely hold on to that hope that in the near future.

Overall economics can totally achieves. it is a fact that the member of the member of the ASEAN have differences in term of political standing, culture and traditions but it's not a problem with our help I know that there're a bright future are waiting for all of us. and that is a reason why History, Science and Technology is important

We use History to learn about others, their culture, their tradition to be understand each other more and more and using science and Technology to help us, our country, our world to be moving forward, to help each other and to give a bright chances and future for everyone, especially kids give a chances to them to study, to go to school, to get knowledge so the next ten years, twenty years to the new up coming year all of them can help each other to pass these chances to other kids go on and on.

TEST 4, WRITING TASK 1

SAMPLE ANSWER

This is an answer written by a candidate who achieved a **Band 6.5** score. Here is the examiner's comment:

> This answer addresses the main features of the redeveloped sports centre, but it could be improved by adding a brief description of the centre as it is at present. Another aspect of the response that could be improved would be to indicate where the various facilities will be situated in relation to each other: from the description above the reader cannot know where for example the gym, the leisure pool and the dance studios will be located. The range of vocabulary is above average, however: [*illustrate | reconstruction | redeveloped | additional | replaced by other facilities | renovated*] and shows flexibility and precision. There is a variety of complex structures such as present and future verb forms, passive forms and relative clauses [*the place where… | It is also clear… that*]. There could be more variety in the language used to express future plans: [*going to*] is over-used.

The following plans illustrate the layout of the university's sports centre at the present moment and the way it will look after a reconstruction.

According to the new layout, the redeveloped sports centre is going to become bigger. First, the gym is going to be larger and an additional changing room is going to appear. Besides, there is going to be a sports shop and a cafe in the reception zone. Apart from that, 2 dance studios are going to work opposite the gym. Finally, the sports centre is going to get a new leisure pool. It is going to be located in the place where the outdoor courts used to be. As can be seen from the new layout, both outdoor courts are going to be replaced by other facilities in the renovated sports centre. Furthermore, a sports hall is going to appear in the university sports centre. It is also clear from the second layout that the redeveloped sports centre is going to be a fully indoor one.

TEST 4, WRITING TASK 2

SAMPLE ANSWER

This is an answer written by a candidate who achieved a **Band 6.0** score. Here is the examiner's comment:

> This script presents some difficulties for the reader. There is an attempt to answer the first part of the prompt (Why is this the case?) although the explanation is not well supported, while the answer to the second question (What can be done about this problem?) lacks focus as it mentions education, clean water and social mobility as well as food. At the same time, it is clear that the writer has some ideas, but lacks the language needed to express them satisfactorily. Ideas are organised into paragraphs and there is some sense of progression, with accurate use of cohesive devices [*Nowadays | According to | for example*] although there is also some inaccuracy [*Hence | In the long team / term?*]. Control over spelling and word formation is weak and there are frequent errors [*itmes | opioin | Captialism | divied | countris | resouse | develping*] for example, causing further difficulty. There are attempts to produce both simple and complex sentence forms, but the error level is high throughout, even in simple forms [*I think it made many problem | the people will be expenditure more*]. Punctuation is also sometimes faulty.

Nowadays, many countries has been tried to develop the Advances itmes to Solves the lack of food in the world by the way why many people around the world still go hungry, In my opioin, I think "Captialism".

Under "the world Order" by USA in 1970 (the cold war) divied the countris around the world in to 3 groups, 1) the frist world like USA, UK, Japan like that, 2) the second word was like Soviet Union and 3) the third word was a devopling countries. I didn't think the captialism is bad, I think it made many problem such as the lack of food in the poor countries.

According to the Economics, the develped countries have a absolute rights to take an adventage from the resouse in the develping countries with the lowest wage, the hardest working and the dangerous places working Hence, the people who live in the develping countries has no oppunities to moblisation their status. the lowest wage they get vice versa the high price of their item product for example 1 dollar US per a day for 1 worker in the develped countries, but 100 dollar US per the item product to be selled, the cap is approximate 99 dollar US goes to the owner who live in the deveoped countries.

The solve of this problem, I think the goverment on each countries should guranted their citizen to have a basic rights, Food, Clear water and Education, for example. The highest price of food that restrize the poor people to access the food, the government need to bare the barrier pices of food won't be high

In the long team of solving this problem, the govement will give more Education fee as free for thie civilan becaus I absolutely think Education comes with mobilisatim the social status when the people has a high Education comes with a hire in a high working. then the government should bare the free of houshold is not high as well. the people will be expenditure more. When the more expenditure the people have, the more money they have we have to solve this problem together, Not the duty of some countries, the problem will be eradicated from the wild. fainally we have to have a hope to solve it, Not despair yet.

Sample answer sheets

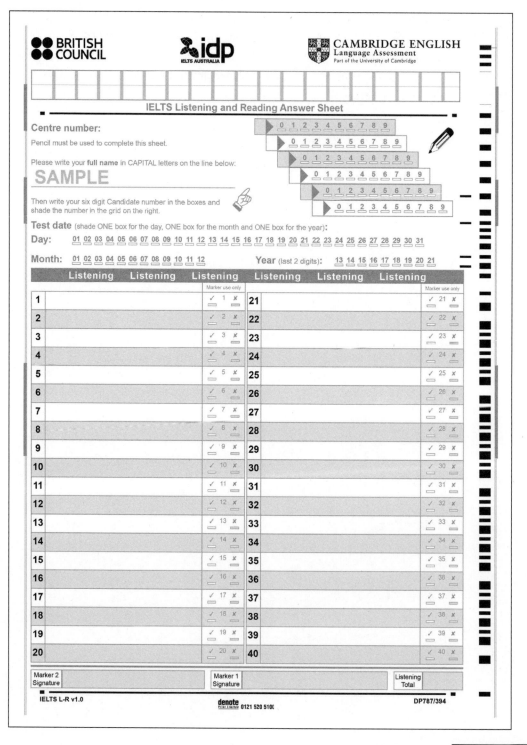

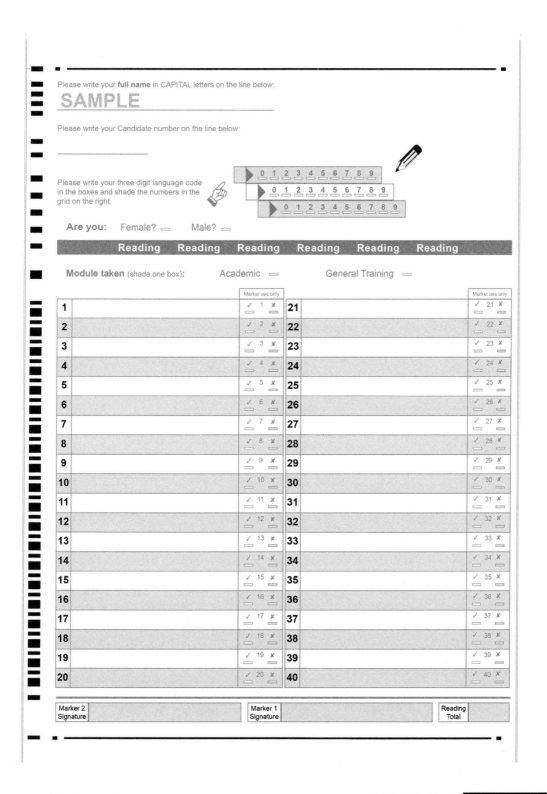

Please write your **full name** in CAPITAL letters on the line below:

SAMPLE

Please write your Candidate number on the line below:

Please write your three digit language code in the boxes and shade the numbers in the grid on the right.

0 1 2 3 4 5 6 7 8 9
0 1 2 3 4 5 6 7 8 9
0 1 2 3 4 5 6 7 8 9

Are you: Female? ▭ Male? ▭

Reading Reading Reading Reading Reading Reading

Module taken (shade one box): Academic ▭ General Training ▭

		Marker use only			Marker use only
1		✓ 1 ✗	21		✓ 21 ✗
2		✓ 2 ✗	22		✓ 22 ✗
3		✓ 3 ✗	23		✓ 23 ✗
4		✓ 4 ✗	24		✓ 24 ✗
5		✓ 5 ✗	25		✓ 25 ✗
6		✓ 6 ✗	26		✓ 26 ✗
7		✓ 7 ✗	27		✓ 27 ✗
8		✓ 8 ✗	28		✓ 28 ✗
9		✓ 9 ✗	29		✓ 29 ✗
10		✓ 10 ✗	30		✓ 30 ✗
11		✓ 11 ✗	31		✓ 31 ✗
12		✓ 12 ✗	32		✓ 32 ✗
13		✓ 13 ✗	33		✓ 33 ✗
14		✓ 14 ✗	34		✓ 34 ✗
15		✓ 15 ✗	35		✓ 35 ✗
16		✓ 16 ✗	36		✓ 36 ✗
17		✓ 17 ✗	37		✓ 37 ✗
18		✓ 18 ✗	38		✓ 38 ✗
19		✓ 19 ✗	39		✓ 39 ✗
20		✓ 20 ✗	40		✓ 40 ✗

Marker 2 Signature		Marker 1 Signature		Reading Total	

Sample answer sheets

BRITISH COUNCIL

idp IELTS AUSTRALIA

CAMBRIDGE ENGLISH
Language Assessment
Part of the University of Cambridge

IELTS Writing Answer Sheet – TASK 1

Candidate Name

Centre Number

Candidate Number

Module (shade one box):   Academic ☐   General Training ☐

Test date

D D   M M   Y Y Y Y

TASK 1

Do not write below this line

100913/2

© UCLES 2018   Photocopiable

BRITISH COUNCIL

idp IELTS AUSTRALIA

CAMBRIDGE ENGLISH
Language Assessment
Part of the University of Cambridge

IELTS Writing Answer Sheet – TASK 2

Candidate Name

Centre Number

Candidate Number

Module (shade one box):   Academic ☐   General Training ☐

Test date

D D   M M   Y Y Y Y

TASK 2

Do not write below this line

100895/2

Acknowledgements

The publishers acknowledge the following sources of copyright material and are grateful for the permissions granted. While every effort has been made, it has not always been possible to identify the sources of all the material used, or to trace all copyright holders. If any omissions are brought to our notice, we will be happy to include the appropriate acknowledgements on reprinting and in the next update to the digital edition, as applicable.

Conde Nast for the text on p. 15 adapted from 'How City Living Is Reshaping the Brains and Behaviour of Urban Animals' by Brandon Keim, *Wired Magazine* 2013. Copyright © 2013 Conde Nast. Reproduced with permission; Taylor & Francis Group for the text on pp. 16–17 adapted from 'Marketing in Travel and Tourism' by Victor Middleton, Alan Fyall, Mike Morgan and Ashok Ranchhod. Copyright © 2009 Taylor & Francis Group. Reproduced with permission; New Scientist for the text on pp. 21–22 adapted from 'Why being bored is stimulating - and useful, too' by Caroline Williams, *New Scientist*, 29.08.2015. Copyright © 2015 New Scientist Ltd. All rights reserved. Distributed by Tribune Content Agency; New Scientist for the text on pp. 24-25 adapted from 'Creative Sparks' by Catherine de Lange, *New Scientist*, 14.01.2012. Copyright © 2012 New Scientist Ltd. All rights reserved. Distributed by Tribune Content Agency; UCSF Memory and Aging Center for the text on p. 37 adapted from 'Memory'. Copyright © The Regents of the University of California. Reproduced with kind permission; University of Minnesota Libraries for the text on pp. 38–39 adapted from 'A Taste of Paradise: Cinnamon' by Troy David Osborne. Copyright © James Ford Bell Library, University of Minnesota, https://www.lib.umn.edu/bell/tradeproducts/cinnamon. Reproduced with kind permission; New Scientist for the text on pp. 42–43 adapted from 'Dark side of the love hormone' by Ed Yong, *New Scientist*, 08.02.2012. Copyright © 2012 New Scientist Ltd. All rights reserved. Distributed by Tribune Content Agency; Harvard Business Publishing for the text on pp. 46–47 adapted from 'Are You Ignoring Trends That Could Shake Up Your Business?' by Elie Ofek and Luc Wathieu, issue July–August 2010. Copyright © 2010 by Harvard Business Publishing. Reproduced with permission; Department for Communities and Local Government (DCLG) and Census for the text on p. 51 adapted from 'A Century of Home Ownership and Renting in England and Wales', Office for National Statistics licensed under the Open Government Licence v.3.0; Bodleian Library Publishing for the text on pp. 60–61 adapted from 'What have plants ever done for us?' by Stephen Harris. Copyright © 2015 Bodleian Library Publishing. Reproduced with kind permission; Smithsonian Enterprises for the text on pp. 64–65 adapted from 'The Many Ways Baby Talk Gives Infant Brains a Boost' by Brian Handwerk, 28.05.2015. Copyright © 2015 Smithsonian Institution. Reprinted with permission from Smithsonian Enterprises. All rights reserved. Reproduction in any medium is strictly prohibited without permission from Smithsonian Institution; Text on p. 73 adapted from 'Electricity – production', CIA World Factbook; New Scientist for the text on pp. 85–86 adapted from 'Endangered earth: The secret battle to save our soils' by Joshua Howgego, *New Scientist*, 07.10.2015. Copyright © 2015 New Scientist Ltd. All rights reserved. Distributed by Tribune Content Agency; Literary Review for the text on pp. 89–90 adapted from 'The Literary Review: Politics of Pleasure' by John Gray. Copyright © 2015 Literary Review. Reproduced with kind permission.

URLS

The publisher has used its best endeavours to ensure that the URLs for external websites referred to in this book are correct and active at the time of going to press. However, the publisher has no responsibility for the websites and can make no guarantee that a site will remain live or that the content is or will remain appropriate.

Praise For

Complete KOBOLD Guide to Game Design

"A must-have book for both those looking to get into this industry, and those who merely want to play."

–NerdTrek.com

"Highly recommended for gaming nerds everywhere."

–citybookreview.com

*Winner, 2012 Gold ENnie Award for
Best RPG-Related Accessory*

KOBOLD Guide to Board Game Design

"I wish I had a book like this twenty years ago."

–Bruno Faidutti, designer of *Citadels*

" I would recommend 'The Kobold Guide to Board Game Design' as the best choice for those considering collectible game design or design for the mass market."

–Joe Huber, Opinionated Gamers

"This book should definitely be on any game designer's bookshelf, but it will most likely offer some insights into some of today's favorite designers for players as well!"

–Game Knight Reviews

Other Books by Kobold Press

Complete Kobold Guide to Game Design

Kobold Guide to Board Game Design

Midgard Campaign Setting

THE KOBOLD GUIDE TO WORLDBUILDING

Introduction by Ken Scholes

With essays by
Keith Baker, Wolfgang Baur, David "Zeb" Cook,
Monte Cook, Jeff Grubb, Scott Hungerford,
Chris Pramas, Jonathan Roberts, Janna Silverstein,
Michael A. Stackpole, Steve Winter

Edited by Janna Silverstein

The KOBOLD Guide to Worldbuilding
© 2012 Open Design LLC

Editor Janna Silverstein
Cover art Malcolm McClinton
Publisher Wolfgang Baur
General Manager Shelly Baur
Graphic Design Marc Radle

"It's a Mystery! How to Design a Mystery Cult" by David "Zeb" Cook originally appeared in Kobold Quarterly #21

"Different Kinds of Worldbuilding" by Monte Cook originally appeared in Kobold Quarterly #23

OPEN DESIGN LLC
P.O. Box 2811
Kirkland, WA 98083

WWW.KOBOLDQUARTERLY.COM

First Edition

TABLE OF CONTENTS

THE KOBOLD GUIDE
TO WORLDBUILDING

Introduction

FOSTER WORLDS TO HIDE AND SEEK IN

Ken Scholes

L ike many of you, I've been visiting new worlds with an eye toward buying real estate for a long time now. My passport has more stamps in it than I can count.

I've been to Barsoom with John and Dejah, then tracked down Carson on Amptor. I took a nice, long walk through Middle-earth with Bilbo, Frodo, and Company before dropping by Arrakis to see how Paul's spice mining was going. I visited Almuric on my way to Hyborea to spend time with Esau and Conan (respectively). And then eventually, I found myself in hot water in Greyhawk's village of Hommlet (I lost two fingers to a giant frog there!) and spent many hours wandering the quarters of Baldur's Gate in the Forgotten Realms.

I am a traveler of many worlds.

I needed to be because this one just wasn't good enough for me. So these others became foster worlds, if you will, where I could play hide and seek with myself through books and with my friends through gaming. And I know I'm not alone. I remember Tim Powers telling my Writers of the Future Workshop that we wouldn't write what we write if we were at home in this world. It resonated with me and I suspect some others.

And somewhere along the way, it wasn't good enough for me to play hide and seek in the worlds of others—I was compelled to join the pantheon of gods who make worlds of their own. I started, like many of us, with my *Dungeons & Dragons* boxed set, a pad of graph paper, and a brain filled with all of the worlds I'd already visited by that time. It didn't hurt at all that somewhere along the way, TSR provided a list of all the other worlds out there that one could turn to for inspiration in creating their adventures. That opened up a door for me to the work of even more world-builders—all of which fueled my fire to create.

And after a bit, it just wasn't enough anymore. I turned to writing where, eventually, I created the world of the Named Lands in my series, *The Psalms of Isaak*, my first foray into the wacky world of epic fantasy.

And I'm wishing I had the book you're now holding right now—*The Kobold Guide to Worldbuilding*—when I started that great and wild ride. Of course, the good news is, thanks to Janna's kind invitation to write this introduction, I'll have my contributor copy handy for the next world I design.

It's going to come in handy.

This volume brings together a fine set of tools, whether you're a game master or an author. In Jonathan Roberts' brilliantly succinct essay, "Here Be Dragons," you'll learn how to very simply, very practically build the map of your world and outline much of its details. Wolfgang Baur will equally amaze in "Designing a Pantheon" and "What is Setting?" with his thoughts on creating gods and religions and settings that create potential for conflict and drive players (or readers) deeper into the story without hampering the game master (or author) with so much detail that there's no room for collaboration.

I'm already taking notes for the world I'll build after I finish with the one I'm visiting now. That makes this a pretty easy book to introduce to you. Whatever worlds you're building, you'll want this one along for the trip.

The essays here, from masters of their craft, form a toolbox with all you need "to create a place that feels real enough to develop an emotional connection to it," to quote Monte Cook's essay, "Different Kinds of Worldbuilding." "After all," he continues, "who wants to save a world that no one cares about?"

So take these tools. Go build more foster worlds we can play hide and seek in. Build them well and take us there. Stamp our passports and make us want to stay forever.

WHAT IS SETTING DESIGN?

Wolfgang Baur

Long ago, I did my first bit of paid design for my friend Jim, who wanted to run a *Dungeons & Dragons* (D&D) game for everyone but didn't want to design a setting and didn't want to pay for a boxed set. He gave me $2 or so, and I did my best with it. I was 12 at the time.

I wish I still had the materials I turned over for my first paid roleplaying game (RPG) design assignment. I remember Jim especially liked the map of the barony or duchy I created using colored pencil, with its castles, forest, lakes, and so forth. He was less enthusiastic about the text; most areas were described with a single sentence, possibly two, which seemed like plenty to me, for I had written them out longhand. The whole must have been maybe 10 or 20 notebook pages. Jim was a little disappointed, but I showed him that I had created a random monster table for the region, and so all was well.

Was it a successful campaign setting? Only Jim could say for sure, but I like to think that most of the ingredients were there, even if they were fairly crude: *location*, *character*, and *conflict*.

A lot of years have passed since then, and I've given a lot more thought to more recent worldbuilding exercises, both complete and partial, from Dark*Matter to Golarion to the Midgard campaign setting.

If you ask me today, I'd say that the goal of setting design is to *create a background or setting for fantasy gaming, one that provides a rich but not unlimited range of choices to both players and game masters (GMs). In addition, the successful design must establish sources of conflict and motivation for heroes and villains who act in the setting to entertain the players.* These character and villain hooks help the GM easily construct adventures, longer-running foes, and a complete campaign arc wherein the characters change the setting in some way and in which they achieve some or all of their own goals of character change or mastery.

Sort of a mouthful, really. Let's break it down and see what really counts in creating a campaign setting.

Background and Dynamite

The whole process of designing a campaign setting is sometimes referred to as worldbuilding, but this is a bit of a trap. "Worldbuilding" implies an encyclopedic approach, and this is exactly wrong. It is giving in to the "clomping foot of nerdism," to use M. John Harrison's memorable phrase.

The gamer's instinct is that of the otaku who must know everything. The designer's instinct should be to provide only that which is relevant, to provide the most immediately useful material and nothing else. The encyclopedia approach may be good for long-term sales and release after release over 20 years. And that level of fan service may be enjoyable for the designer to provide, frankly.

But giving in to that instinct is poison, because it means providing huge reams of useless data along with the nuggets of gold. Completeness is its own reward, but it is a GM's nightmare. If everything is defined (somewhere), the GM has no latitude to invent his own material. If everything is documented, the GM needs to know and master those huge reams of material *just in case* the party goes there. There are no mysteries, and there is no room to maneuver.

The more you detail as a designer, the more lovingly described a region becomes, the more difficult it is for anyone to run it well or feel confident that they know the material. This is why long-running campaigns always reach for the reset button. Burning it all down and starting over is one way to make the setting accessible again for new players, even as it provokes understandable howls of outrage from those who have spent time, effort, and cash on mastering the old version.

No, the goal is not an encyclopedic worldbuilding approach. The goal of good campaign setting design is to stack as many boxes of dynamite as possible, and then gingerly hand the whole ensemble to GMs so that they may cackle with glee at all the tools, hooks, conflicts, dangers, and purely delightful mayhem with which you have so thoughtfully provided them.

Conflict and Instigation

A campaign setting is a work of instigation, of collusion with the game master and with the players, to create something entertaining. Climate charts and trade routes may be useful bits of worldbuilding, but they should be largely invisible to the players. They are the merest foundation on which a campaign setting should be built.

So, what makes for good instigation? All the sources of human conflict: love, war, revolution, murder, betrayal, greed, theft, rape, oppression, religion, national pride, slavery, and the raw lust for power. These are hardly the stuff of real-life amusement (quite the contrary), but for fictional entertainment they are the tools in your toolbox as you consider the main characters and societies. Peaceful hobbity Shires are exactly the sorts of places we all want to live as cheerful, peaceful, kindly neighbors. But your first instinct as a game designer should be to convince the players that it's a fine place worth saving—just before the orcs invade and burn it down.

Good and evil aren't necessarily the best or only source of conflict: consider the dozens of ways you can shape a setting to set nobles against peasants, dragons against princes, merchants vs. pirates, or even wizards against priests. Bake those sources of conflict into the world. Make it clear that some rulers and some nations have big, deep-seated urges to conquer, to rule, or to assassinate their enemies—then make their societies paranoid and trigger-happy. Presto, your campaign setting just got more interesting, no matter whether the player characters are outsiders fighting against the paranoid super-empire, or they are lordlings and mercenaries of the empire, sent to put down the rebellious scum on the fringes.

If your players recognize the social structure as Empire vs. Rebellion, more power to them. The dramatic dynamic itself is part of the design, and it encourages game masters and players alike to choose goals and play adventures with a logical conclusion that shapes the world (the victory of one or the other side).

Build a tinderbox, and game masters and players will beat a path to your door.

So Why Write a History?

Focus on the now, on conflict. Just as set designers for a theatre or movie don't worry themselves overmuch with the history, creation, and narrative of a particular location's part (except as expressed in the present), so game designers really should not bother themselves with history except when it impinges on the current day.

This is one of the greatest traps that designers fall into over and over again. "Ten thousand years ago" sounds like the beginning of an epic history, certainly, but for most player characters, it's just irrelevant. Players don't care about 10,000 years ago until the moment it bites them in the ass. Make sure that for each reference to ages long past, there's some element of that history that is a real and present danger or conflict.

Why is it so hard to follow this rule and focus on the present? Partly this is J.R.R. Tolkien's fault for, in addition to giving us two great works of literary genius that redefined fantasy, he also gave us reams of backstory going back to the dawn of time. It's compelling stuff to read the early history of the elves, and the two trees, and Beren and Luthien, and all the other stories before the stories we know. And so gamers and game designers decided that since this was a lot of fun to read, it would also be a lot of fun to create similar history for gaming worlds.

This was a serious mistake.

Certainly readers of fiction want more and more and take delight in the continuing adventures of favorite characters, and their prequels, and their fanfic; the world is richer and more delightful, and everyone wins. But gaming is not fiction, and when we spend too much time on backstory and prequels and historical sweep and the like, the focus on the actions of the player characters fades. Design effort spent on this material makes the GM less effective in his role of director and entertainer. You'll notice, also, that Prof. Tolkien did not intend the *Silmarillion* and many of his notes for publication.

The worldbuilder's role is to prepare challenges and action for the heroes; time spent creating the details of societies, NPCs, and locales that no longer exist in the game world is time wasted. It may be rewarding for you to see the connections of past and present, and it may be a lot of fun. But as a function of successful, effective design it adds precisely nothing to the player's experience at the game table. They don't know the history, they don't care about the web of connections, and they rarely need or want that sort of information in the course of completing a heroic adventure.

I'd say that there's a minimum amount of history required for a setting for it to make sense, some short overview of how and why empires fell or the gods shaped the world for their amusement. A second category of historical backdrop helps the worldbuilder write adventures or stories in the setting because she has a better understanding of where a secret society came from or why two races still fight. The origins of conflict are usually fairly straightforward to explain and very few require full-blown in-character fiction, diagrams of the relevant battles, or descriptions of just how a coup came about. As gamers, we fall into the trap of over-explaining secret origins as a matter of course.

But almost all of what players need is in the category of *current events*. The secret society has goals right now: those matter. The secret society was founded by Evil Wizard Mastermind 1,000 years ago, and its leaders were banished by the paladins of Undying Light? No one cares. The exceptions tend to be entirely of the sort that bring history into the present: the society's goal is to resurrect its founder. But you'll note: that's a current event. Stick to those and your setting will seem much richer, more active, and livelier to players. Why? Because you are paying attention to the part of the setting

AN APOLOGIA: HISTORY AS HOBBY

I often hear the argument that creating history helps a designer understand his or her creation better, and that it amuses the casual designer who wants to think about the grand scheme of things that the players will never know. There's nothing wrong with generating that extra volume of material if you have time and inclination to do so, and if your primary audience is yourself. I write stuff for my own amusement about various characters—and I know it's really not productive except that I enjoy it.

My primary concern is when that material, like gaming kudzu, overwhelms the work of generating interesting characters and conflicts that might actually appear in the game. Since villains in fantasy can and often are ancient powers from the dawn of time, it's worth knowing something about their origins. But if the horror from the dawn of time does not influence the present, have enough awareness as a worldbuilder to cut that material out of your manuscript and avoid inflicting it on players—unless, of course, the wizard or bard is super-keen on various bits of Lore and Knowledge skills. In that case, you've finally found a use for the genealogical charts you drafted that go back 800 years as well as that sidebar on the court customs of the fallen empires.

Work on those sorts of projects for their own sake, but realize that ancillary material is like Tolkien's appendices: they're fun, but they're not the main goal or part of the final manuscript you present to the public or to your players. It's easy to wander for weeks and years in a setting's history and never ever get around to what makes the setting compelling, what makes it unique as a living, shared experience for gamers.

Don't lose focus.

that matters, the part that the PCs touch. Sometimes they meet or care about matters from ancient times that have survived to the present, as in the evil mastermind being resurrected. Those should be moments of high drama and a conflict of past and present. Pay attention to how you build those NPCs and those encounters in the context of the present, and work on what the motivations and methods of those villains are in the present.

This same argument against emphasis on the ancient past, by the way, also explains why most players (rightly) hate the use of lengthy read-aloud text. I leave the parallels as an exercise for the interested reader.

Ignore the Mechanics

I think that almost any campaign setting worth a damn is largely independent of the game mechanics used to play it.

As proof, I offer you the Forgotten Realms (four sets of mechanics and counting have undergirded the setting) and Star Wars (I've lost track, but last I checked I think it was also four sets of mechanics, and by at least 3 different companies) and even my own Dark*Matter (two sets of mechanics). As roleplaying settings, they have outlived the mechanics beneath them repeatedly. They must be doing something right, and it's not about the numbers. It's about the potential for adventure. So save the encounter-thinking, hazards, monsters, and number-crunching for the times when you are doing adventure design. Setting design is less mechanical but just as difficult.

In campaign settings, the goal is to inspire a GM to challenge a party of players and to inspire players to explore and change the world. Neither of those depends much on mechanics, though it's pretty clear that the experience system is a large motivator for most players. So long as character advancement happens in some form and as a reward for exploration, though, there's also a need to create places worth exploring, societies worth visiting, and villains who are both easy to understand and satisfying to defeat. You need a sense of place (and I argue the same for adventure design in *Complete Kobold Guide to Game Design*).

If you can sketch out enough of a sense of place in a few sentences to inspire a month or a year of gaming, your campaign setting is a success. If your setting design inspires no urge to run a game in the red-blooded gamer, well, try again, while knowing that not every setting is to everyone's tastes.

Summation

World design seems like an opportunity to loll about in an endless vista of vast time scales, epic page counts, and limitless possibilities. That's a lot of its appeal to any homebrewer or GM. Daydreaming of other worlds is rewarding for its own sake. But to design a professional setting for an audience, you need to take a hard look at the space and elements available and maximize the impact of every character, location, and mechanic. We'll discuss this in much more detail in the essay on kitchen sink design and the most important setting choices.

Different Kinds of Worldbuilding

Monte Cook

Worldbuilding is something that novelists, game designers, and game masters all talk about, but when they do they actually mean something slightly different. Or perhaps more accurately, they mean the same thing, but they approach the topic very differently.

World Building for Novelists

Novelists, in particular fantasy and science fiction novelists, work on worldbuilding as a backdrop for their stories. But that's all it is—a backdrop. While they might create a fully-fleshed out, living, breathing world, what ends up on the page is only just enough for the reader to understand and appreciate the story. (At least, if the novelist is any good.) In a way, any worldbuilding a novelist does that doesn't focus on the story they're telling is a waste. Fun, and perhaps rewarding, as it gives them a better sense of place and scale, but still kind of a waste.

Even a worldbuilding-focused writer is better off creating a world where there is one story to tell, with only the briefest suggestion of other stories. For example, take Third Age Middle-earth as related by Tolkien in *The Lord of the Rings*. The appendices, The Silmarillion, and other sources tell us that the author's created a much larger world, but we only get a hint of this in the novels. The worldbuilding that we see is only what's going on around the main characters—only what they see.

World Building for a Game

Worldbuilding from a game designer's point of view is very, very different. A game designer needs to build a world not for one story, but for a thousand. Or more. A setting built for an RPG needs to be huge, with a lot going on. Fantasy GMs who want an evil wizard for a foe need to have not one but many to choose from. Another

GM might want pirates. And another might want a jungle for his player characters (PCs) to explore, with dinosaurs. Another will want all three. And each one of these needs to cover a wide scope—from something that poses a small but interesting threat to something really big and important. Maybe even world-threatening.

So to keep with our Middle-earth example, for an RPG, Middle-earth doesn't need Sauron; it needs five or six, all in different locales with different motives and goals. And a cult trying to resurrect Morgoth, about 20 Shelobs, and I don't even know how many Saurumans. And a few dozen petty warlords, pirate kings, orc tribes, marauding trolls, and plenty of dragons. (Of course I am exaggerating. But you see my point, I think.) This doesn't mean, of course, that any one campaign will use them all. And that's the point. GMs need a lot to choose from to offer their players, and the players need to have a lot of choices themselves. The world needs to be dynamic and broad.

The game designer's world needs a lot broader detail than the novelist's as well. The novelist can mention the ruined city of Karmesh in the Bleak Desert as a bit of flavor, but the game designer needs to describe what's there. The novelist knows his characters aren't going to Karmesh, ever. It's just a part of one character's backstory. But the PCs in an RPG might go there, and they're going to want to know what they find. The GM needs details. Facts. Maps. And he needs them now.

I'm currently working on a worldbuilding project called *The Ninth World*, which is the setting for my new game, *Numenera*. My approach to worldbuilding is twofold. I want to present a bunch of great setting details and adventure ideas, but I also want to steep GMs in the flavor and concepts underpinning the world, to help them create their own details. Sort of the "give a man a fish and he eats for a day; teach a man to fish and he eats for a lifetime" approach to setting design.

This, of course, is a different kind of worldbuilding still. I'm giving lots of detail, but then empowering GMs to create it on their own as well, by giving them an idea of what kind of things they could create. And what would and wouldn't be appropriate for the setting. Or rather, what the implications of different kinds of material will have on the setting. This allows each GM to make his own Ninth World, which is the best of all possible worlds (pun not intended—no, really).

WORLDBUILDING AND THE GM

The GM's worldbuilding sort of falls in between. Ideally, the GM who builds his own world has more than one story in the offing, so that the players have some real choice as to what their characters do in the world (one story = railroaded campaign). But the GM doesn't need to create as many opportunities as the game designer because he's only got his own group to work with. Again, ideally, the GM knows his group and knows, for example, that they aren't going to be interested in pirates but will be particularly eager to go after the undead lord and his zombie horde.

The GM also has the ability to build his world as he goes. Like the novelist, he only needs to present the players with worldbuilding information as they require it—only as it is needed for the story at hand. If the PCs are in a tiny village in Kingdom A, they don't need to know any of the details of the political machinations of the nobles in the kingdom, and they need know nothing at all of Kingdom B and

Kingdom C. The GM is free to wait to add those kinds of details. He doesn't need to pre-build the entire world.

This, of course, can lead to a tricky bit of juggling. The GM has to stay at least one step ahead of the PCs. It's helpful to have chunks of the world that he can toss in when needed. For example, the PCs are on a ship sailing toward an adventure locale. The GM isn't ready for that location, so he has the PCs spot a mysterious island in the distance. He pulls out his old *Isle of Dread* module from way back when and uses that, not so much for the adventure, but for the setting.

Or the PCs are about to cross the border into a new kingdom that they've only heard of by name. Unfortunately, that's all the GM knew about it as well, and the game is in a day and a half. He pulls out a few of his Steven Erikson books (*The Book of Mazalan the Fallen* series), changes some of the names of the Seven Cities, and inserts that region into his game world. A GM, then, has the unique opportunity to incorporate other people's worldbuilding into his own worldbuilding process.

That's not cheating. That's being a game master.

One huge advantage to on-the-fly worldbuilding is that it allows the campaign to be reactive. If the GM creates it all ahead of time and lays it all out before the players, it is set in stone. But if he later decides he wants to have a magical realm with floating mountains high in the sky and dragon-riding knights, but he hasn't created such a place, he's out of luck. But if the world is being built as the campaign goes along, he can add this land in anywhere it suits him and—more importantly—suits the campaign.

PLAYERS AND WORLDBUILDING

But perhaps—just perhaps—there's yet another way to build a world: collaboratively.

Consider the idea that the players actually contribute to the creation of the GM's world. For example, the GM could mandate ahead of time that each PC hails from a different kingdom, land, or region. Each player, then, is responsible not only for creating his or her character, but also for the place the character comes from. The player would develop the rulers, the communities, and the geography. This could involve developing the traits for the PC's race as well. The GM, in turn, takes these player "submissions" and incorporates them into the world he's already built.

Some GMs will want to have the ability to take liberties with the players' creations to make them all work within the larger context. Others will decide to work alongside the players as they develop their homelands to ensure they have the cohesiveness needed for a usable campaign setting.

Once it's in the GM's hands, of course, it's his world to shape. He shouldn't undo what a player has created, but instead he should utilize it. This is important, because the whole point is each PC knows a lot about his or her homeland. If the GM changes it all, there's no background knowledge. But the GM can still make use of the material and create surprises.

For example, say a player with an elf character creates a wasteland that she comes from. In her creation, this was once a beautiful wooded realm, but evil priests of dark gods destroyed the vegetation and almost wiped out the elves. The character's people destroyed the priests long ago, but the realm is still a barren desert. The player, as she creates, names a number of the various important elves in the land, and even creates a relationship with one of them, stating that the queen of the surviving elves is her aunt.

At some point after the campaign begins, the PC needs the help of her aunt, the queen of the wasteland elves. She leads her friends (the other PCs) to her ancestral land. She knows her way around—she knows the dangers of the polluted river and where it is possible to still find game. She even knows you have to pay the trolls guarding the only pass through the mountains to get to the queen's hidden palace. That's all well and good.

But the GM has decided the evil priests were not wiped out long ago. Instead, their agents are still active in the land and they now control the queen with mind-altering drugs, making her their secret thrall. When the PCs arrive, the elf character senses something is amiss—she knows this place and these people, remember—so now the player's knowledge of the realm becomes a hook for an adventure. What's going on with the queen? When the PCs discover she's being drugged, they need to figure out who's doing it and why.

The important thing to take away is that allowing the player to create the wasteland didn't remove power from the GM. On the contrary: it saved him some work, it gave him new opportunities for adventures, and it made the elf player feel more invested in the campaign as a whole. When she senses something is amiss, it's really going to worry her. When she learns that something has happened to the queen, and that the evil priests—that the player herself created—are still around, it's going to be far more meaningful to her than if the GM had created it all himself.

And perhaps that's the most important part of worldbuilding, no matter who does the work. To create a place that feels real enough to develop an emotional connection to it. After all, who wants to save a world that no one cares about?

Inside Out and Outside In

Chris Pramas

There are many ways to build fictional worlds. If you are a talented linguist like J.R.R. Tolkien, you can start by creating new languages and then create a setting to make their home. If you are an artist, you can start with look and feel and then go from there. I am a historian by training, so that's the lens I tend to look through. I want to know not just what is this place, but how did it get this way? In my 20 years of professional game design, I have approached world building in two ways. Sometimes, I start with a local setting and then expand it until the world is fleshed out. This is building from the inside out. Other times, I start with a broad framework that is large but shallow, and then focus in on certain areas to give them greater detail. This is building from the outside in. In this essay I'm going to walk through both processes and talk about their strengths and weaknesses. Remember, though, that there is no one right way to do it.

INSIDE OUT

This approach is the more practical of the two because you are building what you need as you go. It's particularly useful when starting a RPG campaign, though the same applies if you are writing a novel or screenplay. You decide where your story is going to start and you start building up the local area and its surroundings. You can start with something as small as a village or as large as a city-state. Hopefully, you have one or more story ideas in mind, so you can sketch out what you need to support that. Who are the major players in this story? What do they want and what is creating the conflict(s)? When you have some broad ideas, you can start adding details. What is the culture of this land like? Are they religious and, if so, what form does that take? Who are some secondary characters you could introduce for color and sub-plots? What secrets are just waiting to be uncovered? As you start play or write your story, the need for further detail will become apparent and you can fill those in as you go. In this way the setting will continue to grow organically.

The process I just described is the one I used when creating the city of Freeport. It started as the setting for a single adventure (*Death in Freeport*, 2000). I knew I wanted to write a city adventure, since Wizards of the Coast was going "back to the dungeon" with the launch of third edition D&D. I also knew I wanted a place where characters from all over might meet, so that argued for a port and it was a short hop from there to pirates. I thought much of the adventure should be an investigation, which made me think of *Call of Cthulhu*. That led to the creation of a sinister cult (The Brotherhood of the Yellow Sign) and other Lovecraftian touches. In the end I wrote a four-page history of the city, plus the locations I needed for the scenario. Though not lengthy, that 32-page module created a template for Freeport. It was a setting that combined classic D&D fantasy with Lovecraftian horror and pirates.

Death in Freeport was a hit and indeed it put Green Ronin Publishing on the map. We continued to expand Freeport in future products. First, we did two more modules to make a trilogy that told one big story. Those adventures added more locations to the city, and many personalities with their own goals and agendas. Part 3, *Madness in Freeport*, did a lot to introduce the government and ruling elite of the city. We also added details about the ancient serpentman empire and its descendents. After the trilogy, we did the natural thing and released a full-fledged sourcebook called *Freeport: The City of Adventure* (2002).

From the beginning the idea of Freeport was that it was a city you could use in any fantasy campaign setting. The gods were not named, but referred to as God of Knowledge, God of War, and so on. There were references to "the Continent" but that's as far as it went. This was a feature for many game masters, and they used Freeport in many different campaign settings. Some other publishers even put Freeport into their own worlds. There were always folks who wanted to see a World of Freeport though. When it came time to do *The Pirate's Guide to Freeport* (2007), a revised sourcebook about the city, I decided to add an optional chapter that described the larger world and detailed "the Continent." And how did I do that? Outside in!

OUTSIDE IN

The first RPG campaign setting I was exposed to was the original World of Greyhawk folio (1980). I first saw it around 1981, when I was all of 12 years old. The folio contained a 32 page Gazetteer and Darlene Pekul's awesome poster maps of the setting. (Don't underestimate the importance of those maps, by the way. Great cartography helps suck people into your world. See Jonathan Roberts' essay, "Here Be Dragons," for more on the subject.) By today's standards, the World of Greyhawk was sparse on detail but it launched thousands of campaigns the world over. In talking with many Greyhawk fans over the years, I've found that most of them liked the fact that the setting was not overly detailed. It provided a broad framework that they could build on and customized as they saw fit.

The interesting thing about Greyhawk is that it did start small, in Gary Gygax's home D&D campaign. It was originally just the dungeons of Castle Greyhawk and then the nearby city. As his campaign grew, he added more details to the world but he never expected to publish it. He thought each GM would want to create their own setting. As the early modules proved though, there was an interest there, and the decision was made to publish the *World of Greyhawk*. Gary did not want his players learning too much about its secrets, so he made some major changes (like creating a brand new map) and made up a bunch of new material. What he provided in the folio (and the later 1983 boxed set) was a big picture that was ripe with possibilities. Some of those were realized in later products and others in the many home campaigns that used the *World of Greyhawk*.

In the folio and boxed set, you can see many principles of outside in design. The scope is large. In fact, it's larger than the maps! The area covered in any detail represents only a section (The Flanaess) of a much larger super-continent called Oerik. The nations are painted in broad strokes. The boxed set includes a section on the gods and cosmology. And there is history there. Gary describes the migrations of peoples, ancient wars, and apocalyptic events to set the stage for the modern Greyhawk. There is also plenty of mystery in the setting as described, to leave room for further development or just to give GMs ideas for adventures.

Outside-in design lets you think big. I had the chance to do that, in Greyhawk no less, when I was working on the D&D *Chainmail* miniatures game for Wizards of the Coast in the early 2000s. I wanted to set the game in Greyhawk, as it was supposedly the default setting of third edition D&D, but my team was not allowed to use the nations of The Flanaess. We decided to detail the eastern part of the super-continent of Oerik instead, an area about which little had been published. This became known as The Sundered Empire setting, and at its root was a big question: what happens when the God of War dies? My idea was that mortal heroes slew the God of War Stratis in the hopes of creating a lasting peace. Instead, they started a huge conflict, as warlords sought to become the new God of War. That was the premise I started with as I built The Sundered Empire, and it helped inform the competing factions and many other aspects of my world building.

To take this back to Freeport for a minute, outside in was the approach I took to world of Freeport in the *Pirate's Guide*. In fact, knowing I had only a chapter in which to work, I drew inspiration from the Greyhawk folio. The chapter delves into the history of the ancient serpentman empire, the cosmology of the setting (which uses Yig as a sort of world serpent), and gives an overview of the "the Continent." Some things from the folio I chose to leave out, like specific numbers and troop types of the nations (which was a nod to D&D's wargaming heritage). Instead I included entries for each nation like important landmarks. These were just names with no description provided, dangling mysteries for GMs to explore. The elf kingdom of Rolland, for example, has Cairncross Hill, Shrine of the Hunter's Moon, and Windgrass Grove. I have never written those up, but I bet some enterprising GMs have.

If outside-in design has a flaw, it's that it takes some time to figure out the big issues. How large is the setting? What's its cosmology like? Are any big ideas baked into it? What are the cultures and nations like? How did the various peoples get where they are today? Who are some famous and infamous people from its past? If you are trying to get a game or story underway soon, outside-in design may not be the approach for you. If you have the time and inclination to do work up front though, you may find it easier to slot new elements into your existing framework than expanding the world as you go. The other issue is that with all these broad strokes, you will miss a lot of fine detail. That's OK, as you can zoom in on areas to support adventure and story ideas.

CROSSING THE STREAMS

So far I have talked about these two approaches as a binary choice, but it doesn't need to be that way. You can mix and match as you go, and that's just fine. You might design a village one week and create an entire pantheon of gods the next. The important thing is to keep pushing ahead and expanding your world. You can even start with one approach and then move to the other. I was part of just such an attempt, once again (strangely enough) involving Greyhawk.

In 1999 I was working at Wizards of the Coast in Roleplaying R&D. I had been hired to work on the third attempt to do a *Magic: The Gathering* RPG (this time using modified AD&D rules) but when in-fighting between departments kyboshed that project I was put onto the *Greyhawk* team. This led to me writing (with Sean Reynolds) *Slavers*, a sequel to the 1st edition *Slavelords* modules, which were favorites of mine. It also gave me a chance to help craft a plan to bring new blood into *Greyhawk*. Roger Moore, who was working remotely in the Midwest, flew out to Seattle for a week of meetings, the team banged out some ideas, and we put together a plan for the next phase of *Greyhawk*.

Our thinking was that *Greyhawk* needed a new entry point, a way we could ease people into the setting. Books like *Greyhawk: The Adventure Begins* (1998) was great for old fans, but because it tried to summarize the whole history of the Greyhawk Wars and subsequent events, it could be daunting to newbies. Our idea was to start with a local area (say, a town and the surrounding area) in an intro product that was designed to get a new campaign off the ground. Then there'd be a succession of products that widened the scope. The next might detail a province, the next a duchy, the next a kingdom, and so on. This would ultimately lead up to a big book detailing a major slice of the setting. In our case, this was meant to be the Great Kingdom and some of the surrounding nations.

Sadly, this plan was never enacted. I feel like it was a real missed opportunity because then Greyhawk could have been approached either outside in or inside out by different game groups. I think Freeport does that, in that you can ease people into it with the original modules or jump right in to the *Pirate's Guide to Freeport*.

I hope you've found my experiences in worldbuilding helpful. In the end, the important thing is that you sit down and do it. Thinking about how you're going to get there is important, but don't let excessive analysis stop you from getting your creation going. Starting is the hardest part.

HOW REAL IS YOUR WORLD?
History and Fantasy as a Spectrum of Design Options

Wolfgang Baur

One of the frequent cries around fantasy campaigns is the call for more realism or, at least, plausibility and verisimilitude. This is a long tradition in gaming circles and yet a slightly crazy one. Part of the joy of fantasy is the joy of escape from the modern world into the exploration of something new, original, creative, and different from the commute, the job, the children, the parents, the roommate, and so on. No one wants to be reminded of the real world in a fantasy game.

And yet we want things that we relate to: characters, heroes, archetypes that are grounded in myths and legends we recognize. We want "real fantasy," one of those things that makes me scratch my head, though I think we know what is meant. We want to suspend disbelief, and yet we also all have pet peeves, concerns, flashpoints that drag us out of a fantasy. How much you as a player are willing or able to suspend your disbelief with a fantasy setting is a matter of individual character and personality. How much your audience is willing to suspend disbelief and buy into your setting is a matter of supreme importance to a game designer: you need to find the sweet spot where the maximum number of people want to believe.

It's important to include magic and wonder and crazy elements in a fantasy setting. At the same time, there's clearly a limit. When things go too far off the rails, the fan screaming about "so fake" and "stupidly unrealistic" never quite stops. The internet has reinforced this tendency, but it's a strangely specific one. Swords and battle axes as big as a steamer trunk are fine to some people and anathema to others. Elves everywhere and floating cloud cities and massive mountain-sized dragons are exactly what some players and GMs want—and are annoyingly childish or foolish to others.

What does this mean for worldbuilding? It means that, as a designer, you need to consider some choices and consider your audience. And then decide which tradition to follow. Here's a summation of the field and what it means for your own worldbuilding efforts.

Real Worldbuilding

There are at least two clear traditions in fantasy worldbuilding: the real worlds and the pure fantasies. Fans of the two approaches are usually split and sometimes react violently to the wrong flavor. As with all matters of art and creative endeavor, this is a matter of subjective judgments and personal preferences. The quality of the execution carries a great deal of weight as well.

To put it simply, the competing traditions are these: some fantasy worlds are built more closely on real European legends (such as Conan's Hyborea, or an Arthurian variant, or Golarion's many Earthlike cultures), while others are built more clearly on a premise or a conceit (Barsoom or Dark Sun or Spelljammer). A few fall somewhere in between, but let's pretend for a moment that these are entirely different schools of thought with respect to worldbuilding. They're not, exactly, and I'll get to that.

The European Tradition: Historical Fantasy and Real Fantasy

The first great tradition in fantasy worldbuilding takes as its premise all the myths and legends of Europe, and weaves a world on those elements. You can certainly quibble with my categorizations, but the sorts of settings I'm talking about fall into about two large camps. There are the purely historical fantasies, and there are the ones that are clearly more distant cousins to the real world, though the echoes of the real world are visible to anyone who scratches at the surface a bit.

Hard Historical Fantasy

For the historical fantasy settings, I'm thinking of things like Jonathan Tweet's *Ars Magica*, Clark Ashton Smith's Averoigne, Chad Bowser's *Cthulhu Invictus*, Sandy Peterson's *Pendragon*, Lovecraft's Cthulhu Mythos and the related RPG, White Wolf's World of Darkness, and Scott Bennie's *Testament*. These are excellent fantasy worlds, with a specific character, a specific time period, and are built on the firmest ground of realism you can imagine for something that is still clearly a fantasy setting.

What does historical fantasy mean for your design and worldbuilding?

On the one hand, it means that your technology, backstory, and characters are already matters of historical record. The important elements of your design are the ones that introduce alternate history and magic to the setting, the differences from reality. Perhaps there are houses of wizards behind the scenes. Perhaps Arthur's knights do pursue the Grail, or eldritch, sanity-blasting monstrosities wander through Medieval France.

You'll note that this approach is a powerful shortcut to familiarity. It makes these worlds easy to explain to players, and Hollywood uses this formula often as well ("It's the Wild West—but with UFOs!"). This makes it easy to get buy-in from players or readers, and it simplifies your workload and enriches your storehouse of reference material. The real world is weird, wild, and wonderful. Humanity's legends and story cycles are a well of endless inspiration. It's easier to attract an audience with a proven story and setting, or a hybridization of two elements into something new.

This is all great fun for anyone who loves history and alternate history, and a historical fantasy is as realistic as a setting can be, but the style also creates its own limits. Once you are committed to King Arthur and the Round Table, it's tough to work in Cthulhu (though hardly impossible—Mordred and Morgan Le Fey were clearly cultists!). Once you are discussing wizards and medieval Europe, it's hard to suddenly bring in wuxia martial arts. There are limits. A known setting can be bent pretty far, but must never violate the mysterious line where disbelief creeps in.

Because this clarity of focus makes the game easy to explain to others ("It's the Crusades with magic" or "It's the Chinese Three Kingdoms with secret Lotus monks"), it may also limit the size of your audience. Historical fantasy is a rich field but, for many, it's just too historical. *Call of Cthulhu* is beloved by RPG designers, but if you don't love Lovecraft and the 1920s, it's just never going to be your cup of tea. Know in advance that your audience may be small but intensely loyal and likely includes many experts in the period in question.

Your goal might be a somewhat accurate recreation of a historical period, overlaid with just enough fantasy and flavor to make it spicy and sexy—but not so much that you "ruin" it with too much fantasy. How much is too much? This is entirely a matter for you to determine. Some will say James Bond vs. Voodoo zombies is good fun; others will say it ruins the Bond franchise. Some will enjoy Napoleonic adventures with assassin cults; others will complain about the lack of realism in 17th-century social standards.

The approach often taken for this sort of design is to declare that the history of the world is well known—but that there is also a secret history, known only to vampires, or Templars, or wizards.

With historical design, tropes are your friend, and indeed tropes of the period are indispensable. Your job is to take what everyone knows about that time period and combine it with just enough new elements to make it exciting and original. You are both an amateur historian and a stage director, and if you are successful you will make a historical period come alive with credible characters, action, and period details. Too much detail, too much accuracy, and too much minutiae are your enemies. Consider yourself a popularizer of the period, and you'll go far.

"Real Fantasy"

Which brings us to the world that is clearly full of the echoes of history and reality, but divorced from it to a greater or lesser degree by its fantasy conceits. It's one step more fantastical, if you will; its magic is bigger and brighter and its history and sense of earnestness about itself is one step less, while still respecting the roots and traditions of fantasy. There's more Cthulhu, more fireballs, more giant robots, bigger bets on dragons and monsters and the fantastical coming into the open, rather than the Secret History approach.

To quote particular examples, I'm thinking of settings like Robert E. Howard's Hyborea, Jeff Grubb's *Al-Qadim*, Suleiman, Kenson, and Marmell's *Hamunapta*, my own Midgard campaign setting, Bruce Heard's Mystara, David "Zeb" Cook's Kara

Tur/Oriental Adventures, Tracy Hickman's *Ravenloft*, John Wick's *7th Sea*, Games Workshop's *Warhammer* RPG, and Greg Gorden's TORG. Some of these lean more heavily on the real and some more on the fantasy, but in each case, the designer clearly has a shelf full of real-world reference books. Others, like Roger Zelazny's *Chronicles of Amber*, Richard Baker's *Birthright*, and Paizo's Golarion, all lean fairly heavily on Earth and its cultures, so they seem to belong here as well.

Each of these owes a great or lesser debt to the real world's cultures and societies, and the usual points of departure include the world's great mythologies and legends, such as the Egyptian mythos, the Norse sagas, the *1001 Arabian Nights*, the tales of Stoker and the stories of Atlantis and the *Song of Roland*, Grimm's Fairy Tales, pirate tales, the tales of Baron Munchhausen, and the Holy Roman Empire. They're all built on the assumption that the real world is worth embellishing, and that fantasy is a matter of making real places or real legends more exciting. If dragons were real . . . life would be more exciting.

So, what does a real fantasy approach mean for your game design?

In each case above, it's impossible to imagine that fantasy setting without the body of lore that undergirds it. As the designer of such a setting, you must know the basics of that mythology inside and out, and the more of the obscure points you know, the better off you are. At the same time, it's very easy to get trapped in excessive research that players won't care about, and your prose and descriptive detail can become dry and academic. In a historical fantasy, that's more acceptable than in a real fantasy, where the goal is not so much "simulation plus a little fantasy" as it is "experience an improved version of the tales."

Your goal as a designer is to understand what makes that mythology tick, and why it appeals to a modern audience. Once you understand it, your work is to make it both accessible and playable by lifting the best parts of it and making them irresistible to gamers.

That's right: your goal is to do a better job on the Arabian Nights, to improve on the Brothers Grimm, and to swipe the best bits of ancient Egyptian lore from 5,000 years ago, and make it compelling reading for teenagers, college kids, adults of all ages in the 21st century.

No one said it was easy.

THE MODERN SPECIAL CASE

The big obvious exception to all that dissection of historical roots of genre is the modern age. The closer we get to the present day, the more realism is tolerated— nay, demanded! Can you imagine Sandy Petersen's *Call of Cthulhu* being dinged for being too European? Of course not; the idea is ludicrous. The same goes for my own *Dark*Matter*, Rowling's Harry Potter books, Eckelberry and Baker's *Star*Drive*, Naomi Novik's Temeraire series, Mike Pondsmith's *Castle Falkenstein*, Lester Smith's *Dark Conspiracy*, Jordan Weisman's *Shadowrun*, and Steve Weick and Mark Rein*Hagen's *Vampire the Masquerade*.

The closer we get to the present, the more we demand some adherence to reality. Fantasy retreats when the players know all too well what the world is really like, and especially when they may have visited some of the locations involved (or at least, seen them on TV). The ability to suspend disbelief shrinks, in particular around matters of geography and culture.

What do modern traditions mean for your modern fantasy setting?

Clearly, you need to know your time period as well as any historical fantasy fan, but you also probably need to limit the fantasy elements, rather than spend time and effort expanding them. I'd argue that the main work of a setting designer for a modern setting (defined as anything after 1800, perhaps, or at least in the gunpowder-and-photographs age of history) is working out all the implications of their fantasy world's divergence from real world history—as it affects the players. The magic system is top of the list, followed by any secret history, and new cultures with prominent non-player characters (NPCs) (such as aliens, vampires, dragons, or fey).

I could go on at some length about modern campaign settings, but it's a bit of a tangent from the main focus and a specialized topic. Let's just say that they present some unique challenges of balancing what people know and what people want, but no more so than the historical fantasies of older periods. The difference is that we as readers and gamers think we understand the present day and the near past better than we understand the distant past.

THE ASIAN SPECIAL CASE

This leads me, strangely enough, to Asia. There are at least three prominent Asian settings in the history of fantasy RPGs, perhaps more depending on what you count as prominent. To my eyes, these are David "Zeb" Cook's *Oriental Adventures* and Kara Tur, Paizo's Tian Xia setting, and then AEG's Rokugan (and various modern settings, of course, such as *Dragon Fist, Shadowfist*, and *Hong Kong Action Theatre*). To a certain eye, these are purely a type of "real fantasy" as they could not exist without reference to Chinese and Japanese mythology. But I'd say that they form their own corpus of setting types, precisely because their myths are less entrenched in the psyche of the typically American and European audience of people who play them.

To put it another way, even with the rise of Asian cinema, anime, and manga, I'd argue that most Americans and Europeans don't grow up on a steady diet of Chinese and Japanese stories and setting materials. The assumptions about goblins and Shinto and Confucian values aren't ingrained in us as Western gamers. Unless you are a recent immigrant or a huge JRPG fanboy, you have to learn those tropes, from anime, from martial arts films, and from video games. It's a little like historical games, in that we get less of it from osmosis. We might know what a hopping vampire or a kappa is from our bestiaries and monster manuals. We're less likely to immediately recognize the shaman queen Himiko.

Now, I would argue that the more we know the myths and locales of a place, the more allergic we may be to them. Familiarity breeds contempt, and what is more familiar than the stories we grow up with?

Sure, you might argue that we love many real-world tropes, and that druids are real-world historical figures, and paladins are a direct rip-off of the French chanson of Roland. But for the most part, the Druids are an old, old story, but they are invisible because no gamer treats them as remotely historical anymore. They've been absorbed into gaming culture, divorced from their origins.

Some gamers react negatively to what they've seen too often. So, what makes a setting strong, compelling, tied to myths we cherish, but not too familiar? That's the fine line that every gamer and every designer draws somewhere differently.

And the proof of it might be that the Asian fantasy feels exotic and original and new to us, though the legends and tropes are completely grounded in real-world history and Asian traditions. Asia is not something we've seen often, so it comes across as shiny and new. Familiar but not too familiar. It's new to us, as gamers, so there's less of a sense of "seen it, done it." The regular, straight-up, bog-standard vanilla Asian fantasy still feels different and creative to your average Western gamer.

What does all this mean for your Asian setting design?

On the one hand, you get to play with a new box of toys, a new set of research, new sourcebooks, new characters, monsters, societies, and setting elements of all kinds. Nothing is Western, traditional, played-out. If you love novelty, Asia is full of entire cultures that—despite the continuing rise of Japanese, Korean, and Chinese culture—are still largely unknown to your audience as a designer. That's the good news.

The bad news is that as much as gamers react against overdoing the historical part of real-world European history, it's even worse with Asia. No one wants to play a real samurai or ninja. Everyone wants to play the legends as described in film and video games. And a tabletop RPG is never going to be as good at cinematic action as a film or video game about the martial arts.

The solution for a Western game would be to spend some time on the other mythic elements, about character and setting. Western gamers, however, don't want to learn the code of the samurai or mimic Confucian values. They want to kick ass (and rightly so). Your job is to balance mythic materials with modern violence in a satisfying way that neither insults the source material nor loses the interest of your audience, in a culture not necessarily your own. Again, no one said it was easy.

Getting the balance right of a relatively unfamiliar mythos coupled with Hollywood aesthetics is brutally difficult. As proof I offer you the long and stunning history of tightly-designed and lusciously-produced Asian-flavored RPGs, none of which have been a long-term commercial success. The one possible exception is the *Legend of the Five Rings* property, though in that case, we're talking about a card game that occasional puts a toe into RPGs, not an RPG property first and foremost.

Asian settings are full of sexy new toys and delightful new myths and awesome action flicks. Despite this, they have more in common with the small-but-loyal following of historical European fantasy than you might first suppose. Be wary, and know what you want your setting to achieve before committing to a major Asian campaign setting.

THE PURE FANTASY LINEAGES: ANCHORED AND WILD

The alternative to realism in your fantasy is the pure invention of high fantasy. Hippos fly, the sun is dying, spaceships crashed on distant worlds give rise to fantasy caste-based societies of stunning complexity, and lightning rails cover a vast pseudo-industrial continent. Hell, you could say that midichlorians provide a unifying life force for a far-flung fantasy empire of the stars. These are all Big Fantasies.

Within that realm of the high-flung fantasy setting, I think you can probably tease apart two flavors. One of them is more recognizably "realistic" or concerned with plausibility, and the other is more clearly interested in a high concept or message, with less concern for realism or authenticity.

Anchored Fantasy

Anchored fantasy is high fantasy that still takes a grain of simulation to heart. There's a sense of pattern-matching, of making sure that linguistics are reasonable, that armor might matter, or that societies function similarly to human societies already known.

If pressed to name the pure fantasies that are most anchored in some degree of reality, I'd probably list game worlds like Monte Cook's Diamond Throne, Margaret Weis and Tracy Hickman's *Dragonlance*, Jack Vance's *Dying Earth*, M.A.R. Barker's *Empire of the Petal Throne*, Ed Greenwood and Jeff Grubb's *Forgotten Realms*, Fritz Leiber's Lanhkmar, Tolkien's Middle-earth, John Wick's Rokugan, and Lucas' *Star Wars*. They all feature social structures and technology that is somewhat Earth-derived, even if the worlds themselves are clearly new.

In an anchored fantasy, the people act in ways that are semi-feudal, or similar to the Meso-American cultures, or simply in guilds, cities, and societies of knights with fancy swords and mystic codes. They're not familiar, exactly, which makes them thrilling. But we recognize that they are built on models we recognize and the places and structures they inhabit are appealing partly because we do understand them as somewhat like our own history.

What does anchored high fantasy mean for your design?

I would argue that the emphasis here is on creating an entirely new world that obeys most of the same principles and laws we know, with the major addition of magic. You can take huge liberties as a designer in these settings, setting continents adrift, lighting the world from enormous lamp-like trees, mixing alien and human societies together, and hopping from one charming vignette to the next without too much concern for the details of trade and agriculture. Your eyes are on the fantastical, and some hand-waving is fine; your audience will follow.

What seems most familiar is the heroic characters and the societies they come from. These take certain recognized forms, such as feudalism or a caste system, that are based on earth analogues. Humans are largely dominant, but not entirely, and this means that high fantasy is a place for utopian and dystopian realms as bright and dark as you can imagine. These anchored fantasies seem to drift, as a group, easily into Manichean and sometimes racist fantasy, and they are difficult to pigeonhole.

Each is a strange soap bubble, a mix of the familiar and the truly new. As a designer, you have great freedom to explore and experiment.

Wild-Eyed Wahoo Fantasy

Beyond those somewhat anchored fantasy settings are the wild-eyed and the wahoo worlds. This is by no means pejorative, as these include some of my personal favorites, but it is meant to show that there are high-concept, love-'em-or-hate-'em sorts of settings. Call them worlds of pure chaos, places where anything goes and where the usual rules do not apply. They are not meant to be realistic, and indeed that is their appeal. They are settings unmoored from reality and operating by rules of your design—but these settings do have rules.

To provide some examples, think of places like China Mieville's Bas Lag, Pratchett's Disc World, Frank Baum's Oz, David "Zeb" Cook's *Dark Sun* and *Planescape*, Keith Baker's *Eberron*, Jim Ward's *Gamma World*, NCSoft's *Guild Wars*, Andrew Leker's *Jorune*, Michael Moorcock's Melnibone, Jeff Grubb's *Spelljammer*, and Blizzard's *World of Warcraft*. These are places where truly Weird Shit happens, with different rules of physics, alien landscapes, magical wastelands, alien gods, mutants, and cosmologies. It's fun to go out on the edge, and fantasy is always exploring strange places like this. These are the high-wire acts of worldbuilding. They take creative risks, not always successfully, and they endure a higher degree of mockery than the real fantasies or anchored fantasies do because of those creative risks. They also attract a loyal following who love that particular flavor of weird. Just ask any *Planescape* fan.

But what does wild-eyed and wahoo fantasy mean for your design?

First off, it means less worry about matching real history and legend, and complete creative freedom to ask "What if?" This is tremendously liberating to a writer who may have spent a lot of time with more traditional fantasy settings. What if Law and Chaos were universal forces? What if philosophies came with secret societies and belief changed the fabric of the universe? What if wizards could stand on a spaceship's deck and travel among the worlds as starfaring explorers? What if magic creates enormous and impenetrable brambles that are slowly choking the world? What if the world was doomed to die any day now, and magic was a curse? What if Ragnarok already happened, and the World Serpent flattened Europe? What if goblins were all pyromaniacs, or mutations were good for you? What if the world really was flat? (Wait, that's Midgard.)

A wahoo design needs a single, unified premise or series of premises. These must be clearly stated and then enlarged and expanded to their logical conclusion. It needs strange societies that encapsulate that premise, and conflicts between them, and room for both humor and tragedy. Most of all, a wahoo design needs to offer new patterns for GMs to follow; the traditional myths and legends don't apply here, so you need to show people the hooks and the standard tropes of this new world. As a designer, you need to make the bizarre seem not just familiar, but inevitable, encapsulated in a few key locations (Sigil) or characters (dragon kings).

Most of all, you need to know just how far you can push this premise before it all comes apart. Too much humor or lightness, and it all becomes laughable. Too grim, and no one wants to play. Just because you are reinventing the rules of physics, sociology, and biology does not mean you get a free pass to invent anything and everything. On the contrary, you must first describe and explain your premises, and then you must adhere to them scrupulously. Work your premise, and make it sing, and the world will dream the same strange dream you have. Fail to stick with it, or treat your premise with any disdain, and your high-wire act will flop and fail.

A Mix of Fantasy and Reality: Low Fantasy

I said earlier I'd get back to the place where plausible fantasy and pure intersect, and here we are. It's fantasy with grit and plausibility, with a dark streak of cynicism and a love of the double-cross. This is, frankly, where I run Midgard sometimes, in the space of low fantasy. It is not floating cities and unicorns, it is not wahoo very often, it has dirt under its fingernails and bloodstains on its soul. There's magic, sometimes hugely powerful magic, but it's anything but a common or everyday experience to see it.

To quote a few touchstones as I've done earlier, I'd put forward Glen Cook's Black Company, Chris Pramas's *Freeport*, Mike Mearls's *Iron Heroes*, N.R. Crossby's *Harn*, Steve Brust's Vlad Taltos series, Robert Lynn Aspirin's *Thieves World*, and George R.R. Martin's Westeros. Arguably Bioware's *Dragon Age*, Gary Gygax's *World of Greyhawk*, and Ursula Le Guin's *Earthsea* books belong to this camp, though they might be placed in the real fantasy camp instead. But this is my taxonomy, and I think the style and undergirdings of these settings have much in common.

The main thrust of the low fantasy characters and the settings is that there are limits to power, that everything has a price, that human nature is corrupt and salvation uncertain. Maybe you see where I'm going with this. . . . It's very similar to hardboiled or noir, and it requires a certain cynicism about human nature and about the roles of pure good and pure evil. It's a worldview, as much as anything.

What does gritty low fantasy mean for your design?

The interesting thing about low fantasy, or gritty fantasy, is that the heroes in it are absolutely heroes, but the setting is built in such a way as to minimize the potential for munchkinism and masturbatory fantasies of pure power. Instead, the limits of power are quite real: heroes are smaller and less important than other forces (kingdoms, gods, devils, ancient Dragaerans, what have you) but they fight and struggle mightily anyway, knowing they won't always win. This is a hardboiled ethos, a punk ethos of the little hero who comes up from nothing to achieve much. It is surprisingly unpopular in fantasy RPGs, though it is a dominant thread in fantasy fiction as sword and sorcery of the old school and the new (Joe Abercrombie doesn't even bother with magic in his take).

I think gritty settings are more appealing to designers than they are to players. Few players want limits to their character's power and a sense of futility is rarely sexy in an RPG. It's possible to design around this, to make a game compelling even when the death rate is very high and the odds of success low. It's just a lot harder than a game where players can buy magic items out of any book or where any wound is quickly healed. Design for low fantasy if you like, but realize that the majority of the fantasy RPG audience doesn't play this style of game.

An Exhortation

This overview of the major fantasy RPG subgenres presents them as I see them, with reference to particular traditions or styles in setting design. Different designers often work in several such subgenres, and I certainly would not want to imply that one or another of them is superior to the others. They all have their followers, and while the size of the audience is certainly a consideration when thinking about what sort of world to build, it's hardly the most important.

Most of all, I think, as a designer you should be aware of what has come before and how your world design relates to those ancestors. Build a world that wildly reinvents an ancient mythos. Build a whole new mythos and share it. Discuss what you love in other worlds, and think about why you love it. Don't be afraid to crib the best of history, and don't be afraid to run with a high concept if you have one that sets your designer-senses tingling.

When you've done all that, combine old and new in a way that makes it a joy for both players and game masters, but more than anything, create a world that is exactly as real and as fantastical as you want it to be. I want to play in that world.

MIDGARD IN THE TAXONOMY

The Midgard campaign setting started as deliberately not a setting, and confined itself to the Free City of Zobeck, a river town that could be dropped pretty much anywhere into a homebrew campaign. That lasted for about six years, but over time, people wanted to know more and more about what was over the next hill. In 2012, with the publication of the Midgard campaign setting, a goodly portion of the world was revealed. Where does it fit in?

I've suggested here that Midgard is a real fantasy setting, but that's only partly true. It has won the ENnie Award for Best Adventure for *Streets of Zobeck*, which is a gritty low fantasy collection. It includes an entire region where Abominations Walk the Earth, and it is more wahoo in the various corners than I might have expected: especially its Shadow Lands and its Elf Lands. Fantasy has a nice way of upping the ante, and making something strangely real and entirely weird. I ran with those elements, or at least I designed them in for the players who enjoy them. They're easy to ignore for those who prefer their fantasy more realistic. The flexibility is part of what makes Midgard click.

In other words, I thought I was going to write it as sword and sorcery, and it's closer to Greyhawk and Golarion than I thought it would be. Sometimes, in the work of building a world, things may take unusual turns. That's not necessarily a bad thing, and in the case of Midgard, I'd say it's an incredible strength. The setting makes it possible to play real fantasy, anchored fantasy, low fantasy, and even some degree of wahoo fantasy in different regions of the setting. Individual GMs can emphasize or de-emphasize certain regions and elements easily to suit the preference of their group of players. I'd like to see more settings take this regional or modular approach to worldbuilding, and make it possible to scale the level of historical and fantastical elements to suit two or more of the audiences described here.

BRINGING HISTORY TO LIFE

Keith Baker

The paladin leveled his sword, the point lingering in front of the orc's neck. "You shouldn't have come here, beast."

"This was our land first, and my kind who forged that blade in your fist." The gray-skinned shaman laughed. "You don't even know what it is, do you? You think it's just like any other lump of enchanted steel. Go ahead, then. Strike me down. Draw innocent blood with the Sword of Justice, and see what it costs you."

Adventurers live in the moment. As you design your world, you may develop a rich and detailed history. You could produce lineages of kings for each kingdom you create, explore the roots of religion, even establish the global events that led to the current geographical layout of your world. But why do the players care about any of this? How does it impact their experience as they explore the world?

Not every element of history will impact the player characters. Some things are simply about creating a world that feels real. However, there are many ways that history can affect, inspire, and improve your adventures. Consider the following questions as you develop your setting.

WHY DO WE FIGHT?

What are the greatest conflicts in the modern age of your world? Is the most menacing threat an ancient evil—the dark lord lingering in the land of shadows—or conflict between human nations? Are there cultures or races in your world that you want the adventurers to see as implacable enemies—any time they encounter troglodytes, they know it's going to be a fight to the death?

Whether the enemy is troglodytes or the human tribes of the Tralog Hills, it's good to establish the reasons for these conflicts . . . and preferably, to find a way to make those personal for the players. You can tell the players the basic origin of the conflict—

how the Tralog tribes are tree-worshipping savages who have always resisted the civilizing agenda of the Griffon Empire—but after that, work with each player whose character comes from the Griffon Empire to determine their personal interactions with the Tralogs in the past. Was a character's father killed during a Tralog raid? Was the character once captured and tortured by Tralog barbarians, producing disfiguring scars that remain to this day? Was her life spared by a Tralog druid who told her that the fate of both their cultures would one day rest on her shoulders?

The same principle applies even if the threat is an ancient evil. The major villain of the campaign is the Lich-Lord of the Kingdom of Bone. It's been centuries since his undead legions have ventured from the blasted realm . . . but what connects the player characters to him? Is the wizard the last surviving member of his mortal bloodline? Does the paladin hear the voice of the saint who gave her life to defeat the Lich-Lord the last time he rose? Could the thief's terrible nightmares be related to the finger bone he found in the purse he stole from that stranger?

These conflicts may not be so simple and clear cut. It may well be that the Tralog Hillfolk have valid reasons to hate the Griffon Empire. It could be that the enemy in your campaign isn't an exterior foe, but rather rival families within a single kingdom. But the principle remains. Work with the players to determine what their characters know and why they care. Do they embrace these conflicts, or do they have reasons to go against the common flow? Could the adventurers end up forging a new peace between the Tralogs and the Empire? Bear in mind that this doesn't have to be the focus of a campaign at all. The adventurers could be solely interested in exploring dungeons and making a profit. But at least when they do encounter a Tralog, they have a sense that they are tied to one of the big conflicts going on around them—and they have a personal stake in it.

LOST CIVILIZATIONS

In our world, the general rule is that technology advances and, as a result, modern weaponry and tools are invariably superior to those from the past. If you want the best gun money will buy, you buy it; you don't go poking around a dusty crypt hoping you'll stumble on a rifle better than you could find at the gun shop. However, in fantasy RPGs we often want the most potent tools and treasures to be things that cannot be bought—things that can only be obtained through adventures. Logically, how do we justify this? Why are the treasures of old equal or superior to what's produced in the present day?

Artifacts are generally one of a kind, with origins steeped in legends. When you're looking for a broader spread of treasures and challenges, this question can be answered more broadly with the introduction of fallen civilizations: cultures that advanced to a point beyond that of modern civilizations only to vanish from the world. In exploring this possibility, one immediate question is how the civilization fell. Here are a few ideas to consider.

- **The Deluge.** From the biblical flood to the story of Atlantis, there are many tales of civilizations wiped away by a devastating force of nature. An important question here is whether this was a divine punishment, a truly natural disaster, or a cataclysm the culture brought upon itself. Could it happen again? The signs of this disaster could be traced across the world. Lingering elementals or demons may be the remnants of this destructive force. Are there still intact cities from this civilization, or just ruins and artifacts carried far and wide by the waters?

- **World War III.** As a society advances, war becomes more devastating. A fallen civilization could have been wiped out or simply reduced to a more primitive level by military conflict. Who did they fight? Was it a civil war? A war against an extraplanar opponent? Are the survivors still around today, in a more primitive state? Are modern cities built on the foundations of the old?

- **Croatoan.** The fate of the lost civilization remains a complete mystery. Its cities are still virtually intact, and still contain valuable artifacts protected by powerful wards. But the people of the nation simply vanished. This provides both a source of dungeons containing mighty magic and a mystery that could be solved as part of a campaign. Are these ancients going to return? Or could their fate strike a modern nation?

- **Vestiges of Former Glory.** A fallen culture may not have vanished completely; it could still linger in the present day as a shadow of its former self. Perhaps the elves were spread across the entire continent until a curse or war depleted their numbers; now there is only a single occupied elvish city. The elves possess amazing magic, but as their numbers have dwindled and greatest artificers died, they have lost many secrets and magical techniques. As such, they are very interested in reclaiming relics from the ruins of their former empire – but everyone in the world wants elven magic for their own.

While lost civilizations provide an easy source of dungeons and advanced magic, there are many other ways to make a fallen culture relevant in the present day. Monsters that pose a threat in the present may have been created as weapons of war by a fallen culture. A race of savage humanoids could be the degenerate remnants of a previous civilization; their current state speaks to the story of their downfall. Perhaps orcs were once the most advanced civilization in the world; the first human civilization brought down the orcish empire, and it is for this reason that orcs seek bloody vengeance on humanity.

THE STUFF OF LEGENDS

In the present day, who do the bards sing of? What are the stories children demand to hear? Who are the greatest heroes of the past, and what were their treasures and tools?

Legendary heroes may be the foundations of modern nations or religions. Their unique artifacts may be the most powerful magic items player characters can hope to find. But as with war, an important question is how they intersect with the characters. As mentioned above, it's best to discuss this directly with your players. However, if you are designing your world for a mass audience, that may not be an option. But you can still think about different legends that are likely to appeal to different sorts of characters—the tale of great sacrifice and courage that may have inspired the paladin; the story of the master thief whose hoard has never been found; the tale of the first wizard, who stole the secrets of magic from the gods and was cursed for his crime. Share these tales with your players and ask them to pick the ones their characters care about. Aside from revealing something about the kinds of adventure that appeal to them, this can also lay the groundwork for adventures to come. The paladin loves the tale of the king who gave up his life and his sword to save his nation from demons. Now the demons are returning, and the sword must be found. Can the player characters write the final chapter of this tale? And what challenges are involved? Finding the sword may be the easiest part of the challenge. But it must be reforged in the fires where it was first made, and the one who wishes to wield it must be blessed by a particular god and cursed by a fey lord. These details are all spelled out in the original legend, but the player must unravel the riddles and then find a way to follow in the footsteps of the past.

Of course, there's another side to legends: the damage adventurers can do when they interfere in someone else's tales. Perhaps a party delves into an ancient Orc tomb and retrieves a *+2 Blade of Buttkicking*. For the fighter, this is simply a step up from his current weapon. But for the orcs of the region, this weapon has significance far beyond its magical powers. This is the sword of the last true orc king, waiting in his tomb for the day a new king would prove worthy and take it. That a human desecrates the tomb and now swans around with the orcish blade on his belt could be mortal insult. It could drive any orc who sees it into a murderous rage. Or far worse, it could actually be the event that unites the warring orc clans behind a single new king—a king who will avenge this crime.

In the end, legends are a way to add depth to any culture, and to show that the creatures that players consider to be monsters have their own heroes and aspirations. This is even more interesting if the players' lack of knowledge of these tales and customs becomes a direct threat in a scene. Look to the paragraph that opens this article. The paladin had no idea that the *+2 Blade of Buttkicking* is the orcish "Sword of Justice." What *will* happen if he strikes an innocent orc with it? Does he dare to find out?

How Does History Affect You?

As you develop a new world, stop and think about events in our recent history that have had a personal effect on you. Has your life changed because of 9/11? Hurricane Katrina? The civil rights movement of the 20th century? The Holocaust and World War II? The development of the nuclear bomb, itself a consequence of the World War? While I'm never a fan of directly transplanting real world events or places into an imaginary world, if you stop to think about the roots of a real-world event and its far-ranging impact, you can likely create imaginary events that *feel* real. Pearl Harbor and 9/11 are two examples of the impact of a devastating, unexpected attack. Has anything like this happened in your world? Prohibition created a host of interesting stories. Is there anywhere in your world where a powerful nation has set up a similar situation—not necessarily for alcohol, but for *something* people want? How has this affected organized crime? Does it have the support of the common people? And as always, how does it affect the player characters?

These are just a few examples of the impact that history can have on a campaign. The key point is to look beyond the simple facts and find the ways that the events matter to people—the ways in which they shape history, and add life to the enemies and treasures players will encounter in your world.

APOCALYPSO: GAMING AFTER THE FALL

Jeff Grubb

Most fantasy campaign worlds, indeed, most fictional fantasy worlds in general, are apocalyptic in nature.

I know—it sounds counter-intuitive at first. Fantasy is the domain of heroes and wizards, of dragons and treasure. Its tales are set in some distant realm of the past, when life was both simpler and cheaper than it is today. Fantasy is *The Lord of the Rings*, of course, and Elric, and Fafhrd and the Grey Mouser, and Conan, but also *Dragonlance, Forgotten Realms, Magic: the Gathering,* and other series that pepper the shelves.

Apocalyptic fiction, on the other hand, takes place after the fall. Stephen King's *The Stand*, Cormac MacCarthy's *The Road*, and the Walking Dead series falls into those categories, along with *A Canticle for Liebowitz, Hiero's Journey,* and such games as *Gamma World*. In apocalyptic fiction, our mighty civilization has been brought low by war, by pollution, by forces unknown, and the survivors struggle to make their way in a fallen world.

Yet fantasy is as post-apocalyptic as any dark tale of survivors of whatever cataclysm that ended modern civilization. In fact, more so.

Think about it. Your typical *Dungeons & Dragons* campaign consists of adventurers whose lot in life is to raid ancient tombs for lost, powerful treasures. Fair enough. But for there to be ancient tombs, there must have been ancient tomb-builders. And these tomb-builders were relatively powerful, in that they built structures that could withstand the test of time. In addition, these deep places of your world still have guardians, be they undying, unliving, magical, or clockwork, who are still around after all this time to guard their treasures.

Further, these ancient builders, regardless of origin or nature, also had items of wondrous power that one could not get at the local market. Here were magical swords belonging to long-dead heroes, dusty tomes of forgotten knowledge, holy artifacts of lost gods, and riches cast in strange metals.

As a result, these settings, challenges, and rewards all require the existence of predecessor civilizations. Further, these precursors probably met rather sudden ends, as they didn't have much chance to pass along their secrets to succeeding generations and races. Greyhawk, elder-bearded that it is, had its Rain of Colorless Fire, which wiped out the magical empires of the west and set the stage both for buried kingdoms and forgotten wizardry. The Forgotten Realms, grown out of Ed Greenwood's campaign, has had a sequence of cascading failures, as first the dragons ruled, then the giants, then the elves (leaving mythal stones carelessly around like abandoned toys) and now men. It seems that with every change of hands, the rulers of the world become both physically and magically smaller (the halflings and the gnomes of the Realms are standing in the wings, rubbing their hands eagerly, waiting for their big entrance).

Dragonlance, which evolved not out of a single extant gaming campaign but instead was created entirely as a setting for games and stories, underscores this apocalyptic nature even more strongly. In the development of the world, Tracy Hickman drew two sets of world maps for the continent of Ansalon. The first was in the golden age, when the gods spoke to men, and mighty empires such as Istar reigned. Then he (or rather, in the world, the spurned gods) dropped a mountain on Istar and shattered the map. The world of Dragonlance that the players initially encounter is a broken and fallen thing, its glory days the stuff of legend, its magic lost, and its gods no longer in communication.

The pattern continues through the game worlds of D&D and related worlds of its age. Eberron was wracked by recent world war that left an entire nation consumed by magic and lost. Tekumel, the setting for *Empire of the Petal Throne*, has a long history, most of it in the downward direction. It actually is set in the far future (after an atomic war has destroyed most of the Northern Hemisphere of Earth), and the planet of Tekumel is sucked into another dimension, crashing its advanced civilization, and turning most of its devices of the age into magical talismans. (Tekumel's inhabitants also bury and build over their cities every few decades, a cultural phenomenon that guarantees that there will be plenty of underground space to cavort in.)

So the very presence of dungeons in *Dungeons & Dragons* creates the need for earlier, more powerful civilizations, a history that the players can raid and struggle against. They are all fallen worlds, worlds that were once more powerful than they are now, and have struggled to rebuild. Many of the monstrous threats are creations of these ancients, either intentionally as servants and guards, or unintentionally as the result of their wars. In short, the fantasy world is post-apocalyptic. But its roots go back to before the first polyhedral dice were rolled.

Let's go back to the literary forefathers of these game worlds, for it is out of those inspirations that D&D and its kindred games have been woven. *The Lord of the Rings* looms large in all such discussions, of course, and its history consists of nothing but fallen empires and a wistful desire for days that have passed and will never come again. The Middle-earth of *Lord of the Rings* is at the shank-end of its Third Age, the previous ages being much more glorious but destroyed by conflict. The elves are a remnant of their once-great past. The dwarves have lost their ancestral homes, both in the Lonely Mountain and in Moria. And even though Sauron himself is defeated, the time of the old races has gone, and the fourth age belongs to man.

So we are continually faced in *The Lord of the Rings* (and to a lesser extent, in *The Hobbit*) with both fallen predecessor kingdoms and their powerful magical legacy. Once Gondor and Arnor ruled this land, but Arnor is long gone and Gondor is beaten back to a nub of its former self. The dwarven halls of Moria are inhabited by orcs and fouler monsters, and the Lonely Mountain was captured by a dragon. The elves have been in twilight for centuries, their havens reduced to a handful of outposts, most of their people fled across the sea. One of the early chapters of the book is titled "The Shadow of the Past" and is a full-strength infodump as Gandalf unspools the history of Middle-earth, driving home the idea that things were once greater than they are now.

And the "Shadow of the Past" chapter deals with the history of the most powerful magical artifact of Middle-earth—the One Ring. Crafted by a powerful elder being, it cannot be reproduced in this lesser age, and can be only destroyed in the forge of its own making—Mount Doom.

Middle-earth as a result is pervaded with an inherent conservatism and a resignation to its condition, coupled with a longing for this lost and glorious past. The magic of the elves is such that will not be seen again, be it lembas or Galadriel's filter. And though there may be attempts to restore some legacy with the past—it is, after all, the return of the King that is a goal both sought and attained—things will never be the same again. The world has been bent, Númenor has been sunk beneath the waves, and with the passing of Sauron, the work of the wizards is done and magic itself is in decline.

Even fantasy forebears that don't deal in as large a set of issues as *The Lord of the Rings* have had to deal with these fallen empires of their own past. Conan is always finding himself among ancient ruins, or beneath cities in rotted foundations, fighting some terror, or recovering some lost artifact. Similarly, Leiber's Fafhrd and the Grey Mouser stories, though focused in tightly on the two heroes in a low fantasy, has its share of forgotten magics and elder secrets. Elric might escape this, at first blush, for these tales were set when once the world was young, but no, Elric's Melnibone has gone from ruling the world into rot, pulling back to its Dreaming City. *The Sword of Shanara* series inverts the formula slightly, but underscores it—it is our world that has fallen to a nuclear apocalypse, and the elder depths that the heroes plumb are the legacy of our time, though decked out in fantasy tropes.

So why does this fascination with the past play so heavily in our fantasy literature as well as fantasy games? Yes, for the same reason: the need for places in which heroes can fight and recover lost treasures. But our ancient mythology is generally positive. The Greek gods under Zeus rebelled against Chronos and the titans, but the end result was to make a better world, not a fallen one. The Norse pantheon has the Ragnarok, but that is the foretold end of the world for everyone, not a set of stories that explain why Thor isn't hanging around your village. The various hells created for these mythologies are going concerns occupied by the spirits of the dead, not remains of lost kingdoms. Why the fascination with fallen kingdoms and elder civilizations in fantasy?

The reason in part goes back to the European Enlightenment, from whence much of the modern age (including the birth of the modern novel) has come. Here was a time when the civilizations of Western Europe were unifying in political power, advancing in technology and knowledge, and emerging as world powers. Yet they were still dealing with the long shadows of their predecessors—the Romans who ruled many of their lands, and before them the Greeks and the Egyptians. (Yes, there were Persians and Babylonians before as well, but they extend much further back.) It was difficult to sit on Capitoline Hill and look out at the triumphal arches of what was once Rome without feeling like one was in a diminished age, or to see the Sphinx excavated from its desert sands without wondering what else was hidden beneath. Rome, Greece, and Egypt were the real-world equivalent of the fallen empires and ancient treasures later captured in stories, and they were romanticized (yes, the Roman in the name) and held up as paragons of their age—ideals that the then-moderns could only seek to equal. So the neoclassical and Greek Revival architecture aped earlier columns and facades, while teams of explorers and adventurers plundered old tombs to find lost knowledge.

That last bit sounds so very much like a D&D adventure. It is here, in the recognition of previous powers, that the Western literary tradition gains much of its fear and wonder of the riches of the past, which passes down into the fantasy tradition and from there into gaming worlds. Even our electronic game worlds, be they *World of Warcraft*, *Diablo*, or *Guild Wars*, have that same descending pattern: once things were great and the age was golden, but someone screwed up, and we're now all paying the price for it. Apocalypses and Ragnaroks, large and small, litter the past of fantasy worlds, and the landscape is a scar tissue of these previous fallen times.

So where does that leave us when building brave new worlds?

The great, lost past of fantasy provides a strong foundation for storytelling, and provides many of its tropes but, as we see, it has its own baggage. This heritage creates a rich gaming universe filled with great treasure, immortal legends, and lost knowledge, and may account in part for the fact that fantasy gaming universes have succeeded over all other genres—they have universally understood tropes and archetypes. But the apocalyptic nature of fantasy also carries with it the implied statement that the current setting is diminished. That this is a lesser world, living in the shadows cast by the monuments of the past, and that the achievements of its heroes are reduced in the process.

There are a number of ways to approach this. One is to keep the focus tight and the expectations low. Lieber's Lankhmar is a good example, in both fiction and gaming. Fafhrd and the Grey Mouser live in a fallen world of lost treasures, but their goal is merely one of where the next meal (and next drink) is coming from. They may irritate lost gods, tread through forgotten galleries, and recover ancient artifacts, but it ultimately comes down to doing the job. The two heroes' masters may have more the feeling of striking against the darkness of the modern times, but Fafhrd and the Grey Mouser live for the moment. In games, an urban medieval fantasy that worries more about thieves' guilds and internal politics than about quests and ancient curses keeps the scope limited and the story grounded in the practical.

Another method is to embrace the idea of the diminished world whole-heartedly.

Jack Vance's *Dying Earth* series, transformed into a game of the same name from Pelgrane Press, engages strongly with the idea that so many great empires and ages have come and gone that it makes no sense to even worry about them, since we are truly at the end of days and the sun may well go out tomorrow. If there are tombs, they have been despoiled so many times it matters not. If there are monsters, they have been recreated and exceeded. If there are treasures, they are but trinkets that do not matter because the world is about to end. This creates an almost-comic pessimism against which the actions of Vance's protagonists (and the actions of any would-be Vancian hero) are cast against the weight of history, which is so great that it cannot be recognized and as such is merely part of the world.

A third option is to do without these trappings of the past entirely. China Mieville's Bas-Lag books, *Perdido Street Station, The Scar,* and *The Iron Council* all exist in a fantasy universe, but it seems to have moved out of the Age of Enlightment's concern about its predecessor civilization to a more sure-footed thinking of an Industrial Age where new spells and attitudes are considered part of the world. There are monsters, indeed, but they are not the product of ancient apocalypses; rather, they are new discoveries of evolutions of current developments. Indeed, in *Perdido Street Station*, where a monster is unleashed on the city and a group of D&D-style adventurers are assembled to hunt it down, they feel more out of place than the creature that they are hunting. Mieville abandons the tropes of the fantastic past, in particular its apocalypse, for a more progressive view where the actions of the current age are what matters. It is a very different type of fantasy.

Lastly, one approach to consider is the idea of taking on the past and defeating it, of proving the superiority of one's age through besting the ghosts of the previous age. I haven't seen this one as much, but it takes a page from Mieville's work while retaining the presence of the fallen empire and processor ages. Yes, there has been an apocalypse, be it a rain of colorless fire or planetary dimension-hop. And it has spawned all manner of lost kingdoms, dangerous weapons, and lurking monsters. But the ultimate goal of this approach is to create a new world out of the ashes of the old by defeating the creatures of the past, by harnessing the energies of these lost kingdoms, and by exceeding the expectations of these predecessor races.

In this way we can take a particular trope and bend it away from its usual assumptions and the conclusions that come with it—that the world is wounded, and while we may staunch the bleeding, we can never truly heal it. We can build new fantasy worlds with an active viewpoint, that things can change as a result of the protagonists' (and players') actions. That we can shed the tradition-encrusted bonds of the traditional fantasy and move the genre, both games and fiction, forward into its own new age.

HERE BE DRAGONS
Worldbuilding Advice from a Professional Mapper

Jonathan Roberts

Fantasy worlds and cartography have a special relationship. I can pick up a standard whodunit in the bookshop without needing a map, but if I open a fantasy novel, the first thing I look for is the map. If I can't find it, I'm lost.

The need for a map is understandable. Stories in fantasy worlds are stories of exploration. It's no accident that so many heroes are wide-eyed innocents. As they discover new wonders, the world is revealed to us through their eyes. All explorers need a map, and that's just as true for the reader exploring by proxy as it is for the sailor venturing out into the dangerous deep.

WHY DO YOU NEED A WORLD MAP?

If you're like many GMs, you'll start your adventure in a small town with some adventure locations nearby. The adventurers won't venture beyond the confines of this area for at least a couple of sessions and that gives you more than enough time to detail the surrounding area. You *can* manage by just mapping the next area that players haven't discovered yet and build your world as they explore.

But maps do much more than stop you getting lost—they help players suspend their disbelief.

When an author introduces a new world to you as a reader they're asking you to believe the place is real. You need to believe that behind the castles and battlefields there is a functioning world. A good novel hints at events that happen off-screen. A great novel allows you to interpret those hints and predict how events will play out. The unseen workings behind the narrative give the world depth. In roleplaying games this is even more critical. Players are willingly immersing themselves in your world. They can go anywhere and do anything, and they need to believe that if they do that, they will find a rich living world waiting for them. The problem is that no GM has the time to invent that much detail—nor should they. The key is to help players believe that you've got a world of detail at your fingertips, without ever needing to create it.

So what does this have to do with maps? A map is the perfect tool for convincing players there's a functioning world just over the horizon.

I ran campaigns in the Forgotten Realms for years. My players never ventured further than the eastern edge of the Moonsea, yet they knew about the Magocracy of Thay, the vast Anauroch desert, and jungles of Chessenta. When they met a Red Wizard they immediately knew what that meant, even though I'd only mentioned Thay in passing. The map gave them the feeling that they could jump on a ship and sail to the Nelanther Isles or travel the Road to the Dawn all the way to the Plains of Purple Dust. They never did, but they believed that they *could*.

In this way a map provides an illusion, a useful mirage of a world that you don't need to create in exhaustive detail. It also helps you tell the story. Names on a map should spark the imagination and give players a hint of undiscovered wonders, such as the Devastation of Smaug or the Wide Dothraki Sea. The style of the map can tell a tale all its own. Thror's Map tells us at least as much about the cartographer as it does about the Lonely Mountain. A map is a way of providing information to your players, just like a piece of read-aloud text or a bloody scrap of paper in an assassin's pocket. You can add whatever information, or disinformation, you want in the map you show your players.

DESIGNING YOUR WORLD

So a world map is a useful illusion—and as with any illusion the trick is to make it consistent and believable. I approach all world maps in the same order to make sure the features hang together, whether I'm designing my own world from scratch or working up a map for a client.

Grab a couple of sheets of blank paper and a pen, and we'll get started.

Nation Building

City-states war, villages burn, and the future of humanity hangs in the balance. Stories are about heroes and the fate of nations. A country's culture and history is often closely tied to its geography. If we define our countries first, the geography will follow. Note down the countries, city-states, nomadic tribes, and so on that will form the centerpiece of your stories. Here we're interested in those things that are defined by the landscape. Are they a seafaring nation? Is it secluded or does it have regular trade with other countries? Do they have enemies? If so, what stops one or other wiping each other out? Is a nation famed for its metalwork? Its beer? Its light horse cavalry?

Use these answers to get an idea of the geography. A country famed for its cavalry should have lots of plains and rolling hills. It should have fought most of its battles in this terrain, so any enemy needs to be on the other side of those plains, not coming through a steep mountain pass. A country famed for its ships should have a wide coastline it depends on for its resources. It might have little or no farmland, forcing it to rely on imports to its ports. Two ancient enemies might be separated by a range of almost impassable mountains or a strait of water. Any effort to cross this barrier takes preparation and gives the other time to prepare a defense. Think of the English

Channel—fought over for centuries by France and England—or the natural barrier of the Alps that protected northern Italy until Hannibal brought his elephants over.

These questions give you a quick cheat sheet for the type of terrain you need for each country, and also give you quick off-the-cuff content when your players ask questions. Why are the elves of An'Rathor bad horsemen? Their secluded valley is surrounded by mountains so they always fight on foot.

Sketch Your Countries

Now it's time to sketch out our first map. Start by noting down the names of your nations roughly where you want them to be. This isn't so much a geographical map as a map of connections. Mark the barriers between countries and any major geographical features.

Define Your Nations

With this pinned down, my next step is usually a coastline. On a fresh piece of paper, start drawing a coastline. Use your nation sketch as a rough guide. Let your pen wander—coastlines are fractal, so any mistake can become a feature. The aim here is not to be neat. Add jagged edges and wiggles, inner seas and channels. Be careful with large land masses. The continental US is a vast unbroken landmass, and it can be tempting to go in a similar direction with your own world. I'd recommend providing much more coast, like Europe. As a Scot I'm biased towards coasts—you can travel coast to coast in my homeland in a couple of hours. But I'm not just saying this out of national pride—coasts allow for more variety in storytelling. You want to create a rich and varied world, so allow it to be rich and varied! Give countries coastlines to defend, straits to battle over, fishing grounds to feed them, and islands that harbor pirates and kraken. Talking of islands—add in groups of islands off the coast. A fun trick for islands is to use the shape of the coast to help define their shapes.

Add Mountains

Mountain ranges form along tectonic faults. They tend to form long, strung-out lines rather than filling out a region. I'm not arguing that you should figure out the tectonic history of the world to justify your mountains—you have better things to do. I'm just saying that when you lay in mountains, do so in lines. Ranges often lie close to coastlines; as one plate pushes over another it rises up and sinks the other plate beneath the ocean. The Andes are a good example of this.

If you need inspiration for mountain ranges, it's only a click away. Jump on Google Maps, turn off the labels, and switch to the satellite view. Check out the Himalayas along the north of India—they look like a line drawn by a willful god. Remember: mountains are often the lairs of dragons, the home of giants and trolls, one of the places that harbor all those things that lie beyond the light of the campfire. They also provide one of the most formidable natural boundaries that will define the borders of your countries.

Add Rivers

The paths of rivers are determined by the height of the terrain, which is why we've left them until now. Rivers are one of the most important geographical features for nations. They're a means of fast transport, they provide fish for eating, water for drinking, and a means of disposing of the effluent of civilization. When placing rivers, remember the following rules of thumb:

- Rivers always flow downhill. This may sound obvious, but remember this means a river can't flow from coast to coast or over a mountain range.

- Rivers join as they run to the sea, they rarely branch. Deltas are the exception rather than the rule.

- Rivers start in mountain ranges and end in oceans. Lakes without a river connecting them to the sea will be stagnant.

Rivers start inland and end at a sea

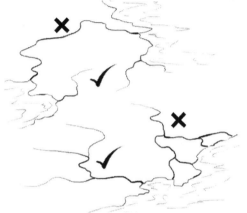

Rivers join, they rarely branch

Climate

You could spend days figuring out wind patterns and climate models for your world, just as you could create tectonic geological histories for your continents. But that's not the plan for this exercise. Once again, you can follow a few basic rules to make sure your climates don't present obvious logical problems.

- In many cases a region will have a prevailing wind. Such winds pick up wet air currents from the sea and travel inland until the rising altitude cools them to the point where it rains. This means that rain tends to fall on the side of the mountains that the prevailing wind hits first. One side of a large mountain range can be lush and fertile and the other side dry and barren.

- Rivers rarely run through deserts, and if they do they must start somewhere much wetter.

- Forests don't border deserts—make sure there's some plains or scrubland in between.

- Climates tend to fall in bands by latitude. Check out Google Maps and use the Earth as a guide. Some latitudes tend to have desert, others rainforest, and others plains and deciduous forests. If you follow these, your players will find it familiar, even if it's only subconscious.

Final Geographical Touches

Great! We now have a world with nations, mountain ranges, deserts, and rivers. We're almost done with the geography. Add in some hills along the edges of the mountains, and anywhere you're going to want abandoned mines (you do need mines for your 1st level adventurers to clear out, don't you?), add thick virgin forest to hide bandits and green dragons, and you're done!

At this point it's best to step back and have a look over your world. Have a coffee, come back, and look at it with fresh eyes. I guarantee you'll see things you want to tweak. A mountain range will give you an idea for a glacial lake, a desert will look like it's in the wrong place. Edit, change, and tweak until you're happy with it.

BUT WHERE HAS ALL THE FANTASY GONE?

We're creating a fantasy world, remember? Now it's time to break the rules.

Brainstorm weird and wonderful locations: pockets of tundra in the center of the desert, rivers that run uphill, great floating ziggurats that hover over an ever-spinning whirlpool. All that work you've done making sure that the rest of the world hangs together means that these features will seem all the more fantastical. They'll be the wonders of your fantasy world, locations that nations will vie over for control. Sprinkle them around, especially in places that your players are unlikely to travel to. Outlandish names and reputations will spark your players' imaginations and make them want to expand their horizons. Suddenly you won't be telling them where to go, they'll be exploring of their own volition, and you'll know you succeeded in selling your world to them.

COMING FULL CIRCLE – PUTTING THE COUNTRIES BACK IN

Take some colored pencils and sketch in the borders of your countries. The borders should follow the natural obstacles. Make sure to leave some areas beyond the reach of any nations. These are the untamed wildernesses of the world, the regions off the edge any civilized map. Quite literally, here be dragons. When your players want to claim a royal charter by taming the frontier, these are the places they'll go.

Cities

A city thrives where there is food, water, and opportunity. Rivers or river mouths are great places for cities, and the reason for the location of many of the greatest cities of our own world (London, Paris). They are often defensible (Edinburgh) or near the source of a valuable trade material, such as a goldmine (Johannesburg). Once your capitals are placed, add in other major cities and fortresses. Keep cities near locations that justify their existence—a spice route, a valuable fishing ground, a naturally occurring source of helium that fuels the airships of a nation. Fortresses similarly are placed along borders, at mountain passes, at the heart of a region's power, or along the coast to watch for raiders.

□ Fort
■ City
★ Capital City

You don't have to name every city. It's easy to get bogged down coming up with names for every hamlet and fishing village. I tend to name capital cities and leave it at that. Create a separate list of five names for forts, five for towns, and five names for inns. When players ask about a place you haven't named, use one from your list and mark it on the map. When you have a moment after the game, update your list so you're never caught out again.

Once you've added your conventional power centers, it's time to add the fantasy ones. This is the time to place the five-thousand-foot pinnacle of ice at the center of the world, the ancient basalt gates erected by an extinct race of titans, and the floating cities of the sea elves.

Roads

The highways of the world define the arteries of trade and commerce. Start by connecting up your capital cities. Roads tend to follow the path of least resistance, following rivers, coastlines, and winding through mountain passes. Once these are done, add a few smaller roads to connect up smaller towns—but don't worry about details. These are more to give an impression of detail than anything fixed.

Finishing Up

You're done! You now have a functioning map of your world, with nations, trade routes, perils, and treasures galore. Use this version for your own reference and sketch a less detailed version for your players. Then, when they scratch the surface and ask questions, you'll have immediate answers. This will give them (and you) a framework that they can use to interpret the world and hint at adventures over every horizon.

A map is a functional object. Its first and foremost purpose is to clearly display information. A good map can be drawn with a marker pen in the back of an exercise book or fully painted across three feet of canvas. It is relatively easy to turn a pen sketch into an old world masterpiece—but that's the subject for another article.

How to Design a City-State, Tribe, or Nation

Wolfgang Baur

I t's fairly widely agreed that the atomic unit of RPG adventure design is the encounter, which governs the conflict between the adventurers and a set of foes in a single social or martial clash. What is the atomic unit of worldbuilding? Well, funny thing about that, as this is quite a bit fuzzier, but I think it might well be the *society*: a unified tribe, city-state, or nation with a shared culture, language, and traditions. You can build a world from smaller units, but in the end, it's the abstraction and concreteness of a particular social milieu that makes a particular place or a resident of that place memorable and unique.

For most human societies, the foundation stone might be the clan or the extended family—but unless your campaign world is about feuding families or highland clans or cattle rustlers, that unit of social organization is slightly too small. For science fictional societies, you might argue that the spaceship or colony is the basic unit of social organization, but for purposes of this discussion, I'm sticking with the larger fantasy setting.

Here's my argument for the tribe or city-state as a foundational unit: it provides political identity, language, a religious context, and a set of skills and traditions related to warfare, mating, magic, and social harmony, and likely a set of laws and a structure or hierarchy that governs proper and improper behavior. Those are, not surprisingly, all the tools you need to govern adventuring, titles, status, wealth, and arcane lore and divine wisdom. Skills, gear, and magic items arise only from a society. Without a society, you have a dungeon board game, a wargame, or a miniatures skirmish game, which might have elements of worldbuilding, but not a full-blown RPG setting.

The tools of the adventuring trade are always embedded in a cultural context, and thus for most worlds, the society is more important than the terrain, the weather, the monsters, or the economic and political relationships between societies.

In other words, the elements of a society are the elements that inform an adventurer's resources and background. You could define just that adventurer's immediate family or clan, and that might be appropriate for a wandering nomad from the plains, newly arrived in the Big City. But for most characters, defining just blood relations means you'd miss some of the options available elsewhere on the social ladder—where that family or clan fits into a wide context. An adventurer isn't always or even often from the upper rungs of society, and his clan or family might be tiny, obscure, largely extinct, or simply of little consequence to the world.

At the same time, the adventurer might have grown beyond that humble origin and made a name in a guild or priesthood, and that reputation defines the character. In this case, those non-familial options and elements of society will tend to be the ones that matter in play, and the character will interact with the various ranks of aristocrats, high priests, and tyrants of the world. Those characters are the ones most often handing out interesting missions, quests, and magic items in an adventure. Even if an adventure revolves around the movers and shakers of the lower classes (master of the thieves' guild springs to mind, as does a beggar prince or a humble monk), you'll need to have designed how that lower stratum of society works to know how adventurers fit into it.

In other words, to loot a world properly as a fantasy tomb robber, you need to have some understanding of where a society stashes its loot, who can tell you where the dungeons are, and how your character can transform raw gold into magical power, political power, higher knowledge, or landholdings, as your character might desire.

How to Design a Tribe

A tribe is relatively simple. The people share a race, language, and traditions, and a ruler. Most of all, the central fact of tribal life is that each tribe contains crucial blood ties among its members, and its most important sources of survival skills, political acumen, history, and knowledge all come from a collection of related people, families, uncles, aunts, and so forth. A tribal population might be a few dozen, a few hundred, even a few thousand, but the way you know these people is through blood ties: "Oh, you are the elder whose cousin was my grandfather! Good to meet you!" Blood and kin matter so much in a tribe because this is how you determine who is a member (you are born into a tribe), and also how you determine your status within it.

One way to think of it is that clan, family, and lodge relationships are an overgrown form of high school cliques and academic infighting. The stakes are small, by some standards, and there is no escaping your family or your birth. Footloose adventurers don't exist in a tight-knit tribe; there might be strangers or loners or visitors or hermits, but they aren't members of the tribe.

The relationships and marriages and feuds of a nomadic or settled tribe are carried along through history, but the wall of unity protects the tribe against all outsiders. The tribe always comes first. Strangers are not to be trusted. The tribe obeys its elders, and those who step out of line are ostracized, exiled, or otherwise shamed. Tribal life is hard: everyone must work together, and the young typically must obey the elders.

This way of living is alien to most modern people, at least on the surface, though it is simply the biological version of us versus them. Designing a dwarf clan or a gnomish family or wood-elves who are hunter-gatherers and rely purely on their own tribe is a great exercise in worldbuilding. Tribal societies are ancient and functional, and still exist today in a few places. They might bear further study for the designer of an interstellar merchant house, or a wandering tribe of elves, or a settled hill tribe of ogres that relies on banditry.

Identify the tribe's headman, matriarch, shaman, or ruler. Identify the tribe's immediate goals or enemies. And identify their system of reward and punishment. Building that society makes it easy to see who would give out quests and rewards for accomplishment, who might be banished and why, and who the tribe fears. Those things are generally enough to place the tribe in a larger context.

How to Design a City-State

The central fact of a city is not blood and family (though those continue to be important, sometimes vitally so), but rather location and residence. The members of a city-state are those who live there. They might be relatives and members of a single tribe or clan, or they might be offspring of two, three, or a dozen distinct tribes. They might be mostly a human population, with an important minority of minotaurs or halflings, and yet still all members of the same city state. So long as they are acknowledged as citizens by some authority or by virtue of residence, the people of a city-state are more mobile and less locked-in than a tribe.

A city-state is a single settlement, and the oldest ones date back to the Harappan civilization in the Indus Valley, roughly 5,400 years ago. Even then, the outlines were clear: agriculture, a settlement, and some kind of ruling class. The cities had baths, jewelry, domesticated animals, drainage, granaries, and much more, centuries before Egypt. This is an important difference from nomadic tribes: the permanent settlement in a single locale means that locale is developed over time and its people can build defenses, temples, armories, docks, shipyards, irrigation systems, mines— whatever helps them to exploit their surroundings and make life a little easier. If a place grows attractive enough, people with no relationship to the city-state's founders will settle there and become assimilated.

And that's the point: a city-state is a place that must attract and retain its people, because urban life is the exception to the rule in middle-ages technology (see sidebar on population). Each city-state will have some advantage and lack others. As a designer, you'll want to know the city's strengths (it has a thriving merchant class and strong breeding of draft animals and warhorses) and its weak points (perhaps it is riven by competing factions or families, and political violence is common). Make those themes apparent in the city's markets, the city's NPCs, and the other day-to-day elements that visitors experience. Think like a tourist: food, shelter, shopping are likely stops, so make one destination in each of those categories stand out.

Then, throw in a twist: the things that visitors wish they didn't have to deal with in the city are as important (and more exciting!) as the things they do want to accomplish there. In a city of political strife, perhaps a fiery orator stirs up a mob. Perhaps the adventurers are mistaken for spies of one faction or another. Certainly they may provoke a fight or be challenged to prove themselves as patriots.

The city's ancient history might lead to adventure hooks, but keep it current. Your focus in designing a city-state is to make it vibrant and alive, to provide that one recurring theme that everyone remembers about the city. If the players are saying, "What is going on with that crazy mob?" when they leave town, that's good. If they are saying ,"Oh, I can't believe it: that was mostly drunken women in that mob! They are some kind of bacchae or crazed amazons!" then you've taken another step in defining the world and its people.

Every city, in other words, is defined by how its people act, whether it's well and generously and honestly, or when they are under pressure, threatened, or cruel. Make it clear what attracts people to the city-state, or why it has become less attractive, and show that citizens can vote with their feet in extremis. Make the city come alive by the stereotypes and repetition of certain patterns of behavior.

How to Design a Nation

Finally, we come to the big enchilada. At the level of a nation, with hundreds of thousands to millions of citizens, the scale of the population alone makes the approach of a tribe or even a city-state difficult to retain. What holds a nation together is largely language and culture and, to a lesser degree, ruling bloodlines, along with an aristocracy that shares common values and common goals. The noble class comes into its own in a semi-feudal, theocratic, or otherwise pre-modern social structure. This is because the king or high priest or tyrant can no longer see the

Fantasy Populations

As citizens of the 21st century, we are used to large cities of a million or even 10 million people. These largely did not exist in the Middle Ages in Europe. Rome is a notable exception (roughly 1 million inhabitants in 100 AD), but it was a huge exception and the high water mark of a global empire.

For a large kingdom, Cordova in Spain had 400,000 inhabitants around 900 AD. Paris was the most populated city in Europe around 1300 and had 200,000 inhabitants—France itself had 17 million. Constantinople had perhaps half a million people in 1400, and it was the greatest city in Christendom at the time. These were the peaks of population in the Middle Ages, and serve to provide a sense of scale for the upper boundary of population for similar societies.

The population was also distributed very differently before modern agriculture and the scientific and industrial revolutions brought people into the cities. For most of human history, a tiny minority lived in cities. Most people were farmers and lived in hamlets, villages, and small towns.

borders of the nation, and delegating administration and government tasks (military, taxation, a penal system, recordkeeping, and so forth) must be performed far from the center of authority.

This means two things for game design: it means that you need to know what the ideals, values, and principles of the nation are, and also how they are subverted or upheld far from the center. How does the king communicate with his vassals? How does the goddess-queen receive tribute and celebrate her victories? Who represents the rulers along the border? What do the nobles want, and are they getting it from the existing order? Is the kingdom peaceful, threatened, or rotting from within?

Choose at least two points of conflict, and write those down for the nation. I'd recommend one conflict within the national borders, and one conflict between the nation and some other group: a neighboring nation, nomads, a secret society, or maybe a dragon in the mountains that is the nation's nemesis. A nation with no conflicts within itself or with external nations is a wonderful place to live, peaceful and prosperous—and boring for gaming or narrative. I would not spend too much of your valuable design time on dull locations with few promising avenues for adventure.

Once you have at least two sources of conflict for your nation, figure out how those conflicts appear in everyday life that characters might see. If the king is a good ruler and taxes are spent well on worthy causes, then perhaps the heir is dissatisfied and vain and seeks power through encouraging banditry and gathering young barons to his cause. Or perhaps a curse afflicts the kingdom's rulers, such that the throne is never held for long, and each king dies a horrible death.

You need to design political dangers, political arcs, or political goals, and to some extent you need to know what the second-rank barons and earls are doing. Because— let's face it—by the time you are talking about a kingdom as big as medieval France (medieval population, roughly 17 million before the Black Death), there's no such thing as a simple city-state. There are multiple city-states, multiple competing interests, and multiple layers of complexity tying them all to a central hub of authority, such as the divine right of kings, a demi-goddess ruler, or simply the iron hand of a militant order of knights keeping down all other power centers.

DESIGNING SOCIETIES: ADDING WONDER TO THE WORLD

The important element in all these societies is not necessarily the details of the ruling house (though those are often compelling), or the secrets of a society's trade routes, but rather that sense of what the society values and cherishes. Are they mad for learning? Are they terrified of ghosts? Are they all tattooed with the names of the elements and seeking to balance great forces of sea and sky? What makes them more than a historical society?

When I seek to design a successful tribe, city-state, or nation, I always attempt to add some element of magic, wonder, or mystery that takes the real world and dials it up another notch. After all, if your readers wanted pure history and careful simulation of known periods, they'd probably play a historical game or read a historical novel. So it's important to add at least one bit of fantasy or SF spice to your creation. That bit of spice might be the first idea you have about the society, and everything else merely works out the consequences. But it's also possible that the spice is mainly visual (a city of gigantic monuments and crocodile-headed statues that walk each night) or that it is largely historical (an empire that the elves abandoned, whose roads are magical).

And that's the basics of society design. With a whole globe and all of human history to draw from, there are thousands of examples of successful and past societies that might be enlivened or explored in games and fiction. Go forth, and bend whole nations to your whims. (For more on the subject of building societies, see Mike Stackpole's chapter, "They Do *What*, Now?")

Empires!

The central fact of empire is conquest. An empire grows by attacking and absorbing the tribes, city-states, and nations around it, as shown by the history of the Romans, Aztecs, Arabs, Turks, Indians, and Chinese empires, to name a few of the larger success stories in empire-building. This need to conquer has several obvious and some less-obvious consequences in worldbuilding.

The obvious one is a need for a large war machine and the ability to marshal the population for conquest, tribute, and then administration of newly-conquered people and territory. The less obvious consequences are the need for cosmopolitanism and a need for extreme bureaucratic skill. Empires need to find ways to deal with both primitive and sophisticated citizens who speak dozens of languages and who share no common culture. They need to find a way to organize entire nations to fit into the existing imperial model of rule. And they need to find ways to feed and house a growing population of their own people, for the more successful an empire is, the longer its borders and the hungrier its many mouths become. At some point, even the most successful empire can be threatened as much by a bad harvest (and bread riots) as by the small states on their periphery.

From a design point of view, an empire is a patchwork quilt of tribes, city-states, and nations, with one of these nations being dominant over all the rest. That's more a matter of applying techniques from the prior discussion than of creating an entirely new category.

THEY DO WHAT NOW?

On Societies and Culture

Michael A. Stackpole

Because discovery plays such a large part in the enjoyment of fiction and gaming, it's important for world designers to present something different. Sometimes it's a complete world, sometimes it's just a pocket universe or hidden valley. The most important aspect of both of these is the society that functions within the world. Getting it right isn't always easy, but failure to do this means the world is simply boring—which kills any entertainment value.

Getting it right is a matter of challenging yourself intellectually, and then following through with all the logical consequences of any decisions you make. The worlds that are the worst are the ones in which a designer decides a visual effect would be incredibly cool, then fails to deal with the consequences of that effect on the people of the world. Not only does this make the world shallow, but it completely misses the chance to create a place which will intrigue players.

For example, in my DragonCrown War cycle of novels, I decided that one class of society in the nation of Oriosa would wear masks. These masks would bear signs of their lives—from religious preference and exploits, down to whether or not their parents were still alive. No need for Facebook in this world; just read a facemask and you were good. I decided that, since wearing a mask was acknowledged to be an honor, it was considered ill-mannered to be seen barefaced by someone who was not a member of the family.

That's all well and good, but it forces more work. Public baths, for example, would have to provide bathing masks so that folks wouldn't ruin their good masks. It meant that when one of my heroes sees a corpse without a mask, he comments, "Because he was without a mask, I couldn't identify him." It required that nobles from other nations would be given a lacy "courtesy mask" to acknowledge their rank. It also meant that to have your mask taken from you was the greatest disgrace to which a citizen could be subjected. Literally he would be having his identity stripped from him—metaphorically they were ripping his face off.

WHERE TO START

The easiest place to begin to shape a society is to look at realities that result from physical form. Sexual dimorphism—the physical differences between male and female—is a prime place to start. And you could easily make that *trimorphism* if you're dealing with a non-human race which has more than one gender/life stage form. Because, for most species in our world, males are bigger and stronger or more colorful, playing with a species where our roles are altered immediately gives players a puzzle.

Imagine a hidden valley where a sisterhood of magicians has existed for eons. When a child is born they determine if it has any magick talent at all. If not, the child is sent with one of the sisters to nearby communities, where such a healthy baby is swapped for one which is not quite so robust, but is brimming with magical energy. Furthermore, they choose their mates from among the world's greatest mages, seducing them or kidnapping them and putting them out to stud for a short time, then returning them to their home. They even give their studs a young, male apprentice as a parting gift, since they've got little use for such a male child unless he turns out to be a great mage—as determined by the world.

There you have a simple society which operates on secrecy, on the sublimation of the individual to the benefit of the whole, with a self-centered morality that justifies the abuse of outsiders. It's a classic reversal of male dominated societies that practice infanticide (and you could toss that in, too). If you were to overlay upon this whole foundation the fact that these women need the best magicians since they are involved in a war to keep the world safe from an invasion of Elder Squidlings that would destroy everything, you have that whole ends-justifying-the-means conundrum to wrestle with.

Going further with this society isn't tough. If the rest of the world is male dominated, or even based on gender-equality, the details here would set them apart. Female gods would move to the fore. Male gods might become demons or serve the females. *Witch* might be a grand title here, whereas it's a term used for criminal female magickers elsewhere. The whole male-problem-solving mode of dealing with difficulties might be completely alien or considered rude. Covens might refer to groups of women who get pregnant by the same man, who bear and co-raise his children. They might not govern through a hierarchical system, but do everything through consensus. If they are holding off the invasion mentioned above, they might see themselves as the she-wolves of legend who are protecting all humanity, and have adopted both that symbolism and have woven legends in a history they accept as real.

DETAILS MAKE A DIFFERENCE

Non-human societies can get stranger even more quickly and are made by the attention to detail. For example, if creatures have three fingers and a thumb on each hand, would they use base 10 for counting? Whereas we might say, "Nine out of ten times," they'd likely say, "Seven out of eight times." If they see outside the visual light spectrum others do, or hear sounds above or below our hearing or are telepathic, these things will be reflected in how they act and what they value.

In the *DragonCrown War* books, I created the *urZreithi*. They occupy the same ecological niche as Dwarves, but they are shapeshifters. They don't shift their shape into animals, but change their shape to suit themselves to whatever they are doing. A miner, then, will make one hand a hammer and the other a pick. A warrior will armor himself and make his hands into blades. Because of this, I decided, they'd not value the physical form of an individual since form has no meaning outside function. So, if a warrior died in battle, they'd leave the body there. Sure, they'd have a memorial for the person, but his physical form and its recovery was unimportant.

Which means that they and their philosophy would be at odds with someone in a religious order that didn't believe in leaving anyone behind. In essence, by taking a concept which is generally considered noble and rendering it valueless, or by taking something most folks consider evil and turning it into a virtue, a design can quickly craft details for a society that becomes a puzzle for his audience.

Another good place to look for different aspects to explore involves history. Many designers work on the now and neglect how things got to be that way. For example, in between World War One and World War Two, Hungary was run by an Admiral. That might not seem strange until one remembers that Hungary is landlocked. Only by realizing that it was once part of a larger empire that had a coast and had a navy does this make any sense. This situation could only grow out of history, so it forces the designer to create some history. From that history, then, all sorts of cool stories can flow.

PLAYING "WHAT IF . . . ?"

Challenging yourself to create these sorts of societies and worlds isn't that difficult. It's the classic "what if" game of science fiction. And there are plenty of books and web sites that offer descriptions of real or curious phenomena which are great starting points for these kinds of things.

Begin with a hidden valley setting—a setting that likely isn't economically viable, but is intriguing enough to hold together for a short visit by your audience. Let's start with, say, a high mountain valley which has, at the heart of it, a massive ship. There's no ocean for many a mile, but this thing looks ship-shape and the folks working on it are as skilled a set of shipwrights as anyone has ever seen. How did it get here? Why is it here? What are they going to do with it?

There are dozens of answers to those questions. Maybe these are the survivors of a Noah's Ark, and they keep the ship going because they know, someday, another flood will take them back down to lands some God has promised them. Or maybe they are the remnants of a mutinous crew, which the captain caught and had exiled to this place hundreds of years ago. He casually remarked that they'd be free once they sailed from the place, and they're ready to fit the ship with balloons or skis and make their great escape. Or a prophet has come among them and convinced them to make the ship—out of true belief, or because he's bilking them of money.

This process is cyclical. You can have many explanations. The Noah's Ark idea may be new to cover the shame of the mutiny story. Maybe they are just waiting for heroes to join them for a grand voyage of adventure beyond the stars. Any designer should be able to rationalize not only the truth of the situation, but the truths of the situation. Wheels within wheels make for very intriguing and entertaining adventures.

Once you have a hidden valley concept down, then look at expanding things to link it to the world. For example, in that mountain valley, where do they get the lumber they need? What is it they trade for such lumber? Once you can make the valley economically viable, it becomes an anchor around which you can build the rest of the world. A portion of anything the hidden valley produces will be traded down the line by the lumber-folk and so on. As you figure out what the next place trades and work out what the implications of that are for their community and the world, suddenly things take shape fast.

Granted, economics is not the only way to connect places. Because I was trained as a historian, I find fabricated history to work quite well. Geography, theology, and species/race relations also function very well in this regard. Economics is just the lowest common denominator, hence a good place to start.

As mentioned above, details make a world real. Dietary preferences determine agricultural methods—and the scenery through which folks walk. Coins, the images on them, their age and stories and slang concerning them can tell a lot about a world. National pride—bearing in mind that nationalism is a fairly late development—can also provide a breeding ground for details. Everyone has slang to demean others— other species, other religions, other nations—so figuring out the how and why of those terms will guide you in exploring the world.

Lastly, challenge the tropes of folklore concerning your world. In my novel Once a Hero I got great mileage out of wondering why Elves and Men would be pals, when Men die so quickly that an immortal race would hardly be inclined to treat them as more than pets. Having your audience explore the world and learn about it, while the world learns more through its interaction with them is terribly engaging. Your audience (as players or through the characters in a story) is invested in seeing to it that the other side understands.

Also listen to your players. Their interpretations/beliefs and even mistake about the world can provide you excellent fodder for future development. As they try to connect the dots, they may not see the image you intended them to see. Sometimes their image is better, and you can use that to your advantage. Tell them they're very insightful, and they'll never noticed you've stolen their idea and made it over as your own. Take their solutions as further challenges, and you'll produce a dynamic world which will satisfy you and them for a long time to come.

How to Make a High Magic World

Keith Baker

Swords and sorcery. Dungeons and dragons. Wizards and warriors. All of these fall under the umbrella of what we call fantasy . . . but the worlds around them can be very different. In many works of fantasy fiction, society hovers around a medieval level of sophistication. Magic is a miraculous thing that has little impact on everyday life.

"High Magic" is generally used to describe a world in which powerful magic is an integral part of society. Wizards aren't isolated hermits; they are influential people whose creations drive the wheels of civilization. Generally speaking, high magic goes beyond the widespread presence of mystical techniques and tools, and also suggests that these techniques are powerful and advanced. Spells such as teleportation and resurrection create a society capable of things we can't accomplish in the present.

In developing a high magic society, there are a number of things to consider. What basic needs of society are fulfilled with magic? Where does this power come from? What impact does it have on daily life? How do the protagonists of your story—whether the heroes of a novel or the player characters in a game—stand out in a world where powerful magic is commonplace? Beyond that, where are things going to go as your story moves forward?

What is the Nature of Magic?

In developing a high magic world, the very first thing you need to do is identify the nature of magic itself. What sort of a tool is it? What sorts of people are capable of harnessing it, and how easy is it to develop new things? Consider the following options.

Magic is a Science. Mystical energy can be manipulated in predictable, reliable ways. It may be that it's shaped using words and gestures, channeled with a pinch of sulfur instead of a copper wire, but if a formula works one day it will work the next—and more important, someone smart enough can take that formula and develop a new one using the same basic principles. In a world in which magic is a science, a high magic society likely followed a logical path of evolution. Just as in our world, there will be inventors and innovators whose discoveries changed the world. Who created the first fireball? Who developed teleportation, and how long did it take to craft a teleporter that could transport someone between cities?

A world like this can still have people who channel magic using faith or innate ability, such as traditional clerics or sorcerers. The key is that the magical tools that are part of everyday life are the result of applied research—and that there are people out there working to improve these tools and techniques, and given time they will likely succeed. In a world like this, you should decide exactly what's holding people back, and how magic could advance further. Are there limited resources—the mystical equivalent of plutonium—whose rarity is holding back certain fields of magic? This is a way to add an unusual form of treasure, or to make a particular region especially important; if dragon bones are the key to the most powerful forms of magic, then any dragon could be worth a vast bounty, and finding a draconic graveyard could create a new gold rush in the region.

Another aspect of scientific magic is the potential that people are tampering with forces they don't truly understand. Is there any possibility of the equivalent of a nuclear meltdown? Say that your civilization uses bound elementals to accomplish basic tasks. What would it take to trigger a mass release of these elementals? What sort of havoc could they wreak before they were banished or contained?

Magic is a mystery. Magic is a vital tool of society. Teleportation is a key part of commerce. Mystical wards defend cities from monsters beyond their walls. And yet, these tools cannot be replicated in the modern age. It could be that they are relics of a previous civilization, and that the current society has simply salvaged them from ruins and incorporated them into its culture. If this is the case, finding a new dungeon associated with the ancient civilization is an incredible opportunity. Beyond finding treasures that may directly benefit adventures—magic swords, staves, armor—explorers may find new tools that can benefit their town or homeland, whether it's the equivalent of a magical microwave (applied *prestidigitation*) or better still, the ritual required to mass-produce such a thing. In this case, an important question is just what happened to the advanced civilization: if it was so powerful, just how did it fall? This subject is explored in more detail in the chapters, "Bringing History To Life" and "Apocalypso."

Another option is that magic is homegrown and may even follow scientific principles, but that the greatest works of magic can only be accomplished by a very select group of people. It could be tied to bloodline—a sound basis for the authority of a noble family—or perhaps there can only be one Supreme Sorcerer in the world at a time, and for a new one to be appointed the old one must die or abdicate. Such an approach makes the people who can produce powerful magic extremely important, while also explaining why magic doesn't advance quite so quickly as it does in an entirely scientific world.

A gift of the gods. Magic is the tool of the gods, and only comes to the mortal world when they will it. In a world where all magic is divine in origin, churches will be very powerful and cardinals may have more power than kings . . . unless nobles also have magical powers derived from the gods. It is a bridge between the two extremes of mysterious magic and scientific magic; it is an active force within the world, but advances only occur when the gods grant them. With that said, there can be traditional wizards in such a world. Perhaps a rogue god taught the first wizard the secrets of magic so that they might one day challenge the heavens—in which case wizards may be feared, with witch-hunters tracking down these vile sorcerers. Or alternately, the gift of wizardry may be a blessing of a god of knowledge; wizards work as they normally do, but should they anger their divine patrons they will lose the ability to understand their spells.

How Does Magic Affect Everyday Life?

"High magic" suggests that magic is a vital force within a society. It doesn't simply exist; it defines a culture. For me, the most important piece of world design is considering consequences. If your world possesses a tool that doesn't exist in our world, what are the results? What does it mean to live in a world where people can reliably raise the dead? Is magic a part of all walks of life, or only used in a few ways? There are flying ships and lightning cannons, but medicine is much the same as it was in the 12th century? Start by considering the following elements of civilization, and thinking how magic applies to them.

Transportation. How do people get from one place to another? How do you transport troops, cargo, or civilians? How fast is it, and is it limited to specific locations—a railroad that follows a specific path, or a teleportation circle that can only take you to one of a handful of other circles? Are there flying ships that can transport large numbers of people, or flying carpets that only transport a few? Is personal teleportation a casual, commonplace thing? Are there any limitations on who can employ magical transportation—only wizards, only people with specific training or heritage—or can anyone steal a flying carpet?

Warfare. Critical questions arise when it comes to battle magic. First is the obvious question of just how powerful it is. Is the magic that can be deployed on the battlefield the equivalent of a grenade or a nuclear weapon? Can a mundane force challenge a mystical enemy and have any hope of winning—overwhelming them with numbers or employing superior tactics—or is battle magic the absolute king of the battlefield? One common solution to this is to have spellcasters cancel spellcasters; as long as you have a sorceress on your side she can cancel the spells of the enemy wizard, at which point the grunt soldiers remain relevant. Of course, if the enemy spellcasters are brought down, your spellcasters can dominate the field— making wizard-hunting a logical job for your elite group of heroes!

Beyond the bigger picture, there's the question of how magic changes personal combat. In this world, do people still use bows, or does everyone carry a wand? Are there things that make both valid choices—a wand can hold a powerful spell, but only a single charge of it; a "musketeer" might carry a pair of wands, but once they are discharged he'll turn to his trusty sword.

Another vital question is just what mystical tools a nation brings to the battlefield.

A nation of necromancers and a nation of pyromancers may both rely on magic to win the day, but the weapons they employ will be very different.

Medicine. How advanced is magical healing? Can you regenerate lost limbs? Cure any disease? Raise the dead? If so, are these tools in the hands of a particular group of people—for example, only divine spellcasters—or are they services available to anyone who has sufficient funds?

A world in which it's possible to reliably raise the dead is going to be dramatically different from the one that we live in. The people who control resurrection will have tremendous influence, and if anyone can buy their services, a wealthy person becomes extremely hard to kill. Think about the limits of resurrection. Are there ways to kill someone permanently, whether by inflicting a certain form of damage or using a particular tool? Does it require a particularly rare component, which would make a nation that possesses that substance extremely influential? If it's something that can only be performed by divine spellcasters, will the gods only return those who have served them faithfully in life? Take a moment to consider what sort of impact you want resurrection to have in your world—the purpose you actually want it to serve, and what limitations it needs to have to make that work.

These are three of the most vital services, but there are others. If magic is used for communication in your world, how effective is it? Can anybody send a telepathic message to a friend, as they might with a cell phone today? Or is it more like a telegraph—say, an air elemental that swiftly carries a message from one message station to another? Is magic employed to provide light and heat, and if so, what form does it take? Do you have lanterns that burn with cold flame, or are buildings themselves constructed from luminescent materials? How about crime and punishment: do the forces of the law use divination magic to interrogate criminals? What sorts of techniques are used to imprison people?

The questions are as endless as the options. The important thing is to decide how far you want to go. Personal teleportation and reliable resurrection create a society that will feel futuristic to us, while airships and fireballs aren't so different from airplanes and bombs.

WHAT IS THE ROLE OF THE PROTAGONIST?

In a world where sorcery is completely integrated into modern life, being a sorcerer may seem less exciting. Obviously it's good for the protagonists of a world to stand out in some way. How do you make them feel special in a world in which the magic around them is more powerful than what they can personally produce?

One way is to emphasize that the arcanist or priest is more attuned to the infrastructure of the world than other types of characters. In a world where arcane magic is everywhere, the wizard can fill the role of a hacker or tech-head in a cyberpunk story—the person who understands the way the world works, who can identify the dangers and potentially seize control of the reins of power. Normal people can't fly a magical galleon, but if you get to the bridge your sorcerer can take control. In a world where high magic is a gift from the gods, a cleric may simply be the person who understands the system and has connections in the church hierarchy. In a world where magic follows purely scientific principles, the cleric may be special precisely because his faith-based magic isn't bound by the normal rules.

With that said, if you want your spellcasting protagonists to truly stand out in the world, you can focus on their roll as innovators. If magic follows scientific principles, your wizard may be the one who takes teleportation to the next level. If magic comes from the gods, your priest may be chosen to act as the personal hand of a deity or a wizard may be the first one taught to use arcane magic, the sole student of the rebellious god.

For characters who don't employ magic, part of the question is how its presence affects their lives. A warrior is an expert in combat and weaponry. If magic wands are the primary ranged weapon in your world, then you may want to adapt the skills of the fighter to allow him to be a wandslinger instead of forcing him to employ bows. If magical wards are commonplace, the rogue may have specialized tools for bypassing them, both when it comes to disarming traps or countering a wizard's defenses before making a surprise attack. These don't have to be innate abilities of the characters; the assassin may have to buy his ward-breaking powder. But given that wizards aren't assassins, think about the tools they might create to enable assassins to do their jobs. Regardless of the role of magic, there will always be a place for intelligent people who know how to create and repair the tools society relies on, tough people prepared to endure the dangers of battle and exploration, and clever folk who can trick the others. As you create your world, just make sure to think about those roles, and the tools that might exist for each class.

WORLDS AND TECHNOLOGY

Wolfgang Baur

Humans are creatures of technology, and yet many imagined worlds do their best to ignore this. Fantasy, in particular, seems to exist in a never-never world of easy farming, simple animal- or wind-powered transport, and natural and divine medicines that actually work without all the annoyance of a scientific or industrial revolution. Most fantasy RPGs are, in a sense, a deep denial of the facts of pre-modern life, and instead they substitute a rosy and glorious past of daring adventure and magic.

And that's OK. In fact, that's sort of the point: it's a fantasy. Living in a time of starvation, plague, and burdensome travel would be a boring, deadly grind. Gritty is only fun if your character doesn't die of dysentery.

Yet what technology you do highlight as a worldbuilder is important to the flavor of the world, the logic of its stories, and the drama of its best moments. Where and how technology fits into the picture is very much a personal decision for a worldbuilder, and very much a matter of taste. Here are four main elements to consider that will make a huge difference in your worldbuilding: movement, knowledge, war, and living standards.

TECHNOLOGIES OF MOTION: TRANSPORT & COMMUNICATIONS

One of the primary technologies of any world is the simple matter of getting from here to there—and in the era before phones or digital communications, this puts a hard limit on the speed of news as well. The news of a revolt or a queen's untimely demise or a wizard's hideous demonic assassins only moves as fast as a horse and rider, or as fast as a messenger pigeon. This can be quite entertaining when the PCs arrive at the site of some earth-shaking event too late because they chose to walk rather than spend their gold on fast steeds or a swift eagleback flight. Things in a fantasy world can happen quickly in distant places, faster than the heroes can get there. It seems to me that you could probably write an adventure that assumes the

PCs are travelling toward the site of some great disaster, and they closer they get, the better the information about it becomes. And of course, the information makes it sound worse and worse, racheting up the tension every time the PCs learn more of what they are getting into.

TRANSPORT

You may be familiar with the idea that most peasants never went more than 20 miles from where they were born in the medieval period. It's a stunning fact. And most people in a fantasy setting stick near their thorps and hamlets as well. Are they homebodies? No—it's simply too hard to get around when walking or riding a horse are your best options.

For most heroic adventurers, these limits don't matter. They have fistfuls of gold and magical horses to carry them and their heavy gear wherever they choose. The GM points them at an adventure hook, and off they go. Journeys are little more than a series of random encounters. The world has no freeways, but transport is simple. Just ride and fight some monsters, and—boom!—you are at the next dungeon.

This is very, very functional and good for advancing the story. But it misses several worldbuilding opportunities. In the early development of Midgard, for example, I proposed the existence of sand ships to sail across the desert. This was met

TECHNOLOGY AS A STYLE MARKER

One reason that worldbuilders get tangled up in their technology is that sometimes we want to present something that is out-of-period or inappropriate for a particular culture, locale, or stage of scientific development. The usual problem is airships for sky-borne adventuring, or cannons for pirates, or a system of long-distance rail travel in pre-industrial times. Explaining how that much steel, helium, or coal is available in a semi-feudal society with only animal-powered machines is quite a challenge.

The usual solution is to shortcut the whole problem by saying "it's magic." This may seem like a copout (and on one level it certainly is), but it's also timesaving and extremely functional. You want lightning rail connecting the five nations of a vast continent in Eberron? No problem! You want some cannons but not wholesale gunpowder? Bring on some rapid-fire Spelljammer ballistae! And so on.

The use of a particular element of Renaissance or early modern technology that is handwaved as a sort of magic is really perfectly fine if it gets you the result you want. This is fantasy and, up to a certain point, your audience will usually grant you one or two elements of super-science-disguised-as-magic. You can get very hung up on trade routes, mining, labor requirements, and so forth, but this is largely an exercise in futility because the players of the game don't care about that. They care about flying in airships, or zipping across continents, or unleashing a thunderous cannonade. If your world caters to those heroic styles, don't worry too much about who built the lightning rail.

with quite a bit of acclaim from the project's backers, more than I expected. Why? Because sandships are romantic, practical, and exotic.

Some of your modes of transit should be similar. Perhaps there are companies of giant-eagle riders that take passengers over the mountains for hefty fees, though it requires exotic saddles and hard weight limits. Or you may have vast herds of migrating manta rays that pull ships across whole oceans, but only twice a year and only for those who build the right sort of harneses and ships. Or you might have ancient shadow roads like those of Midgard, dangerous to traverse and yet tempting because of the speed they offer. Make travel itself a little more interesting.

You'll notice from the examples chosen here that "technology" in the sense of transport is typically either animal-powered or magical or waterborne. Adding machine transport to a setting can be done (airships or the mysterious underground transports of Tekumel, for instance), but most transport technology of fantasy settings involves animals, water, or magic for the very good reason that these technologies all function in the absence of decent roads.

Though a few historical empires like the Incas and Romans did build great road networks, these are key exceptions. Most nations didn't build roads because the engineering involved is expensive and difficult. Going over hills or through marshes is harder still. Bridging rivers and crossing mountains is yet more challenging. Modern humans in developed nations forget just how damn hard it is to get anywhere, so I would advise providing some sort of transport technology to a gamer audience—and making it very clear that once characters are off that transport grid, getting anywhere is much, much harder.

TECHNOLOGY OF KNOWLEDGE: LITERACY AND PRINTING

Possibly the most disruptive technology of the medieval period was, of course, the invention of movable type by Johannes Gutenberg for the printing of indulgences. It was primarily a religious technology to begin with, but was soon adopted for secular uses as well—and it spurred the growth of radical politics, changes in faith and doctrine, and the rapid growth of a literate population. Before the printing press, most people couldn't read—perhaps for the rather practical reason that there wasn't very much interesting reading material.

I jest, but not by much. Whether or not your fantasy world has literacy and who controls that literacy is a major building block of the setting. Historically, only two classes ever developed literacy to a high degree before the printing press: the priests and the merchants. In a few cases, you might argue that the kings and tyrants used literacy but, in practice, they farmed that work out to priest-scribes and merchant-accountants.

So, what's the difference between a priestly literate class, a mercantile literate class, and an aristrocratic or general literate class with a printing class? Well, everything.

As literacy governs history, science, knowledge, accounting, debts, records, land claims, justice and the law, it's fairly crucial to civilization. The people who control the written word control a lot of power. They are in a position to dictate divine or secular law to others. Their hands are on the levers of power.

A priestly literate class may exhort donations to the church, and they control the divine word, with which to bully nobles, kings, and upstarts. A mercantile literate class controls the flow of wealth, grain, goods, and taxes. They decide who starves and who prospers.

All that being the case, the decision as to who reads and writes, and who does not, says a great deal about power and influence in your world. It may well be that multiple groups read and write, but do so differently or only within a secret society or guild (see "It's a Mystery! Designing Mystery Cults" and "How to Design a Guild"). It may be that all nobles read and use this as a mark of civilization and superior breeding against all lesser creatures. Or it may be that almost no one but wizards reads and that the act of reading itself is nearly magical. Whatever your preference, this is a technology that requires only sheepskins, papyrus, oak gall, soot, and goose feathers, but it can change your world. Don't ignore it just because there's no fire, steel, or large animals involved!

Technology of Warfare: the Keystones of Heroics

Speaking of fire, steel, and large animals: one of the primary drivers of technology has always been warfare. Armor, weapons, horses, elephants, siege weapons, and even the development of arithmetic are down to the need to crush someone else's skull in a hurry. Where do your world's societies stand in the ranks of the military power?

The easy answer is that they are stone age, bronze age, iron age, or carbon steel-using societies, but that only helps us so far. And it's not that less advanced societies are necessarily less interesting. For instance, the idea that a society is metal-poor was explored in the Dark Sun campaign setting. It made for some great gaming.

From a worldbuilding point of view, what you need to know are two primary factors about a society: what is its apex warrior using, and what is the levee conscript using? By apex warrior, I mean the most decked-out badass of that society: perhaps a mix of steel armor, pure-magic blades, and healing leeches that are born next to the skin. You'll notice that this is a combination of metal, magic, and quirky technology. I like to mix it up in fantasy societies and give each culture at least one thing that doesn't have an Earth equivalent.

Just as interesting is the typical levee. This might be a peasant in formed-chitin armor with an iron-tipped spear and a set of signal banners for communicating. Perhaps this army is better-coordinated and better-led than most. What does that mean to an adventure in this world? It might mean that signal flags are a real danger, like more-familiar gongs or bells. It might also mean that the weapons of the place are more often spears than swords.

Make some interesting choices in warfare, in armor, weapons, animals, signals, and battlefield medicine. The role of the exotic and magical should not just be in everyday technology. Quite the contrary: the most advanced technology a society has is generally found either in the hands of its rulers or its armies. Make it stand out in physical appearance, in price, and in what skills or wealth is required to bring it to bear. Make the capstone technology hard to find, and players will be more eager than ever to get their hands on that stuff, especially if the world's high-status elite rulers have it and flaunt it.

Technology of Life, Food, and Medicine: Crucially Useless Technology

Growing crops for people and livestock is crucial and difficult work when you don't have tractors. It's even harder without routine access to fertilizer, herbicides, or even irrigation.

Growing food is also incredibly un-heroic in terms of dramatic adventure. It's important that someone have mastered that technology; you can make a nod to irrigation and fertility magic in your worldbuilding if you like, but the nitty-gritty of wheat, sorgum, rye, millet, and barley? Deadly dull. Not worth your time. What you need to know from a worldbuilding perspective is who has good food technology, who starves, and who grows fat. Food is money and power in a society where people still frequently die of starvation. At the same time, agricultural technology is slow, dispersed, and takes a vast array of peasants to implement. It's necessary, but rarely heroic, to tend an orchard. If you have to arrange conflicts in your worldbuilding, stick to livestock. At least they are susceptible to theft and feuds.

Medicine, on the other hand, is a technology with immediate, practical usefulness for every adventurer. Herbalism, disease cures, the understanding of binding up injured adventurers are all chances to provide some special technology or twist—but at least in D&D and Pathfinder and similar standard fantasy settings, it is almost always replaced by magic from a very early stage. Why? Because the technology is so important that any realistic system of healing and recovery is too slow, too complex, and too fiddly to really further gameplay. Being wounded is dramatic. The recovery is often not.

Avoid the technology discussion of medicine unless there is something special there, such as a race of healers (that can be played or befriended by player characters), or a particular techno item of powerful healing (for PCs to pursue).

The Many Uses and Dangers of Unobtainium

Many science fiction stories feature a particular technology or substance that is critically valuable and impossibly rare. The fandom term for this is "unobtainium," as in, you'll never obtain any. This is a key concept in worldbuilding for gaming but a decidedly mixed concept. If you decree that something in the setting is vitae, spice, arcane dust, or power gems that enable all the cool technology—well, it's instantly what players want. But the moment they get it in the setting, the power curve of gameplay changes. This is what many players think will happen with gunpowder or lasers, for instance (in practice, those are often just longbows with expensive arrows and shinier optics).

If the PCs never obtain any of the wonder material, they'll be disappointed. If they do obtain the technological or arcane wonder-power material, they have a key to new technology and great power. It's a nightmare for the gamemaster who has made access to it too easy. It's a frustration for players who can't ever find the stuff.

So, if you do decide that your technologies depend on such a thing, I recommend two elements in your tech design: 1) the material must be available and outrageously expensive, 2) it must be quickly consumed, and 3) the powers it grants must be designed into the rules set. [1]

Here's why:

1. If the material isn't available, ever, you're just annoying everyone with powers available only to NPCs. Shame on you for not sharing the coolest toys.

2. If the material doesn't burn up at a furious rate, you will always have cases where once it is found, the campaign never returns to its lower-power state, and you essentially bifurcate the whole setting into haves and have-nots. If that's your goal, great, but for most settings, the difference is not that stark.

3. The power has to be helpful, but it should not overshadow the heroes themselves. It should, ideally, be a technology that is additive to the heroes existing powers, enhancing what they already do, rather than replacing what they already do. Make them a little faster, hit a little harder, see a little further, talk a little smoother. But don't give this techno-powerup a whole new set of epic powers.

WORD CHOICES: THE LANGUAGE OF TECHNOLOGY

A lot of what bothers players of a fantasy RPG about technology sometimes boils down to language and word choice. If your guns are called "bolt-throwers," that's OK, even if they are ranged weapons that require slow reloads just like a rifle. If your grenades are "manufactured in a workhouse by human slaves" that's much more offensive to the ear than if they "were distilled and enchanted by kobold alchemists." Similarly, a kevlar vest is a very different tool than a suit of boiled leather or lamellar armor. In statistical terms, the differences may be minor. In worldbuilding terms, the differences are huge.

I would argue that many of your choices in technology are such matters of terminology rather than effect. Some players simply react violently and irrationally to words that trigger modern or technological associations (see "Gunpowder" sidebar). That's really their issue, but as the audience, it's their fantasy, and it's worth considering right at the very start whether you want to appeal to players with that technophobia (and appeal to their sense of magic and avoid technological trigger words), or you want to go full steampunk or arcane-techish (and garner a different audience). It's difficult or impossible to please both groups, and which way you jump is one of those creative decisions that shapes the world. Use the right trigger words in your design, and you enable a thousand daydreams of howdah pistols, spiked bronze gauntlets, or tiger-striped bolt-throwers.

In this sense, some of what you think of as design decisions (whether to include some weapon or not), may be more of a naming decision. The look and attitude of a weapon is an important part of that technology and defines the character who carries

---

[1]For more on the idea of magic needing to be designed and the elements that need to be considered, see Michael A. Stackpole's essay, "Designing Magic Systems," in *The Complete KOBOLD Guide to Game Design*, Open Design, 2012.

it. The stats underneath might be the same, but the guy carrying the rapier is not the same as the guy carrying the bronze spear. Choose your names for technology carefully, because they deliver an important charge of emotional resonance and cultural memory for the GM and players.

SUMMATION

While every technology decision has clear consequences, and there's no exact right solution for all cases, this is what makes worldbuilding fun! Some technology is vital to life but deadly to heroic adventuring. Other technology is best presented by its absence—it adds nothing to the game experience. Choose your words carefully, present technology as both exotic and critically useful to the tasks that the players set for themselves, and your worldbuilding will be much the richer for it.

WHY HATE GUNPOWDER?

Nothing is more divisive among some fantasy RPG players than the presence or absence of gunpowder in a setting. It seems to irritate or even enrage some fans; its presence is seen as "spoiling" a world of pure magic and imagination. I admit for a long time, I was one of those players, and I see and sympathize with the problem.

For many gamers, fantasy RPGs are about the pre-modern and the magical, the age before industry and automation, the time before science and standardization. There is little that is more scientific, industrial, or standardized than firearms. Sure, gunpowder in warfare dates to the medieval period (look up bombards sometime), but gunpowder weapons don't feel medieval to us. At best, they feel like part of the Renaissance or early modern period, when arquebuses and flintlocks changed warfare from single combat to massed ranks of faceless individuals. They destroy the sense of heroism.

This argument is a load of horsepuckey. Ask any soldier, read any account of the American Civil War; it's not the weapons that make for heroism or its lack. On the other side, I think that the stories of the pure individual heroism of the Golden Age are rather suspect, because before the age of gunpowder there were plenty of faceless levees, spear carriers, and mooks in the Pharoah's armies, as well as famous heroes.

However, that's not the point for those who hate gunpowder. Gunpowder is a potent symbol and signifier of modernity, of an era after the fall from romantic rose-colored medievalisms, and of an industrial age. It's not the game effects of gunpowder that are the objection: it's the meaning of gunpowder, the flavor, that's the problem. Which side of the gunsmoke you land on in your worldbuilding depends on what flavor of world you are building, not the weapon's deadliness on the field of battle.

WHY NO MONOTHEISM?

Steve Winter

Writers who create campaign settings for roleplaying games seem to love describing the gods of their worlds, and I do mean "gods." One seldom sees a fantasy setting where a monotheistic religion has taken hold the way Judaism, Catholicism, and Islam reigned in Europe, the Middle East, and northern Africa during the Middle Ages. This seems odd upon consideration, because everything else about most RPG settings borrows heavily from late Roman and medieval European cultures. One type of character, the cleric, has its roots deep in Christianity, but the class has evolved well away from that idea. I'd like to look at why that is and what the implications would be for an RPG that adopted a widespread monotheism.

THEOLOGY 101

First, let's recognize that religion can be tricky to talk about and let's clarify some terms.

Monotheism is the belief or doctrine that only one god exists, so monotheistic religions, like Judaism, Christianity, and Islam recognize a single entity as the one and only deity in existence. That deity can exhibit more than one aspect, like the Trinity of Catholicism, but the being is, by definition, the *one* and *only* god.

In contrast, polytheism posits many gods, and polytheistic religions recognize more than one deity. They might be equals, or they might be ranked in a hierarchy. Each deity typically has its own portfolio of interests: harvests, love, war, prosperity, industry, fertility, death, birth, creation, sunrise, sunset, storms, and so on. Individual cities and families sometimes have their own unique patron deities. The gods might get along with each other, ignore each other, try to undermine each other, or fight openly (in their divine realm, of course). They are frequently anthropomorphic (humanlike in appearance or characteristics), but not always. When a pantheon's gods are anthropomorphic, they tend to display behavior that reflects our ideals and foibles magnified to godly intensity.

Two Kinds of Polytheism

It's worth distinguishing between two different types of polytheism. The first is *henotheism*, in which worshipers choose one god from a pantheon and focus their worship on him or her. This is how most RPG worlds tend to work. The god of nature and the goddess of war might be brother and sister, but Rildar the Devout wears the holy symbol of just one and never the other.

Contrast that with *kathenotheism*, in which people worship all of the gods at different times as the situation demands. A farmer might pray to the lord of sun and rain when his crop is growing and to the harvest mother when the crop is ready, but he's not an exclusive disciple of either one. This brand of polytheism is less common in RPGs, even though it has been more prevalent in history.

Animism doesn't necessarily recognize any particular deity. Instead, animists believe that many parts of the natural world have spiritual lives or are inhabited by distinct spirits such as dryads and nymphs. In RPGs, druids are the most common animists, even though very little is known about the beliefs and practices of the historical druids—or maybe that's their appeal.

Dozens of variations exist: *pantheism* (the universe is a deity), *syncretic monotheism* or *syncretic polytheism* (the melding of different, sometimes contradictory religions into one), *paganism* (not modern paganism but a generic term, usually for someone else's religion).

So, Why No Monotheism?

Why don't we see more monotheistic religions in RPG worlds? I attribute it to six reasons.

1. In the Beginning . . .

Those familiar words come from the Old Testament, but I'm stretching them back to an earlier age. Polytheism is much older than the big three monotheistic religions of Judaism, Christianity, and Islam. We associate godly pantheons with ancient civilizations such as Sumeria, Persia, Egypt, Greece, and Rome. The Nordic pantheon is a popular exception, since it flourished well into the Middle Ages (and continues to this day). Monotheism is a more recent arrival.

Most fantasy settings try to evoke a sense of great antiquity, of a world predating history. Conan's Hyborean Age isn't medieval Europe and Asia, however much it might look the part. It is a time "before the oceans drank Atlantis" that bears a superficial resemblance to the Middle Ages but greatly predates Moses, Abraham, and the rise of Christianity. In such ancient realms, fierce gods still rule in pagan splendor and sometimes demand unwholesome rituals from their followers.

Contrast that with modern, monotheistic religions that preach compassion, peace, and love for your fellow man, and consider which offers more avenues for wild, heroic adventure.

2. Mythology

In games, we care about what the gods do for us, not their doctrine or how they're worshiped. We're really interested in mythology rather than religion. Mythology is where we read about gods fighting monsters, scheming against their rivals, traveling the world incognito, and handing out favors (and magical weapons) to mortals.

Put simply, player characters want their gods to reward them in this life, not the next. It's in the mythology of the great pantheons of Greece, Rome, and Scandinavia where that happens most often.

3. I Serve the God of War

Roleplayers look for ways to make their characters unique. By necessity, the deity of a monotheistic religion must be all-encompassing. That means my cleric is a lot like your cleric, and they're both in league with Bob's cleric, and no one likes Bob's cleric. If there are multiple deities to choose from, a player's choice can say a lot about the character's personality. A character who worships the god of war is likely to have different goals and take a different approach to things than a character who worships the spirit of the meadow.

4. Options, Options, Options

Gamers love options that make a difference. Characters worshipping dissimilar gods can receive unique abilities and benefits from the rules. Priests of the god of thunder and the god of luck can operate very differently on the battlefield or in a city bazaar. That sort of specialization makes a lot of people happy.

5. The Great Escape

We tend to roleplay as a means of escaping from the mundane world that surrounds us 24 hours a day. Monotheism is a familiar part of that world for most of us. Why extend it into our fantasy settings when there are so many other, more exotic choices?

6. I'm a Little Uncomfortable with This

Finally, there's social pressure. Religion is a serious issue for a lot of people—the most serious, in many cases. Anything that impugns a religion's dignity, treats it flippantly, questions its tenets, or trespasses its sacred ground can generate unwanted heat. If you prefer to avoid offending people, or treat everyone's beliefs with respect, or share those beliefs yourself, then why invite unnecessary trouble? A purely fictitious pantheon of gods evades problems before they begin.

DESIGNING FOR MONOTHEISM

Those are all sensible reasons for fantasy worlds to have a multitude of gods, but do they exclude monotheistic religions? You can argue, for example, that henotheism (a pantheon of gods where most people worship one and ignore the others) isn't much different from several competing monotheistic churches. That would be one workable model.

That model doesn't, however, represent true monotheism. It allows something like monotheism, but then it undermines the whole concept by not allowing the monotheists to be right.

That is, after all, the foundation of monotheism—that our god is the only one. If the practitioners of any other religion can demonstrate that its deity actually exists by, say, performing miracles (spells) in his or her name, then a theology denying the existence of all other gods topples like a house of cards.

Happily, as problems in fantasy world design go, this one is not as insurmountable as it sounds. The solution is twofold.

First, even the one true faith can be split into sects. All we need to do is look around the modern world for examples of what happens when people who worship the same god disagree over the finer points of canon. You might love the sinner and lament the apostate, but there is neither forgiveness nor salvation for the heretic.

Second, a religion can be false and still have power. In other words, not all gods need to be gods. Fantasy stories are filled with beings who masquerade as gods but aren't. Demons, dragons, ancient sorcerers, monstrosities from beyond the stars, and other entities can have power dwarfing that of men while still falling far short of omnipotence. Many things can be supernatural without being divine, and such entities make excellent foes for adherents of the one true faith.

This, then, can be the shape of a thrilling campaign: a world that is the domain of a single, enigmatic, omnipotent (or near-omnipotent) deity whose followers agree on the big picture but split into factions over the details. Some churches coexist more-or-less peacefully despite their differences, while others scheme against opposing sects, persecute heretics, and wage war against nonbelievers. Around the periphery and hidden in the shadows are the secretive demon worshipers, beast cults, and pagan temples where powerful, supernatural, but mortal entities pose as gods to manipulate mortals, feed their egos, and fuel their dark agendas. Religious conflict could easily take front and center in such a campaign, rather than being a background element.

DESIGNING A PANTHEON

Wolfgang Baur

T he construction of a decent pantheon of gods is one of those tasks of worldbuilding that delights me. Though I'm not religious myself, the mystic or spiritual impulse is one that fascinates me, and I'm a fan of comparative religion, mythology, and a dilettante in all the mysterious ways that humans have communed with the divine over the ages.

Which is why the standard D&D pantheon makes me so angry. It presents both a failure of imagination and a misunderstanding of pantheistic belief, all in the name of some shoddy mechanics and attempts at character building. It's hugely disappointing. I think that a thoughtful worldbuilder could do much better by trying things that reflect human nature and that offer new game mechanics.

WHAT'S WRONG WITH MONOTHEISTIC PANTHEISM

The implicit presumption of standard D&D religions is that from among an array of gods, priests choose to follow a single god and no other. This is a pure import from the monotheistic worldview, and in particular of the second commandment in Judaism and Christianity: "You shall have no other gods before me." (Exodus 20:3).

But of course the whole point of a pantheon and a pantheistic worldview is that a believer in a system like this can and does believe in many gods and offers sacrifice to them. The "Go Team Thor!" approach of the implicit or explicit RPG pantheons aligns characters with gods the way that we choose sports teams or political parties: you can be a Democrat or a Republican, but not both at once. You can follow the Chicago Bears or the Green Bay Packers, but cheering for both is pure madness.

Pantheism and Belief

Pantheistic belief isn't like this cheerleading approach, and it's annoying to have games that assume the gods of every pantheon are all as jealous as the God of the Bible.

Imagine, then, a world where a priest follows a constellation of many gods, as in Midgard, or in many still-extant cultures of Earth. Polytheism is not just a pantheon of many gods; it is the worship of multiple gods at once. While a priest might specialize in the propitiation of a particular divinity, a pantheist priest need not.

Now consider the gaming consequences of this idea. Religious life is a constellation, a menu that can be consulted more than once, a multiplicity of possible divine connections and characters ideas. It makes, frankly, for a very complicated priest class in an RPG, but it also delivers a very rich character in a novel and possibly in an advanced fantasy game. And of course that's one direction I pursued in the Midgard campaign setting, because paganism has rarely gotten an interesting set of rules and worldbuilding in *Dungeons & Dragons*.

Mysteries and Multiples

The constellation of belief is one way to design more interesting faiths. The other is to reintroduce a degree of mystery and uncertainty in religion. The old religions of Greece, Rome, and elsewhere frequently kept some of their teachings as mysteries offered only to the initiated; the rites of Bacchus or Mithras would be revealed slowly to the faithful, and presumably the more devoted members of those faiths would know more than those who did not follow those gods. This could easily become a set of feats, divine spells, or special abilities for both clerics and non-clerics who follow a particular path.

But notice: the mysteries of these ancient cults were not exclusive. Or rather, some were limited to only men, or only women, in ways that designers seem reluctant to do with fantasy religions. The gods of a pagan pantheon, though, are not meant to be all things to all people. They don't have to be, because there are so many of them. Instead, they are targeted to particular functions (expressed as domains and keywords in game terms), and they are meant to address particular needs in people in various life stages. Young boys and young women could and perhaps should follow entirely different gods than mature men or elderly women.

Why, then, can't a character who begins as a young man have an initiation in one god and then gain a second focus of worship? Or rather, it's possible, but it's not encouraged. The character sheet in a Pathfinder game or D&D game has only a small place for "Patron God", and it's always listed as a singular. In Midgard, that character sheet offers several lines, and it should be "Patron Gods," plural.

In many cases, this makes better sense in-game than the weird monotheism of PCs. A multi-classed wizard/rogue character might follow both the god of magic and the god of thieves, or the god of her home town and the goddess she discovered among the elves.

GNOSTICISM RATHER THAN REVEALED TRUTHS

The other big problem for D&D religion is that everyone knows the gods are real. There are no plausible atheists, though perhaps there's room for the agnostic or the skeptical in some form. I'll just say that skeptics in a fantasy world might just say that the gods might be powerful beings, but not truly divine.

For our purposes, that doesn't matter. The gods exist; what's important for gaming is how player characters interact with the divine. For the most part, this has been treated similarly to a phone call or a business transaction; clerics input prayer and get back spells; paladins tithe and uphold a code, and are granted power to smite evil. All this is terrific and direct. The trouble starts when designers say, "The gods exist *and they explain themselves to humans.*" I take issue with that second part.

The existence of fantasy gods in gaming is usually interpreted as meaning that gods are perfectly understandable, and that they spend a lot of their time briefing the clergy and the high priests. Presumably they do this to make sure that the tenets of the faith are not only well understood but also unified and clear and the same everywhere the god is worshipped. This leads to cartoon gods, like a comic-book Thor (totally unlike the Thor humans actually worshipped) and a cartoon Raven Queen, Lolth, or Moradin (cardboard cutouts rather than sources of awe and mystery). The gods are easy to understand. Faith is really a matter of making the right offerings and getting the right gifts in return. There's never any mystery in the divine world.

I understand why designers do this. It's the geek compulsion to make everything neat and orderly and put all variables in a box. But I also think this is a huge wasted opportunity, because religion is inherently not neat and easy to put in a box. Faith is ephemeral; doubt is crucial. Religious strife is a great motivation both between faiths and within a single faith. Splinter groups, heretics, and mystery cults with different inner mysteries are loaded with gaming potential. But they don't work if everyone can call on the gods and get a straight answer.

In Midgard, I take a different perspective on this, though there are other ways to deal with the problem. My solution is to make the gods both opaque in their motivations and essentially inhuman and unknowable because of their divine status. That is, everyone knows that the gods exist but no one really understands them. They are mysterious. Their answers change over time; their appearance is inconsistent. Their motives are irrational by our standards and often seem completely insane, trivial, bizarre, or obsessive. Why do the gods want what they want? No one knows. But they do want those things.

And that's one of the keys to the Midgard approach to the gods. Most of the time we design around the player characters; what do these powers do for a PC? How soon does he access them? What elements enhance or diminish those powers? How do followers act and what symbols do they wear?

But it's just as legitimate to say that a divine being has demands. This concept first appeared in the *Zobeck Gazetteer* for the Midgard setting, and it has expanded ever since. The gods want things from worshippers; the Christian god, to name the obvious example, wants belief, an exclusive relationship, a code of conduct, confession of sin, forgiveness, and a certain percentage of income. No D&D god makes anywhere near this level of demands, nor should they. Roleplaying a priest should not require weird cultic knowledge—but it should require some sense of respect and humility on the part of a PC and some sense that a god is not an entirely known quantity.

Let me expand on that slightly, by reference to the real world. A certain level of confusion or uncertainty or doubt is part of the religious experience for many real-world believers. Those who are entirely too certain of themselves are labeled zealots or fanatics.

Indeed, the lack of certainty is a feature that leads to religious strife and conflict. In the real world, sectarian strife is often fatal, horrible, community-destroying. Think of the Wars of Religion between Catholics and the Lutherans, or the Crusades, or even the Cathar Crusade of one Christian sect against another as historical examples. Think of the most current, ripped-from-the-headlines massacre or genocide. In a fantasy game, these are terrific motivators and sources of deep conflict, engines that power story, campaigns, entire civil wars and slaughters.

What is reprehensible in the real world can, of course, be strong, strong fuel for roleplaying games. Treat it with caution, but don't ignore it!

Here, then, is how I bring some uncertainty and strife to religious topics in Midgard.

Masks of the Gods

The first key point of a fantasy faith is that it have at least two faces, and possibly many more. If a religion is entirely revealed and all its adherents are certain of exactly who said what, when, and why, you've lost a powerful source of confusion and conflict within or between faiths. So, in Midgard I made certain that gods were not entirely clear to mortal eyes—indeed, mortals aren't sure who the gods are, because one god may wear many masks. This is similar to the Roman and Greek practice of syncretic religion, where local gods of conquered tribes might be associated with existing Roman gods. Thus the fertility goddess of the Gauls might be seen as simply another name and a different church for the same divine wellspring.

The theology of this is less interesting to me than the practical consequences for game design. One of the generally unfortunate results of any long-running campaign setting is its tendency to spawn new gods yearly, monthly, and even weekly. Every new god requires a new write-up. Every new write-up requires a community to support that god, of priests and followers. Eventually, it just becomes tiresome to say "here's the tenth Forest God"—people tune out.

The idea of gods wearing masks leads to a syncretic solution that means new names might have existing powers, and it also hints at an underlying connection between divine wellsprings. Perun is the god of war and thunder in Midgard. Mavros is a war god first, but similar to Perun in most respects. Thor is the god of thunder first and foremost, though also a god of war. They are three masks of the same god.

Competing Faiths

At first this might seem to mitigate against conflict. After all, the three churches and followers understand each other—but their small differences can also be the source of conflict and misunderstanding about the true faith. It might be as simple as which branch of the church deserves to have one of Mavros-Perun-Thor's holy hammers, or which of their paladins are the bravest and boldest, but suddenly there is room for additional tensions between characters and within the setting.

This is even more the case when the exact nature of the divine conflict is shrouded in mystery. The gods in Midgard can and do murder one another, but how this happens and how their faiths survive a deicide is not understood by any mortal mind. What's clear is that a pantheon is always in flux, and that the gods that are most alike are most likely to fight.

The design decision here was that there cannot be more than one sea-god in Midgard without the two of them being either two masks of a single source, or being eternal enemies. Masks are sources of strength, and confusion, and that's fine. Whether the two sea gods are the same figure or two eternal enemies, either way, the setting is more vibrant and more dangerous. This is the deliberate result of a pantheon designed for conflict rather than designed to have an encyclopedic summation of separate gods in endless rows.

Your own design work may adopt the model of masks and mysteries, or may take on completely different theological properties. The point, though, is that you should design your world for conflict among at least some of its major religious forces, and think through the implications of both the theology and the nature of divinity in your setting. Gods at rest, granting powers to worshipping in a predictable way, could certainly also be harnessed for maximum conflict. An example from the world of novels might be John Scalzi's *God Engines*.

Religious strife is a boon. Make sure to find the right levers for it.

Uncertain Prophets

One such lever of strife that deserves a little more attention than most is the idea of religious oracles, leaders, and prophets. Some of them are likely bringing divine revelations in a fantasy world. Some of them may well be complete frauds. In either case, they are primary movers and forces for change in a setting.

Whether your prophets are more like Christ, Mohammed, the Sibyl, Buddha, Joseph Smith, or Joan of Arc, they are not keepers of the established order. New religions are inherently destabilizing to the established order. This is why the birth of a religion is often violent or filled with zeal—it takes a lot of energy to overcome entrenched religious orders such as Jesus against the established Jewish priesthood and Roman state, or Mohammed preaching against the idol worshippers and existing sects of the Middle East, or even Joan of Arc asking merely for a divine blessing for her dauphin and king. On the line between wild legends and history, Hercules and Achilles were thought to be semi-divine, and they certainly did shift the world. Think in those terms, and you'll have something like the Saints and Legends of Midgard: mythic characters whose actions are larger than life.

This need not involve physical action and adventure, of course. Oracles and prophets change the world with every word they utter. People move, and nations totter. Give voice and thought to these figures in your setting, whether they are forces for good and life or forces for oppression and fear. Old religions will defend themselves against new ones, and new ones will seize land, temples, and treasures through rhetoric, mob action, great battles, or miracles. A world without miracles and without gods present and active is certainly possible, but many fantasy readers and gamers enjoy the idea of real gods acting, siring children, demanding sacrifices, and blatantly favoring their own few city-states and chosen people.

The idea of divine patrons is as old as religion, and the gods are always on the side of their people. This makes them unique worldbuilding options as super-heavyweight political actors. Consider them a valuable portion of your design toolkit, and revisit, reinvent, and rediscover the variety of human belief systems to enrich your world building. Leaving religion as just a reservoir of spells and healing is not just boring, it is in direct contradiction to real, lived religious experience.

Make your world's religion risky, active, and lively. It's far more fun to play in a setting where the religious order is novel and dangerous than to play in setting where it just functions as an alternate magic system.

IT'S A
MYSTERY!
How to Design a Mystery Cult

By David "Zeb" Cook

Do your players greet your religions with a yawn? Are your temples predictable? Do your powers of description fail whenever the party interrupts a temple's solemn service?

"You've managed to slip in unnoticed while the priest is leading the ritual."

"What's happening?"

"Umm . . . A priest's standing in front of a statue on an altar, and he's chanting. The rest of the worshippers are watching him."

"Okay, it's another priest in funny robes waving his hands in front of a big statue. We've seen this before. Let's stop him . . . because we all know what happens next."

You sigh and ponder: Whatever happened to the wonder of such scenes? Where did the majesty go? The thrill of the unexpected? The mystery? Fortunately, there is a cure for this. It comes straight from myth and legend, and yet it's firmly grounded in the world's ancient history. It is both known and documented, but its details remain cloaked in superstition and guesswork. In other words, it's real enough to fit into a campaign setting, while still being fantastical enough to provide the catalyst for strange and wonderful adventures.

What am I referring to? Why, the ancient tradition of mystery cults, of course.

On the surface, a mystery cult is quite simple. It is a group of believers who practice secret rituals to worship their god or goddess. The key word here is secret, thus the *mystery* of mystery cults. Now, that may sound like any given campaign's batch of evil cultists, whose clandestine cults are littered around most fantasy settings.

So what's so wonderful about that, you rightfully ask? Here's the thing: You can get more mystery out of your mystery cult by digging into the whys and wherefores of them, and that means delving into some history and sociology. Fortunately, you just need a little knowledge—no Ph.D.'s worth of studying is required!

HISTORICAL MYSTERY CULTS

Historically, the best-known mystery cults have their roots in ancient Greece and Rome. Among the most well-recorded were the Greek Eleusinian, Dionysian, and Orphic mysteries and the Roman cults of various eastern gods—Isis, Mithras, and a few others.

These weren't secret societies in that nobody knew about them. On the contrary, writers of the time provided most of the information we have about them, and archaeologists filled in the gaps. A quick Internet search will uncover several sites about them, ranging from scholarly PDFs to New Age sappiness, and worse. (Consider yourself warned.)

So, although they are called mystery cults, it wasn't because their worshippers hid their membership. Instead, the mystery surrounded the specifics of the rituals they performed. Only those initiated into the cult learned and took part in the rites. So while a fair amount is known about the cult of Dionysus or the Eleusinian Mysteries, the nature of their ceremonial rites remains guesswork. For this reason, all the scholarly research about them becomes, at some point, pure conjecture.

In ancient times, the mystery cult was simply part of the community's everyday fabric. As a way to describe this, scholars divide religious worship of the time between public (or state) religion and personal religion.

Public religion was the official stuff—big temples with organized priest hierarchies and the like—that everyone was expected to belong to. The holy festivals, sacrifices, and prayers of these temples involved everyone in the city or community.

The other stuff, the *personal* religion, is the meat of mystery cults. People could join whatever cult they wanted, and there was no *official* role for these organizations. Being a member was more like an extracurricular activity in today's terms, and a person could join several different mystery cults—although this could prove tricky if each cult's goals opposed or competed with one another.

In gaming terms, a game setting's public religions, the *official* ones, are the standard temples with their attending clerics—say, a temple to Athena in a setting using Greek traditions. Such public religions include even the dark gods that the orcs venerate, as well as the gods that other non-humans worship. These public religions hold services for the good of the community or the health of the tribe. At the same time, the setting's mystery cults are more akin to joining a secretive club to gain certain benefits.

For example, Kleitos the Grocer joins a mystery cult because he's looking for extra good luck, fortune, and influential friends. Adventuring types may be interested in pledging membership to gain divine favor or, as outlined below, for more nefarious reasons.

HOW TO DESIGN A MYSTERY CULT

Adding a mystery cult or two to a campaign is a good way to add variety to those anonymous high priests, blank temple facades, and stereotypical holy days. On top of that, they can be a great source for adventure. After all, nothing gets the pot boiling like a little mystery.

Creating a mystery cult doesn't have to be a difficult thing; all it takes is a little planning. Who (or what) is the object of the cult? Why does the cult exist? What do they do? How do player characters join—if they can at all? Creating the answers to these four simple questions should provide more than enough ideas for multiple adventures.

1. Who–or What?

The first question is the easiest: What is the cult's object of worship? Most often this should be an existing deity in your campaign. While any god or goddess can have a mystery cult associated with them, they are most common for very old gods or very new ones. If worship has been long established, the mystery cult emerges from all the tradition, legends, customs, and quirks that time helps accumulate.

Alternatively, if the religion is new to the area, the *mystery* of the mystery cult can attract worshippers dissatisfied with their current choices. Decadent, dying, and minor religions are all other good choices. Decadent ones offer more interesting adventure possibilities, while dying religions work effectively because the mystery cult becomes a kind of last-ditch attempt to keep the god's memory alive. Minor religions suit because they don't usually have all the obligations of an official religion, and therefore they can experiment with their ceremonies and do things a little differently.

A mystery cult doesn't have to be about a god; it can instead be about a philosophy or an ideal. A cult seeking enlightenment through stoicism (or debauchery!) might embrace several related deities as part of its rites. The Orphic Mysteries of Greece (which apparently involved purification of the soul through rebirth) called on Dionysus and Persephone, deities of fertility, wine, and rebirth as part of its rites. So a mystery cult might promise a "conquest" of death, offer the rules for leading a just life, provide a path to divine power, or allow a perfect communion with all nature rather than assure worshippers the grace of a particular god.

Clearly though, the choice of god (or philosophy) initially defines the cult. The cult of the Wolf Warriors of Wotan (as god of battle) isn't likely to be contemplating the wonders of nature as its purpose in life, after all. They're going to contemplate savage war.

2. What's the Goal?

With the who or what answered, it's time to choose a goal. Basically, why is the cult mysterious, and what are they trying to accomplish? This is where the cult's real adventure hooks take shape, as the choices you make here determine the challenges the PCs may face and the rewards they may gain.

Mystery as Temporal Power

The simplest goal is power—not in the next world, not through rewards in the afterlife, but simple power in the here and now. This is the easiest motive to use when building adventure hooks. While power can take many forms, its appeal is certainly easy to understand.

Because the mystery cult has goals in the real world, its members can often seem like a secret society of schemers. However, a mystery cult is not a group of Masons with a secret handshake and a funny password. They seek divine enlightenment to guide their actions and to give them the power to overcome their obstacles, whether those difficulties are mortal enemies or life's everyday difficulties.

The Old Ways: The nobles of the city support a mystery cult that seeks to maintain the "old ways" of a fading religion—the city's god now being eclipsed by new beliefs. The cult wants to keep the old traditions alive, as these traditions have, over the ages, ensured its followers positions of power. The new ways threaten the nobles' dominant grip in their community, and they pray for the divine power to crush their enemies and rivals.

This kind of cult is grimly conservative and is hostile to new ideas. Their secret rites reinforce the idea that worshippers are elite and special—and most of all—right in all things. Newcomers, outsiders, and upstarts are potential threats to their power. Such a group might include vigilantes and witch-hunters who seize heretics for secret trials and purification (in other words, torture) as part of their rituals.

The mystery cult might provide the "old" families with the justification and tools needed to take down nouveau riche threats to their status and influence. Not surprisingly, the cult has rigid restrictions on membership, especially for the true initiates.

Cult of Commerce: A mystery cult for the god of commerce might include aspiring merchants and tradesmen in the town who simply hope to be blessed with extra fortune, more business, and the opportunity to make useful business connections.

Of course, there is always the chance for trouble when two business rivals strive for the same good fortune. Adventurers may suddenly be useful to the cult to ensure one of the competing businessmen fails to properly observe the secret rituals needed to gain the god's favor. To succeed in this task, the player characters must learn what those rituals are to know how to effectively sabotage them.

The Slaves' Mystery: In an oppressive society, slaves turn to the mystery cult of their homeland as a means to acquire freedom from their masters. Through the cult's practices, they seek freedom in this world or the next. Their secret rites inspire acts of rebellion and sabotage, as their god's divine power possesses them to perform such feats. The masters want the cult crushed and the leaders revealed to them. Do the player characters join the rebellion, or do they hunt down the cult's ringleaders? And if they chose the latter, how do they fight the power of a god?

Mystery as Knowledge

This type of mystery cult typically seeks forbidden knowledge, the secrets man was not meant to know. Its members might do so for power (see above), enlightenment of the spirit, obtainment of a small portion of the god's power, or for internment of that god on Earth. The knowledge sought is not that simply found in books or unearthed in ancient crypts. It comes from esoteric practices requiring years of training and ritual to unlock, such as learning how to read the secrets of perfumed smokes, translating the flights of birds, or learning to write the divine alphabet, where vast knowledge is contained in the curves of a single letter.

Not surprisingly, given the obsessive and demanding nature of the work, such cults tend to be small and favored by wizards, sages, and monks, as well as the deranged.

Mystery of Magic: The mystery cult of a deity of magic will naturally favor wizards of all sorts, though more rational-minded ones find the whole idea a foolish waste of time. Nonetheless, these "dreamers" may gather to intone secret chants on nights when the planets are aligned perfectly. Members may even practice in isolation as shut-ins in their studies or as hermits in the mountains, where they can fully devote themselves to their god and rarely, if ever, meet another follower of their cult.

Cult members may do all these things in search of pure truth, the grand understanding of everything, or even transfiguration into the divine. The path to such knowledge is difficult, so there are always those looking for a shortcut to that same enlightenment. If only they knew what was done in those secret rituals, they would certainly learn the answer they seek!

Secret Knowledge: A lay cult for everyday citizens may seek to spread enlightenment through knowledge and instruction. The knowledge must be taught in secret; without proper instruction and guidance, the great insights are corrupt and useless. In other words, "If everyone knew what we know, they would simply misunderstand and abuse it."

Such mystery cults are usually harmless unless their need for secrecy causes them to take extreme measures against those who no longer follow their ways. And, of course, there are always those—like avaricious wizards or suspicious priests—willing to pay for their secret knowledge.

Mystery of Rebirth: The mystery cult of a dead god's followers pursues the literal secrets man was not meant to know in order to resurrect their deity. This deity is naturally something awful, horrible, and elder, a god so alien that its return would threaten mankind's existence. The mystery cult is led, naturally, by a mad genius who has deceived his followers into believing they are bringing about a wondrous new age for mankind. If those outside the mystery cult knew what the cultists were up to, they would take great efforts to stop him. In this case, what the cult is up to is quite literally a mystery.

MYSTERY AS PROTECTORS

Just as there are mystery cults trying to bring about the end of the world, there are others just as determined to save the world. These mystery cults exist to make sure key rituals are observed to:

- Keep a terrible evil safely locked away forever
- Keep a terrible evil appeased, so it leaves them alone
- Strengthen a deity in its constant celestial battle against a terrible evil
- Ensure terrible secrets man was not meant to know stay secret
- All of the above and more

The cult could keep is rituals secret for a variety of reasons, but it most likely does so because exposure would give its enemy (the terrible evil) the information needed to eradicate it.

Cults of this nature also tend to be far more secretive about everything. Where they meet, why they meet, who goes to the meetings, and even who they revere are things they are not likely to discuss. After all, they are engaged in a covert war to protect the rest of mankind, and they can trust no one outside their inner circle.

• The mystery cult's secret rites invoke the power of a fertility goddess to keep the minions of death at bay. This means more than ensuring a good harvest, for if the cult fails to keep the favor of the goddess, the barriers to the kingdom of death will fall, and nightmarish horrors will overrun the land. It's not just that crops will fail, it's that an eternal darkness of cold and gloom will settle over the land until everything living withers and dies. Because active agents of the death god stalk them, the cult must keep its rites mysterious and secret to avoid detection.

The cult exists in a world that seems safe and secure. The gods have their proper places and are venerated by everyday folk. Everything seems as it should be.

However, the truth is the gods are weaker than known and are under threat from elder forces even greater than they. Were this common knowledge, it could lead to despair and chaos among the people. The cult exists to ensure that select true believers can aid their god in times of weakness. Only the highest initiates of the mystery cult know this secret, and it is their purpose to aid their gods in fighting these enemies.

Clearly, stout-hearted, pious adventurers seasoned at facing horror and death would be a great asset to such a cult. Just as true, corrupt individuals would be of great use to elder forces in bringing about the fall of the cult and its protectors.

• The mystery cult is a small local group charged with observing specific rituals in order to keep the wards strong on an ancient tomb. Inside rests a vampire lich, sealed away by a long-dead high priest. To guarantee the tomb remains sealed, the priest created the cult to serve his god and to keep the seals refreshed and intact. By faithfully discharging their duties, the initiates gain favor in the next life.

The cult keeps its practices secret as a precaution against tomb robbers or foolish adventurers who hope to earn fame and glory. Of course, the mystery cult is surrounded by rumors that they are hiding a fabulous treasure hoard or an artifact of fantastic power.

MYSTERY AS DIVINE POWER

By far, this is the most common reason a mystery cult exists: To offer a deity special veneration in return for divine favor, whether in this world or the next. The mystery of the cult is not the rites that are its path and practice (although these are secret). The true mystery is the nature of the divine itself—it cannot be explained in words or simply by watching a priest performing at the altar. Trying to reach the divine without observing the cult's rituals only leads to failure and misunderstanding, or possibly even to madness or death.

Understanding the divine can only be done by experiencing it, and the only way to experience it is to take part in the cult's secret rites. In ancient Greece, the mystery cults of Dionysus involved wild dancing, wine, and sex to reach a divine passion and communion with their god. It also led to unfortunate results of madness, riot, and murder when the rites got out of control. Even the most basic dealings with gods are not without risk!

• The mystery cult is a classic "Orphic" group. The followers meet at a sacred grove and perform wild rituals to bring about the perfect state to allow their god to possess them. However, being possessed by a god has its drawbacks. Those possessed may go permanently mad or embark on a murderous rampage—after all, who can predict the whims of a god?

However, followers who succeed (and survive) can be imbued thereafter with divine power and understanding, making the reward worth the risk. Of course, the local lord may have other ideas about the value of madmen, raving rioters, and divinely-powered peasants roaming the countryside. In fact, he might really want to suppress such a group, if only he can find someone foolish enough to try.

• The mystery cult lives in an isolated monastery far from contact with civilization. Here the worshippers come to perform the rigorous purification mysteries to become one with their god. Those successfully preserving through the arduous task may venture into the world to lead others to the true glory, or they may remain in seclusion to contemplate their god. In any case, rumors abound about a trove of great wealth and great power within the monastery, just lying in wait for anyone arrogant enough to attempt to seize them.

• The mystery cult is well-known, not hidden or isolated in any way. Common citizens are members, and through secret rituals, they find a path to inner peace and harmony, making their everyday lives better. In this, the cult is very successful, and its prosperity threatens the established order of the other temples, priests, and gods in the region. Discrediting the cult or quashing it is all possible work for adventurers. Doing so does not come without risks from enraged worshippers and displeased gods, though.

3. Joining

For any mystery cult, you have to join before you receive its benefits, and membership is not automatic. A character cannot just walk into the temple, say a prayer, and move on. If joining were that easy, there'd be less mystery! Joining has two requirements: You must be the "right type" of person and thus invited to join, and you must undergo an initiation.

Invitation to Join: The "right type" entails meeting whatever requirements the cult deems appropriate, leading to an offer to join. Some mystery cults are very forward thinking, allowing anyone to join—men, women, slaves, elves, trolls, or whatever. Other cults may be extremely restrictive, allowing only wizards, males, females, full-blooded elves with blue eyes, or only left-handed redheads into their membership.

Ultimately, the GM decides the requirements, but if the GM wants the PCs to join the cult, then the PCs must obviously meet them, or the GM must provide an option to trick or infiltrate the cult in some way. At any rate, the GM can use membership as a PC reward or challenge. The mystery cult of a god of battle such as Wotan might only accept warriors who have killed a man in battle. The mystery cult of a god of learning might allow only literate scholars with high IQs (although this creates an interesting question of how they would determine that). The cult of a goddess of sorcery might only accept females, regardless of all else. Obtaining membership alone can catalyze potential adventure hooks.

Initiations: Meeting the cult's requirements is only half the battle in joining it, though. Undergoing an initiation is paramount to being fully accepted. Historically, the initiation proved the followers' worth, and it prepared them for the revelation of the mysteries to come.

Initiation didn't necessarily happen immediately upon joining either. Often, time and training in more basic rituals to prove oneself might be involved before a follower was initiated into the secret mysteries.

For example, a follower might have to donate money or service to earn the rite of initiation. In a campaign, this depends on how long the PCs should be involved with the mystery cult and how difficult the process is supposed to be. As the focus of a single adventure, the initiation rite should take place fairly quickly. In a long-term campaign, the process can be drawn out to build additional adventure hooks and to ground the PCs in the world setting, meeting and impressing cult leaders and other members.

The initiation itself can range from a simple, harmless ritual to something dangerous and challenging for the PCs. Just what must be done is a secret, part of the cult's mystery. Those passing their initiation don't talk about it, or they tell imposing stories to increase the majesty of the cult.

What the initiation requires depends on the cult and the GM's imagination. It should most certainly involve pomp and ritual appropriate to such an important occasion.

For example, a simple initiation may involve reciting specific charms or prayers, along with viewing sacred objects important to the cult. A more complicated one may require the PCs to undergo an examination of their faith. A truly hard initiation might demand the PCs provide a suitable sacrifice, killed by their own hands, or complete a dangerous physical challenge. The Wolf-Warrior cult of Wotan may say that killing a man in battle is not enough; instead, they require the head of an opposing chieftain as proof the novice should learn the inner secrets. Again, the initiation process is another source of possible adventure.

4. The Secret Part

And what are those secrets only initiates know? That's the point: Nobody knows! For the GM, that means making them whatever he wants. "Congratulations! Now you know the secret handshake" might not be satisfying enough, but learning the prayers to call for a divine blessing, the rites to send oneself into a battle frenzy, or even how to shape-change into a wolf on certain holy days might be useful. With secrets comes responsibility.

Once initiated, there's no going back. The character is a member of that cult. Forever. Lapsed cultists are never popular with their fellows, and cultists who reveal a cult's secret rituals do so to great peril. They may be shunned by others, driven from town, or even hunted by assassins seeking to silence betrayers.

This last part is an important adventure hook for characters who have to infiltrate a cult. Infiltration implies betrayal, since the characters are only pretending to join. Once they complete their treachery—revealing the mystery, stealing the magic widget, or turning over the cultist to the authorities—the PCs are going to have enemies, lots of enemies. They won't necessarily know who those enemies are—some prominent members might not be open about their affiliation.

Potentially, their enemy list will include an offended god or two. And while a god might have better things to do than show up and blast the PCs for their crime, even a distracted god can make life very challenging for player characters.

And that just leads to a whole new set of possible adventures.

How to Design a Guild, College, or Secret Society

Wolfgang Baur

Most worldbuilding is about people, places, magical changes on a global scale. But a smaller and more focused aspect of any setting is its collection of social structures: orc tribes, bards' colleges, thieves' guilds, vampire bloodlines, and even its church hierarchies and knightly orders. How does one design these elements to make a world a little more compelling and a little more playable? I'd say that the social design of these societies is crucial to drawing players further into the world and into the game.

Here are the key elements to consider when you are designing a society or guild. These points can be applied to most RPG settings and, indeed, to most worldbuilding.

Distinguishing Shared Goals and Exclusion

Unlike a tribe or nation, a society is essentially voluntary and not necessarily defined by a particular locale. Priesthoods, wizards' councils, artisanal guilds, and orders of paladins may pick and choose who is a member, and that membership generally doesn't come until after an apprenticeship or proof of qualifications. In other words, societies like this are essentially clubs, and like all clubs, they may add members frequently, rarely, or never.

The founding members are usually among the most influential members for obvious reasons (longevity, institutional knowledge, and sometimes the rewards of dispensing patronage), and sometimes it is simplest to design with the assumption that their goals are the group's goal. Picture, for instance, the archmage who wishes to enslave the queen of the djinn, the master of the goldsmith's guild who wishes to create the finest work of art ever seen, the legless and secretive alchemist who hopes to climb a mountain and build a shrine to his sainted wife. Each of these founders has a personal goal and might be persuasive, powerful, or wealthy enough to convince others to share that goal.

Most of the time, though, a group's goals are broader and more ambitious, and for a society to survive the death of its founding generation the goals certainly must be larger than any personal goal. They need to be goals that transcend individual ability, that require team effort, that change the world in some way. They need to be big goals, because people are less likely to join up and struggle to achieve lesser goals. And, well, we can presume that monsters require similar levels of motivation.

So what might those big goals be? The details depend on your world as a whole, but perhaps they involve waking a sleeping and imprisoned god, raising a library to contain all knowledge, exploring the distant corners of the world, collecting all forms of magical ore and gemstones, serving as healers to the poor and the sick, protecting elven lands from the bite of the ax and saw, destroying all trace of a blasphemous heresy. Or perhaps the goals are more specifically about power: restoring the proper bloodline to the throne, enslaving all humanity to the rule of the lich-queen, or instituting the theocratic state under the One True Demon-God.

Initiation and Acceptance Rituals

Who undertakes these goals? Those who volunteer their efforts as apprentices and journeymen, who are born into the cult or society, who pay some fee or perform some task, or who are initiated through some ordeal.

The key element for play is when a player character attempts to join one of these groups. This should be a moment of at least a little drama and a little suspense. After all, the character's application to join might be rejected by a blackball vote, a divine refusal, a terribly augury, or poor omens. A longstanding foe might contrive to frustrate the player character's attempt to join, delaying it, or making sure the application is forever rejected. Getting in should require a little work. Here are 10 possible ways to frame the entrance or initiation itself:

1) **Soaked in Blood:** The initiation might be one of trial by combat, requiring the initiate to fight a real or symbolic battle against an illusory foe, a horrible monster, or a journeyman of the society. Winning might be perfunctory—unless a rival has swapped in a real monster for the fake one. And in the case of combat against an armed foe, the goal might be to show toughness, steely calm, or good breeding, rather than victory itself.

2) **Strength of Mind:** The initiate might be tested in memory, courage, and knowledge of arcane matters, questioned for hours by examiners, asked to sing or recite, asked to answer questions in ancient tongues or to declaim long-dead histories, and to theorize

on the construction of spells and artifacts long lost to the ages. The goal might be the world's most excruciating oral defense, or the goal might be to roll skill checks until the initiate fails. Indeed, strength of intellect is a fine way to judge candidates for more cerebral societies, and ever-increasing target numbers for those skill checks can provide a sense of rising tension and difficulty in a game session.

3) Generous Ring-Giver: The initiate might be asked to show great generosity of spirit and an open purse. The initiation might involve bribes and gifts to a guildmaster, endless rounds of drink for newfound brothers and sisters in the order, even gifts of minor magic, symbolic animals, or perhaps jewels, rings, knives, or other items of significance to the society. The richer the initiate, the more generous the gifts are expected to be; the exact amount might be stipulated as so-and-so many horses, gold pieces, necklaces, or what have you. Failure to provide sufficient gifts might result in a blackballing by a soured supporter of the initiate, especially if the generosity requires a vote (as in 8, Acclaimed by Peers).

4) Bound by Magic: The initiate might be required to swear a powerful magical oath or undergo rituals of binding and compulsion, to ensure that the society's secrets will never be revealed to outsiders, or to encourage obedience to a guildmaster, or simply to ensure honesty among the members of a thieves guild. ("When you have sworn this oath, you may never lie to your brother or guildmaster.") This binding need not be entirely negative or compel certain action: the members of a wizard's guild might all gain the ability to detect or read magic on entrance to the guild, and the members of a thieves' guild might all see in the dark like cats.

5) Ceremonial Sacrifice: The initiate might be asked to sacrifice something of great value to join the society: a magical item, an heirloom, blood and hair. The initiates might all be eunuchs, or they might all be sworn to chastity or poverty. These things are surely something the initiate would know ahead of time, but knowing it and roleplaying giving it up are two different things. Make the point clear in the design so that it is clear in play.

6) Divinely Anointed: The initiate must enter some sacred place, undergo a religious ritual, or enter some ordeal with meaning to members of the faith, such as a knight's vigil or a priest's anointing. The candidate might be accepted or rejected by higher powers, or might even be expected to return with a vision, prophecy, or sign blessing his or her entrance into the society. Failure to gain such a sign or vision might be cause to dismiss the candidate permanently or until a new season returns to open the society's doors again.

7) Returned from Darkness: The candidate might need to withstand some drug-induced trauma, long fasting, deliberate poisoning, time spent in isolation or darkness, or other harrowing rituals with some real physical or psychological risk. The candidate might be tempted to spiritual or secular corruption, offered solace, water, food, or other succor that he or she must refuse.

8) Acclaimed by Peers: The candidate must charm, beguile, or work hard enough to win over the founders, leaders, or peers of the organization to vote him or her into the next rank of the society's hierarchy. Failure to convince them means the candidate does not advance, whatever his or her merits.

9) Given a Lock Without a Key: The candidate is given secret knowledge, items, a companion animal, or new magic, and must master them or learn to command them in some fashion. Until he or she solves the riddle of this test, he or she remains an initiate and cannot enter the society fully.

10) Tested and Marked by Fate's Hand: The candidate is thrown into the sight of some powerful entity—a demon, angel, dragon, archmage, or arbiter of some kind—which peers into the initiate's soul and divines whether he or she is worthy to join the order. If the candidate fails, he or she is cast back into the world, rejected, and told to attain some quest or higher understanding before returning. "You have not pleased the Secret Master—go forth and grow in skill and wisdom before you return!" If the candidate succeeds, some mark of the test appears on his or her body: a tattoo, halo, horns, eye color, or badge of some kind that makes it clear that this person is one of that Secret Master's followers.

OPEN, NESTED, AND SECRET SOCIETIES

Craft guilds and thieves' guilds, knightly and priestly orders, mage's colleges, cults, aristocratic clubs, and secret societies: they are all organizations devoted to some form of group action and purpose. But they are not structured the same way when facing the public. The craft guilds keep their methods secret and the wizards hide their arcane lore. The knights might have an open face to the world, but hide their martial techniques and their battlefield commands, banner codes, or special maneuvers and training methods. Priesthoods are known both for a public face and their inner knowledge (see Zeb Cook's essay on Mystery Cults for more on this practice of the ancient world). And cults and secrets societies are certainly secretive in what they do and do not reveal to others, especially if their goals are malevolent.

As a consequence, you'll want to think carefully about any society's public face and its private behavior and trade secrets. The most charitable, honest, and good-hearted society might still have secrets it prefers to keep to its upper echelons, the dirty laundry of its funding, its politics, its careful cultivation of wealthy donors, or its harsh rule against men and their place in the order. Likewise, a cult of animal and human sacrifice might take clear and obvious steps to prevent any public knowledge of its real activities from reaching the public.

As a game designer, you need to consider what secrets your organization has and how it keeps them secret. Peer pressure, economic self interest, shame and guilt, powerful sworn oaths, threats to family or friends, magic compulsions, invisible demonic surveillance: something helps the society keep its inner workings secret.

In general, your society might be open to all, with all its information largely known but for a handful of relatively important details of finance, theology, or magical lore. Or it might be that while admission might be open to all, it might well be closed to all but a handful of the most devout. That is, anyone can join, but not everyone joins the higher echelons, because a society might well have an inner and an outer circle. The inner circle knows the society's true goals, while the outer ring works at some other public goal, perhaps related, perhaps merely a cover. In other words, a society might have multiple levels of involvement and initiation. At each layer deeper, the character becoming initiated into more of its secrets will have an "ah-ha" moment that explains some of the society's previously mysterious behavior. The design goal is to make it clear what information is accessible at what level.

Finally, the purest form of us-vs-them thinking in a society is that all within it keep all its information secret, and those outside it are all viewed as dangerous, unbelievers, threats to the society's greater goals. The everyday word for a society structured this way is a cult, though in some advanced economies the term "Wall Street banking firm" might also apply. If you are designing a vampiric bloodline, a Cthulhu or Mythos cult, or a similar group, consider both the secret lore and the penalties for sharing it carefully. These are likely to become plot points for gamemasters or story points in shared fiction for the setting. It might be wise to specify a particular form of punishment or retribution used against those who betray a cult's secrets: death by drowning for former devotees of Dagon, careful assassination by sunlight or vampiric bleeding for those who cross an ancient clan. If this is part of the world lore, it can be used in adventure and story design down the road.

Status and Command

Once you have determined what the types of entry to the guild or society are, you might consider the hierarchy within the society. The medieval guild master, the archmage, the vampire prince, or the baron who leads an order of knighthood are all fairly straightforward. Who are their primary supporters? How does an initiate move up the ranks from apprentice to page to squire to knight to master-sergeant to commander to marshal? How many ranks are there in this cult, anyway?

Give them some titles, make it clear that the organization acknowledges those titles, and provide the world bible with a sense of who typical members are at each of these ranks. You might not spell out every rank of a weaver's guild that is tangential to your setting, but if your worldbuilding is all about a secret organization of monster hunters, you need to sort out who signs the expense reports when someone goes overboard on ammunition costs while tracking down bigfoot.

Finally, make it clear how many minions a group has, and how widespread its influence is. This might be as simple as assigning a number of members to a thieves' guild, or it might be as complicated as drawing a full chart of sires and ghouls in a city's vampire population. Note, as well, that a small organization need not be less important or less influential than one with thousands of members. The Circle of Eight in the world of Greyhawk was central to that world's lore and mythos, and all its members were important. You might well design a similar small group of power brokers for your next world.

The Need to Design Competitors

One of the less-appreciated aspects of designing a guild or society is designing its rivals, competitors, and nemeses. After all, if it were easy to accomplish their goal, the society would already have done so. Perhaps they are opposed by another particular society, or perhaps their goals are so vile that all right-thinking people oppose them. It's also possible that a nation-state or city-state knows of their plans and opposes them. It might be a single archmage who keeps them in check, or a loose confederation of street urchins and clever adventurers.

It's less important exactly who their opponents are than that they have some opposition who know what they are up to. When player characters join a society, they are also taking on those opponents as their own. This gives a gamemaster an easy source of conflict—as long as the opposition is clearly designed and spelled out for use, with its own goals, hierarchy, tools, spies, and special magical items. Ideally, design a simple membership test that adventurers might be able to pass or subvert to "join" the opposing society in disguise.

Repeated Signs and Recognition

Part of designing any college, guild, or society is designing how it looks to players in your game. I find that the simplest solution is to use a single symbol, article of clothing, code word, or other identifier, and just beat it to death. The Cult of the Red Star uses a red star, the Loyal Guild of Alchemists uses a pelican, the Order of Undying Light uses a sun symbol.

13 Unusual Societies for Worldbuilding

1. An alchemist's guild that really has discovered the fountain of youth

2. An order of inquisitors that can sniff out any lie

3. A brotherhood of minotaurs and rangers who specialize in dungeon delving—and banditry

4. An order of paladins devoted to robbing the rich

5. A group of holy slavers who believe their slaves are better off in servitude

6. A secret society of werewolves or weretigers, intent on gaining power over populations of unsuspecting victims

7. A wizard's guild entirely devoted to becoming liches and clock-wraiths

8. A thieves' guild that performs great works of charity for orphans

9. A dwarven merchant guild that specializes in transport by airship and griffonback

10. A society of singers devoted to maintaining the wall that surrounds the world, keeping hell's legions from overrunning civilization

11. A priestly order devoted to the advancement of knowledge and the mapping of the world

12. A society of women who between them are oracles and prophets, and who seek a world of greater peace and stability

13. An order of assassins devoted to maintaining a secret fortress where lie the roots of Yggdrasil and the Fruits of Knowledge

They are obvious, of course, because they are meant to be easy to recognize at a glance. And for wizard's colleges with their lions, snakes, ravens, and badgers, it becomes easy to use those symbols as shorthand for character and personality. There's nothing wrong with saving yourself the explanation every time: "You see a man with pale hair and a serpent tattoo" is an easier way to communicate that the person the heroes are dealing with is a member of House Slytherin than a more roundabout way of doing it. This works well for all open, public societies to help them recognize each other—and of course, it makes it easy for villains to recognize and target the heroes of the game.

Conclusion

Why go to all this trouble? Because secret societies are both the greatest villains and greatest heroes of a world you build. They outlive any attempt to kill them. The archvillain who is a member of a society can be killed: his followers may live to strike again in vengeance. The hero who falls in the service of the Order of St. Arik knows that though his life is sacrificed, another will pick up the banner and the cause.

Well-designed societies can echo and resonate throughout your worldbuilding. Make them mythic, epic, mysterious, secretive, or vile, but make them clear, organized, active, and passionate about their aims. The results will stir conflict, drama, and great games.

HOW TO WRITE A WORLD BIBLE

(or, How to Keep it All Straight)

Scott Hungerford

When I worked for WizKids Games on brands like *MechWarrior* and *Mage Knight*, I was one of the folks in charge of putting together world bibles—large collections of facts, histories, maps, pictures, character backgrounds, and other bits of information that summarize a game world. Such a document is part of the package that game company management teams use to set up business deals with potential partners. Industry outsiders probably won't read and understand every nuance of a 200,000-word first-draft document. But by providing an organized world bible of information that agents, licensors, and other business folks can flip through quickly, a game company gets that much closer to making the deal.

Additionally, through developing world bibles, my daily process of generating accurate game and website content became much easier. The bible helped to ensure that all the writers, editors, game designers, and artists I worked with had the right answers when it came to the amazing worlds we were building together. While you may have slightly smaller aspirations than writing up a four-hundred page document detailing everything in your game setting before you start to play, for the content editors and continuity managers who work at game companies, these world bibles are the lifeblood of a creative enterprise.

LESSONS OF THE BIG SCREEN: WORLD BIBLES IN ACTION

In order to meet WizKids' business goal of bringing our game brands to Hollywood these world bible documents were an essential part of our strategy. If one of our games got picked up for a movie treatment, the bibles would define exactly what Hollywood could do with our property.

During this process one of the Hollywood producers I talked with wanted to take our capitol city in *Mage Knight* (which magically floated a thousand feet off the ground in our fantasy world) and have it fall out of the sky and be destroyed in spectacular fashion at the climax of the film. It was comparable to Spiderman's New York City being nuked and forcing Peter Parker to move to Los Angeles in future installments of the franchise. If we didn't have things carefully written out in our bibles defining what Hollywood *could* and *could not* do with the property, they would discover loopholes that would undermine all of our work—just like your players will if you don't think through all the details of your worlds!

Whether you're making your own RPG sourcebook, writing short stories, or even working up a wealth of source material for a string of novels, world bibles are a great way to help you organize information about large groups of characters, plots, and monsters into a manageable reference guide. While some us might be lucky enough to see our work on the big screen, for the day-to-day work of generating a great world filled with detail, intrigue, and adventure, a world bible is an important tool for game designers and writers alike.

Living Documents

A good world bible is a living document, rarely staying the same for more than a few weeks at a time. At both WizKids and Wizards of the Coast, the ongoing process of designing new game sets, contracting with authors for new novels, and even the process of adding or removing cards or figures during game testing could trigger new rounds of bible revisions. Specifically at WizKids, the weekly tournaments that we sponsored worldwide drove important parts of the official ongoing storyline. For example, one faction in the game could gain more political control if its players managed to win enough matches at the gaming table. This meant that the content team had to plan for every contingency, and the content bible had to be regularly updated to reflect the outcomes of every storyline tournament.

For your own worldbuilding, a completed first draft of a world bible is a fantastic accomplishment—but you should be prepared to update it as you get new ideas, develop new plots, or especially when your test groups make interesting or erroneous assumptions about your setting. A world bible is never truly done, but you can (and should) save and print dated drafts when you reach certain milestones in your creation so you can easily look back to see how you did things before the last few rounds of edits.

> **Hint:** *A good old fashioned three-ring binder can be a handy and quick resource when designing worlds—and it offers the added feature of allowing you to scribble notes in the margins as things happen during a game or when you wake up in the middle of the night with a new idea.*

World Bible Sections

I break down bibles into three parts—**World, Cast**, and **Appendices**—though creating each section and all the materials within isn't necessarily a linear process. One of the toughest parts about creating a world bible is putting the exact right facts in—and just the facts that matter. It's an easy trap to just start to write and dump the entire kitchen sink into one monstrous document. But if you focus on presenting just the key facts and start to train your brain to think about the specific details that matter rather than just jotting down everything that comes to mind, you'll come out with a great resource at the end.

Section One: The World

World Name: Even if you don't have a final name in mind when you start the project, choose a placeholder name up front that summarizes the theme and mood of your world. If you don't choose one, I guarantee your players will!

Introduction: Create a one-page summary, a foundational five-paragraph essay detailing what the game world is about. In my experience this will likely be the first part of the bible you write, and will be the last document you touch when everything is said and done. Be sure to summarize not only the world and characters in this page, but talk about the central point of conflict in the game world in detail as well.

> *Hint: The first time an important vocabulary word appears in your world bible, such as the name of a city or a bit of new terminology, bold it so you can see at a glance if it is the first time the word is mentioned.*

Races and Cultures: Whether mortal or monstrous, initially limit yourself to one page per race and/or culture in this section. Start with a one-line summary at the top of the page, and then flesh out the rest of the page with information on languages (both spoken and written) and how factors such as illiteracy, customs, taboos, and religion ties in with daily life. Be sure to think about political or religious factions within each racial or cultural group, and how those mainstream or splinter movements might affect the future of each kingdom, nation, or dictatorship.

> *Hint: Lifespan is one of the more telling indicators for how a culture thinks and thrives, as a race of Dwarves that lives 30 years at best is going to have a very different outlook and philosophy than Elves that live for thousands of years.*

Magic and Technology: First write up a one-page summary of how magic, science, and physics works within the world. Once that's done, devote one or two pages to each category of science or magic that you find interesting. Be as creative as you like, but don't fall into the trap of focusing only on how your world is different from the real world. In your setting, imagine daily life for those living at the lowest level of income as well as for those who are very wealthy. How does magic and science affect what they eat, how they travel, and how they earn their daily bread? Once you have the basics down for how the average person lives daily life, then you can dive into how the upper and lower classes deal with magic and technology in greater depth.

Fleshing Out Races and Cultures: Once the previous two sections are finished, go back and write up a one-pager for each group that utilizes science or magic in their culture. As a good example, did you know that the Aztecs used wheels in their children's toys—but didn't use wheels for transporting goods from place to place? (It's because they didn't have any domesticated animals that were capable of pulling carts.) It's these little facts that can really make a culture interesting, and will give your players a sense of wonder when they play in a world they've never visited before.

Currency and Economy: Give yourself a few pages to work out the details of coins, currencies, payment systems, barter, and the relative prices for food, materials, weapons, gifts, and services within the world. You don't need to finalize every last price in the marketplace in advance—but knowing whether a gold coin is called a carpa or a therpa is just as handy as knowing that one of these coins buys a cup of coffee and the other one buys a sizable estate in the countryside. Each culture will likely have its own form of currency, and they may have a trade currency they use specifically with their neighbors. Whether it's in the form of hard metal or sea shells, or written deeds of what is owed and owned, a culture's currency defines them just as much as their style of government.

Section Two: The Cast

The Cast of Characters: Next you want to write up the character-by-character breakdowns, not just of your bartenders, bad guys, and friendly fixers, but who the key rulers and masterminds are who run things, either publicly or behind the scenes. Initially, force yourself to one page per character, though most will require more space later on as you outline their age, parentage, social standing, genealogy, family curses, business endeavors, romantic interests (both welcomed and unrequited), and other such information.

> **Hint:** *I'd suggest using italics to note "secret information" in your world bible so you can keep track of all those pesky conspiracies with greater ease.*

Monsters and Menaces: If your world has antagonists, whether dragons or giants, giant ant colonies or sentient plagues, be sure to include a zoological summary of each kind of entity, one page per type. Above and beyond game statistics and the obligatory picture, provide a concise summary of what (or who) they eat, where they live, and what drives them to continually act against the races and cultures of your world. With a little bit of work you can create an interesting menagerie of creatures and critters, both mundane and supernatural, which will add even more flavor to your game world.

Section 3: The Appendices

Appendix A: Timelines and Histories: Be sure to include a timeline of events in your world bible, whether dating back thousands of years or just a few months since a certain historical event or disaster happened. Initially, just include the big events, then be prepared to insert, remove, and update entries as you—and others—continue the creative work.

Later on, as your world evolves and more pieces get added to it, you may find yourself with new events that require you to detail out sub-sections of the timeline. Whether by running multiple gaming groups or, as in WizKids' case, having new comics, promotions and characters being continually added to the brand, you'll need to leave enough space in your history to allow for the expansion of your world.

Also, giving major events a name (Day of the Black Rose) or having holidays publicly or secretly celebrated (Dead King's Solstice) can be a great way to continually remind players that it's only been a few years since King Ferdinand was assassinated—and that their homeland has been subjugated by an enemy king ever since.

Appendix B: Cartography: Even if it's just an untidy sheet of ruled paper with a few scrawl marks, include a map with key borders, coastlines, mountain ranges and landmarks clearly pointed out. You don't have to be able to draw to create a simple map, and there are a lot of real-world maps online that you can pull inspiration from. You will likely continue to update your maps as you continue your work, so don't feel ashamed to add or remove sections as you go. (See Jonathan Roberts' essay, "Here Be Dragons" for insight into creating maps.)

Appendix C: Glossary: At the very end of your document, maintain a glossary of key terms. While you should eventually have a sizable alphabetized dictionary covering every last person, monster, spell, and place in your world, at the very beginning of this section be sure to feature a one-page entry that covers the thirty or forty essential words and terms the player or reader needs to know.

BRINGING IT ALL TOGETHER

If you're adding to your world bible after every game, then making upgrades to your manuscript after every session should work out pretty well. But if you're building a world from scratch, then I have a couple of other ideas to help you assemble your masterpiece!

For the initial generation and assembly of concepts and ideas, I've put whiteboards, bulletin boards, and chalkboards to good use over the years. However, there are lots of different programs today that let you sort your ideas in non-linear fashions, almost like organizing index cards on a tabletop.

For myself I've painted twenty feet of wall in my office with a brand of magnetic paint, so I can stick magnets and index cards to it by the hundreds in whatever order I please. This way, as I make notes on index cards, scraps of paper, or diner napkins, I can stick them up on my wall until it's time to sort it all out. Including question cards is also a good idea, especially if you don't know an answer just yet but need to figure one out before you start.

PLAYING IN SOMEONE ELSE'S BACKYARD

Worldbuilding in Licensed Worlds

Janna Silverstein

I t starts with a compelling universe. For me, it started with *Star Trek*, then *Star Wars*. Once we're fans, those of us with a creative streak want to go play in those worlds we grow to love. Some of us turn to fan fiction. Some of us become authors creating our own worlds. And some of us, once we have the skills and the knowledge, begin to work in beloved universes created by others.

But entry is neither easy nor cheap.

My first foray into working in other universes was during my time as an editor at Spectra, Bantam Books' science fiction imprint. It started with my working on the reissues of the very first *Star Trek* novels ever printed. That project was at the shallow end of licensed work. The books had already been published. They merely needed new cover images to freshen them up for a new generation of readers. Thus was I introduced to the licensing department at Paramount Pictures. During my time working with the good folks there, I began to truly understand the requirements of licensed work: the approvals, the contract details, the protective approach toward beloved properties.

But it wasn't until I started editing *Star Wars* novels and books based on DC Comics that I began to understand the breadth and depth of the difficulty and the challenges involved in creating new material for known, beloved, even flagship properties. Once I moved to the other side of the desk, working at Wizards of the Coast on *Magic: the Gathering* and WizKids on *MechWarrior* as a licensor rather than a licensee, I got the full 360-degree view: why companies choose the designers and writers they choose, the tools they may (or may not) provide to make that work possible, why and how they protect their properties, and why the bar to entry for creative types is so high.

HEY YOU KIDS, GET OFFA MY LAWN!

Let's start by talking about terms: property, licensor, licensee. A property is a creative conception, for example, *Dungeons & Dragons, Greyhawk, Eragon,* Harry Potter, and so forth. A licensor is the entity which owns the property. A licensee is an entity which purchases the right to produce material based on a licensor's property. This relationship is usually governed by a strict and binding contract that sets out rules about the material to be produced, the approvals and permissions required, not to mention the money involved, and much more.

If there's no agreement between a licensor and a design studio, a game company, or a game designer producing new material based on the licensor's property, then it's against the law to do so. It's copyright infringement. The creative entity can be prosecuted if the licensor chooses to pursue that route. (That said, the rules for fan fiction have loosened up considerably since the early days. Fanfic is ubiquitous on the web now, and some licensors don't pursue prosecution because most fan writers aren't trying to sell their work, and because fanfic fans the flames of customer enthusiasm, which is ultimately good for business. If they do try to sell their work, however—and some have tried—and the licensor finds out, they're in for a world of hurt. This applies not just to fan fiction but to games and all other sorts of derivative works. Better to be a law-abiding citizen. Seriously.)

Of course, there are two other cases with regard to producing material that's not contracted for with a licensor that are worth mentioning. The first is the sanctioned approach, one that some game publishers have taken and used to great effect to find new writers. I'll talk about that a little later. The second is the idea of producing unrequested material to submit to a licensor with the idea that they'll acquire it once they see it. Let's get this out of the way right now: This idea is a pipe dream. The reasons will become clear shortly.

Why are licensors so strict about protecting their property? Because it's their lifeblood. The money made from big-name properties is often what keeps a company in business. It's the reason big companies seek to extend the life of the copyright on flagship characters and worlds. If the property isn't protected, that financial engine will run out of gas. They may also lose the legal right to call the property their own. We all want to be paid for our good work; we deserve it. Legal protection and prosecution is the way businesses—licensors—sometimes must do it.

INVITATIONS TO PLAY

Still, licensors want to expand and exploit their properties so they work with licensees to create books, games, toys, and so on—products that may not be the things they are most expert at producing. How do you get that gig? How do you keep that gig? What's involved?

I talked with Mike Selinker, founder of Lone Shark Games, about that. He's worked with an enviable catalog of licensors and properties: Disney, Harry Potter, Marvel Comics, *BattleTech,* and *Pokémon,* to name just a few. He gave an answer to that question that sets the bar pretty high. In the context of meeting with J.K. Rowling's company about Harry Potter, he asked to meet first with the creative team rather than the business types. He said, "We were the best creatives in the world in our respective realms, and so we forged a bond about our mutually interactive skill sets. That's how you make someone entrust their world to you. Of course, you have to actually be the best creatives in the world at what you do first."

Remember how I said that entry is neither easy nor cheap? This is what I was talking about. Working in a licensed world usually requires experience—proven chops and powerful results. When I worked on the *Star Wars* novels at Bantam, we brought in only authors who had track records: they had already produced finished work, had a record of good sales, and had shown a strong work ethic over and over again. Whether we're talking games or novels, that's what licensors are looking for—in a word, professionals who can deliver. Their properties are world-class, and they want the related, licensed products to be in the same category. "The licensor is looking to be blown away," Selinker says. "They get mediocre all the time."

Earlier I mentioned one way that less-experienced creatives could break into working in licensed worlds. This is one corner of the licensing business where the game industry has been smart and proactive. Some property owners do accept unsolicited work for review. *Kobold* Quarterly, for example, accepts submissions based on the *Pathfinder RPG* and the Golarion setting. But here's the rub: if they like it and want to publish it, the Golarion material still has to be reviewed and accepted by Paizo Publishing, which owns the Golarion setting. The licensor has the last word, and often the word is "no." A sale is a rare occurrence. But it does happen. Occasionally.

PLAYING BY THE RULES

So, you've got the gig: the owner of *Aqualung Airship* wants to work with you to create a game based on their world. And you, the licensee, ask the first, most obvious question: Can I see the world bible? You want to know everything that the licensor knows about the universe, and you want to be sure you're getting it right. Even if you're a die-hard fan who has followed *Aqualung Airship* from its inception, it's a stone-cold guarantee that there's information you don't have and, presumably, a bible—that tome of secrets reserved for licensed creatives—will reveal it all. Scott Hungerford talks about what a world bible is and how to put one together in his chapter, "How to Write a World Bible." It's a practical guide to keeping the facts straight on any universe—and apparently one that many licensors could use.

The truth, says Keith R. A. DeCandido, is that "there is almost never a bible, and when there is, it's more often than not useless." DeCandido knows whereof he speaks. He's an award-winning author who's worked with properties including *World of Warcraft, Dungeons & Dragons, Resident Evil, Star Trek*, and *Doctor Who*, just to name a few. "And you will almost never get a list of what you can and can't do," he continues. "You find out what you can't do when you try it and they tell you no."

Selinker told me the same thing. But he added a crucial point: "The one thing the licensor is guaranteed to be good at is knowing what's 'too far.' The goal, then, is to expand their comfort base with everything that you can imagine fitting into that box."

And that's a challenge. Without a bible, the licensee has to take what they know and extrapolate what could work, which means pushing the boundaries and exploring new territory. "You can't be afraid to push up against that wall," Selinker says. "They want you to. They may not tell you that's what they want, but they do. Their job is to rein you in. You can't come 'pre-reined.'"

One way to expand boundaries and build out an already-established world is to use locations and concepts where the original medium can't go by virtue of inherent limitations. DeCandido says, "My Leverage novel involves wild animals, which is something a TNT show doesn't have the budget for." Similarly, in a novel he can take his characters to locations where a TV show might not be able to afford to travel. Games can take characters not just to other locations on Earth, but under the sea, off the planet, even to alternate universes, as long as it makes sense in the context of the original property—until the licensor says, "That's too far." The job of the licensed creative, then, is to find that darkened, unexplored corner of a universe and shine the light in to show what's possible. Game mechanics are a great way to do this, reflecting the way a universe works, but revealing some truth to it at the same time[2].

One thing is certain: Whether or not a licensor has a world bible, they've given great thought to what will and won't work for a property, whether because it's a TV show with a tightly-woven plot thread planned out at the beginning of each season or because it's a game with a tournament structure that directly influences sanctioned storytelling. If that's the case, then acceptance and approval of licensed material becomes a trial in how good a licensee is at shaping material to the requirements and—more importantly—the restrictions of the world. This is one of the reasons so many licensors won't look at unsolicited material from unknown writers and designers. No matter how clever or how original, if the material doesn't fit into the plan, it can't be used. Furthermore, any licensor who looks at unsolicited submissions could open themselves up to legal action if they produce stories or products that even vaguely resemble that unsolicited work. When I said earlier that selling work to a licensor without a license to produce it was a pipe dream, these were the reasons I was talking about.

I'VE PLAYED HERE BEFORE . . . OR HAVE I?

Despite a need to not pre-rein oneself, DeCandido still approaches each universe with some caution. If you're working on a property that you really know and love, there's a danger. "The hardest thing is to resist the temptation to fanwank yourself into insensibility—doing that thing you always wanted to see the characters do, and forcing them to do it whether or not your plot actually calls for it." So it's one thing to have the cultural literacy required to work on a property; it's another thing to overlay that literacy and enthusiasm with a professional's eye for what will and won't work, and why.

Finding that sweet spot is a skill that needs to be developed. At the same time,

---

[2] See Colin McComb's excellent chapter, "Basic Combat Systems for Tabletop Games" in the *Complete Kobold Guide to Game Design* for great thought and detail on game mechanics that reflect story elements.

some universes come with a history that's deep and broad, like the Marvel or BattleTech universes, and are full of territory for expansion without encountering the kind of dangers we're discussing. Such enormous scope provides the creative with great freedom and tons of possibilities. The BattleTech/MechWarrior property, for example, is nearly 30 years old. Its story is galactic in scope and spans nearly 1,200 years of history, and has manifested itself in RPGs, board, computer, and card games, more than 100 novels, and a TV series. There's a lot of room to move in such a world. Pick a planet from the map that's been mentioned only once or twice in campaigns or other properties, create a likely scenario, and go from there—provided, of course, that the licensor approves.

Of working with Marvel, Selinker says, "That's a company that completely understands that its characters express themselves in hundreds of different formats, and that each format has different needs. They also have by far the richest environment ever created. . . . On marvel.com, I can read ten thousand comic books for a single subscription fee of $60. . . . You can immerse yourself in the world because they make the world available to you."

DeCandido says this is key: "Whether you're coming to it cold or know it like the back of your hand, it's always best to immerse yourself in the universe in whatever way is best, to have it all swimming around in your brain as you sit down to write." So even without a bible, most properties are their own resources. Your ability to absorb and produce material appropriate for a world depends upon your capacity for research and synthesis.

THEIR RULES . . . AND YOUR RULES

If licensors have boundaries, licensees should, too. Even if you're working on a universe you love, as a creative you need to know when to hold the line and when to walk away.

On holding the line, Selinker is talking about a specific phenomenon he's seen over time. "Sometimes, your licensor wants *your* job," he says. "We game designers have all the fun. Day after day, they're looking at mediocre expressions of the thing they own, struggling to stay awake through pitch meeting after pitch meeting. The project you're working on with them is their creative outlet. The licensor that wants to design your game for you conveniently forgets that you've had years of training to get good at what you do. They have not. But since they approve everything, they have this human nature thing of liking what they come up with. The trick is to not be surprised about it, and not get mad about it. But you have to stand your ground. Your job is to give the licensing company what they want, not your licensing *contact* what they want.

"That said, a completely hands-off licensor is no good either. If they give you no feedback at all, just simply trusting you to do whatever it is you do, then your game can completely miss the mark. It's a balance. Everything's a balance."

And sometimes, no matter how much you want it, you have to step away from work. Knowing when to do that is the sign of a true professional. DeCandido says that he's only walked away from projects in specific circumstances. "The only time

I've stepped away from a project is by never saying yes in the first place. I've done that a few times, and those instances were usually cases where it wasn't going to work logistically—too tight a deadline, too little money, both—and I just wouldn't be able to complete the project."

Selinker has walked away from projects when the project itself wasn't right. "I got asked to work on an NFL card game. I love football, and can quote chapter and verse about players, seasons, rules, everything. I listened to what the design team had done. They had abstracted out the offensive line, the defensive line, yardage, and penalties. I said, 'Guys, I would love to work on an NFL game, but I can't help you. The things I need a football game to do can't fit in the space you've given it.' And I regretfully walked off the project."

Reflecting on Playtime

Worldbuilding in licensed universes, obviously, comes with a lot of baggage: oversight by licensors, understanding the rules of someone else's universe, finding the right place to set your piece of the larger picture. It also comes with a pretty high bar to entry. Most of the skills discussed in the rest of this volume certainly are applicable to the process: understanding the setting, its assets, and its limitations. Your licensor can be either your collaborator or your adversary; collaboration is always preferable, because your licensor also holds the keys to the kingdom—a playground full of equipment we all want to play on. You've just got to earn the right to play, and with the right attitude and skill set, you will.

THE LIMITS OF DESIGN

Wolfgang Baur

G ame design is about making decisions within constraints. There are only so many pages to describe a world, and that means only so many pages and so much art. Even if you distribute a setting as a PDF or video game download, the issue is still there: only so much time to write, playtest, rewrite, test again, edit, proof. Only so many dollars for art and maps. So one of the greatest challenges for game design is to provide as much useful, entertaining, inspiring, and worthy material as possible, given that it can never be a complete description of a world.

There are two ways that game designs generally attempt to solve this problem. Novels generally follow one of them.

PLEASE FANS AND STILL FAIL

The first method, and the one most commonly attempted in RPGs in particular, is the attempt to be all things to all people. Monte Cook talks about this in his chapter, "Kinds of Worldbuilding," the need to provide three variant jungles, many dungeons to delve, a canvas for the game master and players to choose from. This buffet includes all possible player races, typically at least three and often a dozen non-human races in a fantasy world, the sort of variety that makes Barsoom or Earth look relatively humanoid-poor by comparison.

The goal for these settings is called kitchen sink design (KSD), and it is an abdication of design responsibility. Instead of making choices for what to highlight and what to leave out, the objective of KSD is to provide every possible option, a terrain of every flavor, nations and wilderness to suit every possible adventure that a GM might run, cultures, societies, and religions by the yard and by the ton. Everything a gamer *might* want should be included. The ideal kitchen-sink world should fulfill all possible gaming desires and cover all subgenres, periods, and peccadilloes.

This solution means that none of the places, cultures, or races are given as much room as they might be if the worldbuilder made the harder choices. Instead, the worldbuilding takes a turn into what a software builder might call "feature creep". Instead of three core races, there are 12 or 15. Instead of 20 major kingdoms we have 100. More is always assumed to be better.

Surprisingly, this "garbage pizza" or "everything bagel" approach does please a significant portion of the audience. Sort of. For a while.

WHY THE KITCHEN SINK MESS SUCCEEDS

To my eyes, the attempt to do kitchen sink design is always futile. It is an abandonment of a designer's responsibility in favor of selling out to the marketing department. The goal is to provide something for everyone and to bring in the largest possible audience. That way lies madness, because human preferences and subjective likes and dislikes will always vary across a wide, wide spectrum. Even if you please 95% of the audience, that vocal 5% will complain about the lack of rules for aasimar, or the lack of a decent matriarchy, or the lack of a gay prince or a couatl princess.

There's a good business reason why setting sprawl is often baked in at the start, and I'm sure you know what it is. The more individual races and nations and cults that exist in an RPG world, the more game supplements a publisher can provide. For example, *Vampire: The Masquerade* started with a core set of two major clans and about a dozen bloodlines, and it has added more over the years. I'd argue that this splintering and increase in factions was good for business (more clanbooks, yeah!), but bad for the community in the long term. (I gotta learn about *another* prince and *another* secret history and set of powers? Ugh, I'm out.) The encyclopedic nature of worldbuilding is a golden business opportunity. But this is both a weakness and a strength.

The strength is that with "something for everyone" your audience is, possibly, larger and you can please everyone for a while. Gamers lobby for their favorites, and the publishers produce the most popular supplements. Over time, everyone wants official emphasis on the content that interests them. Publishers become stuck supporting the less popular elements, for the sake of completeness. To a certain degree, this reflects the RPG hobby as a collector's hobby rather than a game-playing hobby. Players want the full set of the clanbooks, class splatbooks, or kingdom books. They may really play with just one of them, but it's fun to read all that detail about the setting. The urge for completeness has given us the *Silmarillion* and *Unfinished Tales* and 12 volumes of the *History of Middle-earth*. It has given us 50 or 100 volumes of the Forgotten Realms.

And that's a real strength. People who buy and read setting books are enjoying the RPG hobby without engaging in it the same way that players do. You can see that both types of audiences exist, and there are times when a roleplayer may be looking for a new group when reading adventures and supplements is a great way to keep in touch with the hobby.

The Death of the Kitchen Sink

At the same time, this all-things-to-all-gamers approach is self-defeating. Instead of presenting a smaller number of locales in detail, it skims over dozens or scores of different worlds all mushed together. None of them necessarily make a lot of sense as neighbors, none of them are well-designed as nations or useful for gameplay—but they provide a lot of variety and novelty. That novelty alone is considered reason enough to provide more acreage, more slightly-different humanoids, and more gods in an ever-growing pantheon. This satisfies the human itch for the new and the fleetingly interesting—at the cost of making the setting less and less internally coherent.

The alternative is to do a setting with focus. With emphasis on the most prominent, most compelling, and richest sections of your world, you increase the chance that gamers will care about the setting rather than grazing it lightly with an emphasis on browsing for the outré or the unusual. They might grapple with the material when it covers a small nation in depth and a large nation lightly and swiftly. The reader will want more material on a great setting—but you don't have to provide it all at once and in depth. The goal of worldbuilding with focus is to deliver the goods in a coherent way over time.

So resist the urge for completeness and categorization and a wild open volume of material. Make the material you create matter. At a certain point, the kitchen sink approach collapses of its own weight, and there are simply too many tomes of setting material for any new player to see them as anything but an incredible obstacle to learning the world.

The publisher reaction is usually to release a new edition or hit the story reset button in some fashion. "Here's the world, but new!" is the rallying cry. It is accessible again for new gamers! But at the same time, the fans who mastered the old version of the setting may easily become alienated or annoyed. Tampering with the core expectations, characters, and joys of the setting is always exciting, and always dangerous. It may become too tempting to ignore the business proposition of setting the core book to the same audience again, but if a publisher hits the reset button often enough, fans give up on it. The world they first fell in love with has changed, and the fans find a shiny new world next door to explore.

Core Worldbuilding vs. Dead Worlds

The opposite approach to the kitchen sink is "fire-and-forget" or "limited canon" worldbuilding. This is what happens with most indie RPGs, since many of them are entirely self-contained and never produce a supplement. It's also the case with RPG settings such as Al-Qadim, Dark*Matter, or the latest version of Dark Sun, which were produced as limited-run books, without any promise to the reader about future support beyond a year or so.

I find it quite telling that indie and story gamers find nothing unusual in an RPG that delivers its setting in 32 pages or 100 pages, and that includes all the rules to play and all the setting needed to play. These story games assume that the game is four hours long or perhaps a half-dozen sessions for a "long" game. There's no need to provide a lot of reference material to produce a playable roleplaying game. It is a habit and a tradition grown from the fantasy novels of Tolkein and from the traditions of Greyhawk and the Realms. But it is by no means a requirement of the form.

THE MIDGARD SOLUTION

The goal for Midgard was emphatically not a kitchen sink. There's seven major regions covering a variety of cultures and appealing to the most likely styles of play, but some things just don't really exist. Elves and halflings are minor races. The 50 kingdoms are built on themes from the core fantasy inheritance, and yet the world is not itching for 50 splatbooks to explore it all. The pantheon is expressly designed to resist the sprawling deification of every theme, domain, or human concern (see the chapter "Designing a Pantheon" for more on this subject). The world has focus because it does draw a line. The original design spec was even more constrained than the final version, but yes, I gave some ground to please the inevitable demand for encyclopedic reams of options.

I may yet regret that, but for the most part the solution was to deliver those variants (halflings, for instance) as a small and largely obscure PC race. They are playable, but they are not famous, not central to the setting, and can easily be ignored. Their role in party dynamics is largely taken over by kobolds, a race that does figure more prominently in the worldbuilding, the lore, and the dynamics of the setting (dragon-rich as it is).

The goal is explicitly to present a rich world that does not need 20 supplements to prosper.

Perhaps this is a foolish business decision. But I think it is a wise creative decision to keep the setting accessible and to avoid the encyclopedic sprawl and steep learning curve that inevitably dogs settings after a few years of development. There's richness and depth here, and plenty of time to expand on the elements that people find most appealing.

I hope that adventures and a smaller stream of support material will keep Midgard out of the kitchen sink category, while still making it accessible to gamers who want a setting they can learn quickly and play the way they want.

It's a bit of a shame that a setting designed to resist splatbook sprawl is the exception rather than the rule. This seems to be more the case in mainstream fantasy

INDIE AND STORY FOCUS

The existence of indie games provides an interesting counterweight to the encyclopedic kitchen sink settings. They are featherweights in word count and in options, often providing a single locale, highly constrained player character options, and tell a single story or a primary kind of story. For instance *Fiasco* delivers an experience in which Murphy's Law rules, things fail horribly, and that's the entertainment. If you want to play it with a different setting or culture, buy another playset—usually in an entirely different world or genre.

settings, though, and there is one other place where worldbuilding is tighter and much more focused, namely indie games and story games (see sidebar).

CONCLUSION

Worldbuilding can be an enjoyable hobby for its own sake, and many game designers still treat it as a way to explore various social or narrative issues in dozens of environments and cultures, spinning out ever-greater quantities of material for an existing setting. My own view is that this can be enjoyable but is ultimately self-defeating, as the best worlds are memorable without requiring a 12-volume set for beginners. Kitchen sink design, then, feeds fan desires in an unhealthy way, and ultimately abdicates the primary function of game design—to make choices that focus the game experience—by emphasizing all choices equally and providing narrative and playspace for both popular and niche interests.

CONTRIBUTOR BIOS

KEITH BAKER is best known for creating the Eberron Campaign Setting for *Dungeons & Dragons* and the storytelling card game *Gloom*. He's produced a host of games, novels, and RPG supplements, including the novel *The Queen of Stone* and the card game *Cthulhu Fluxx*. Currently he's hard at work on a brand new world. Keith can be found online at Keith-Baker.com, or on Twitter as @HellcowKeith.

WOLFGANG BAUR is the founder of Kobold Press and a long-time designer and editor in the field. His writing is firmly in the mainstream of RPG design, with credits on *Dungeons & Dragons, Alternity, Call of Cthulhu,* and the *Pathfinder RPG*. He has edited *Dragon* Magazine, *Dungeon* Magazine, and *Kobold Quarterly* magazine. The periodicals business is where he learned the value of repetition and the usefulness of dealing with difficult freelancers by keeping a straight razor in his boot.

Wolfgang is known for his world-building in the fan-favorite "Kingdom of the Ghouls" adventure as well as placing the foundation stones for Thassilon, Qadira, the River Kingdoms, and most of the Storval Plateau in Golarion, the core setting of the Pathfinder Campaign. As his worldbuilding talents have grown, he has likewise upgraded his boot armament to simple two-shot Derringers.

The Midgard setting is Wolfgang's third complete published world, following on the Origins-nominated-but-obscure *Kromosome* SF setting and the Origins-award winning *Dark*Matter* campaign (with Monte Cook). He enjoys writing travelogues of imaginary places and doesn't plan to stop anytime soon.

DAVID "ZEB" COOK Videogame and RPG designer, along with occasional writer – has been mysteriously employed making games for 30+ years. In that time he's taken a swing at most every kind of game except sports, so there's still another challenge left. Starting at TSR, he was the designer of AD&D 2nd Edition, *Oriental Adventures, Planescape,* and a slew of modules and other things. Since leaving TSR, he has been in videogames working numerous titles including *Fallout 2, Lords of the Realm III,* and *City of Villains*. He is currently working the upcoming Elder Scrolls Online MMO for Zenimax Online. He hopes someday to be an Elder of Gaming, mostly by living long enough.

MONTE COOK has worked as a professional writer for almost 25 years. As a fiction writer, he has published numerous short stories, two novels, a comic book series from Marvel, and has attended the Clarion West SF&F writer's workshop. As a nonfiction writer, he has published the *Skeptic's Guide to Conspiracies*. Most notably, as a game designer, he has written hundreds of books and articles. Best known for D&D 3rd edition, he also designed *Heroclix, Ptolus, Arcana Evolved, Monte Cook's World of Darkness,* and many more. His new project is *Numenera*, a science fantasy game set in the far future coming out from Monte Cook Games. In his spare time, he investigates the paranormal as one of the Geek Seekers. Check out his work at montecook.com.

JEFF GRUBB is a veteran game designer, author and worldbuilder. He was one of the co-founders of the *Dragonlance* setting, a co-creator of the *Forgotten Realms* setting, and has built campaigns ranging from the *Al-Qadim* to *Spelljammer* and has contributed to the recently-published *Midgard*, from Open Design. His novels include seminal works for *Magic: The Gathering, Warcraft, Guild Wars*, and *Star Wars*. He has been most recently helping build the world of *Guild Wars 2* from ArenaNet. Interestingly, his training is as a civil engineer, and he has gone from building structures to building universes. He likes to dream big.

SCOTT HUNGERFORD has worked for Wizards of the Coast and WizKids as a game designer and content editor for card, board, and miniatures games. He eventually transitioned to the electronic gaming industry as a designer for casual games, MMOs, and strategy games for the PC, Xbox, iPad, and Facebook. In his spare time, he gallivants around the countryside with his wife, or works on photography, music, or other artistic projects. He typically writes one to three full-length novels a year, often longhand. Having written epic fantasy, paranormal, urban fantasy, and a number of YA manuscripts, he's that much closer to achieving his dream: seeing one of his books on a bookstore shelf!

CHRIS PRAMAS is an award-winning game designer, writer, and publisher. He is best known as the designer of the *Dragon Age* RPG and *Warhammer Fantasy Roleplay*, 2nd Edition, and as the founder and President of Green Ronin Publishing. He has been a creative director at Wizards of the Coast and Flying Lab Software, and was the lead writer on Vigil Games' *Dark Millennium Online*, the Warhammer 40K MMO. Green Ronin continues to thrive under his leadership, publishing games like *Mutants & Masterminds, DC Adventures*, and *A Song of Ice and Fire Roleplaying*.

JONATHAN ROBERTS grew up in a medieval farmhouse between a ruined castle and a Bronze Age fort. Jon has illustrated maps of real and imaginary worlds for a wide range of clients from Wizards of the Coast and IDW comics, to George R.R. Martin's Lands of Ice and Fire and the World of Midgard for Open Design. Along with his own illustration work for books and games, Jon has curated gallery shows of maps by illustrators around the world.

KEN SCHOLES is a renegade GM turned writer. After nearly a decade of worldbuilding through short stories, he's now wrapping up his five volume series, *The Psalms of Isaak*, critically acclaimed as "a towering storytelling tour de force" by Publishers Weekly.

Ken cut his teeth on the TSR gaming craze of the early 80s, creating diverse campaigns within the *Dungeons & Dragons, Gamma World, Top Secret* and *Boot Hill* RGPs to play with his friends. Ken's eclectic background includes time spent as a label gun repairman, a sailor who never sailed, a soldier who commanded a desk, a preacher (he got better), a nonprofit executive, a musician and a government procurement analyst. He has a degree in history from Western Washington University and is a winner of France's Prix Imaginales for best foreign novel and of the Writers of the Future contest.

Ken is a native of the Pacific Northwest and makes his home in Saint Helens, Oregon, where he lives with his wife and twin daughters. You can learn more about Ken by following him on Facebook or visiting www.kenscholes.com.

JANNA SILVERSTEIN has worked for more than two decades in the publishing industry. As an acquisitions editor for Bantam Spectra, she had the privilege of working with authors including Raymond E. Feist, Katharine Kerr, and Michael A. Stackpole among others, and working on properties including Star Trek, Star Wars, Aliens, Superman, and Batman. She also worked at Wizards of the Coast on *Magic: the Gathering* fiction and at WizKids on fiction based on *Mage Knight* and *MechWarrior*, both in print and online. For Open Design, she edited *The KOBOLD Guide to Game Design, vol 3: Tools & Techniques*, and the ENnie Award-winning *Complete KOBOLD Guide to Game Design*. Along with Open Design, she has edited projects for Night Shade Books and Pocketbooks. Her own writing has appeared in *Asimov's Science Fiction, Orson Scott Card's Intergalactic Medicine Show, 10Flash Quarterly,* and in the anthologies *Swordplay* and *The Trouble With Heroes*, among others. Though she'll always be a New Yorker, she lives in Seattle with a princessy calico cat, many books, and a respectable—if somewhat smaller—collection of games.

STEVE WINTER began working for TSR, Inc. in 1981, and has managed to make a living from D&D ever since. His many roles have included editor, designer, novel author, creative director of AD&D, web producer, editor-in-chief of *Dragon* and *Dungeon* online, and community manager. His current gig is as an independent writer and game designer in Seattle. Steve's reflections and speculations on D&D, RPGs, and game design can be read at www.howlingtower.com, or you can follow him 140 characters at a time on Twitter as @StvWinter.

18466234R00068

Printed in Great Britain
by Amazon

MARTHA GRAHAM

Choreography and Dance
1999, Vol. 5, Part 2, p. iii
Photocopying permitted by license only

© 1999 OPA (Overseas Publishers Association) N.V.
Published by license under
the Harwood Academic Publishers imprint,
part of The Gordon and Breach Publishing Group.
Printed in Singapore.

Contents

Choreography and Dance
1999, Vol. 5, Part 2, p. v
Photocopying permitted by license only

Foreword: A Poem

Martha did die
What to write
What to dance

The messenger has arrived
standing at the threshold, his presence announced by a
terrible silence. An angel's wings folding to his back
not awaiting an invitation he descends to all fours and
like the tiger or the wolf stalks his prey

It is only afterward, days or weeks, that we finally hear
the bell and feel the solemn thud of the funeral cadence.

Donlin Foreman[1]

---

[1] Donlin Foreman, *Out of Martha's House*, page 16.

Choreography and Dance
1999, Vol. 5, Part 2, pp. 1–5
Photocopying permitted by license only

Introduction

Alice Helpern

Writing a book with a title *Everything You Always Wanted to Know About...* was somewhat of a fad in America's publishing world. The responsibility of filling this journal about the choreographer, Martha Graham, led to similar temptation, soon resisted.

In the years since Graham's death in 1991 a number of books and articles have been published by and about Graham. The core of this issue came from a 1994 Symposium at which several members of Graham's "Dance Group" from the 1930s and 1940s talked about their experiences. The Symposium, jointly sponsored by the Brooklyn Academy of Music and the New School for Social Research, was designed to accompany a season entitled RADICAL GRAHAM, part of the Next Wave Festival of the Brooklyn Academy of Music. Graham's work was no longer considered radical in 1994 but the emphasis that season was to rediscover what was revolutionary about Graham in her pioneering years.

The panelists whose words are published here were well into their seventies and eighties when they spoke, and yet they made the time come vividly alive. During the day the audience had the opportunity to see those dancers perform on film in footage taken in the 1930s and 1940s. Sadly, shortly after the symposium, Erick Hawkins died. Those who listened to him realized that this was, perhaps, to be his last public appearance. In 1996 Dorothy Bird died; Marie Marchowsky followed in 1997. These dancers who helped to shape dance history in the twentieth century were generous in helping us comprehend the enormity of Graham's contribution to dance.

Insights into Graham's creative process were confined primarily to those who worked with her in the studio. For this reason the dancers who shared that privilege are enormously important as primary sources. Thus Helen McGehee's piece, "An Opportunity Lost," which focuses on the making of *Clytemnestra*, is included in this volume. McGehee provides the same thing that the panelists provide: personal reflections which are rarely found in printed form.

Scholars today have another major source of Graham's creative life, the *Notebooks*, published and unpublished, which she kept during her choreographic career. Nolini Barretto's essay provides the historical background for those reading about Graham's early years, and also elucidates the references which inspired Graham's intellect and imagination. Going back even further, Mark Wheeler's paper provides the background for Graham's fascination with the East, sparked by her contact with Ruth St. Denis. Ideas prevalent in American intellectual and artistic thought were carried to great heights once tempered by Graham's creative energy.

Although there are several sources providing a chronology of Graham's dances, there are few listings of published materials on Graham as comprehensive as the one compiled by Leslie Getz, which has been updated for this issue. Getz includes all doctoral dissertations written in the United States relevant to Graham.

Donlin Foreman was a principal dancer in Graham's company at the time of her death. Also a poet, his writings are included here in part because they so eloquently express the impact Graham had continuing into her latest years when she was no longer dancing.

Graham wanted to be remembered first as a dancer, as the most extraordinary performer that she was. It has been left to others to acknowledge and document her contributions as a creative force in twentieth century dance and theater.

New York
August 1997

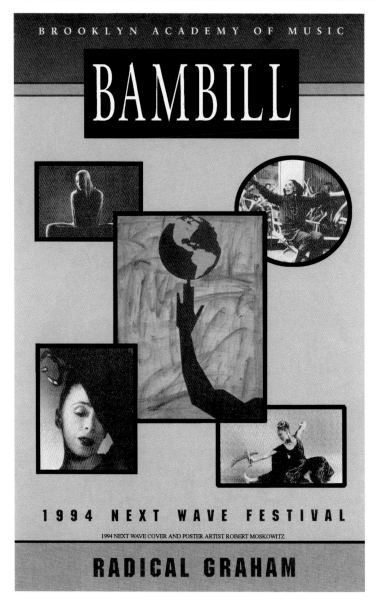

Figure 1 Program cover, Brooklyn Academy of Music, 1994 Next Wave Festival, RADICAL GRAHAM: Martha Graham Dance Company. Credit: Robert Moskowitz

The Brooklyn Academy of Music's 1994 NEXT WAVE Festival in cooperation with
The New School presents

RADICAL GRAHAM:
A ONE DAY SYMPOSIUM
on the work of Martha Graham during the 1930s and 1940s

Saturday, October 1, 1994
Tishman Auditorium of The New School
66 West 12 Street, New York, New York

PROGRAM

11:00 am   Morning Session

Welcome: Harvey Lichtenstein, President, Brooklyn Academy of Music

Panel: **Martha Graham's Early Technique and Dances: the 1930s**

    Moderator: Deborah Jowitt, Critic, <u>Village Voice</u>

    Panelists: Members of Martha Graham Dance Group:
        Thelma Babitz, Dorothy Bird, Jane Dudley,
        Frieda Flier, Marie Marchowsky, Sophie Maslow.

Excerpt of Julien Bryan's film, <u>Steps in the Street</u>

1:00 pm   LUNCH BREAK

1:45 pm   Afternoon Session

Slide Lecture: " Martha Graham: Abstract Expressionist of the Dance ."
Dr. Stephen Polcari, Director, Archives of American Art in New York, the Smithsonian.

    Introduced by Don McDonagh, New School Faculty

2:45 pm   Rare Films of Martha Graham and Dance Group

        <u>Frontier</u> and <u>Steps in the Street</u> by Julien Bryan
        Introduced by Sam Bryan, International Films

4:00 pm   **The Dance Theater Pieces of the 1940s**
        "A Conversation with Jean Erdman and Erick Hawkins,"
        conducted by Francis Mason, Editor, <u>Ballet Review</u>.

5:15 pm   Closing Remarks

    Curator of Radical Graham Symposium: Alice Helpern
    On-Site Coordinator: Laura Kaminsky, The New School

Figure 2   First page of program for "Radical Graham: A One Day Symposium", New York City, October 1, 1994.

THE DANCERS:BIOGRAPHICAL NOTES

Thelma Babitz Genecin was born in New York and moved to Los Angeles, where she began dancing. She came to New York to study further and danced with Martha Graham's Dance Group from 1936 to 1939. She is now living in Los Angeles, where she teaches dance to senior citizens.

Dorothy Bird Villard is from British Columbia. She was a member of the Dance Group from 1931 to 1937. She went on to dance on Broadway, and later formed a trio with Jose Limon and Beatrice Seckler. Dorothy taught for 25 years at the Neighborhood Playhouse in NYC. She is now working on a book of memoirs about her life in dance.

Jane Dudley joined Graham in 1935 and was a member of the Dance Group and Company until 1946. She returned to dance the role of the Ancestress in Letter to the World in 1953 and 1970. A member of the New Dance Group Studio, she performed with the late William Bales in the Dudley-Maslow trio. Jane now teaches at The Place in London.

Jean Erdman is from Hawaii and first met Martha Graham while studying at Sarah Lawrence College. She danced with her from 1939 until 1945. Jean made her choreographic debut on a program shared with Merce Cunningham at Bennington in 1942. Director of her own company for many years, she co-founded The Open Eye with her late husband, Joseph Campbell.

Frieda Flier Maddow grew up in Los Angeles and studied ballet from a very young age. She came to New York with Thelma Babitz and was a member of the Martha Graham Dance Group from 1936 to 1941. Frieda now lives in Los Angeles.

Erick Hawkins was the first man to join the Dance Group, and was a member from 1938 to 1950. He created many significant roles in the 1940s, taught, and directed the Martha Graham School at 66 Fifth Avenue. He opened his own studio in 1951, and has been director of the Erick Hawkins Dance Company since that time.

Marie Marchowsky was the youngest member of the Dance Group when she joined in 1934. She left in 1940 to do her own choreography, returning to dance in Primitive Mysteries in 1944. Marie directed her own companies in Los Angeles and Toronto, and returned to New York in 1978. She continued teaching independently, and at City College and the High School of Performing Arts.

Sophie Maslow joined Martha Graham in 1931 and danced with the Group and Company until 1944. She taught at the New Dance Group for many years, performed with the Bales-Dudley-Maslow trio, and directed her own company. Sophie lives in New York and continues to stage her work around the world.

Special Thanks to: Joseph Melillo and Scott Watson, Brooklyn Academy of Music; Dean Elizabeth Dickey, The New School; Diane Gray, Martha Graham Dance Company; Sam Bryan, International Films; Michael Stier, Cunningham Dance Foundation; David Guion, Erick Hawkins Dance Company; Helen McGehee Umana, former member, Martha Graham Dance Company; Rose Carol Washton, The Graduate Center-City University of New York; Elizabeth Harris, University of Virginia.

The Radical Graham Symposium, a part of the 1994 NEXT WAVE Festival, is sponsored by Philip Morris Companies Inc., and is produced in cooperation with the New School.

The 1994 NEXT WAVE Festival and the Martha Graham Centennial Celebration are sponsored by Philip Morris Companies Inc.

Figure 3 Second page of program for "Radical Graham: A One Day Symposium": biographical notes of the dancers.

Choreography and Dance
1999, Vol. 5, Part 2, pp. 7–31
Photocopying permitted by license only

Martha Graham's Early Technique and Dances: The 1930s, A Panel Discussion

Alice Helpern

Moderator: Deborah Jowitt, Critic, Village Voice

Panelists: Dorothy Bird, Sophie Maslow, Jane Dudley,
Thelma Babitz, Frieda Flier, Marie Marchowsky

D. JOWITT: I'm sure many of you recognize the people on stage here with me. On the far left is Dorothy Bird; next to her is Sophie Maslow, then Jane Dudley, Thelma Babitz, Frieda Flier, and Marie Marchowsky. These are all women who joined Martha Graham's Dance Group in the 1930s. Dorothy dates from 1930, Sophie from 1931, Jane from '35, Marie from '34, and Frieda and Thelma, who came from Los Angeles, both joined in 1936. I thought a nice way to start introducing these women to you would be to ask each of them what her first glimpse of Martha Graham was, what she was doing at the time, and what she thought. Dorothy, do you want to begin?

D. BIRD: I first saw Martha in Seattle. I had never heard of her; I had never heard of modern dance. I came from Canada. They had showed me a photograph of Martha. At that time, my mother was always fixing my hair on my forehead and 'round my face; that was sort of what everybody was doing. I looked at this picture of Martha with hair straight back, sharply cut off and head turned to the side, showing her strong neck, and I said, "My God, she looks like a horse!" But I loved horses! So that took care of that. I met her and she was absolutely spell-binding. She was very intimate with us, not at all stand-offish, very direct. The first thing she said was – she didn't wait to be introduced – "I want you all to call me Martha and to call Mr. Horst, Louis. We have no time for manners and artificial behavior; we've got a very important thing to do." We were going to work on a dance for a production of *Seven Against Thebes*, at the Cornish School.

D. JOWITT: The Cornish School is a very important school of theater and dance in Seattle. Merce Cunningham was a student there and Martha and Louis had come out in the summer of 1930 to teach. This was the first exposure [to modern dance] for these ballet-trained girls.

S. MASLOW: The first time I saw Martha was in a performance. It was a date I had while I was still going to high school, on a Sunday night. They didn't have regular performances on Sunday at that time. Theaters were closed, so the dance performances took place on Sundays. My mother was told that I'd be home early enough to attend school the next day. I saw Martha perform with three girls. I don't remember all of the three names...

D. JOWITT: The three girls were Betty McDonald, Evelyn Sabin, and Rosina Savelli.

S. MASLOW: I was very much impressed by the performance. I didn't see Martha again until she became my teacher at the Neighborhood Playhouse of Theater and Dance. I had been in the children's classes there. At that time it was on Grand Street in the heart of the ghetto section [on the lower East Side]. I used to come from Brooklyn to go to the classes. This was to be a full-time, three-year course in theater and dance. We also studied composition with Louis Horst; Martha taught the technique.

The first time I saw her was at a meeting where she was introduced to the students. There were nine of us at the time. I was very impressed by the way she looked, very fashionable. She had on a cloche hat that went all the way down so you couldn't see her, really, unless she lifted her head up. She didn't say very much. Once she started to teach us, it was clear she had a powerful personality. She made you do more than your best in class. You would find yourself doing things you didn't even know you could do, and you wouldn't dare do any less than your best. If she told you to take three leaps and jump out of the window, you would've done that too. She did ask us to do impossible things at certain times in class. She was very busy beginning to find her way, finding a new way of moving. That way was to make the human body an instrument that would be capable of expressing all things in human experience, not just pretty things. Sometimes they were ugly things. The movement was strong, sometimes very angular. We never turned our legs out, as you do in a ballet class; we always had parallel feet. We didn't have classes that were particularly good for making the body strong. She did whatever she was interested in at the time. Most of the time I had sore muscles. I know that, because we would do things using the thighs, over and over and over again, and the next time we might do jumps in the air. You did get to be very strong and you learned how to work as a dancer, seriously, to use every minute and every bit of energy you had, in the class.

Louis taught us composition; he was a very serious task master. There were lots of times when people were crying. You had to perform your own dances in front of your peers and that was a very delicate situation. He was interested in making dance an art form, and he based his teaching on musical forms. We had to do things to conform to certain musical forms, which made you aware of what form was, so that you wouldn't just get up and do something that was a feeling without anything else. You had to put it into some sort of shape.

J. DUDLEY: The first time I saw Martha, I was still in high school, and I was studying something called rhythmic dancing. It was natural, late [Isadora] Duncan... I mean after Duncan... but it never would have happened without Duncan. I used to work in a studio on Fifty-sixth street that the Neighborhood Playhouse had moved into temporarily. I used to see Martha coming up the stairs as I came down. She had long hair and she always smiled at me. I was very, very impressed that she smiled at me; it made me feel important. I also realized that she was quite shy. I asked if I could watch her teach a class. The class had about eight people in it and they all looked like Martha. They wore their hair exactly the same way. At that time she was teaching in a short tunic.

The one technical exercise that I remember – she demonstrated the whole class through – started on the floor. There was a movement called pleadings. In this particular sequence you came up with a rounded back and then you stretched your back. You extended one leg out in front of you, so your weight was on the bent knee. Then Martha took another contraction and lifted her weight completely up to a standing position on the under leg, so that her other leg was in the air in an extension to the front, parallel. Then she rounded her back and went down to the floor with a leg in the air, returning to her original position.

I don't know how many of you have ever been able to lift your weight on one leg, but that was what the whole class was doing, not very successfully. She was by far the most successful. She had an enormously beautiful plié. Her Achilles tendon was so long, she didn't have any problem going close to the floor.

The next time I watched a class was when she was teaching actors at the [Neighborhood] Playhouse. By then they'd moved to Madison Avenue, in another temporary set-up. Gertrude Shurr was her assistant; I don't know whether Martha actually came to that class. These were actors, but what a sequence they did! [Sitting on the floor], you put one foot ahead of you and took a contraction. You tilted your body so one shoulder was forward, toward the front leg. And you reached back and took hold of the heel of the back leg which was on half toe. Then you took a half turn in your torso, without letting go of your heel so the body was parallel to the ceiling, looking up, bridging in a high arch but holding onto your heel. Then you contracted back again. You did that about four times, and then you took a release and you came [sat] up. Remember these were actors! But they honestly managed to do it! They trembled, I'll admit that, and some of them lost their balance, but they did it! And that's something I've never understood because now fourth [swastika] position is a dirty word. I taught actors at The Playhouse too and they were all in fourth position in the floorwork, and there were men there too. No one asked a question about it being bad for your hips, bad for your knees – it was just part of the scene. That was my first experience.

D. JOWITT: Then you joined the company. You became one of those people on the floor!

J. DUDLEY: That's right! That's right!

T. BABITZ: I came to New York because I wanted to study with Martha. I'd been dancing all over Los Angeles and Hollywood in films and in plays, and having a wonderful time. I saw a picture of Martha and I thought, Wow! That was it. Somehow I came to New York; I wanted to see all the New York dancers. I saw Hanya's [Holm] group, and I saw Humphrey and Weidman, and others. I thought: "Lovely. That's lovely. I can do that." But when I saw Martha's group I thought: "Ah! I can't do that." I immediately went to her class and I kept going until I was able to do that, do it with all my heart and soul. I adored Martha all the way through it.

F. FLIER: I feel that I never really met Martha. I came to New York to be in a show and everyone said, "Oh you'd be perfect to be in Martha's company, but you mustn't go to Martha directly, you must first go to Gertrude Schurr and study. She'll tell you when to go to Martha." So I went to Gertrude Schurr and we sat down on the floor. We never got up for three months. We kept doing these exercises. I'd never seen floor work before in my life. I'd done ballet, and some kind of tension-relaxation modern before. Finally, I was told, "You can go to Martha," which I thought was really exciting. But I didn't meet her. I remember I was in the back of the class, some place, and I wore a bathing suit; I didn't even have the right kind of leotard. Later they taught me how to make a leotard with this piece of jersey: you made a crotch and you made your armpits with little triangles and then you sewed it all up. That was your outfit for the class. After about two months, Martha said , "Would you like to be in my company?" I said, "Wonderful!" So that was it. I didn't really know her.

M. MARCHOWSKY: My first introduction to Martha's technique was through Lily Mehlman. She was my dance counselor in camp. I was fascinated by the technique; I just thought it was so powerful and strong. That was the first time I heard the words Martha Graham.

When we got back to the city Louis [Horst] told me that Martha was going to give a concert at the Craig Theater. I went and it was absolutely overwhelming. I told Lily afterwards that I wanted to study with Martha. She said "Well I don't know, ..." – I was in high school – "I don't think there's anybody there who goes to high school." Lily thought I was very talented and she knew I wanted so much to go. She asked Martha, and Martha said "You know I don't want children around, but if she behaves herself and acts like an adult, she can come. But the moment she behaves like a child she will have to leave." I came there and saw Martha with this short tunic, and long hair. Everyone was sitting on the floor; that's how we started the class. I never opened my mouth, as long as I was there. I was so afraid she would think I was a child.

D. JOWITT: Sophie started to speak very eloquently about the early technique: how the stance was parallel and how the thighs did so much work. I'd like to talk a little more about the technique in relation to certain dances. Dorothy, I'd like you to tell the story about the rock, and also tell about some of that movement that you thought she was using for [*Moment*] *Rustica*?

D. BIRD: We did a tremendous amount of absolutely stationary work, a tremendous amount of work without moving visibly, until we were totally related to every hinge and every muscle in our bodies. And we worked on breathing. Then she got us ready for initiating movement. This was in Seattle; we were all total beginners and most of us very young.

We did swings. We did a lot of swings. Later on, people didn't do swings, I think, but we did a lot of swings. The swing came from the hip hinge. You swung your arms up and you rose up on your heels. You reverberated, and then you arched and rounded. It was tremendously violent and suspended, and it came on a breath. The first swing was just in place, up and down. When we got that pretty well set and were whiplashing like crazy, she said, "Now we're going to do the lunge. The swing is going to be done in a long lunge." We had to keep our feet on one board on the floor. Absolutely one line, not parallel. They were parallel for the first swing; the second swing was on one line. It was very difficult to balance, so we pulled back. She said, "use the front foot like a Russian heel or boot. Draw in and curve and then when you do the swing, swing your arms back and lunge forward and throw your head up. The force is forward and back, and forward and back. When you go forward, there is a point below your belly button where your energy comes out." So here we are, we're going to throw forward and thrust our energy out to the audience. Then she said, "You know, they brought down the walls of Jericho with sound." Somehow or other she associated us with the idea of this force. "The force of that body when it comes out is going to be enough to break a huge rock!" So we worked and worked on it. It was ferocious! One morning we went to the park, very early, to run. We were practicing running up and down the green lawns of Volunteer Park in Seattle. We saw this great big rock. We lined ourselves up at different angles. We pulled back and we threw, terribly forcefully, and we waited. We did it again and again and again. We finally went back to class and I said to Martha, "We did it! We all tried it! We said 'Ready, set, go!' But we didn't break the rock!" Martha said, "Well you did learn to initiate movement with energy, didn't you?" Which we did.

D. JOWITT: Sophie, you were speaking about the parallel aspect of the technique. When you started, it seems to me there was almost no twist. Is that true that the contractions were mostly front and back?

S. MASLOW: No there was a twist too, within the contractions. You could do them not only front and back but also, against the parallel legs that went one way, the body would twist and go the other way.

D. JOWITT: I guess it was the spiral that I was thinking of.

S. MASLOW: That was different. That came later.

D. JOWITT: And jumping those many many jumps. Sophie is responsible for the restaging of the parts of *Chronicle* that you saw [at the Brooklyn Academy of Music] and was involved with *Celebration*, the original reconstruction, not the one that is being performed now. Now you hear of Graham in connection with the floor, but the amount of jumping with those dances seems to me such a potent part of them. What was that all about?

S. MASLOW: We did jumps in dances. We did leaps in classes, but not very many. It depended on the period. There were times when we never went in the air, and then there were times when she'd concentrate on jumps. But what was extraordinary is that dancers didn't get hurt. I don't know why, because we didn't use pliés very much. There was no particular training for using the feet a certain way, but we did. We could all jump and come down silently, which I've been trying to get dancers to do for years, and can't.

D. JOWITT: There's a beautiful Barbara Morgan photo of you with Jane and Frieda in *Celebration*; all of you just look like arrows. (*See Figure 5*).

S. MASLOW: I call it the three graces.

D. JOWITT: Very contemporary grace, right?

J. DUDLEY: The first thing is that you concentrated on jumps the way you do in a ballet class, before you leave the center. I think that the technique so trained the whole body, and particularly the torso, that the weight was held up in a very strong and supporting way. I don't think some of the jumps that we did were remarkable. The simplest one, for example, was from parallel first position out into second. Sometimes you alternated first and second and sometimes you just landed in second and opened and opened again and again. There was always an end. You landed in plié, held it, and straightened, a little coda of three counts. There was another wonderful jump. You start in parallel and you went into the air and turned out like a frog. You came down and landed in fifth, and then you jumped again in parallel. There was another jump which was absolutely impossible to do. It's in *Celebration.* You jumped in the air from a parallel position, took the frog position in the air, tipped your body in the air then took a parallel extension in second. Jumping into the air again you brought your legs down and together.

In the most impossible jump in *Celebration,* – I don't know if you would have noticed it – you did that jump, extended your leg out, landed, and swung it around and pulled back into a fourth position, with the front leg up in the air. It was really beautiful, but it needed a lot of strength. I don't think those jumps are taught any more. They're quite difficult!

D. BIRD: In Seattle, one of the first things Martha did was talk about the feet. First we got down on our hands and knees, we put our hands near the floor, and we felt the floor before we touched it. Then we got down again and didn't touch it, just felt it. We felt the sensitivity in every finger. Martha said, "you're not going to dance in a ballroom; you're not in a court situation. We're not interested in courtly behavior, in ballrooms. This is ground, these are pebbles, these are rocks. Your feet have to be so sensitive that they adjust to all the different things." That's why we could land silently, because we landed so delicately on the toes and the ball and the arch, with barely any weight on the heel. We had the feeling that we were sensitive to the ground; that's how we were able to get these wonderful feet. I think we had wonderful feet.

D. JOWITT: I think that during the period when Martha was working in Seattle, in 1930, she was making a lot of discoveries. People have wondered if her interest in jumping was sparked by being the Chosen Maiden in Massine's production of *Rite of Spring.* Her solo, which she supposedly worked on a great deal by herself, involved constant jumping at the moment of the final death dance. So, that's a possibility.

F. FLIER: In jumping, she used the floor like in falling. You didn't fall on the floor, you bounced. You were resisting the floor. And the way you jumped, you bounced away from the floor.

D. JOWITT: She said somewhere that the floor was like a drum.

F. FLIER: Yes, a drum; it was a beat. As opposed to ballet where it's even, down and up, this is a pounding, a bouncing ball.

M. MARCHOWSKY: About the feet: We didn't point our feet until *Celebration.* The foot was always flexed in all of the earlier work.

F. FLIER: In jumping?

M. MARCHOWSKY: We didn't jump very much.

D. JOWITT: That was 1934.

M. MARCHOWSKY: We all had really to learn to point so we didn't come down heavily on the floor. But always, feet were flexed.

D. JOWITT: Thelma, when you say you were drawn to it because you couldn't do it, was it that strength that drew you?

T. BABITZ: Martha's technique was for her body and we had to become her body. And I was never turned out; I never could do a decent fifth position, or a pirouette. I watched her and studied what she was doing and what the other girls were doing. I used to go home and do that getting up from the floor with one leg out and coming down again. I really beat my bottom something awful, but finally I got to do it! And I always felt that I was at a disadvantage because I didn't have the hip turn-out. But it was so wonderful doing it after I got it.

D. JOWITT: Some of you had interesting roles in Graham's company and you had special little things. I don't know what your best memories are, but I wondered if you'd each like to talk about one particular dance you were in, or about the way she worked on it that excited you, or the way your role was developed.

D. BIRD: I didn't have any very big roles.

D. JOWITT: Oh yes you did. You were reminding me that you did get to stand in for Martha in *Heretic* when John Martin presented a program to acquaint the New York public with Graham's work.

D. BIRD: Yes, I did right here in the New School, downstairs in the little auditorium. Yes. Yes, that's when modern dance wasn't modern dance. Martin didn't want it to be called modern dance. He said that's a terrible name for it. It'll be passé right away. He and Louis were going to educate the public, educate all the dancers, and everybody would give demonstrations at the New School. The audience could ask questions afterwards. Martha was furious! She was wild; she was so full of rage. She didn't want to do this. And Louis said "You've got to do it!"

D. JOWITT: That's because Mary Wigman was also going to do something on the same program.

D. BIRD: Wigman did it first and she was wonderful. Martha wasn't going to do it, but she said, "All right, we'll do it. We'll do a demonstration. And we'll do some dances and some technique and I'll answer a few questions." And at the last minute, with no preparation, she gave Lillian Shapero her role in *Primitive Mysteries* and she told me to do her role in *Heretic*. Well I was no Joan of Arc. And I didn't even think they were persecuting me unfairly about being Joan of Arc. She just said, "Take four steps forward, hinge back, fall this way, lunge that way, run around there, stop, lunge ..." I counted out the steps, did the lunges, and I figured that was what I was supposed to do. Afterwards John Martin whispered to Martha, "You know, I felt like telling those other girls, 'you better stop that you old meanies!" I was doing the role so unsuccessfully, that he felt that they were persecuting me unfairly.

D. JOWITT: What was the dance that you enjoyed most being in?

D. BIRD: I loved *Primitive Mysteries*, absolutely loved it. I was very involved at that time, which was 1930 and 1931. It was a wonderful experience for me, but it would take me an hour to begin to tell you about it, it was so extraordinary. We took almost a year to develop the walk.

Nothing was ever to be done in any dance that was already done in another dance, because Louis said, "You don't get oak leaves on a maple tree. You've got to have maple leaves for a maple tree; nothing is to be moved from one dance to another. Nothing." Wasn't that a law?

J. DUDLEY: Yes.

D. JOWITT: In the early days. Later it was different.

D. BIRD: Right. We worked on this walk a thousand ways! A thousand ways! Without music, of course. It was all done without music. Music came later. Right Anna? [to Anna Sokolow, sitting in the audience]

S. MASLOW: I loved *Primitive Mysteries* too. I remember Martha spoke about the source of it. She had gone to the Southwest and seen some Indian dances. It was a combination of American Indian life and rituals, – the Catholicism that the Spaniards had brought to United States and the American Indian rituals, both together. That was about the only thing that she spoke about. For the rest, it was the quality of the movement itself. I couldn't say why it was so appealing. It was very direct, very strong. I did the last section of *Primitive Mysteries*, which is called "Hosanna": the two of us were in the center and worked together while the people were dancing around. The only directive she ever gave me in that was when she said, "It's like a picnic." That was it!

D. JOWITT: Marie, you said you had a memory of that.

M. MARCHOWSKY: I remember her saying that this was a ritual. A Penitente group, Indians, would hang a boy on a cross for twelve hours – not nailed. And in the second part , we were supposed to be tearing our clothes off.

D. JOWITT: Did she [really] say anything like that? Marie, you were this young, shy person, so maybe she really had to express what she had in mind. Is this "Crucifixus" you're talking about?

M. MARCHOWSKY: "Crucifixus," yes.

S. MASLOW: Oh, "Crucifixus." Well, Jane and I were on each side of her, pointing to Christ on the cross. All I remember was that my neck was absolutely aching! We continually did a little step forward. It took, I don't know how long, to get to the front.

J. DUDLEY: [It took] the whole section.

S. MASLOW: It was a whole section that we stood that way, looking up at the cross. Martha had a way of giving a speech while you were working at something, to make you do it better, but sometimes when I left I didn't remember what she had said. It didn't seem to be apropos of the dance, but it was always inspiring, and you always did the thing much better. I did know it was American Indian ritual and the Christian religion.

I re-did it many years later [for the Louis Horst Memorial Concert in 1964 at the American Dance Festival in New London, Connecticut] when she consented to have it reconstructed. (She was never interested in doing any reconstructions.) She came back from Israel, to see if the dance was good enough to be performed. During a rehearsal, she began to talk to the new people who were working on the dance, and she talked about the Sabbath Queen. That's what the Jewish ritual calls Saturday, the coming of the Sabbath Queen. All the time she spoke about the Sabbath Queen, and I was really floored.

D. JOWITT: She had come from Israel?

S. MASLOW: Yes, she had just come from Israel. And it was inspiring to everybody who was dancing. But she had the capacity to make you always want to do whatever it was she was working on, even if it seemed far-fetched in the way she spoke about it.

D. JOWITT: Jane, you worked with her on some really important parts, like the Ancestress in *Letter to the World*? Do you want to talk about some of those dances?

J. DUDLEY: I'd like to talk about *Letter to the World* because that was the first really important role that I had during my period with Martha. The dance is based on the poems of Emily Dickinson and her life. The Ancestress was the figure of a Puritan. Martha was the poet and Jean Erdman was the speaking Emily Dickinson. I was the symbol of the Puritan strain, the strong repressive force in Emily Dickinson's life. I thread through the work; my role changes depending on the section of the dance. I come in at the very beginning as the figure of death: "It's coming – the postponeless creature – It gains the block – and now – it gains the Door – "[1]

At that period, the Group Theater was an important theater repertory company on Broadway. How they ever succeeded in surviving, I don't know. They were working on the Stanislavsky method.

---

[1]   Emily Dickinson, Poem # 390. In Thomas Johnson, ed. *The Complete Poems of Emily Dickinson*. Boston: Little, Brown and Company, 1960. Page 186.

My husband had formed a film group and they were very much impressed with the way Stanislavsky talked about structuring what he called it "the spine" of a role, or of a play.

What I tried to do was to thread the character of the Ancestress through, on the basis of this inner line of what she stood for. In the beginning, it's really the power ... the feeling of death I used to feel as I walked forward in this walk that Sophie was talking about, where you step on the heel and bring the other foot up, with arms out. When I first did it at Bennington, there was a ramp, and a big door opened; I came down on this little stage, right to the audience. I always came right down to the audience. I used to feel as though I were a big black cloud that completely absorbed the stage and the space in front of me. Then, the Ancestress gains the block, and now she gains the door. Louis played a wood block, so it was like a clock, ticking off the time. I remember I lifted my arm. Then I turned toward Martha. She was at that beautiful white bench that Arch Lauterer had designed, that Puritan white bench. The whole line in that piece was that. I wanted her to be completely dominated by me, subservient to me, have no will of her own, to return to being a child. It ended up with her going into my arms and rocking back and forth very stiffly. It was the power of [love] – Erick [Hawkins] – who brings her back to life. That was really the next dance.

Later, I was like a governess. "'Tis "Conscience" – Childhood's Nurse" – [2] was the line, and I remember looking down at the chair as if it were a cradle and there was a child in it. Later, I broke up the relationship. I always felt that, throughout, I was a kind of a dark, closing-in force. Martha really felt that Puritanism was the death element in life, and sexuality was the life element in life. That conflict is very important in her work.

Another interesting thing: she never played to the audience. When she was on stage, it unconsciously satisfied something in her, so that she was completely integrated, completely unselfconscious. She got her ego satisfaction in that she constructed everything around herself.

I remember having this tremendous feeling of security with her, because we had a very close relationship in *Letter*. It was a very interesting experience to dance with her on stage. She didn't upstage you; she was completely honest and direct, with no mannerisms. She never, ever used her face, for example. I don't ever remember it. She used to say the face was a mask.

D. JOWITT: Thelma, what about you? You had a good part in *American Document*, which was kind of a turning point.

---

[2]   *Ibid.*, Poem # 1598. Page 661.

T. BABITZ: It was delightful to work on that because Martha was doing something that she'd never done before: working with a man partner. That was important to her and to the dance. Isn't that the one where we had the end men?

D. JOWITT AND OTHERS: You were on the end.

T. BABITZ: Anita and I. We did our little thing, and our little dance, and it was always so much fun.

D. JOWITT: That dance was based on a minstrel show, very very loosely speaking. In the minstrel show line-up there are always the end men and these were Thelma and Anita, who were two small bouncy women, I guess. Right?

T. BABITZ: We were supposed to tell the jokes. Martha didn't actually say that but she did say, "Have you ever seen a minstrel show? Do you know what the end men do?" We'd all seen something of it in films, and we knew what she wanted.

There were other things, the earth things that she did, where we kind of dug into the ground. It was a pleasure to watch her with Erick. They really did something new, because they were so involved.

D. JOWITT: In each other?

T. BABITZ: In each other and in the dance. That was my favorite dance. I think I left after that.

D. JOWITT: That was a high point. It's a very interesting idea to take some particular kind of American form, like a minstrel show, and then tell a completely different story through it: of American history and the emancipation of slaves, and robbing the Indians of their land. Yet, it incorporates the lighthearted idea of the walkaround.

F. FLIER: The most thrilling thing to me was when I started to dance with Martha. There were twelve of us; we could all move in our way, and yet be together, completely. The unison part in *Celebration* was the first dance that I learned. It was just thrilling to feel twelve women all at once in the air, and yet each was an individual. You didn't feel like you were imitating anybody. You could express yourself through her technique. That was a miracle to me, not to try to be like someone else.

D. JOWITT: Marie?

M. MARCHOWSKY: The dance I loved was *Primitive Mysteries*; I think that was one of the most thrilling experiences. I was taught the dance in 1934 by Gertrude Shurr. There was one moment in which four of us had to fall straight down on our faces. It was supposed to be a front fall. Did any of you ever do that? Well maybe you were the tall girls. It was just amazing to see them all go down wham! right on the floor. It was a very, very frightening thing to do, but somehow we were so hypnotized by the dance, that we just went right down on our faces. That was it.

D. JOWITT: It has a lot to do with those walks in silence that go between the sections. When you have those twelve women, all walking in perfect rhythm together in silence, it binds the group together. The music, when it came, was very spare.

J. DUDLEY: Yes. At that time, the dance came first and the music was written afterwards to counts. That process has changed now, but in all of Martha's early works, Louis wrote to her counts. That was true of *Primitive Mysteries*. I think some of the most important music for Martha was the music that Louis Horst wrote.

S. MASLOW: *Heretic*, particularly.

J. DUDLEY: Yes.

T. BABITZ: "The Old Breton Song," which separated each whole group of movements. We all moved together. I remember when we were on tour, we'd come to a high school auditorium, and the young men from the football team used to move the curtains or set. One of them came up to me and said, "How do you give the signals?"

D. BIRD: The entrance to *Primitive Mysteries*, of course was silent, and we worked and worked and worked on this walk, in silence, forever. We weren't allowed to hold hands; we pressed our hands together. We weren't allowed to count, and there wasn't any music. So it was pretty difficult. Each group came in and backed out, and came forward, and backed out and gradually assembled itself. It was a spellbinding thing to do. And when Louis' little flute music came, it was heavenly. Wasn't it, Frieda?

F. FLIER: The other important thing was that you never interpreted the music. The music came afterwards, so the dance was the important thing. I had grown up with the idea that you hear something and then you dance to it. Martha never did that.

D. JOWITT: Well I think that was partly Louis too, in those days, saying that dance must be strong and independent. The music was only going to emphasize what the dance values were.

D. BIRD: They thought maybe it should be like punctuation. If you did something and then 'pa-paaaa!' The music would be an exclamation mark. You did something else and a little comma would come in, and that would be the music. That was Martha's idea of what she'd like.

D. JOWITT: Then later, of course, with composers like Aaron Copland, who wrote the beautiful score for *Appalachian Spring*, the dance and music were sort of going at the same time. That is, they [Graham and Copland] were corresponding all the time about what shape the dance was taking, about what shape the music was taking. In fact, Copland even gave input into some of her ideas about the dance, and of course she gave him a lot of feedback on his music.

J. DUDLEY: When I first came to study with Martha, there was a pianist whose name was Dini De Remer. With one finger in the bottom register of the piano, she played the counts, "unh, unh, unh, unh." And when the class was over, she did a little trill at the top of the piano! It's not what's being done now at the studio for class.

S. MASLOW: I would like to add something to that. At one time Martha needed a pianist, and Leonard Bernstein came to audition for her. He had not yet conducted anything; he was just a talented musician. She didn't take him! We then had a party and he played jazz all evening.

D. JOWITT: I would like to ask these women, too, a little bit about the arts, the theater scene in New York during the 1930s when they were in the company. It was a very productive time in the arts. It was also a very penurious time for people in general, and for artists unless they happened to be painters with a good WPA [Works Progress Administration] job. What are your strongest memories? What, if any, influence you felt that had on Louis Horst and on Martha. What was the picture like in New York then?

S. MASLOW: It was pretty terrible, actually. I think the statistics were that one out of every four people had no job at all. There were people who lived along the river, along the East River, in houses built out of cardboard boxes and pieces of tin. They would make meals in tin cans with whatever they could find. There were long lines at churches and synagogues where people got free food. There were apples being sold on street corners for five cents, by people who had no jobs.

In a very strange way, the whole situation in New York was different from other places. There was a kind of camaraderie among artists who didn't have too much at the time. In any case they were never part of society getting jobs and so on. They got along as well as they could. They began to do things together. There were dance groups that began to work at unions. There were unions that were interested in cultural things. There was a big union movement. People were starting unions or trying to make strong unions. They were working together at it and they had cultural things in the unions. They had choruses; there were little theater groups for the playwrights and actors that attached themselves to unions. There were dancers' organizations. Somehow the terrible situation that almost everybody was in, began to have something else too: some sort of hope for the future. There was a world that could be better. You could work for it and in some way express that feeling. The Works Progress Administration that was instituted by Roosevelt was very important during the thirties. For the first time, the United States began to support artists in a way that it had never done before. Everybody got the same amount of money – I think it was twenty-six dollars a week – no matter what they did. The seamstresses got the same as the dancers and the technicians got the same as the designers. Everybody got twenty-six dollars a week, which was more than a lot of other people were getting.

In the process, there were certain things that would develop in theater that had never taken place before. There was a "living theater" for the news that was going on. Whatever was current was put into a theatrical form. Orson Welles and John Houseman had a group of black actors in Harlem; they did Shakespeare and other plays. There were musicals done. There were hundreds of theaters, all over the country being supported by the government. There were national theaters: English theater, Yiddish theater, Greek theater, Chinese theater, children's theater, and circuses.

Just a few years ago, there was a college in Virginia, George Mason University, that got wind of the fact that the materials used at the time in all these theaters were housed in an empty airplane hangar somewhere in Washington. Someone there managed to get people interested enough to support a search. They wanted to acquire all these things. They got enough money together to go there and take out the scenery and the costumes. Everything had been pulled out of these theaters very quickly, because the WPA plan was just dissolved instantly while it was still in effect. The collection even included ashtrays that had been left in the lobbies, and cigarette butts, and everything else. They put all that stuff into trucks and brought it to Washington.

The whole group at George Mason managed to get some of that, and they had a big festival. They invited me to come down and talk about the period. I was not on WPA because to qualify you had to not have a job, and I was in Martha's company at that time. I didn't get paid, but I had a job. You couldn't be in WPA if you had a job.

WPA did Helen Tamiris' *How Long Brethren*, and it was very good. They did a living newspaper thing, called *One Third of a Nation*. People went to the theater for twenty-five cents. And a whole new audience was built: for theater, for dance, for music. Visual artists were also involved. They sent artists out to paint murals in railroad stations and other public places. They sent writers to different areas in the country to write about specific places. They had photographers who went all over the country to produce books of photography of different areas.

It was an extraordinary time. It finished suddenly, when Congress decided it was too radical, that there was no longer a need for it. I think we were about to go into World War Two.

There's a wonderful story about the production of Marc Blitzstein's *The Cradle Will Rock*, that was supposed to open. You can read about it in John Houseman's book.[3]

D. BIRD: I was going to say that even in Seattle, they had this whole wonderful thing going on. Everywhere you went, in libraries, in railroad

---

[3] John Houseman, *Run-through: A Memoir*. New York: Simon and Schuster, 1972.

stations, in public buildings, there were paintings, some very good, some not so good. Everywhere you looked, there was art. Very exciting.

D. JOWITT: Maybe Jane can answer this. How much do you think Martha and Louis took in of the total art and theater scene? I hear from people about her interest in Ernst Barlach.

J. DUDLEY: Yes Barlach for *Lamentation*, but although Martha was not a joiner, she definitely had an uncanny sense of the *Zeitgeist*, the feeling of the time. And…she danced, by the way, at affairs at *The New Masses*, a very left wing magazine; she appeared on a benefit for them.

Sophie choreographed and I performed in the last big pageant done for Earl Browder, before he was sent to jail. It was performed at Madison Square Garden, and it was very impressive. When we got to California, the local paper in Los Angeles did show a little picture of the dancers in the pageant and said: "Did Martha Graham realize" – and they showed a little picture of something in the pageant, of the dancers – "I…did Martha Graham realize that she had two communist members in her company?" That's how it was put. And Graham never said a word to us.

She was the first person to bring black dancers into a big company, although Sophie says that's not true. Mary Hinkson was the first black dancer to be a member of a major modern dance company.

Chronicle definitely made a very strong social comment. Also *Panorama*, when she first did a season at Bennington.[4] Martha didn't go to Germany, by the way, when she was invited by Hitler to come and perform.

D. JOWITT: Yes, but none of the dancers wanted to go either, right? This was the Berlin Olympics in 1936, when the company was invited to perform. I should point out that *Chronicle* was made in the summer of 1936, at the time the Spanish Civil War broke out. As Thelma reminded me, Graham's company also danced at benefits to raise money for the International Brigade.

T. BABITZ: Sophie covered just about all of it. I just wanted to add that the ILGWU [International Ladies Garment Workers Union] put on a wonderful revue, *Pins and Needles*. It ran and ran. At Orson Welles' Mercury Theater, for instance, four plays were going on at the same time, and you could go from one to another for a quarter each. The whole atmosphere of New York City – the same thing was going on in Los Angeles and San Francisco, – was alive with theater, art, music. It was heartbreaking when they turned it off.

---

[4]   Description of these dances written presumably by Louis Horst can be found in Barbara Morgan, Martha 'Graham: *Sixteen Dances in Photographs*. Dobbs Ferry. NY: Morgan Press, 1941, 1980. Page 160.

D. JOWITT: Louis Horst was also very influential in getting Martha to hear modern composers, to hear the latest in music, and to see art exhibits.

T. BABITZ: Louis used to chide me because I would like to go to symphony concerts, because I was brought up in a musical home. He said "Don't listen to that, that's dead stuff. Listen to the new music."

S. MASLOW: I once asked him why we never used any of the musical forms that were later dances, like the waltz, and why he never used any romantic music. He said, "there's nothing as old as yesterday's newspaper." Period!

D. JOWITT: He had spent a few months in 1925 in Vienna, so maybe he'd had his fill of waltzes and Schubert.

S. MASLOW: No, I think that was his point of view, and Martha's music was always modern music. I would never have admitted to anybody that I really liked Tchaikovsky, which I did, or Rodin; I wouldn't confess to that either.

D. JOWITT: Everything had to be modern. If the dance was going to be modern, the music had to be modern and the decor. Alexander Calder and Isamu Noguchi were some of her first designers.

T. BABITZ: It was a radical moment.

J. DUDLEY: But, it's interesting to look at her early programs. In 1928 and '29 she did use Debussy and Scriabin.

D. JOWITT: As soon as she did *Heretic*, about 1929, the modernism became very pronounced, although it had been growing. She did, however, continue to perform some of those early dances on tour, with some of the same three women that were part of her first trio. At some out-of-town engagements on which she couldn't take the whole group, she did those early works.

Frieda, what is your vision of living in New York then, of the cultural scene in New York?

F. FLIER: Well I have a personal vision again. It was hard to live on ten dollars a week, and we didn't get paid. So, I went to an audition. It was after Martha invited me into the company, but I hadn't started rehearsing. Someone said, 'Oh there's an audition on Broadway for Balanchine's *On Your Toes.* So I auditioned, and I was selected. I was supposed to sing "I'm in the Mood for Love." I couldn't do that, but they took me anyway. I came to Martha and said, "Isn't this wonderful? I have a job!" She said, "My girls don't work." And that was it. That's the end of the story.

D. JOWITT: Frieda , you had some interesting stories, too, of early touring days and some of those colleges where you played, where you couldn't find the performance.

F. FLIER: I couldn't find the rehearsal. Once we were in Ann Arbor, Michigan. We were in a new place, a dormitory. We'd been on the train all night. Somebody knocked on the door and yelled 'Rehearsal!

Rehearsal!' and everybody ran away. Marie and I were getting dressed. We went to wash in the sink. This faucet fell off, and the water was pouring up. Marie left and I thought I couldn't leave, I had to deal with the faucet. I finally found somebody who would take care of it, and then I didn't know where the rehearsal was. This was a huge campus and I kept trying to find where the music was playing. Finally I did; of course, Martha was very angry that I was late.

M. MARCHOWSKY: I remember we were in Salt Lake City and we had a performance. As you know you just can't eat before you perform; it's rather impossible. There was a little reception afterwards and we were all very hungry. The ladies had these dishes, little plates with these little tiny sandwiches with the crust cut off. In about ten minutes, everything was gone!

The women were so distressed, and so disturbed by this. They didn't have anything more to give us and we were just like animals. They must have thought, "Oh! what kind of people are these?"

T. BABITZ: They were Mormons and weren't allowed to have any drinks. We didn't want any liquor, we wanted something like a Coca-Cola at least. They didn't have that.

D. JOWITT: But you all said that touring in those days was a luxury compared with the life you had in New York.

SEVERAL VOICES: Of course. It was heaven.

D. JOWITT: Because you were paid twenty-five dollars a week? And traveled on a train, and slept in hotels and had a good time.

M. MARCHOWSKY: Thirty-five [dollars]! I came home with a lot of money. I remember I had never been out west. On the train, Martha came over to me once. We were in the desert. She said, "Do you know, there are many rattlesnakes in the desert!" She was educating me about the west!

D. JOWITT: These women spanned the period from the early 1930s into the 1940s. All of them had left the company by the time of *Appalachian Spring*, and some of them were gone by the end of the thirties. I thought it might be interesting to talk about what changes you observed in Martha's work during that time. What kind of new developments or discarding of old things happened?

Dorothy, you were there from 1930 until '37. You were there when the sort of "American" strain developed.

D. BIRD: Yes, it was definitely "American dance." She was breaking the mold. We were American pioneers and when we got our parallel feet we were like railroad tracks that never came together, either back or front, out into the distance. There was a lot to do with distance. The whole thing changed, of course when Erick came. They turned out and pointed their feet, which was just unheard of. Then they got delicate arms and hands. I was shocked!

D. JOWITT: Many of the women did leave the company at that time, right? They didn't feel they could weather that transition.

S. MASLOW: I don't think that was the reason they left. I think that people individually left for different reasons. I was pregnant, that's why I left.

D. JOWITT: But you were in those dances of the forties, for quite a while. You were in *Letter to the World*, right? You were in *Deaths and Entrances.*

S. MASLOW: And *American Document*. I think that Martha was always changing; she was always going into another phase. What happened in the world interested her and made her do different things. What happened in her own life also made her do different things. She was never interested in going back or reviving anything old.

It's just lucky that things are somewhat preserved and you can see them from the past. But at the time that we were there, at the very beginning, things were very harsh in texture, in movement. She was considered ugly by a lot of critics. We were called "Graham Crackers," and we were supposed to all look like Martha.

As she became more accepted and better known, she began to round out her technique. She began to include things that were more flowing, rounder, feet pointed, turned out positions, and it became a much healthier kind of class to go to.

D. JOWITT: Was that true even in the forties? Or was that much later?

S. MASLOW: It was true in the forties. That already had happened. And then it continued to change even more afterwards.

D. JOWITT: Do you think that Erick Hawkins, having been in Balanchine's ballet company, brought some mild tolerance of ballet to her?

J. DUDLEY: Yes, I think that was the first time we ever stood in fifth position. One of the interesting things in working with Graham is that each fall there were new things in the technique. She would have worked by herself over the summer, and new things in the technique would be added to the class.

I remember when we first did a spiral. A spiral had been absolutely out. The torso had been twisted, but it never turned on the hips on a high release, as it was called. And, later the arms, instead of being straight as they were in a lot of the floorwork, suddenly became a port-de-bras. At one point we even held our arms ahead of our heads the way one does in ballet, so that the face could be seen on either side. Before that the arms were held way back so the chest was very open.

Interestingly, Graham was extremely careful about placement, and about turnout, and about how the arms were held. I think it's important to know that she was a meticulous teacher. She was not only inspiring, but she never let a class just go through things. I remember walking into the playhouse one day. I was teaching and I guess I wasn't doing a very good job. Everyone was sort of going through it mechanically. She said, as she stood at the back of the room, "There's no Kundalini in the class. That's what's lacking." And I don't know if you know what Kundalini is. It's the energy that, like a serpent, starts at the base of the spine and goes up through the spine to the base of the head. Then she said: "Now each of you choose some verse, some lines which you're studying in acting, and say them while you're doing the turns around the back."(The turns were so named, turns in which the hip turns the torso.) The class immediately came alive. Before that they were working quite mechanically. At that point it involved the whole of them and they were suddenly people doing something, not just going through patterns.

D. JOWITT: That meant something to them. It's interesting what you say about the arms. I studied at the Graham school at a much later date, and we did a certain kind of barrel leap with the arms like this [demonstrates]. In the early pictures and films, the women did the leap with fists as they jumped.

Thelma, you were only actually in the company three years. But you saw the changes that came with *American Document*. Did you observe much happening in those years, not necessarily to the technique, but to Graham's ideas?

T. BABITZ: It was four years. She started to talk about the American, not so much the culture, but about the nature of America, the democratic ideas. She just would touch on it. She never said anything directly; she always would approach it from how she felt about things, and how she moved. I could see that. Everyone could see that. *American Document* was quite a different thing from what we had done before.

F. FLIER: As we began to turn out and do more balletic things, it got more comfortable for me. I didn't have to struggle. It was a struggle to be straight and very percussive. To be lyrical and open was more natural to me. I think at the time Martha started enjoying Tudor's choreography and she was going to see [ballet]. Before that she hated the ballet; then she started accepting it more, in a certain area.

D. JOWITT: She did admire Tudor and he admired her very much. Marie, you were there from 1934 to 1940, so you saw that change.

M. MARCHOWSKY: Yes. At one time we began doing things for her Greek dances, from her Greek period. Do you remember that, Jane? *Tragic Patterns*, I think. And it was all very two-dimensional. Everything was done with very, very strong contractions. It was very powerful. She told us all that we should go to the Metropolitan Museum, and see the Greek figures.

D. JOWITT: So she did tell you to look at art some times.

M. MARCHOWSKY: She would say, looking at a museum statue: "Look at this boy there, and you will realize how you should be! You should take it from there!" It was a very wonderful period.

D. JOWITT: In those early thirties, Graham herself was involved in Greek plays because she was working with the actress, Blanche Yurka, in *Electra*, performing, and doing choreography. You couldn't get farther from archaic Greek than *Every Soul is a Circus*, right? That was Merce Cunningham's debut in the company.

M. MARCHOWSKY: Right. That was really very strange; there were four of us and the rose. There was also this furniture on the stage and there was a real problem. What are we going to do with all this furniture on stage? There was a sofa, a couch and a stool.

F. FLIER: We had to move things.

M. MARCHOWSKY: Yes, and Louis said, "Well, the stage hands will do it." Martha said no; she didn't want to break up the continuity. She said, "We'll have the girls do it." And so we were carrying all this furniture on and off the stage, prancing all the way through.

D. JOWITT: And that's a far cry from *Primitive Mysteries* with that absolutely bare, pristine stage, no plot, and no props, getting from that to *Every Soul is A Circus* in 1939, with characters called Empress of the Arena and The Acrobat, and all that furniture.

[*At this point, the discussion stopped, and audience and panelists were shown a film by Julian Bryan of excerpts from* Chronicle *(1936), notably the "Steps in the Street" section and fragments of "Spectre 1914" and "Prelude to Action." It was this footage that Maslow used as a source when she re-staged sections of* Chronicle *for the current Graham company season at the Brooklyn Academy of Music. All the panelists appeared on the screen dancing, and exclamations of – "There's Sophie!" and "I think I was in the back line ..." and "Remember those jumps?" – erupted from the women from the panel who were sitting in the front row.* Chronicle *was made just after civil war broke out in Spain, and its abstract lines of force suggest marching and retreating, holding firm against pressure. The women's forthrightness in dancing and their lack of indulgence created an image of a self-sufficient female tribe – needing no men to express social and political verities. Graham dancers of the 1930s didn't have the finesse of today's Graham dancers, that gloss of ballet training. Their dancing on the film bore out what their words had earlier conveyed: their strong bodies were molded by the conviction that this was the best dancing in the world and that to be doing it was less a job than a mission.*] DJ

Figure 4   Martha Graham and Dance Group in *Primitive Mysteries*. Photo © Barbara Morgan, 1941, 1980.

Figure 5 Jane Dudley, Sophie Maslow, and Frieda Flier (l. to r.) in *Celebration*. Photo © Barbara Morgan, 1941, 1980.

Figure 6   Members of Martha Graham Dance Group in *Celebration*. Photo © Barbara Morgan, 1941, 1980.

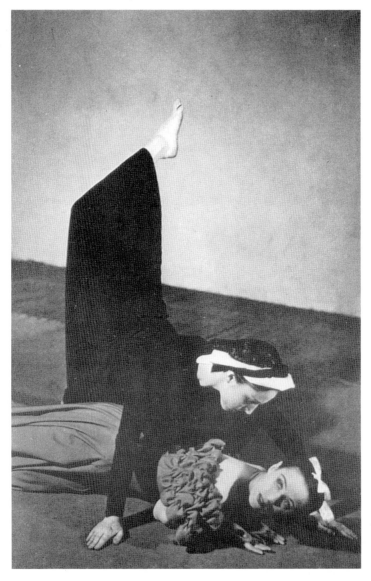

Figure 7   Jane Dudley as The Ancestress with Martha Graham in *Letter to the World*. Photo © Barbara Morgan, 1941, 1980.

Choreography and Dance
1999, Vol. 5, Part 2, pp. 33–40
Photocopying permitted by license only

The Dance Theater Pieces of the 1940s: A Conversation with Jean Erdman and Erick Hawkins

Alice Helpern

Moderator: Francis Mason, Editor, Ballet Review

F. Mason: Good Afternoon. I'm Francis Mason. It's a pleasure and an honor to have two magnificent witnesses to [Martha Graham's choreographic process]: the great Erick Hawkins and the great Jean Erdman. They are both crucial to the 1940s, and to the subject of Martha Graham in general. This morning six wonderful women were here talking about Martha Graham's work and we saw films of these wonderful women ["Steps in the Street" and other excerpts]. Now suddenly there's a man in the picture, Erick Hawkins.

Erick, I think we'd all be interested to know what motivated you, a classical scholar who graduated from Harvard majoring in Greek. You'd gone to Europe, you'd seen the ballet, you'd seen Harald Kreutzberg, and you wanted to dance. Then you worked with Balanchine. You were the first male student at the School of American Ballet. You watched him make *Serenade* and other great pieces.

E. Hawkins: I was in *Serenade*.

F. Mason: Suddenly, Martha Graham. Why did you seek her out?

E. Hawkins: I haven't been in this auditorium for many years, but it was here that I saw José Limón. Up to that time the dance was for women. Limón gave me the concept that a man could be a modern dancer. And then I saw ... a Hindu dancer.

J. Erdman: Shankar?

E. Hawkins: No, not Uday Shankar. It was later on. But I still remember, a kind of *tour jeté* that had such ease! And then, sitting back there, I also heard E. E. Cummings recite his poems.

F. Mason: This place [The New School for Social Research auditorium] brings all of it back, doesn't it?

E. Hawkins: Yes, but the most appropriate thing is that it was in this auditorium that Martha had a vision. I wasn't here at that performance, but I certainly heard about it afterwards. She had a kind of debate with Fokine.[1] Martha said there is such a thing as a New American Dance!

F. Mason: She was talking and Fokine rose to ask a question. He began to argue about how it was impossible to have New American Dance. She didn't know who he was, and it didn't matter to her. What he said was important.

Erick, the *Herodiade* premiere took place at the same time as *Appalachian Spring* – at the Library of Congress in Washington, did it not? They were commissions you arranged.

E. Hawkins: We were at Bennington. That was about 1943, I wrote a letter to Elizabeth Sprague Coolidge, who had a foundation in the Library of Congress. I went up to the Jennings rehearsal hall; Martha was mad at me because I was late. But I guess in my own opinion I was doing something very important. Because I wrote that letter to Coolidge, she asked Martha and me to come to Washington. That led to *Appalachian Spring* and *Herodiade* and a piece by Milhaud [*Imagined Wing*].

The score for *Herodiade*[2] was wonderful, but it was the relation of the movement with the music that jelled it. When that music was right, it added up to something.

The Milhaud [*Imagined Wing*] wasn't a very good piece. We did it just once in the Library of Congress. We had composed it in the halls, because there wasn't a rehearsal space.

F. Mason: You and Martha put it together in the halls?

E. Hawkins: I remember that's the first time I knew Yuriko, who was in that dance. I don't know if Martha ever forgave me for being late to that rehearsal, but I was doing something very important. Martha had had some very fine music beforehand, but it was not orchestrated fully, and some of it was a bit scrappy.

I think the other night at Brooklyn Academy of Music, they really distorted Martha's idea. You couldn't doctor it up; you had to preserve it clearly.

F. Mason: But *Appalachian Spring* was done by Aaron Copland for nine or was it thirteen instruments, as you specified, so you could take it on tour.

E. Hawkins: The original score was for thirteen instruments: four violins, two violas, two celli, a contrabass, flute, clarinet, bassoon, and

---

[1] Hawkins is referring to the Lecture Demonstration with the Graham group and John Martin in 1931. The occasion is also referred to in Vitale Fokine, ed. *Fokine: A Ballet Master*.

[2] The Hindemith music, also entitled *Herodiade*, was commissioned by Elizabeth Sprague Coolidge for the occasion. Its original title was *Mirror Before Me*.

piano. I don't think there was percussion. *Herodiade* had the same instrumentation. So those were very fine products of something you call modern dance.

F. Mason: Erick, could you tell us a little about Martha's work process in putting *Appalachian Spring* together, and the role you had in it? You had a major role in most of the pieces of the forties, most of the pieces from 1938 through the 1940s. How did this work?

E. Hawkins: Well, when it came to lifting her, as in *American Document*, I had to do the lifting.

F. Mason: You didn't say, "Martha, can I lift you here?"

E. Hawkins: So I put in my two cents to guide her as to what was possible. That finally led to *Night Journey*, which has some quite extraordinary lifts, I think. There was a way of composing the duets that was rather different.

F. Mason: No question about it. I think that's what we're interested to hear you speak about. I think Jean Erdman also might have something to say. You watched the creation of some of those pieces yourself.

J. Erdman: Yes. Of course I wasn't around when they were rehearsing their duets, but in *Every Soul is a Circus*, I was given my first solo. I had a little entrance. I walked in, and bounced around, and did a few turns, not really dancing, because I had to go up and sit in the place on the set that was for an audience. I was the audience for the show that was going to come out on the stage. I was very upset at not being involved in anything more than that, but nevertheless I made the most of it.

E. Hawkins: Yes she did. I still remember her.

J. Erdman: I just wanted to find out whether anyone saw what I was doing. And Martha had told me to change my headdress every now and then. One of the changes I had was a piece of blue jersey. You know how stretchy jersey is – just that, over my whole head; another one was different kinds of hats. I decided to do the changes at the right time, of course, which is what she wanted me to do, but I would do it suddenly, or I'd make a move when someone came near me. I just hoped that the audience knew I was on stage.

F. Mason: They very definitely did; you were The Ideal Spectator, as it was called.

J. Erdman: Yes, my name was separate. I had a character.

F. Mason: And then you became a speaking person.

J. Erdman: When she [Martha] did *Letter to the World*. Do you want me to go on?

F. Mason: Yes, please!

J. Erdman: I just have to tell you that because Joseph Campbell is my husband – everybody knows about Joseph Campbell now – I was married. We got married on a Thursday because Joe said it had to be the fifth month of the year, the fifth day of the week, the fifth hour of the day. And I said, 'Why?' And he said because that's Thor's day, thunder! Thunderclap in James Joyce's work, means the end of an eon. Well, Joe knew it was going to be the end of Joseph Campbell as he'd always known him. He knew now that he was a married man it was a different life. Then I had the opportunity to start dancing with Martha. We married on Thursday, we went out to Woodstock for the weekend to have our little honeymoon, and when he wasn't in school at Sarah Lawrence on Friday, the president, Constance Warren said, "Where is Mr. Campbell?" Everybody said, "This is his day off!." Friday was his day off. Monday came and we came back to the city. Joe started teaching again at Sarah Lawrence and I started rehearsing with Martha Graham. It was as if life began at that moment for me.

F. Mason: As a member of the audience said to me twenty minutes ago, Martha Graham was wonderful in the thirties, and the women were wonderful, but something happened in the forties that broadened the picture and made the work more universal.

Erick, we all know that Martha Graham was the best read dancer that ever lived. I think it was Ben Bellitt at Bennington who said that she was a dancer to whom words were important. She knew about literature. So did you. We're interested to know your view of what Martha, the intellectual, was like when you came to know her, and how she cogitated the future of her dances.

E. Hawkins: Martha was a wonderful person; she was very bright. Otherwise I wouldn't have stayed around.

F. Mason: Clearly. Would she wake up in the morning and say, "Erick I have this fantastic idea."?

E. Hawkins: No, it never was like that.

F. Mason: What was it like?

E. Hawkins: Something just grew.

F. Mason: She'd work in the studio?

E. Hawkins: Yes. When she did *Herodiade*, I remember reading Mallarmé in French with her. I could read the French, but I'm still wondering what it meant. I don't know what Mallarmé really meant. It was very esoteric. But I remember, up at the Jennings house, Martha went through real agony to do *Herodiade*. I was working downstairs, and she was upstairs, she was with Helen Lanfer.[3]

F. Mason: This was at Bennington?

E. Hawkins: Yes. Anyway, Helen was a very wonderful colleague of Martha's. It was agony for Martha to divine what *Herodiade* meant, but going into that mysterious movement was part of Martha's genius.

---

[3]   Helen Lanfer, musician, accompanied Graham in the 1940s. She was also well known as a piano teacher. Lanfer died in 1995.

F. Mason: As she evolved *Appalachian Spring*, which came first, the movement or the music?

E. Hawkins: The music was done first. Yes, and that was a wonderful development in the dance art, that the movement should take the first place, and the music should come afterward. But there were not very many composers that were able to do that.

J. Erdman: Louis Horst could do it; Louis Horst could really do that!

E. Hawkins: Yes, and the only other person is Lucia Dlugoszewski.[4] It really takes a true love of the dance, and also perception to understand that this sound has to go with the impulse that made the gesture, Now, since that time, except for Lucia, I've not found anybody whom I could trust, who wouldn't wipe out what I was trying to do in the dancing by adding some other element.

Music right now is in a terrible state. For a long time, at Bennington, there was a real hope that music could become an amalgamated part, but that was soon lost. That's why something like *Primitive Mysteries* was so elemental, but just right. It didn't wipe out what the dance was doing. Well, I'm going around the bushtail.

F. Mason: No, no, you're right on the point of what we're interested in – different works and their relationship to the music.

E. Hawkins: *Appalachian Spring* and *Herodiade* were very wonderful works. They're playing something with *Appalachian Spring* as background on television now, and it's gotten sifted down.[5]

J. Erdman: Was that music easy to dance to?

E. Hawkins: Yes. Well, it was real music. The state of music today is very difficult, because so many kooky ideas have come into what music is supposed to be. That's why a lot of people have gone back to using baroque music. From the very first dance I ever did, called *Showpiece*, with the Ballet Caravan, when I was at the School of American Ballet, I knew. If you were going to use new music, you had to have a new dance, and if you were going to have a new dance, you had to have new music.

F. Mason: You're the only one now who still says that, and who also says it must be live music.

E. Hawkins: Yes.

F. Mason: That is a great thing.

E. Hawkins: Well, I paid a price for upholding this tradition, because the musicians have to be paid. It takes away a little bit from the dancers salary, but it's worthwhile.

---

[4] Lucia Dlugoszewski, a composer who collaborated on many works with Hawkins, was also his wife.

[5] Hawkins is referring to music for an automobile commercial shown on television in 1994 which uses the Shaker hymn theme from *Appalachian Spring*.

F. Mason: Erick, there is so much interest in the dances of the 1940s. Last night, at the Brooklyn Academy of Music, we all saw *Dark Meadow*. Today we've heard some notions of what it's about.

E. Hawkins: *Dark Meadow*. It just happens, Martha didn't work very hard on it. I remember, in a studio in Philadelphia, I was kind of embarassed about it. I said, "Martha, let's go in there, and ..." I practically made up the movement myself. Maybe she was just tired. Maybe she was just literally tired, or just figuratively tired, but except for the beginning dance, I don't think Martha worked hard enough on it. It didn't come out of her whole being.

F. Mason: It was an idea that you had discussed and you both knew what the piece was about.

E. Hawkins: Yes, *Dark Meadow* came from a phrase in Greek mythology.

F. Mason: "The dark meadow of the soul."

E. Hawkins: That's poetic. And when it's poetic, you can't say what it is exactly. You have an intuition. It refers to something that's quite concrete, but you can't put it into words. Poetry is like that.

F. Mason: You put it into dance.

E. Hawkins: Yes.

F. Mason: Someone said it's a piece about renewal, regeneration, the earth, through love. Is that accurate?

E. Hawkins: Well, I was in it.

F. Mason: What were you doing, standing there all that time?

E. Hawkins: I remember I went behind a long thing that Noguchi made. At the right moment I pulled a string, and a flowering branch came up.

F. Mason: And the piece ended. That's what happens.

E. Hawkins: I've never seen it since that time.

F. Mason: Well, you should see it, It's really an incredible and very powerful piece. Martha knew all about the Greeks and all about Greek philosophy before she did *Night Journey*. Speaking of Greek subject matter, did you talk with her about this, or is this something she came upon that she wanted to do?

E. Hawkins: Well, my reading matter was very often going back into some of the subjects I had in college, and so I probably introduced her to a lot of things. I remember reading some Greek plays, but I don't know whether I literally ... I think it was a very fruitful idea for her to investigate, in terms of subject matter, because it's mythic.

The problem is we don't have a mythic atmosphere in our art. Just lately, three years ago, I used a Navajo myth, because we didn't have a myth today that I could use. The Greeks thought mythically.

F. Mason: Jean Erdman, did Martha Graham talk with Joseph Campbell about this kind of thing?

J. Erdman: Oh yes, quite often, but I never listened in on the other phone. Of course Joe was so enthusiastic about what he was doing himself: working on mythology; working on the relation of how mythology supports the world and so forth; and discovering that no matter what mythology he studied, from whatever culture, whatever period of time, there were things that were constant.

It was really based on the circle of life and/or the hero's journey. He divided the circle in the center and then named the parts. He got these names from his studies. He didn't make them up: ethereal, telluric, and cathonic. And so when you're in the belly of the whale, in the lower world, hell or wherever you want it to be, that's cathonic. And on the earth in human context, that's telluric. When it's in the spiritual realm, it's ethereal. He developed a whole idea about aesthetics, in that every mythological element has a corresponding aesthetic element.

I've been thinking about this because Martha really developed a kind of aesthetic in her own body technique, in her dance technique, that was unique to her and her style. She used it throughout. According to Joe's idea about the relation to mythology, you would be changing the style for each subject. He kept saying that telling a mythological story was not acually making a piece of work mythological, having a mythic proportion. The storytelling was just a secondary thing. For instance, in the *Lamentation* which I saw the other night, there were, unfortunately, three renditions: the people on the side could see one side, but not the frontal, which I think you needed to experience *Lamentation*. *Lamentation* is a mythic dance; Joe would agree. Also, *Frontier*. Telling the story of a Greek myth as narrative did not automatically make it, from Joe's point of view, aesthetically a mythic piece. Martha's own stylized body was already in the aesthetic mode that created the connection between the aesthetic element and the mythic element in many of the pieces that she did with the Greek stories. But the fact that it was a Greek story didn't make it mythological.

F. **Mason**: Both of you dancers, – choreographers, artists – are working on narratives and myths yourself. Looking back on Martha's work, what would you say was the seed that she gave that helped you go on to do wonderful work? Erick has gone on to form his own company and his own school which is still flourishing.

J. **Erdman**: She knew something nobody else in the world knew, and that was how to dance with the whole body! She created a style that was as opposite to ballet as you could possibly be. Ballet was all ethereal, and wanted to be – it's a beautiful art! Martha found something else entirely. It was cathonic. I only studied ballet after I'd been in Martha's company, so I had to learn it from the outside, so to speak. And I realized, of course, that the center is where you have your center of balance. But Martha had the idea of an active center. We really created expression by using the torso in a way that was never dreamed of in ballet because they weren't interested in that aspect. They were doing something else. Martha's gift to all of us is the awareness of that enrichment of the human body in movement.

F. **Mason**: One thing that occurs to me, looking at her pieces at Brooklyn, and looking here: there is a persona involved in Graham's work. She seems always to be asking the question, "Where do I fit in? What am I a part of?" At least that's the power the pieces have for me. She's relating to something else; she's not just a glamorous beautiful performer. There is a center in the head as well as in the solar plexus, that is asking that question and engaging the spectator, as a performer.

J. **Erdman**: It's almost as if she were not afraid constantly to be the heroine in search. Not afraid at all. Always doing it.

F. **Mason**: And always changing. Perpetually changing and renewing herself. And a lesson, it seems to me, for all wonderful artists. You're always renewing yourself; you're always making new pieces. You're making new pieces; you're carrying on.

As you contemplate the work you've done, Erick, and continue to do, myth carries a lot of weight, doesn't it?

E. **Hawkins**: You speak of the myth. There's another aspect of it which I call poetry. The reason it means something to us is that it's poetic. I don't know what one means exactly by poetry, but it does have something. With students, after they've come along a ways, I can see whether they have a poetic way of moving, or if they're humdrum; or whether they're just doing the movement that they've been taught, or if they add something to it. Poetic essence is very intangible. That's why most people don't like it, because they are crude and are not willing to go inside to see what is life-giving. Poetry always does give life.

I still remember Martha's confrontation with Fokine. She did say that there is an area, a genius in American dancing. I think we've been part of that. And the point is whether it's going to change, but I don't want it to deteriorate. So that is the laugh of the Gods that we constantly keep our openness to speaking poetically.

Choreography and Dance
1999, Vol. 5, Part 2, pp. 41–51
Photocopying permitted by license only

The Orient in America: Fertile Soil for Martha Graham

Mark Wheeler

Both choreographic notes and references to literature contained in *The Notebooks of Martha Graham* render *The Notebooks* an index into Graham's considerable contact with the Orient. Placing in broad cultural context the inspiration Martha Graham (1894–1991) drew from the East, this paper offers a survey of America's growing awareness of the East up through the middle of the twentieth century. Because Ruth St. Denis (1877–1968) constitutes an important source of Graham's contact with the East, brief discussion of St. Denis and of the Denishawn company is presented as part of the general survey of those aspects of the East accessible to the American artist of Graham's generation.

The discovery of gold at Sutter's mill north of San Francisco in 1848 triggered the first large scale immigration of Asian people to the United States. While only a negligible number of Chinese were in America in 1848, by 1852 there were twenty thousand, by 1860 one in ten Californians was Chinese, and by the end of the 1860s there were sixty-three thousand.[1] Chinese workers lured by the gold rush to Gold Mountain, as they called America, later were instrumental in the building of the Central Pacific Railroad, with work on that project beginning in 1867. The first Chinese temple was built in San Francisco's Chinatown in 1853, and more than four hundred were on the west coast by the end of the nineteenth century.

As for the Japanese, the shoguns' policy of isolation had forbidden Westerners to come closer to Japanese life than a Dutch outpost at Nagasaki, and the 1870 census found only seventy Japanese in the United States.[2] Finally in 1854 Commodore Perry and two warships negotiated a treaty with the Japanese, and in 1860 the first Japanese

---

[1] Rick Fields, *How the Swans Came to the Lake: A Narrative History of Buddhism in America.* Boulder, Colorado: Shambala, 1981, pages 70–71.
[2] *Ibid*, page 76.

envoy visited America. In 1868 when non-official Japanese citizens first were permitted to travel abroad, a stream of workers began going to Hawaiian sugar plantations. By 1890 two thousand thirty-nine Japanese were on the United States mainland, some having come directly from Japan, some via Hawaii. At the turn of the century Chinese and Japanese worked in service capacities throughout the western United States. Absent in Allegheny, Pennsylvania, these Asian gardeners, laundrymen, and cooks fascinated fourteen year old Martha Graham when her family moved to Santa Barbara in 1908.[3]

Fifteen years earlier, at a critical time in Ruth St. Denis' artistic development, the image of ancient Egypt was very much in the air. Napoleon's excursion to Egypt in 1798 resulted in the discovery of the Rosetta Stone and in subsequent excavation and scholarly research on ancient Egypt. Books about Egypt such as two in the Dennis home in New Jersey – *Egypt Through the Ages* and *The Idyll of the White Lotus* – were common. Already moved by the Palisades Park pageant *Egypt through the Centuries*, Ruthie Dennis attended an 1892 matinee performance by Genevieve Stebbins which closed with the pantomime *Myth of Isis*.[4] A year later an American dancer billed as Little Egypt appeared in the midway attraction *The Streets of Cairo* and inspired a generation of female dancers to explore the sensual lure of hoochy-koochy or belly-dancing. Augustin Daly had set the stage for Little Egypt when he brought a troupe of Indian Nautch dancers to New York in 1881.[5]

Musical variety entertainments parodying some aspect of the Orient were remarkably common during the years 1890–1915. The cheerful mocking of an Asian culture and playful exaggeration of aspects of Japanese style of Gilbert and Sullivan's *The Mikado*, which achieved great success in England and here in the 1880s, set the example for much that was to follow on the New York commercial stage. An unknown Isadora Duncan reluctantly sang in Augustin Daly's *Geisha* in 1898.[6] David Belasco mounted a production of *Madame Butterfly* in New York in 1900.[7]

---

[3]   LeRoy Leatherman, *Martha Graham: Portrait of the Lady as an Artist*. New York: Alfred A. Knopf, 1966, page 34.

[4]   Suzanne Shelton, "The Influence of Genevieve Stebbins on the Early Career of Ruth St. Denis." *Essays in Dance Research: Dance Research Annual IX*. New York: Congress on Research in Dance, 1978, page 41.

[5]   Arthur Todd, "The Rise of Musical Comedy in America," *Dance Magazine*, Vol. 24, No.12, December 1950, page 25. Coomaraswamy provides the derivation of the term Nautch in a 1917 commentary on what he describes as being the first performance in the United States of authentic Nautch dancing, by Roshanara and her associate Ratan Devi: "Indian culture – like that of the old Greeks – employs a single name for the common art of acting and dancing; and this word *Natya*, in its Indian vernacular form becomes *Nautch*."

[6]   Isadora Duncan, *My Life*. New York: Boni and Liverwright, 1927, page 40.

[7]   Oscar Brockett, *History of the Theatre*. Boston: Allyn and Bacon, Inc., 1968, page 514.

The following shows were produced in New York: *Wang* (1891); *A Trip to Chinatown* (1893); *The Wizard of the Nile* (1895); *The Fortune Teller* (1898); *A Chinese Honeymoon* (1902); *The Sho-Gun* (1904); *A Trip to Japan* (1909); and *Chin-Chin* (1914). The Oriental specialty number was a common feature in vaudeville shows and, in the first quarter of the century, editions of the *Ziegfeld Follies* and *Greenwich Village Follies*.

A product of this era of popular variety entertainment, St. Denis was first enamored of ancient Egypt and was doing library and other research on Egypt when the Coney Island attraction *The Streets of New Delhi* brought India into her theatrical vision. St. Denis recruited individuals of Oriental descent for an Indian dance which was to become *Radha*. Early in 1906 *Radha* and later that year *Cobras* and *Incense* were seen in New York, creating a sensation. Following some touring on the East coast, St. Denis spent two years performing in Europe. In Germany she was able to do considerable research in Egyptian and Oriental history in the libraries and museums of Berlin, and *Nautch* and *The Yogi* were created there. One of her first projects upon returning to America would be the full length *Egypta*.

In the spring of 1911, when Graham was seventeen, her father took her to Los Angeles to see her first dance performance. The dancer was Ruth St. Denis and the dances seen by Graham that night were three solos from *Egypta*, followed by *Incense, Cobras, Nautch, The Yogi,* and *Radha*.[8] (Ted Shawn had first seen St. Denis only one month earlier, during her week's run in Denver.) St. Denis became Graham's idol. The young Graham's first amateur dance appearance took place the following August as one of thirty-seven "geisha girls" in a Santa Barbara theater production, *A Night in Japan*.

In 1913 Graham left home to enter the junior college of the Cumnock School in Los Angeles. After graduating in the spring of 1916, she enrolled in the Denishawn School which St. Denis and Ted Shawn had opened in 1915. Along with her fascination with the Orient and sense of awe of St. Denis, Graham brought to Denishawn an elongated torso, giving her a natural affinity for the Oriental dance styles taught by St. Denis.[9]

Graham's first appearance in a professional dance company was later that summer of 1916 in St. Denis and Shawn's *A Dance Pageant of Egypt, Greece, and India* presented at the Greek Theater on the University of

---

[8] Ernestine Stodelle, *Deep Song: The Dance Story of Martha Graham.* New York: Schirmer Books, 1984, page 11.

[9] Ernestine Stodelle, "Anna Sokolow in Japan," *Dance Magazine*, Vol. 41, No.1, page 78. Reporting on Anna Sokolow's 1967 residency at the American Cultural.

Center in Tokyo and on the ongoing association between Graham and the Center, Stodelle writes "there is no doubt that the Japanese dancer's body has a built-in adaptability for the intricacies of modern dance movement, especially of the Graham school."

California, Berkeley campus. By early 1918 Graham was teaching and living at the Denishawn studio. Through early 1920 Graham had danced only minor roles with Denishawn, such as that of a Japanese house-boy assisting St. Denis in a dance about flower arranging.[10] But later in 1920 Graham became a Denishawn soloist, performing Shawn's *Xochitl* and other numbers on vaudeville and concert tours. Producer John Murray Anderson saw Graham dance in New York during the 1922–23 Denishawn tour and hired her for his *Greenwich Village Follies*.[11] One of the two numbers featuring Graham in the 1923 edition of the Follies was *The Garden of Kama*. Like a St. Denis–Shawn piece with the same title, which had premiered in San Francisco eight years earlier, the *Follies* "Garden" choreographed by Michio Ito[12] was inspired by the *Indian Love Lyrics* of Laurence Hope.[13]

Clearly, Graham would have to go further than Broadway to escape the surface Orientalisms she had known at Denishawn. In New York on April 18, 1926, Martha Graham gave her first independent concert. The eighteen piece program "contained romantic and exotic numbers reminiscent of her Denishawn days,"[14] including *The Three Gopi Maidens*, an excerpt from *The Flute of Krishna* to be produced the following month at Eastman School of Music, which had recently been established in Rochester, New York. Having seen Graham on the 1922–23 Denishawn tour and in her 1924 season with the *Follies*, Rouben Mamoulian hired her to teach at the Eastman School.[15] Graham began teaching there in September of 1925, commuting between New York and Rochester. Mamoulian productions for which Graham was responsible for choreography were almost all ethnic or period pieces, among them *Scene Javanese* and *The Flute of Krishna*, the latter staged and filmed in May of 1926 and "obviously Denishawn-inspired as far as theme and style were

---

[10]   Leatherman, pages 47–48. "Her convincing performance led to a plan to turn her into a Japanese boy who was to be billed as a great Denishawn discovery. Her protest about what would happen when her breasts were fully developed was brushed aside: she would simply be bound up. Her mother learned of the plan and said no and saved her from an ambiguous early career."

[11]   Ruth St. Denis, *Ruth St. Denis: An Unfinished Life*. New York: Harper and Brothers,1939, page 174. Graham was the second Denishawn dancer to join the *Greenwich Village Follies*. Among Denishawn alumni St. Denis lists Ada Forman, a featured dancer with the *Follies* for many years.

[12]   Michio Ito was a Japanese dancer who worked in New York (1916–1929) and in Los Angeles (1929–1942).

[13]   Stodelle, *Deep Song*, page 44.

[14]   *Ibid.*, page 48.

[15]   Mamoulian sought Graham as a contributor to theatrical projects fusing all of the theater arts into an organically conceived whole. The director would come to realize this artistic principle in the original stage productions of *Porgy and Bess* (1935), *Oklahoma* (1943), and *Carousel* (1945), the latter two choreographed by Agnes de Mille.

concerned."[16] In performance later in 1926 Graham would present *Three Poems of the East*, and early in 1928, *Chinese Poem*.[17]

Graham's earliest work in independent concerts and at Eastman was not a dramatic departure from her roots; however, in the years to come her continued interest in the style and philosophy of the East would be influential in the development of the Graham technique and of the choreographer's theater aesthetic. Since joining the *Greenwich Village Follies* in 1923, Graham had rented an apartment on Ninth Street in Greenwich Village, not far from the Gotham Book Mart. The store's owner, Frances Steloff, had an interest in Eastern philosophy and religion, and the store had a sizable collection of books on Oriental subjects. Graham was in the store frequently, and learning of their mutual interest in the East, Graham and Steloff formed an important friendship.[18] In 1925 Graham met the Japanese sculptor–designer Isamu Noguchi who designed twenty-three Graham sets beginning with *Frontier* in 1935. Steloff and Noguchi were, for Graham, important personal links with the growing extent and intensity of America's awareness of the Orient. Graham's references to the Orient in *The Notebooks* reveal other sources of her ongoing dialogue with the East.

Little in-depth understanding of the Eastern worldview had been possible until Sir William "Oriental" Jones deciphered Sanskrit and established the Royal Asiatic Society in India in 1784.[19] Hymns to Hindu gods translated by Jones came to be reprinted in American magazines, and one of these made a deep impression upon seventeen year old Ralph Waldo Emerson when he read it in 1820. It was in Emerson's library around twenty years later that Henry David Thoreau first discovered Oriental thought. From 1842 to 1844 Emerson and Thoreau regularly published excerpts from Hindu and Buddhist classics in *The Dial*, the literary journal sponsored by the informal Transcendental Club which met at Boston and Concord. The work of Walt Whitman shows Eastern influence as well.[20] The English journalist and poet Edwin Arnold's *The Light of Asia*, published in Boston in 1879, told the story of Buddha in a manner consistent with Victorian taste. The book's eighty editions sold between a half million and a million copies. One of those copies belonged to Ruth St. Denis whose autobiography identifies the book, along with a translation of the *Bhagavad Gita* and Mary Baker Eddy's *Science and Health*

---

[16]   Stodelle, *Deep Song*, page 46.
[17]   *Ibid.*, pages 300–302.
[18]   Steloff was instrumental in financing Graham's first independent concert.
[19]   The British had been in India since 1612 and William Jones, a justice in the Supreme Court of India, had been sent there to apply his knowledge of Sanscrit to learning the nature of the Indians' disobedience to the Crown.
[20]   Fields, pages 64–66.

(1875), itself influenced by Indian mysticism, as constant companions in her travels.[21]

Turn of the century America's acquaintance with the religions of the Orient was furthered by the World Parliament of Religions, part of the Columbia Exposition of 1893 in Chicago. Among delegates was the Ceylonese Buddhist Anagarika Dharmapala, the leader of International Buddhism, and the Japanese Soyen Shaku, the first Zen master in America. Among results of the Parliament were Dharmapala's lecture-tours of the United States in 1896 and 1902–04. During the latter visit Dharmapala lectured to William James' class at Harvard, outlining the major Buddhist doctrines. Following Dharmapala's speech James observed to the class: "This is the psychology everybody will be studying twenty-five years from now."[22] Another outcome of the Parliament of Religions was the friendship between Zen master Soyen and Open Court Press editor Paul Carus. Carus needed a translator and editor for a new series of Oriental works, and Soyen suggested his student D.T. Suzuki for the task. Early in 1897 when Suzuki arrived here to work with Carus on their 1898 English translation of Taoism's "bible," the *Tao Te Ching* of Lao Tsu, Suzuki began *Outlines of Mahayana Buddhism*. Suzuki's first book in English, this commenced his ongoing direction of the West's attention toward Buddhism.

Ernest Fenollosa, a native of Salem-Boston and graduate of Harvard, arrived in Tokyo in 1878. While at Harvard he had attended the first lecutures in the new field of art history, and once in Japan became enthralled with Chinese and Japanese art. Instrumental in the rediscovery of countless art treasures locked in Japanese temples for two hundred years, Fenollosa convinced not only the West, but also the East itself, that the traditional art of China and Japan were resources to be treasured. By 1884 Fenollosa had acquired enough Chinese and Japanese art for the Boston Museum to have the greatest collection of Far Eastern art in the world, West or East, and in 1890 he became curator of the museum's Department of Far Eastern Art.

Translations of Chinese poems within Fenollosa's posthumous text *Epochs of Chinese and Japanese Art* led American ex-patriot Ezra Pound to expound a theory of poetry which has had profound influence on modern poetry and on the concept of Oriental art and its relationship to modern Western art. Ideas in Fenollosa's essay "The Chinese Written Character as a Medium for Poetry," which Pound would publish and embrace as a manifesto, appear throughout discussions of the art of the East and of the constructivist tendency in modern art. Pound was

---

[21]   St. Denis, pages 48, 306.

[22]   Bhikshu Sangarakshita, *Anagarika Dharmapaula: A Biographical Sketch*. Kandia, India: Buddhist Publication Society, 1964, page 78.

responsible for the publication of other posthumous works of Fenollosa including *Noh* (1916), which Graham quotes in the *Notebooks*. It is possible that Graham's influential contact with Noh dates from her 1923 work with Michio Ito, who had met Noh enthusiasts Ezra Pound and W.B. Yeats in England.[23]

Arthur Wesley Dow, Fenollosa's assistant at the Boston Museum, became Director of the Fine Arts Department at Columbia University's Teachers College in 1903. Dow's students at Teachers College – among them Georgia O'Keefe who enrolled in 1914 – read Fenollosa's *Epochs of Chinese and Japanese Art* (1912) and his review of Gonse's *L'Art Japonais* (1833) and were thus influenced by Fenollosa's "curious mixture of notions derived from Emerson and Thoreau together with Buddhist quietism and detachment."[24]

Ananda K. Coomaraswamy, to whom Graham referred in *The* Notebooks, was born of English and Ceylonese parents and spent his youth in England and Asia. Coomaraswamy brought his entire personal art collection to the Boston Museum in 1917, founding, within the department Fenollosa had established, the first sub-department of Indian art in an American museum. Coomaraswamy's career as museum curator, art historian and critic, and scholarly spokesman of an Oriental worldview was eminently distinguished. St. Denis notes that Coomaraswamy's *Buddha and the Gospel of Buddhism* (1916) had traveled with her "year after year"[25] and Erick Hawkins pays homage to Coomaraswamy in his essay "Pure Poetry."[26] The Coomaraswamy works cited in *The Notebooks of Martha Graham* are *The Mirror of Gesture*, first published in 1917 and in a second edition in 1936, and *The Transformation of Nature in Art*, published in 1935. His translation of the *Abhinaya Darpana of Nandikesvara*, an early compendium of the *Natya Shastra*, *The Mirror of Gesture* offers photographs of Indian dance in sculpture.

The year 1927 marked the publication of *The Tibetan Book of the Dead* (*Bardo Thodal*), edited and compiled by W.Y. Evans-Wentz, another scholar cited by Graham. An American who had earned his degree in folklore at Oxford, Evans-Wentz traveled in Asia in 1919 and the 1920s. In 1919 in Tibet he met the actual translator of the text with whom he prepared the English edition. In light of the profound influence of the

---

[23]   Stodelle, *Deep Song*, page 44.

[24]   In his *The Meeting of East and West* (1946) cited later in this survey, F.S.C. Northrop distinguishes between "art in its first function" and "art in its second function," noting in the art of the Orient a tendency toward the former. Northrop's study, avowedly instrumental in Erick Hawkins' constructivist philosophy of "Pure Fact" and "Pure Poetry," singles out some of the paintings of O'Keefe as instances of "art in its first function."

[25]   St. Denis, page 247.

[26]   Erick Hawkins, "Pure poetry." In *The Modern Dance: Seven Statements of Belief*, edited by Selma Jeanne Cohen. Middletown, Connecticut: Wesleyan University 1966, page 51.

work of Carl Jung upon Martha Graham, Evans-Wentz' publication of *The Tibetan Book of the Dead* is highly significant for the choreographer. Graham's "myth period" of the 1940s was predicated upon her own realization, through Jungian psychoanalysis with Dr. Frances Wickes, of the rich truth of Jung's psychological commentaries on Western, Chinese, and Indian thought, on archetypal symbolism, myth, and religious art. Jung wrote in his "Psychological Commentary" to *The Tibetan Book of the Dead*: "For years, ever since it was first published, the *Bardo Thodal* has been my constant companion, and to it I owe not only many stimulating ideas and discoveries, but also many fundamental insights."[27] Already in 1916's *Psychology of Consciousness*, which Graham quotes in the *Notebooks*, Jung was deriving information and insight from the literature of the East. The extent of involvement of Jung's work with Eastern thought by the early 1930s had warranted the interest of Coomaraswamy who found Jung's work in the same vein as his own and with whom Jung shared some personal correspondence.[28] Richard Wilhelm's German translation of *The Secret of the Golden Flower: A Chinese Book of Life* (1929) included a "European Commentary" by Jung. Published in English in 1931, the joint work was among those classics of Eastern thought which Jung was instrumental in introducing to the West.

The 1930s saw the beginnings of growth in Americans' awareness of Eastern movement forms. Uday Shankar, the Indian dancer who had appeared in New York and London as Krishna in Anna Pavlova's balletic *Radha-Krishna* in 1924, returned to India in 1930 to be instrumental in the renaissance of Indian classical dance which Denishawn's 1926 visit had helped to spark. In 1933 Shankar's troupe appeared in New York, creating a sensation.[29] The research and performance of Indian Bharata Natyam by Russell Meriwhether Hughes (La Meri) developed throughout the 1930s, with St. Denis and La Meri opening the School of Natya in New York in 1940. In addition to La Meri's twice weekly performances at the school 1946–48, Abrahams cites sixty-seven New York City performances by thirty-one Asian dance soloists or performance groups from

---

[27] Carl Jung, Psychological commentary. In W.Y. Evans-Wentz, *The Tibetan Book of the Dead*. Oxford: Oxford University Press, 1960 page xxxvi. What most impressed Jung was the clarity of the book's psychology, the way it instructed the dead, as well as the living, to recognize all appearances and visions, whether beautiful or terrifying, as reflections of consciousness. With *The Tibetan Book of the Dead*, Evans-Wentz opened the doors of the West to the art and culture of Tibet which in the 1960s and seventies contributed imagery to the "psychedelic" cult surrounding use of the drug LSD.

[28] Ananda K. Coomaraswamy, *Coomaraswamy: His Life and Work, Vol. III*, ed. Roger Lipsey. Princeton: Princeton University Press, page 203.

[29] Kisselgoff, Anna "Uday Shankar recalls prior U.S. interest in India," *The New York Times*, 16 October 1968, page 36.

1921 through 1950.[30] Graham's numerous references in *The Notebooks* to "Bali arabesque," "Bali attitude," "Bali position," "Bali turn," "Javanese foot movement," "Javanese step," and "lotus position" could derive from work with St. Denis, from photographed representations of Asian dance and sculpture such as those in *The Mirror of Gesture*, or from exposure to the concertizing cited by Abrahams.

Dissemination of an Asian worldview through scholarly discourse continued. The 1927 publication of D.T. Suzuki's *Essays in Zen Buddhism* and two subsequent editions of the work by 1936 had secured Suzuki's reputation in England and the United States. In that year Suzuki lectured in England at the World Congress of Faiths, enchanting a young Englishman named Alan Watts. In the early 1950s Suzuki's lectures at Columbia University inspired a generation of psychologists and artists, including Erick Hawkins, Merce Cunningham, and John Cage, the latter two actually present at the lectures. While *The Notebooks* make no reference to the work of Suzuki, Graham's philosophy of dance technique as expressed in "A Modern Dancer's Primer for Action" and in the film *A Dancer's World* (1957) shows evidence of her contact with the growing dialogue between Zen and psychology initiated by Jung.[31]

Notes from Heinrich Zimmer's spring 1942 and spring 1943 lectures at Columbia University yielded Zimmer's *Philosophies of India*, published posthumously in 1951. Graham quotes the work, alternately referring to Zimmer; to Joseph Campbell, editor of the book; and to E.B. Havell, the scholar whose unpublished "The History of Aryan Rule in India" is referred to significantly by Zimmer and Campbell. The remaining author

---

[30] Ruth Abrahams, pages 116–152.

[31] In the "Primer for Action" Graham identified the three-fold purpose of technique: strength of body, freedom of body and spirit, and spontaneity of action. She proclaimed that "freedom may only be achieved through discipline," that "spontaneity is essentially dependent upon energy, upon the strength necessary to perfect timing … the result of perfect timing to the Now." The discipline which Graham glorifies extends deeper than mere physical tuning, for "your years of training and discipline in your craft and in the cultivation of yourself as a human being have made it possible for you to be free." "And when a dancer is at the peak of his power he has two lovely, fragile, perishable things – one is spontaneity. … The other is simplicity." In her citing "spontaneity," "freedom," and "simplicity" as desired qualities of the dancer and in identifying discipline as the only way to achieve them, Graham echoes Suzuki, in the following instance addressing the 1957 Conference of Zen Buddhism and Psychoanalysis in Cuernavaca, Mexico.

As Suzuki explained, psychologists talk a great deal about spontaneity, but what they are talking about is a child-like spontaneity, which is by no means the spontaneity and freedom of an adult human being. As long as he is unable to give up his childish freedom, he will need the help of a psychologist, but he can never expect to be free and spontaneous if he does not go through years, perhaps many decades of self-discipline. (See D.T. Suzuki, *Essentials of Zen Buddhism: An Anthology of the Writings of Daisetz T. Suzuki*, edited by Bernard Phillips. London: Rider & Co., 1962, pages 20–21.)

dealing with the Orient whom Graham cites in *The Notebooks* is Santha Rama Rau, an Indian whose *Home to India* was published in 1945.

The West's increased awareness of the Buddhist worldview came via Dwight Goddard's highly influential *The Buddhist Bible* (1932) and his publication throughout the 1930s of many of the *sutras*; through Suzuki's numerous publications throughout the thirties and forties; and through Alan Watts' *The Spirit of Zen* (1946). War between the United States and Japan provoked the publication in 1946 of F.S.C. Northrop's *The Meeting of East and West: An Inquiry Concerning World Understanding*. The fact that such a multi-leveled comparison of "The Meaning of Western Civilization" and "The Meaning of Eastern Civilization" could be written indicates the vast amount of information regarding the East available to the interested American – Martha Graham, for one – at mid-century.

Martha Graham's strong affinity with a non-Western worldview was nurtured through the exploration of Asian culture evidenced in *The Notebooks*. During the 1930s and forties the choreographer's appropriation of the Orient – in terms of both technique and theater aesthetic – passed from surface imitation and thematic inspiration à la Denishawn to a more physically and aesthetically integrated assimilation of the East. The depth of Graham's identification with the meeting of East and West carried with it stringent artistic goals.

There is something here it seems of the struggle between the Atlantic and Pacific cultures. It is the Pacific that emerges stronger – but with a sustained note of the other under it like a vibration. There is a unity. Almost it seems there sounds the sacred syllable that is a symbol of that unity. How can that be communicated? What symbols of theatre can I employ to make it evident?[32]

Bibliography

Abrahams, Ruth K. "Performance chronology of Asian dance in New York City 1906–1976. In *Asian and Pacific Dance: Dance Research Annual VIII*, edited by A.L. Kaeppler, J. Van Zile, C. Wolz, New York: Congress on Research in Dance, 1977, pp. 109–171.

Brockett, Oscar G. *History of the Theatre*. Boston: Allyn and Bacon, Inc., 1968.

Caldwell, Helen. *Michio Ito: The Dancer and His Dances*. Berkeley: University of California Press 1977.

Coomaraswamy, Ananda K. *Coomaraswamy: His Life and Work, Vol. III*, ed. Roger Lipsey Princeton: Princeton University Press, 1977.

Coomaraswamy, Ananda K. "Oriental dances in America." *Vanity Fair*, VII, 61, May 1917.

Coomaraswamy, Ananda K. *The Transformation of Nature in Art*. Cambridge: Harvard University Press, 1935.

Duncan, Isadora. *My Life*. New York: Boni and Liverwright, 1927.

Ewens, David. *New Complete Book of the American Musical Theater*. New York: Holt Rinehart and Winston, 1978.

---

[32]   Graham, during work on *Dark Meadow*, cited in *The Notebooks*, page 190.

Fields, Rick. *How the Swans Came to the Lake: A Narrative History of Buddhism in America.* Boulder, Colorado: Shambala, 1981.

Graham, Martha. "A Modern Dancer's Primer for Action." In *Dance: A Basic Educational Technique,* edited by Frederick Rand Rogers. New York: The Macmillan Company, 1941.

Graham, Martha. Narration for film *A Dancer's World, 1957.*

Graham, Martha. *The Notebooks of Martha Graham.* New York: Harcourt Brace Jovanovich, 1973.

Hawkins, Erick. "Pure fact in movement, technique and choreography." *Dance Observer* 25, 9, November 1958.

Hawkins, Brick. "Pure Poetry." In *The Modern Dance: Seven Statements of Belief,* edited by Selma Jeanne Cohen. Middletown, Connecticut: Wesleyan University, 1966.

Jung, C.J. Psychological commentary. In W.Y. Evans-Wentz, *The Tibetan Book of the Dead.* Oxford: Oxford University Press, 1960.

Kisselgoff, Anna. "Uday Shankar recalls prior U.S. interest in India," *The New York Times* (16 October 1968), p. 36.

La Meri (Russell Meriwhether Hughes) *The Gesture Language of the Hindu Dance.* New York: B. Blom, 1941.

Leatherman, Leroy. *Martha Graham: Portrait of the Lady as an Artist.* Photographs by Martha Swope. New York: Alfred A. Knopf, 1966.

Martha Graham Centennial: The First Hundred Years. New York: Martha Graham Center for Contemporary Dance and the Philip Morris Corporation, 1994.

Rose, Barbara. "O'Keefe's Trail," a book review of *Georgia O'Keefe by Georgia O'Keefe. The New York Review of Books* (31 March 1977), pp. 29–33.

St. Denis, Ruth. *Ruth St. Denis: An Unfinished Life.* New York: Harper and Brothers, 1939.

Sangarakshita, Bhikshu. *Anagarika Dharmapaula: A Biographical Sketch.* Kandia, India: Buddhist Publication Society, 1964.

Shelton, Suzanne. "The Influence of Genevieve Stebbins on the Early Career of Ruth St. Denis." *Essays in Dance Research: Dance Research Annual IX* New York: Congress on Research in Dance, 1978.

Sherman, Jane. "Denishawn Oriental Dances." *Dance Scope,* 13, Nos. 2 & 3, 33–43. 1979.

Sherman, Jane. *The Drama of Denishawn Dance.* Middletown, Connecticut: Wesleyan University Press, 1979.

Stodelle, Ernestine. "Anna Sokolow in Japan," *Dance Magazine,* Vol. 41, No. 1, 40–42, Jan. 1967, pp. 78–80.

Stodelle, Ernestine. *Deep Song: The Dance Story of Martha Graham.* New York: Schirmer Books, 1984.

Suzuki, D.T. *Essentials of Zen Buddhism: An Anthology of the Writings of Daisetz T. Suzuki,* edited by Bernard Phillips. London: Rider & Co., 1962.

Todd, Arthur. "The Rise of Musical Comedy in America" *Dance Magazine,* Vol. 24, No. 12, December 1958, pp. 23–25, 38.

Choreography and Dance
1999, Vol. 5, Part 2, pp. 53–67
Photocopying permitted by license only

The Role of Martha Graham's Notebooks in Her Creative Process

Nolini Barretto

Journal entries made by Martha Graham from the 1940s to the mid 1960s have been transcribed and edited in *The Notebooks of Martha Graham*. The dances they reference represent Graham's post-Americana period – a shift of focus from exploration of American consciousness to a wider perspective, the use of Greek myths and philosophical texts as a way to explore the roots of the unconscious mind and soul. Graham's entries in the Notebooks give insight to the first stages of her creative process and provide understanding of the multiplicity of meanings inherent in such ballets as *Dark Meadow*. Notations for specific ballets, together with quotations, images and phrases give the reader a sense of her creative intent. The paper shows that while often little from the *Notebooks* was actually used in the final dance, the musings act as a springboard to the next phase of creation of the dances, and make evident that Graham's dances were an expression of deep philosophical inquiry.

Martha Graham deliberately destroyed most of her early journals, notes and personal letters. Her copious and enigmatic work notes written in a dense penciled script on six by nine inch coil-bound steno pads, were intended for her personal use only. In 1965, however, hounded by Lucy Kroll,[1] Graham finally agreed to have fifty notebooks published. *The Notebooks of Martha Graham* contain ideas and studies for ballets like *Errand into the Maze, Deaths and Entrances, Dark Meadow* and *Clytemnestra*, spanning the period from the mid 1940s to mid 1960s. Coincidentally, this period is one of transition and an important shift of focus in the creative life of Graham. Many of her dances prior to this period testify to her work as a uniquely American artist. As a reflection of the American consciousness and of the political changes in the world, her early dances were, in a sense, outward directed. The *Notebooks*, and the dances they inspire, are inward looking, as Graham begins to use archetypal Greek

---

[1] Lucy Kroll was the producer of the film *A Dancers World*.

myths and philosophical texts to explore the changing "inner landscape" of her mind.

In 1935, a collection of essays by leading modern dancers attempted to explain to a new audience the significance of "modern dance," and the nature of its aesthetic implications. In it Martha Graham gives voice to her conviction that it is the task of the American modern choreographer to create a "dance form in a manner and style typically American."

Nothing is more revealing than movement. What you are finds expression in what you do. The dance reveals the spirit of the country in which it takes root. ... America does not concern itself now with impressionism. We own no involved philosophy. The psyche of the land is to be found in its movement. It is to be felt as a dramatic force of energy and vitality. ... As we begin to take more and more honor in the interpretation of the American scene, our dance takes deeper and deeper root. ... An American dance is not a series of new steps. It is more, infinitely more. It is a characteristic time beat, a different speed, an accent, sharp, clear, staccato. We know the American expression; we see the American gesture. Of things American the American dance must be made. ... To seek then the essential spirit of the country, to impart its sense of life, to enrich, illuminate, and intensify the American scene becomes then the object of the American dancer.[2]

In keeping with this philosophy, for the next ten years Graham's dances were inspired by contemporary American subjects and reflected the social spirit of the country.[3] Program notes for *Panorama* indicate the three main motifs of the dance: "The Theme of Dedication," based on the "early intensity of fanaticism with which our Puritan fathers sang their hymn of dedication," "The Imperial Theme," an expression of people in bondage; and the "Popular Theme," the awakening of social consciousness of the American people. The 1935 program observes, "In every country there are basic themes of thought and action. These themes are part of the national consciousness and form an inheritance that contributes to the present."

In *American Document* (1938), Graham introduced the first male dancer, Erick Hawkins to her all female company, thereby changing forever the dynamic of her work. The dance was her version of American history, and in it for the first time she used spoken texts to provide a background of reference for her audience. The narrator in the dance quoted from the Declaration of Independence, Lincoln's Gettysburg Address, the Emancipation Proclamation, Walt Whitman's poems and a letter from Red Jacket of the Seneca tribes among other texts, in order to illuminate Graham's themes of Revolution, Puritanism, the exploitation of the Indians, Emancipation and Democracy. It was a colorful and affirmative dance documentary, in the manner of the old minstrel

---

[2]   Virginia Stewart, editor, *Modern Dance* (New York: E. Weyhe, 1935), pages 101–106.
[3]   See Chronology of Dances at the end of this article.

shows. "In performance, its patriotic message was clear and emotionally compelling."[4]

During this period, like American artists John Don Passos and Ernest Hemingway, Graham was moved by the atrocities of the Spanish Civil War to make her own artistic protest. She choreographed *Chronicle* in 1936, *Deep Song* and *Immediate Tragedy* in 1937, as her personal and powerful statements on the horrors of war. *Deep Song*, a dance of unspeakable sorrow, is one woman's story of the anguish and suffering all women and mothers experience when their men are brutally killed in war. The solo is performed to hushed audiences to this day, and its universality transcends "any suggestion of propagandistic doctrine in its personal grief-stricken cry against untimely death."[5] *Chronicle* was a group piece in three sections, opening with "Spectre – 1914 (Drums – Red Shroud – Lament)," continuing with "Steps in the Street (Devastation – Homelessness – Exile)," and ending with "Prelude to Action (Unity – Pledge to the Future)." It was a dance that remembered a past war, grieved about present horrors, and gave warning of coming violence. In 1938, determined to help the cause, Graham (who almost never shared a stage with another choreographer), performed with choreographers Anna Sokolow, Helen Tamiris and Hanya Holm in a benefit concert to aid Spanish democracy.

Frontier, which premiered in 1935, is "a radiant dance of the American pioneer woman, strong, courageous, young and free. It is a dance full of space, in which any momentary sense of wilderness or loneliness is quickly overcome by the sense of opening vista and the fullness of the woman's life."[6] The spare and yet evocative sets designed by Noguchi for this piece, consisted of two thick ropes extending obliquely from opposite ends of a small log fence, to give an illusion of vastness and endless distance. The dance is a celebration of the pioneering spirit, and conveys Graham's sense of wonder about the endless landscape.

Graham's American motifs found their most lyrical and joyous expression in *Appalachian Spring*, danced to Aaron Copland's Shaker inspired score. Ernestine Stodelle writes: "In contrast to *Frontier* with its suggestion of a vast western wilderness to be conquered, the eastern environment of *Appalachian Spring* called for a domesticated interpretation of Americana."[7] Graham as the pioneer bride, with Hawkins as her new husband, together dance a tale of hope, exaltation, the promise of a new land, the pride of possession, and the freedom of the Appalachian landscape.

[4]   Alice Helpern. *The Technique of Martha Graham* (New York: Morgan & Morgan, 1994), page 16.
[5]   Ernestine Stodelle, *Deep Song: The Dance Story of Martha Graham* (New York: Schirmer Books, 1984), page 120.
[6]   Margaret Lloyd, *The Borzoi Book of Modern Dance* (New York: Knopf, 1949), page 55.
[7]   Stodelle, page 125.

It remains one of her most unforgettable ballets, timeless and still evocative of the innocence and optimism of the new world. McDonagh calls *Appalachian Spring* the "cap of Graham's Americana period" after which "she did not return again to personages of American history or to the events of the American expansion for subject matter," but instead "closed her chapter on the American experience with a strong affirmative response to its history and development."[8]

In the mid 1940s, Graham embarked on a very different voyage of discovery. She read insatiably, and moved further away from her early influences to feed her imagination. The change was the result of several contributing factors. First, Erick Hawkins was playing an increasingly major role in her life. He had been a student of Greek literature at Harvard, and was primarily interested in drawing on the Classics for choreographic inspiration. He "awakened her to the dance potential of Greek tragedy. Once embarked on her own Hellenic journey, she was to enter her Greek period and create theater works that matched those of the great poets for character analysis and majesty of vision."[9] In addition, she was introduced to the philosophy of Carl Jung by Joseph Campbell who was married to one of her dancers, Jean Erdman. Campbell aroused her interest in Jung's "unconscious memories of the race," and of myths as manifestations of the psyche. Graham also became a close friend and regular correspondent with Dr. Frances Wickes, lay analyst, writer and Jung's mistress. The late dance critic, Joseph Mazo writes,

After *Appalachian Spring*, Graham turned from her democratic inclinations; the dances she was making required figures of a more lonely constitution. She was engaged in tragedy, and left the secular religion of Americanism for that of psychoanalysis. ... Her retellings of legends during the late 1940s and 1950s interpreted mythology through psychological theory. It was as if she had taken to heart Jung's dictum that one should trisect one's life and spend the last segment meditating on one's self and the world.[10]

Indeed, in the mid-1940s, Graham was in her fiftieth year, and at a stage when physical limitations led her to "turn her thoughts to large-scale ideas in which she would cast herself as a symbolic figurehead within the expanded ensemble she now had at her disposal."[11] Since she could not perform physically demanding roles with the ease of her youth, she increasingly began to create roles in which she used her consummate acting ability and commanding presence to fill the stage. It was therefore inevitable that her dances would focus on externalizing her internal search for a new purpose as a performer and creator.

---

[8] Don McDonagh, *Martha Graham: A Biography* (New York: Praeger, 1973), page 177.
[9] Stodelle, page 145.
[10] Joseph Mazo, *Prime Movers* (New York: William Morrow, 1977), page 179.
[11] Stodelle, page 101.

Graham immersed herself in Greek mythology, and writing late into the night, copied quotations from Campbell's *Occidental Myth*, Gide, Jung, Rilke, and Coomaraswamy, among others. These notes were the fodder from which her dances grew. Her notebooks contain page after page of quotations from mythology, sociology, anthropology and philosophy. Often, the front pages of the notebook contained quotations, images and ideas about a ballet, while the flip sides had notations or written notes once the dance had been set. Graham justifies her extensive use of quotations from different sources, saying:

I am a thief – and I am not ashamed. I steal from the best wherever it happens to me – Plato – Picasso – Bertram Ross...I am a thief – and I glory in it – I steal from the present and from the glorious past – and I stand in the dark of the future as a glorying & joyous thief – There are so many wonderful things of the imagination to pilfer – so I stand accused – I am a thief – but with this reservation – I think I know the value of that I steal & treasure it for all time – not as a possession but as a heritage & as legacy.[12]

The *Notebooks* along with some unpublished journals from the Martha Graham archives, testify to her boundless curiosity, depth of inquiry, and to the multilayered workings of her mind. They give a privileged insight into the very first stages of the creative process. Some notes are the development of ideas in the form of stream of consciousness associations, or a repetition of images and symbols that offer a glimpse into her mind's journey. The different forms of the entries illustrate her different approaches to fleshing out her ideas. She uses the notebooks to develop and work through a central idea or preoccupation, and to anchor and record her mental associations and the path along which they lead her. She uses her notes to record her research and gathering of primary texts which illuminate the narrative she is considering, and to create and people a mythworld of her own devising.

I get the ideas going. Then I write down, I copy out of any book that stimulates me at that time any quotation, and I keep it. And I put down the source. Then, when it comes to the actual work I keep a complete record of the steps. I keep notes of every dance that I have. I don't have notation. I just put it down and know what the words mean or what the movements mean and where you go and what you do and maybe an explanation here and there.[13]

Very few entries are revealing of her personal life or of events preoccupying the world around her, though they may contain the seeds of her personal philosophy and beliefs. Finally, she uses the notebooks to

---

[12]   Martha Graham, *The Notebooks of Martha Graham* (New York: Harcourt Brace Jovanovich, 1973), page 303.
[13]   Graham, quoted in McDonagh, pages 161–162.

conceptualize ideas for theatrical and visual cues, casting, stage direction and as a dance notation. The primary value of the notes, however, remains in their ability to shed light on Graham's method of creation, and while doing so reveals that her dances were, in fact, an expression of deep philosophical inquiry.

The notebooks provide considerable insight into the depths and multiplicity of meanings inherent in Graham's ballets. For instance, *Dark Meadow*, one of her most abstruse works, has been variously interpreted as an exploration of the rites of fertility and sexuality, of the seasonal cycle of death, mourning and rebirth. There is no overt narrative or scenario for the audience to follow. The characters are, 'She of the Ground' (May O'Donnell), 'He Who Summons' (Erick Hawkins), 'One Who Seeks' (Martha Graham), and 'They Who Dance Together' (company of nine dancers). The program notes for a performance in 1946 state:

The action of Dark Meadow is concerned with the adventure of seeking.
This dance is the re-enactment of the Mysteries which attend that adventure:
Remembrance of the ancestral footsteps, –
Terror of loss, –
Ceaselessness of love, –
Recurring ecstasy of the flowering branch

Graham's penned notes on the program call the Dark Meadow, "a world of great symbols, the place of experience, the dark meadow of ATE, the Meadow of choice, the passage to another area of life." The origin of these cryptic thoughts can be directly traced to Graham's initial working out of the ballet in her voluminous notes. In the *Notebooks*, she compiles pages of quotations illustrating the many emotional and philosophical threads she is attempting to weave into the content of the ballet. Among them are:

The Journey of the Soul in search for Immortality

"But the Soul which hath seen most shall pass into the seed of a man who shall become a Seeker after the True Wisdom, a Seeker after the True Beauty, a Friend of the Muses, a True Lover…"

"What after all is the secret of Indian greatness? Not a dogma or a book, but the great open secret that all knowledge & all truth are absolute & infinite, waiting, not to be created, but to be found:"

Coomaraswamy

"The Philosopher as conceived by Plato is an ardent lover. He lives all his earthly life in a trembling hope, sees visions, & prophesies."

"The head Sublime, the heart Pathos, the genitals Beauty, the hands & feet Proportion."

Blake – Marriage of Heaven & Hell

"The Soul is conceived as falling from the region of light into the 'roofed-in Cave', the 'dark meadow of Ate'" –

frag. 119,120,121

"All visible things are emblems" – Carlyle – Intr. Pierre XXXII

I seem to feel in the first part – the opening – a memory of standing in the wind on the top of the Mexican pyramid – And then to remember the descent afterwards – There was an awareness up there of ancient rites – sacrifices – prayers – but enduring through all – the sun, the wind, the rain – "

"God is our own longing to which we pay divine honors"

Unconscious – Jung

I will not be released from this bondage until I have released myself. No man can do it for me.

The Path – the landscape of the journey is life – the Dark Meadow – the place of retribution – Destiny – Karma[14]

Through these and other entries in the journal, Graham begins to work out on paper the characteristics of the players in her mythworld. 'She Of The Ground' was initially mentioned as a possible character inspired by Semele, the mother of Dionysus. Later in the notes she becomes further defined as the "Guide … the Oracle of Dreams … The Smileless One." Similarly, the 'One Who Seeks' was at first simply "The Wanderer." Later Graham muses about "The flight of the alone to the Alone … One who seeks & finds by means of love … The Poet Woman … There is about her the directness of the primitive – enter the priestess, the prophetess or the artist."[15] The characters became so vital and alive in Graham's mind, that when the time came to translate them into physical movements on the dancers, she "composed them quickly. There are several witnesses to the effect that she accomplished long passages in a single evening."[16] The *Notebooks* make evident the conclusion that the ballet is the distillation of the literary and philosophical subtexts in Graham's mind, and that on one level, *Dark Meadow* can be interpreted as the artist's search for fulfillment and her passage towards self realization. Graham is portraying herself in the role of the 'One who Seeks'. Her genius lies in her ability to translate, interpret and make meaningful these preoccupations in a highly charged physical medium. The poet Ben Belitt, who often collaborated with Graham contends:

Whatever she does because she is a dancer will turn everything into dance. You can then have the most complex ideograms and mythological correlations, the labyrinthine meditations of Clytemnestra, because the charge is the charge of a whole lifetime that needs

---

14 *Ibid.*, pages 176 to 206.
15 *Ibid.*, page 189.
16 Agnes de Mille, *Martha* (New York; Random House, 1991), page 268.

Figure 8   May O'Donnell as 'She of the Ground' in *Dark Meadow*. Photo: Cris Alexander.

these polarizations and "stations" in which she can move in the execution of her "errand."[17]

In the notes for the section entitled "Dark Meadow of the Soul," Graham makes fourteen references to Jung's writings. She quotes his Psychological Types, essays on analytical psychology, the unconscious, Apulius, Firmicus, etc. Along with her readings on Eastern philosophical concepts

---

[17]   Ben Belitt, interviewed by Theresa Bowers. Part of the Oral History tapes of the Bennington School of Dance, Columbia University, 1979.

Figure 9 Members of Martha Graham Dance Company in Sarabande from *Dark Meadow*. Women (l. to r.) Ethel Winter, Pearl Lang, Yuriko. Photo: Arnold Eagle.

like Kundalini, Jungian philosophy gave a new dimension to the workings of Graham's mind. Campbell said, "Martha truly is the only one who can translate this material into a masterpiece with her perception. Here psychological linkings are worked through her own experience to emerge fresh and living."[18] Of *Dark Meadow* Graham says, "in a way, it is tracing the lineage, the genealogy of the soul of man, like a graph.

---

18   De Mille, page 278.

It stems back to our remote ancestry going into the barbaric, the primitive, the roots of life, coming out of racial memory. It is concerned with the psychological background of mankind."[19] Indeed, the initial working title for *Dark Meadow* was *Ancestral Footsteps*.

The depth to which Jungian concepts influenced Graham's interpretations and character development is also evident in *Cave of the Heart* which premiered in 1946. *Cave* is Graham's dramatization of the Greek myth of Medea. The action is focused on the terrible destructiveness of jealousy, and of Medea's alliance with the dark powers of humanity. In Graham's treatment of the myth, Medea, in a particularly riveting study of jealousy, kills her rival and is then herself trapped in a prison of flaming spikes of her own imagining, from which she can never escape.

The section on *Errand into the Maze* in the *Notebooks* illustrates how Graham's process of free association of images leads her from the exploration of an initial set of ideas to a pared down essence that works in the physical idiom. For example, Graham writes;

"The temptation of the Hermit" (Bosch)
"Terrible frivolities of Hell"
7 Deadly Sins –
Anger Vanity
The Hay Wagon (Bosch)
(1) An Episode of the Struggle for life
(2) Of Dragons...
Magdalene...
The various ways –
The neophyte to God – dedicated
The Aphrodite – the dream of men –
          Lady of the Labyrinth
The Sibyl – ancient one –
The Young One – (The Virgin –)...
The negation of the Lord of Death (Devil) –
Battle between poet & death...

In the final staging of the dance, *Errand into the Maze*, Graham discarded most of the above images, keeping the idea of the labyrinth and the battle. Program notes from the performance clarify, "There is an errand into the maze of the heart's darkness in order to face and do battle with the Creature of Fear." Pearl Lang, who was principal dancer with the company during this period, explains that Graham believed having an abstract title and theme for a ballet makes it difficult for the audience to relate to the work; therefore, Graham often presents the theme to the audience in the context of a known myth or story.[20] In this case, she uses

---

[19]   Lloyd, page 44.
[20]   From the author's interview with Pearl Lang, New York, November 1995.

the story of Ariadne and her confrontation with the mythical monster, the Minotaur, that lived within the depths of a labyrinthine cave, in order to contextualize the central conflict – be it the individual's battle with her most secret terrors, the fear of the unknown, the fear of abandonment, or the artist's fear of the lessening of her creative powers. The title *Errand into the Maze* came from Ben Belitt's poem *Dance Piece*, an homage to Graham. Belitt says, "She can see a whole script in a phrase like "errand into the maze" and rediscover the force of the word errand. Her images are scripts, "errands," threads to the labyrinth; she unfolds images with the instincts of a sibyl and the physical omniscience of a dancer."[21]

In her notetaking, Graham would find images and phrases that she repeatedly returned to. In the section entitled "The Trysting Tent," images of the "Early Dark," "Deep Dark," "Storm at Night," and "Moon Set" recur through the pages as a mantra, building up the imaginary landscape in her mind. Gradually, through repetition, the images coalesce into:

1. Early Dark –
   First gesture like cry – lifting arms into shaft of light like a sarabande of primordial meaning –
   > formal
   > nonpersonal
   > cry in the night
   solo beginning ...

Later in the notebook, the first section becomes:

In first – night Fall – Early dark –
almost all solo –
> passing, repassing of people –
or
use of tent & cypress tree (like dwarfed pine)
> done by unidentified forces –
> change of landscape – as tho by terrors of mind.
means are unseen[22]

As she wrote, she would find the poetic phrase that could trigger visual images. She would then start laying down a scenario that could encompass the form of the idea that was beginning to take shape in her mind.

The notebooks hold invaluable notations for ballets including *Clytemnestra*, *Night Journey* and *Judith*. The notations are in words, the Graham idiom, terms like "cave turns," "knee crawl" "stork position," "2 knee vibrations," "traveling fall" "March jumps." The terms are clearly understandable for anyone well versed in the Graham technique,

---

21   Ben Belitt, interviewed by Theresa Bowers.
22   Graham, page 219–227.

but would make little sense to a lay reader. The notations also include stage directions, number of measures, and music cues. Howard Gardner believes that "on their own, neither the quotations nor the mechanistic instructions are particularly revealing. But taken together one senses the kind of work that Graham was trying to create between these 'poles' – a work where the bodily movements, facial expressions, sets, props, and musical accompaniment captured the ideas embodied in the text."[23] For purposes of reconstruction however, the notations are not always useful. The dances frequently change in minor and major ways from the time Graham put them in her notebook. For instance, some steps were changed to accommodate a different cast of dancers, or Graham herself. The *Appalachian Spring* that Graham danced with Stuart Hodes when she was in her sixties, was technically different from the version she originally danced with Hawkins. Since she could no longer perform some of the movements she had choreographed earlier with equal facility, she changed them in her later restaging; this, then, became the version the company performed for several years thereafter.

At various points in her notes, Graham imagines the development of the dance in definite visual terms. For instance in *Phaedra*, she writes of a suspended bed from which Phaedra descends into the action, and to which she returns climbing a small staircase. In *Voyage*, she imagines a grilled gate upstage right, platform, steps, Shoji screen, the interior of a room where each object becomes something different when turned. In "I Salute My Love," (*Ardent Song*, 1954) she includes lighting cues: "as the curtain opens she is standing gazing into an intense light – only her face seen – She sings – As she sits or sinks into darkness of the doorway the scene in the room is lighted." She visualizes the dancer wearing a large outer cape with a veil, a fan or a "small crotali." The stage directions are by no means final; however, they do serve to illustrate that even in the earliest stages of developing a dance, Graham envisioned it in the fullest theatrical sense.

The notebooks are Graham's phase of "theoretical meditation"[24] in the creation of a ballet. She is close, private and brooding at this premature phase. She works at home, alone, and seldom discusses her thought processes with anyone. She is, essentially, voyaging into her inner self until she finds the destination she seeks. Howard Gardner calls the *Notebooks* "a place where she develops the 'space' of her works. Space between literal step description and quotes from literary texts whose animating ideas and emotions she was trying to embody in her works."[25] The notebooks are in effect a springboard from which she launches into the next phase of the

---

[23] Howard Gardner, *Creating Minds* (New York: Basic Books, 1993), page 295.
[24] Richard Wagner, quoted in Leroy Leatherman, *Martha Graham, Portrait of the Lady as an Artist* (New York: Alfred A. Knopf, 1966), page 53.
[25] Gardner, page 295.

creation of the dance. From here she devises a script for the composer she is commissioning, a script which is, in many ways, similar to the notebook entries. The script may contain plot development, quotations from readings that may have inspired the piece, a specific sequence of solos, duets or group sections, and sometimes a time frame for the sequences.

The script was often left open, both so the composer could have the space to develop his music, and Graham the room to depart from her original ideas if necessary. In a letter to Aaron Copland she wrote, "I do know that when I hear your music, it will give a new and different life to the script. Once the music comes I never look back at the script ... Now it exists in words, in literary terms only, and it has to come alive in a more plastic medium ... It seems that I have written miles of words ... The story is not so important, of course, as the inner life that emerges as the medium takes hold of the germ of the idea and proceeds to develop."[26] When the score or stage set came back from the composer or designer, Graham never suggested changes or reworkings. Instead she would change or develop her choreography if necessary, working it around the music or stage sets. "The final result is that characters and the action are so directly and intimately related with the design that they give that sense of the naturalness of the whole."[27]

Once the music was composed, the final part of the creative imaginings that began in the notebooks is worked out in the studio on the bodies of the dancers. Pearl Lang remembers that very little from the notebooks was directly brought into the studio. "Martha might throw in a color, or light, a quality of movement, but she usually had already formulated the way she wanted the piece to work."[28] At times work in the studio might lead to a completely different direction. In 1943, Graham was working on *Deaths and Entrances*, an introspective study of the life and loves of Emily Bronte. During this period, she wrote to her designer, Arch Lauterer, saying, "I have not quite finished the thing I am working on. I hesitate to say the Bronte because it is no longer that I feel. It has become something else more general, I think. I see how far I am away from my scenario when I read it again ... . It has become an experience of the emotions involving that part of us that is responsible for the creative dream."[29] By the 1940s, Graham had so trained her company to respond to her choreography and technique that she could trust a few select dancers to develop movements for their own parts, which she would later either accept or reject. As she had with the composer, she increased the space of the creative field by allowing her dancers to add to it with their own inventiveness.

---

[26]   Martha Graham, *Blood Memory* (New York: Doubleday, 1991), page 228.
[27]   Leatherman, page 124.
[28]   From the author's interview with Pearl Lang, New York, November 1995.
[29]   McDonagh, page 162.

The *Notebooks* close with *Circe* and *The Witch of Endor* which were performed in 1963 and 1965. This corresponds with the closing of yet another chapter in the creative life of Graham. She had originally intended to play the role of Circe herself, but "despite the force of Martha's personality and theatrical showmanship, it was becoming obvious that the light she shed on stage was beginning to dim."[30] Reluctantly she had to relinquish the role of Circe to Mary Hinkson. After *The Witch* of *Endor*, she created a few more ballets, the most notable among them being *Cortège of Eagles*, a monumental mythological reworking of Hecuba's tragic life. Graham gradually retreated into a period of emotional withdrawal while she wrestled with realization that her life on stage was inescapably over. "Between 1971 and 1973, Martha Graham fought her way out of the belly of the whale. Psychologically speaking, her reemergence can be viewed as one of the greatest creative acts of her life."[31] She returned triumphantly in 1973 with *Mendicants of Evening*, to begin yet another creative phase. Choreographing for the first time solely for dancers other than herself, she embraces youth, affirms life, and for the next two decades creates works that are characterized by a new lyricism, athleticism and luminosity.

Few critics have attempted an in-depth study of the *Notebooks*. Some find the book more "misleading than revealing." Howard Gardner writes that he "does not find that the notebooks provide much additional insight into the development of Graham's dances as a visual-gestural-bodily expression of her own person."[32] Even if her many quotations do not seem to be directly related to the final dance, however, they are all used as inspiration in the development of character, content and context. Agnes de Mille values them for their richness of suggestion, and as an "annotated explanation of many of her more obscure allusions, symbols, and ideas."[33] Entries in the notebooks on "Techniques of Ecstasy" for instance, read like a virtual bibliography of the dance. One feels that if one read all that Graham was reading, one might be able to follow the road her mind was embarking on. She quotes the "Magic Prison" of Dickinson, the legend of Orpheus and Eurydice, the sound of spheres from Campbell, and most tellingly, from Bacon, the passage, "For he who recollects or remembers, thinks; he who imagines, thinks; he who reasons, thinks; and in a word the spirit of man, whether prompted by sense or left to itself, whether in the function of the intellect, or of the will and affection, dances to the time of the tho'ts."[34] The *Notebooks* mark Graham's shift in thought and focus from a conscious expression as an American artist to a wider perspective from which she seeks to explore

---

[30]   Stodelle, page 237.
[31]   *Ibid.*, page 260.
[32]   Gardner, page 295.
[33]   De Mille, page 395.
[34]   Graham, *Notebooks*, page 30.

the roots of man's unconscious in order to understand the history and psychology of the race. The notebooks make evident the fact that her dances are indeed the cumulative result of years of intellectual curiosity, poetic sensibility, and a never ending search for meaning.

In the *Notebooks*, Graham comments, "It seems to me that the only point of writing even a so-called autobiography ... is to point a way to others who follow ... The only justification for the pain & embarrassment of self-revealment is to point a way – perhaps to point *a way from* – rather than a way toward."[35] The *Notebooks* illuminate the byways and turns on the path Graham took from her early evocations of the American landscape, to the labyrinthine explorations of the human psyche. Above all, she maintained,

You must keep alive the wonder. You must listen to ancestral footsteps, but you must never look back. You must move ahead believing movement never lies, searching for truth, letting your body speak...[36]

Chronology of Selected Dances

1934	*Celebration*	1948	*Diversion of Angels*
1934	*American Provincials*	1951	*Judith*
1935	*Frontier*	1953	*Voyage*
1935	*Panorama*	1955	*Seraphic Dialogue*
1936	*Salutation*	1958	*Clytemnestra*
1936	*Chronicle*	1960	*Alcestis*
1937	*Immediate Tragedy*	1962	*Phaedra*
1937	*Deep Song*	1963	*Circe*
1937	*American Lyric*	1965	*The Witch of Endor*
1937	*American Document*	1967	*Cortege of Eagles*
1940	*El Penitente*	1968	*The Plain of Prayer*
1940	*Letter to the World*	1969	*The Archaic Hours*
1942	*Land Be Bright*	1973	*Mendicants of Evening*
1943	*Salem Shore*	1975	*Lucifer*
1943	*Deaths and Entrances*	1980	*Judith*
1944	*Appalachian Spring*	1981	*Acts of Light*
1946	*Dark Meadow*	1984	*Rite of Spring*
1946	*Cave of the Heart*	1986	*Temptations of the Moon*
1947	*Errand into the Maze*	1988	*Night Chant*
1947	*Night Journey*	1990	*Maple Leaf Rag*

---

[35]   *Ibid.*, page 269.
[36]   Martha Graham, Excerpts from The Opening Night Address at the Mark Hellinger Theatre, New York, April 15, 1974.

Figure 10   Helen McGehee as Electra in *Clytemnestra*. Photo: Antony di Gesu.

Choreography and Dance
1999, Vol. 5, Part 2, pp. 69–77
Photocopying permitted by license only

An Opportunity Lost[1]

Helen McGehee

McGehee describes the creation of *Clytemnestra* and her role in designing the costumes, first for her own character and then the other women. Martha Graham's *Clytemnestra* was the culminating achievement of her illustrious career. An enormous success, with every performance sold out, there was an opportunity, unprecedented for modern dance, to have an indefinite run on Broadway. Regrettably, management turned it down. Another lost opportunity was the building of a permanent studio-theater within the Martha Graham Studio, as designed by lighting designer Jean Rosenthal. In the end, it was Martha Graham who, like Siva, had the power to create or to destroy.

The originator of a unique and hitherto unknown kind of theater in America was Martha Graham. Through the use of new movement, new music, new sculpture, new costuming, a new approach to theatrical lighting, a new concept of dancer-players playing in a dance-play, she created a kind of theater which illuminates the spectator, moves him to catharsis through unpredictable and shocking visions to a single total vision of human reality. Undoubtedly the creation of that masterpiece which is Martha Graham's *Clytemnestra* was the culminating achievement of this country's pre-eminent genius, the crown of her illustrious career, both as dancer and, more importantly, as choreographer.

Our long Asian tour had ended in the Spring of 1956.[2] Then followed a fallow but not infertile period, a period of brooding which led to the hatching, in 1958, of *Clytemnestra*. This was an enormous success. All the critics wrote enthusiastically but the special measure of success was the acclaim from the general public. Every performance was sold out.

---

[1]   This article was originally an address delivered at the University of North Carolina at Greensboro, North Carolina, in November 1989. It was published in Helen McGehee, *To Be A Dancer*. Lynchburg, Virginia: Editions Heraclita, 1990.

[2]   The Martha Graham Dance Company made its first tour of Asia in 1955–56 under the sponsorship of the United States Department of State. The tour included performances in Japan, the Philippines, Burma, Thailand, Java, India, Pakistan, Iran, and Singapore.

Sailors were buying tickets, not only the *cognoscenti*. The theater management was anxious to extend the run of *Clytemnestra*; nothing was sched-
uled to follow us into the theater. *LIFE* magazine was ready with
beautiful photographs and a cover story. They were waiting only for con-
firmation that the run was extended. The work could have run indefinitely, but our own management turned it down. The reason offered was
that Martha had to help Katharine Cornell. *The First Born*[3] was not going
well in out-of-town previews, her costume was wrong, etc.

Our management was tired and timid. Martha could never accept
capable managers. She never entertained the idea of having a manager
who was not a friend who could be dominated. She had to be surrounded by somewhat lesser people. She preferred to do everything by
herself and this she did until the work became so large that it was utterly
impossible for her to do it all alone. She still had to retain absolute say
over every aspect and for this she had to have a staff of personable people around her, but people who were subject to her will. This leads to
frustrations and tantrums. She believes that "every act of creation bears
within it the seeds of destruction." Of course, this is true, but she loved
this idea and at times it became the excuse for some rotten behavior.

Unbelievable though it may seem, she is shy; all performers are. They
are "at home" only in the theater. She always held herself to an image of
the perfect person. I remember my first inkling of this when I was
demonstrating for her class in the very beginning of my association with
her. She had been working all day and still had to teach an intermediate
class at 6 PM. She ordered tea from Schrafft's and placed it on the floor
near her chair. She made a sudden move to get up to go to correct a student and overturned the tea. This caused her to "over correct" the student, leaving red hand prints on the surprised girl's thigh. I feel sure that
Martha was taking out her embarrassment over not being perfect, over
spilling the tea, and was punishing the student for it.

We, the company, when we learned that we were not extending the run
of *Clytemnestra*, were crushed at this wasted opportunity. It was unprecedented for modern dance to have an indefinite run on Broadway. We
knew the opportunity would never present itself again. We were devas-
tated. We each telephoned to anyone and everyone we knew who might
be able to change this decision: to Isadora Bennett, director of publicity; to
Jean Rosenthal, lighting designer; to Gertrude Macy, theatrical producer;
to Sydney Kingsley, playwright; and to his wife, Madge Evans, the movie
star. But *no*. Craig Barton, Martha Graham's manager and personal

---

[3] Katharine Cornell played the role of Anath Bitniah in *The First Born*, written by
Christopher Fry. She was also producer along with Roger L. Stevens. The play opened at
the Coronet Theater, NYC, on 30 April 1958.

representative, always had an unreasoning dislike for, or lack of faith in, *Clytemnestra*, or perhaps it was a failure of confidence in the public's response to it. I must be careful here. Martha was always able to shift the blame for whatever might be distressing the company to the current manager. She was remarkably adroit in passing the responsibility to the manager and at the same time defending him like a tiger. I remember when Erick Hawkins was her partner he helped her so much with the enormous labor of producing the new works, raising the money, putting on performances, arranging tours, etc. and thus, without being officially called "the manager," he functioned as such in order to get the work done. Consequently there were times when he, too, shouldered the blame. It took years and years for me to realize this. In 1982, Erick performed his masterpiece *Plains Daybreak* at Sweet Briar College. I had not seen him for many, many years. I was very moved by his work and, of course, went backstage to greet and congratulate him. While I was waiting for him to come out of his dressing room, I looked around backstage. The atmosphere was so familiar: the idea of working together; the dancers helping to pack up; the hat boxes identical to the ones I was accustomed to in the Graham company. I then realized what Erick had given to us.

And so I must be fair to Craig Barton, a gentleman of considerable charm. Craig was more "personal representative" than manager and yet was forced to function as manager. Nevertheless his true function was companion-escort and as such he protected her privacy and made many personal decisions for her.

In 1954, we had our first London engagement. Many photographers swarmed around backstage during performances and took pictures during numerous photo-calls and all of them were wonderful. Ten years later I had dinner at Craig's apartment and he said he would show me something beautiful if I would keep it a secret. This turned out to be four or five incredible photographs of Martha taken at that time in London by an old Chinese photographer. She was wearing a very quiet fur-lined brocade Chinese robe which she used to wear in her dressing room. She was virtually without make-up and she was beautiful in a way very few have ever seen. There must have been an instant rapport between the Chinese photographer and Martha. She was luminous, filled with spiritual energy. She is able to kindle this spark at will (in the same way that Eleanore Duse, the great Italian actress, could blush), but in these photographs there was something special which brought tears to my eyes. Craig said, "She has never seen these and she must not ever." "But why? They are so wonderful!" "No. They are not her image of herself." I sometimes wonder what she would have thought had she ever seen them. And what has become of those photographs?

Craig Barton always resisted scheduling *Clytemnestra* wherever he could. Wherever we went in Europe in 1962, it was always the most successful program, and he never failed to be amazed. In 1967, in Lisbon, we performed mostly in the elegant opera house, but one performance was in the huge Coliseo. The circus had just finished and I had the elephants' dressing room. Cats would run across the stage at intervals. "Better than rats," explained the stage manager. The price of tickets ranged from twenty-five cents to eight dollars. Many thousands packed the sold-out house. Craig was horrified that we were doing *Clytemnestra* instead of one of the "easier" programs. It turned out to be one of the most successful performances of *Clytemnestra* and the last time that I performed the role of Electra. Americans tend not to recognize that the Greek heritage is very much a part of the European's heritage – it is not an elitist culture. It exists deep within their beings, and in us, too, for that matter. The danger for us is not to recognize this, take it to heart, and live more richly for it.

To go back to the creation of *Clytemnestra*: We had just completed our Asian tour which started in Japan and ended in Israel in early Spring 1956 and the company was free to travel home as it pleased. Umaña,[4] my husband, and I went to Greece. It was the first time my travels had taken me there. Martha, Craig, and Leroy Leatherman, novelist and author of an important analysis of Graham as artist, also manager and director of the Graham school, went to Greece as well; our paths crossed on a boat to Crete. It was wonderful to have some leisure, after months of having to ration our time and guard our energies for performing. It was wonderful; to see and feed on everything unhurriedly.

Back in New York there was a period of not performing, not even rehearsing. This was strange for the company, a bit unnerving. But it was not a sterile time. Martha Graham's mind was churning. Soon she was ready to talk about a new work and then to cast it. And so we began work on *Clytemnestra*. It was a rich and wonderful time for all of us. This masterpiece is so full of important characters requiring imagination and acting ability from everyone. It contains a remarkable number and variety of richly wrought roles. Solo by solo, duet after duet, group following group, scene by scene; it began to take shape. Once in a while we would get to see what others had been working on. Ethel Winter and I were in the kitchen rummaging for something to eat when Martha came in and said, "Come look at this." She and David Wood had just finished his cross-over as the Messenger of Death near the beginning of the piece. She had, as usual, gotten a length of jersey from the costume room and

---

[4] Umaña was a painter and sculptor, who designed for the author. He and Charles Hyman, husband of Ethel Winter, served as stage managers for the Graham Company on its Asian tour. He also made also made the mask for the Seer and the headdresses for the Furies in the film of Graham's *Night Journey*.

twisted and pulled it around his buttocks and through his legs to form a constricting kind of skirt for him to struggle against. This and a staff and the addition of terrifying make-up were his costume. The sequence was wonderfully choreographed and performed, and it sets the mood for the entire full evening length work. Ethel and I were so happy for Martha and David; we knew that *Clytemnestra* was on its way.

Weeks later, the work almost complete, I began to feel, as usual, the need to get started on my costume. I had developed, over many, many years, the habit of making myself something to wear, because I could not bear to stand around in pins just before curtain time, unable to warm-up or to collect my peace of mind. First I made a black wool jersey sleeveless leotard and then I began to drape the same fabric into a skirt. I started with the "Angels" drape, but I wanted it to be somehow different. I draped it low in back and pulled it up high in front and tacked it here and there to form small draped folds just like the sculptures, and I pinned the leg parts around the ankles. I was very excited and thought I was truly on the right track because it did look so Greek and yet every line and breath of the body was clearly visible. I didn't show it to Martha for approval because I wanted to finish it first. So I took it off, hid it away, and began working on a stole-a simple length of black silk jersey to hang from shoulder to floor in back. Then I began to make a "painting" for the end of the stole using appliques. I made a gold background with an elaborate red and olive green frame. On the background I applied black lions rampant (Mycenae's Lion Gate) facing each other, separated by a red fire. I was very pleased with this and then I thought it would look wonderful as an inner skirt hanging from inside the back of the outer skirt. This would make even clearer the design of pants in front, skirt behind. And so I made another "painting" very much like the stole. I cut, pinned, and stitched all these appliques myself. When I had finished sewing I put the whole costume together, took a good look, cut off one shoulder to leave it bare and I was ready to face Martha.

She loved it. "But what about Matt, and Ethel and Yuriko? Would you make something for them, too?" I made the basic dresses all the same, black but with different colored "flags" appropriate to the different characters. For Matt Turney as Cassandra I used a snake as symbol for the prophetess. For Ethel Winter as Helen of Troy, sister of Clytemnestra, I used two swans face to face. For Yuriko as Iphigenia I showed her being sacrificed. All the women, the characters, the chorus and Athena, wore the same dress, providing another "unity" for this enormous work. Martha's costume was a little different but still black. Later it evolved quite handsomely. I pinned every one of these costumes myself. In order to give me credit in the program the credit had to read "women's costumes inspired by drawings by Helen McGehee," because I did not belong to the costumers' union.

Isamu Noguchi had designed the set but was out of the country by the time the pieces were delivered. Charles Hyman[5] made a beautiful blue platform which formed a stage within the stage and could be placed differently in each act. Isamu's crossed spears were perfect and the throne and the various "rocks" were fine. We did not get the net until we moved into the theater. There was general dismay when we saw it. It was supposed to have been a gold net. What it turned out to be was a rope net that was sprayed with gold paint, looking not at all gold but rather like a tired, muddy tennis net. I remember sitting on the stage floor near Jean Rosenthal who was looking extremely pensive. I suggested to her that we get gold ropes from Thirty-eighth Street[6] and hang them from the beautiful curved bamboo bar and that the net robe could be made from yards and yards of red and Tyrean-purple fabric strung between two of the bamboos. I don't know if it was my suggestion and maybe Jean was having similar thoughts, or if Martha had the same idea. I mention it only to illustrate how involved we all were in wishing to make the piece work.

Martha had always made us believe that your commitment to the outcome of the piece will make the piece work and will enhance your own performance. This simple truth does work, but the difficulty lies in inspiring dancers to believe in that kind of participation. She was able to do this and she created a truly unique company, the company of the late fifties and the sixties. I would like to quote extensively from the critic John Martin's article for *The New York Times*, because he, with his outside eye, rather than a member of the company, makes this so objectively clear:

Martha Graham's season, which closes tonight at the Fifty-fourth Street Theater, once again has been an artistic event of epic stature. It is the third season … since what may be called, without too great a stretching of the literal truth, her apotheosis. It was in 1958 that she emerged from a protracted interlude of trials and frustrations … to take her place among the Olympians with a serenity won by ordeal. Like her fellows on the celestial mount she has created a universe.

Its activity of life is projected in a repertory that is *sui generis* in form, in style, in scope, perception and philosophy; its embodiment can only be Martha Graham herself. Out of this latter inescapable truth has evolved her company, as not merely an aggregation of supporting artists but actually an extension of Martha Graham. This is perhaps the final miracle; the instrumentality for the full projection of her conceptual explorations has been achieved. It is herself extended into outranging dimensions.

Such a consummation must have been inevitable, since only the inevitable comes to pass, but it was certainly not to be predicted when the young Martha Graham came flashing

---

[5]   Charles Hyman is the husband of Ethel Winter. A talented artist, he was the original set designer for Graham's solo, Judith (1950).

[6]   Thirty-eighth Street in New York City is where many stores can be found that sell trimmings for the garment industry, located in the neighborhood of Thirty-fifth to Fortieth Streets from Fifth Avenue west to Eighth Avenue.

forth thirty-five years ago as an individual of striking self-containment. She was pre-eminently the soloist – seer, pathfinder, spirit possessed.

When she first felt the necessity for a company to assist her, it was made up of devoted disciples who collaborated wholeheartedly in being transmuted into what were popularly known as "little Martha Grahams." It seemed inevitable that they would always lay aside their wills and become robots to be manipulated. That kind of self-immolation, indeed, may have provided their great opportunity to become part of the creative process.

But you cannot make living art of the merely obedient; on the other hand, those who developed individuality and creativity quite regularly rebelled against obedience and walked out in bitterness. It was a vicious circle, and one that of all circles seemed least likely ever to be squared. How Miss Graham managed to achieve the impossible is probably unknown even to herself; it was no doubt by magic.

The present company consists of artists, without a robot among them. From year to year we see them grow in power, scope, collaborativeness, depth. Most of them have been trained from the start by Miss Graham, but some of them have careers of their own and have come to her because of an apparent appreciation of the greatness of the association and the immeasurable rewards of such collective creation.

Though the Graham vocabulary of movement, its training processes, the emotional processes behind it, the theatrical approach, the musical approach, the dramatic approach, the relationship to adult human experience, are all completely emanations of the Graham mind and the Graham body, they have become naturalized with conviction and authority by every one of the participating artists. As an ensemble and as individuals they are consciously and creatively an extension of Martha Graham. Here is dedication, indeed, but not immolation.

In these later seasons, Miss Graham has thus made it possible for herself to perform only the roles she chooses to perform in a general theatrical relationship as she has conceived it. She no longer needs to be the soloist, the voice in the wilderness which alone can speak the word. It is her mind, her power, her curiously individual vision, that is the soloist, whether she is on stage or off.

It is impossible to think of a time when she will not dance. May she go on, indeed, for a hundred years! And she probably will. But how much she dances or how long is for her to choose; as long as her creative power and her directorial command are objectified on the stage she is herself present.

As for the marvelous individuals who constitute the composite self, at least four have developed before our eyes into truly great dancers. Helen McGehee and Ethel Winter on the feminine side of the roster, and Bertram Ross and Paul Taylor on the masculine, are vivid, sensitive, highly personal artists, wide in range, who must rank with the top dancers of our time.[7]

Unfortunately, instead of being gratified, Martha Graham set about in "Medea" fashion to destroy her creation. Through manipulation she implanted personal jealousies among the individuals, turning the company first against this one and then against that one, until finally one by one they all left.

During this period plans were drawn up, instigated by Jean Rosenthal, to enlarge the scope of the school, to build a theater in the big studio and part of the garden according to Jean's design, and to

---

7   *The New York Times,* Sunday, April 30, 1961.

encourage the development of choreographers who would thus have access to a workable theater and the availability of numerous dancers with whom to work. Martha made pretenses of wishing this to happen and some effort was made to raise the money, but nothing came to fruition. I feel certain that she was jealous of her company, her creation, and jealous of the idea of really helping to extend and thereby keep alive her incredible achievement. In a way I can't blame her. It was so difficult for her to achieve, why should she make it easier for others? But this is where I think the limit to her genius lies. For all her "vision" she did not envision the establishment of a tradition of theater in this country. For example: the Old Vic became the English National Theater; the Sadler's Wells Ballet became the Royal Ballet Company; in Russia the Kirov and Bolshoi ballet companies continue their traditions, in France the Comédie Francaise; in Japan the Noh and the Kabuki, etc. A tradition of theater does not mean a "dead" theater. Even the Comédie Francaise, as long established as it is, grows and changes and incorporates innovations and experimentations from outside itself.

I often wonder what would be the cultural climate in this country today had she wished to extend *Clytemnestra*'s run and had she wished to develop a theater within her school. The presage that this would never be happened backstage after performance many years before when Antony Tudor asked Martha whether she preferred to be remembered as a great dancer or as a great choreographer and she replied, "Dancer." "I pity you," said Tudor.

The legacy she leaves is the legend of herself as theater-innovator, as dancer-actress, as choreographer-creator, but, having it in her power to establish a tradition of theater unique to this country, she chose not to. I cannot quarrel with her wishes. How can she be different from what she is, other than herself? Is it not enough to have had the genius to create what she did achieve? Of course it is, but it is regrettable that she did not wish to extend it. On the other hand we may look positively at all this. The way is open for another sufficiently endowed artist to re-produce this theater. It must all be done again.

Figure 11 Helen McGehee as Electra in *Clytemnestra* (with Bertram Ross and Martha Graham in background). Photo: Anthony Crickmay (London).

Choreography and Dance
1999, Vol. 5, Part 2, pp. 79–85
Photocopying permitted by license only

Martha Graham: A Selected Bibliography

Leslie Getz

This is a compilation of English-language materials about Martha Graham. It covers the dance book literature as well as all the academic/scholarly periodicals in the field from the United States, Great Britain, Canada, and Australia.

The popular/commercial magazines, such as *Dance Magazine* (U.S.), *The Dancing Times* (U.K.), *Dance International* (Canada), and *Dance Australia* (Australia), are used only in the case of special birthday or anniversary issues, memorial numbers, or to cull out series of articles that could be considered of monograph length. I have chosen to concentrate on the academic/scholarly journals as these are the specialist periodicals that reflect a consistent depth of research and analysis. In addition, they have been produced in far fewer number than the popular/commercial magazines and are frequently difficult to find even in major urban areas.

Although there are many excellent and very informative book reviews, I decided these would not be appropriate to this list. The purpose of this bibliography is to guide people to materials, not analyses of them.

This list is an updated/expanded version of the 'Graham' entry in my book *Dancers and Choreographers: A Selected Bibliography.* It was completed 13 August 1997. The material is used with the kind permission of the publisher, Asphodel Press/Moyer Bell, Wakefield, Rhode Island, 1995. The book is distributed in the U.K. by Gazelle Book Services Ltd., Lancaster, England.

Ackerman, Gerald. "Photography and the Dance: Soichi Sunami and Martha Graham." *Ballet Review* 12, no. 2 (Summer 1984): 32–66.
Alderson, Evan. "Metaphor in Dance: The Example of Graham." In *Society of Dance History Scholars Proceedings*, pp. 111–118. Sixth Annual Conference, The Ohio State University, 11–13 February 1983.
Aloff, Mindy. "Family Values." *The New Republic* 213, no. 11, Issue 4,208 (September 11, 1995): 30–36. Martha Graham and the art of succession.

Anderson, Jack. "Some Personal Grumbles About Martha Graham." *Ballet Review* 2, no. 1 (1967): 25–30.

Apostolos-Cappadona, Diane. "Martha Graham and the Quest for the Feminine in Eve, Lilith, and Judith." Chapter 9 in *Dance as Religious Studies*, pp. 118–133. Edited by Doug Adams and Diane Apostolos-Cappadona. New York: Crossroad Publishing Company, 1990.

Armitage, Merle. "Graham." Chapter 10 in his *Dance Memoranda*, pp. 55–58. New York: Duell, Sloan & Pearce, 1946.

——. ed. *Martha Graham*. Los Angeles: Merle Armitage, 1937; reprint New York: Da Capo Press, 1978.

Bliss, Paula M. "A Natural Collaboration." In *Society of Dance History Scholars Proceedings*, pp. 82–87. Twelfth Annual Conference, Arizona State University, 17–19 February 1989. The collaboration of Martha Graham and Isamu Noguchi.

Brown, Jean Morrison. "Graham 1937." In her *The Vision of Modern Dance*, pp. 48–53. Princeton, N.J.: Princeton Book Company, Publishers, 1979.

Coe, Robert. "The Martha Graham Dance Company." In his *Dance in America*, pp. 134–153. New York: Dutton, 1985.

Cohen, Selma Jeanne. "The Achievement of Martha Graham." *Chrysalis* 11, nos. 5–6 (1958): 3–11.

Corey, Frederick Charles. "Principles for the Use of Stylized Movement During the Interpretation and Performance of Literature Based on Martha Graham's Use of Classical Tragedy in Modern Dance." Unpublished dissertation, University of Arizona, 1987. Ann Arbor, Mich.: University Microfilms International, 1987. Order No. 872,6813. DAI 48-09A, p. 2193.

Costonis, Maureen Needham. "*American Document*: A Neglected Graham Work." In *Society of Dance History Scholars Proceedings*, pp. 72–81. Twelfth Annual Conference, Arizona State University, 17–19 February 1989.

Croce, Arlene. "Tell Me, Doctor." *Ballet Review* 2, no. 4 (1968): 12–18.

Dance Magazine 65, no. 7 (July 1991). A special memorial issue celebrating the art of Martha Graham. Feature articles: Joseph H. Mazo. "Martha Remembered" (pp. 34–45). Marian Horosko. "Martha's Prince" (pp. 46–47). Tim Wengerd. "Martha's Men" (pp. 48–52). Walter Sorell. "Martha and Myth" (pp. 53–55). "Martha's Dances: A Catalogue of Graham's Works from 1926 to 1990" (pp. 56–57). Gary Parks. "Martha Affirmed" (p. 58).

Daniel, Oliver. "*Rite of Spring*, First Staging in America: Stokowski-Massine-Graham." *Ballet Review* 10, no. 2 (Summer 1982): 67–71. An extract, in somewhat different form, from Oliver Daniel's *Stokowski: A Counterpoint of View*. New York: Dodd, Mead, 1982.

Dell, Cecily. "Random Graham." *Dance Scope* 2, no. 2 (Spring 1966): 21–26.

de Mille, Agnes. "Martha Graham." Chapter 15 in her *Dance to the Piper*, pp. 144–160. Boston: Little, Brown and Company, 1952.

——. *Martha: The Life and Work of Martha Graham*. New York: Random House, 1991.

Dendy, Mark. "Graham's Season." *Ballet Review* 19, no. 1 (Spring 1991): 36–42.

——. "Graham Without Graham, 1991." *Ballet Review* 20, no. 3 (Fall 1992): 29–35.

Dixon-Stowell, Brenda. "Ethnic and Exotic Aspects in the Choreography of Selected Works by Ted Shawn and Martha Graham." In *Society of Dance History Scholars Proceedings*, pp. 21–28. Seventh Annual Conference, Goucher College, Towson, Maryland, 17–19 February 1984.

Fischer, Barry. "Graham's Dance 'Steps in the Street' and Selected Early Technique: Principles for Reconstructing Choreography from Videotape." Unpublished dissertation, New York University, 1986. Ann Arbor, Mich.: University Microfilms International, 1986. Order No. 862,5670. DAI 47-10A, p. 3595.

Foreman, Donlin. *Out of Martha's House*. Foreword by Jacques d'Amboise. Italian translation by Elisa Rondoni. Rimini, Italy: Guaraldi/Nuova Compagnia Editrice, 1992. Bilingual: English/Italian.

Foster, Susan Leigh. "Martha Graham." In her *Reading Dancing: Bodies and Subjects in Contemporary American Dance*, pp. 23–32. Berkeley, Los Angeles, London: University of California Press, 1986.

Fowler, Carol. "Spellbinder." In her *Dance*, pp. 28–51. Contributions of Women. Minneapolis, Minn.: Dillon Press, 1981.

Fraser, John. "Martha Graham: Into the Cool Lucid Light of a Seer." *York Dance Review* Issue 2 (Fall 1973): 23–29.

Gardner, Howard. "Martha Graham: Discovering the Dance of America." *Ballet Review* 22, no. 1 (Spring 1994): 67–93. Reprinted from *Creating Minds: An Anatomy of Creativity Seen Through the Lives of Freud, Einstein, Picasso, Stravinsky, Eliot, Graham and Gandhi* by Howard Gardner. New York: Basic Books, 1993.

Garfunkel, Trudy. *Letter to the World: The Life and Dances of Martha Graham*. Boston, New York, London, Toronto: Little, Brown and Company, 1995.

Gibbs, Angelica. "The Absolute Frontier." *The New Yorker* 23, no. 45 (December 27, 1947): 28–32, 34–37.

Goldberg, Marianne. "She Who Is Possessed No Longer Exists Outside: Martha Graham's *Rite of Spring*." *Women & Performance* 3, no. 1/Issue 5 (1986): 17–27.

"Graham." *Dance Magazine* 48, no. 7 (July 1974). A four-part Dance Magazine Portfolio. Tobi Tobias. "The Graham Season: April 15–May 4, 1974" (pp. 44–45). Jean Nuchtern. "Martha Graham's Women Speak" (pp. 46–49). Doris Hering. "But Not for Clytemnestra: Comments on

The Notebooks of Martha Graham" (pp. 52–55). Joel Shapiro. "Martha Graham at the Eastman School" (pp. 55–57).

"Graham, Martha." *Current Biography Yearbook 1944*, pp. 251–253. New York: The H.W. Wilson Company, 1945.

"Graham, Martha." *Current Biography Yearbook 1961*, pp. 182–185. New York: The H.W. Wilson Company, 1962.

Graham, Martha. *Blood Memory*. New York: Doubleday, 1991.

——. *The Notebooks of Martha Graham*. New York: Harcourt Brace Jovanovich, 1973.

Guillermoprieto, Alma. "Martha Graham: Sacred Monster." *The New York Times Magazine*, November 24, 1996, p. 68.

Hall, Fernau. "Martha Graham." In his *An Anatomy of Ballet*, pp. 141–149. London: Andrew Melrose, 1953. Published simultaneously in the United States by A.A. Wyn, New York.

Hastings, Baird. "Martha Graham: The High Priestess of Modern Dance." In his *Choreographer and Composer*, pp. 176–184. Boston: Twayne Publishers, 1983. [On cover: Choreographer and Composer: Theatrical Dance and Music in Western Culture.]

Helpern, Alice. "The Evolution of Martha Graham's Dance Technique." Unpublished dissertation, New York University, 1981. Ann Arbor, Mich.: University Microfilms International, 1982. Order No. 812,8214. DAI 42-07A, p. 2937.

——. "The Technique of Martha Graham." *Studies in Dance History* 2, no. 2 (Spring/Summer 1991). Revised Edition, Dobbs Ferry, NY: Morgan Press, 1994.

——. "Wilson's *Snow on the Mesa* and Graham's Repertory." *Ballet Review* 24, no. 1 (Spring 1996): 38–40.

Hodes, Stuart. "Three Brides in *Spring*." *Ballet Review* 18, no. 4 (Winter 1990–1991): 91–94.

Holder, Geoffrey. "Martha Graham: American Original." *Show* 3, no. 11 (November 1963): 86–87, 118–120.

Horan, Robert. "The Recent Theater of Martha Graham." *Dance Index* 6, no. 1 (January 1947). Also in Paul Magriel's, editor, *Chronicles of the American Dance: From the Shakers to Martha Graham*, pp. 238–259. New York: Henry Holt, 1948; reprint New York: Da Capo Press, 1978.

Horosko, Marian, comp. *Martha Graham: The Evolution of Her Dance Theory and Training 1926–1991*. Pennington, N.J.: A Cappella Books, 1991.

Jackson, Graham. "The Roots of Heaven: Sexuality in the Work of Martha Graham." In *Dance Spectrum: Critical and Philosophical Enquiry*, pp. 50–60. Edited by Diana Theodores Taplin. Waterloo, Ontario: Otium Publications; Dublin: Parsons Press, 1983.

Jackson, Paul. "Martha Graham." *Dance Now* 5, no. 2 (Summer 1996): 39–46.

——. "Radical Graham." *Dance Now* 5, no. 3 (Autumn 1996): 14–18.

Johnston, Jill. "Martha Graham: An Irresponsible Study … The Head of Her Father." *Ballet Review* 2, no. 4 (1968): 6–12.

Jowitt, Deborah. "In Memory: Martha Graham, 1894–1991." *Tulane Drama Review* 35, no. 4/T-132 (Winter 1991): 14–16.

Kriegsman, Sali Ann. *Modern Dance in America: The Bennington Years.* Boston: G.K. Hall & Co., 1981.

Lamothe, Kimerer Lewis. "With Dance in Mind: Reflections on Theology and Dance via Gerardus van der Leeuw and Martha Graham." Unpublished dissertation, Harvard University, 1996. Ann Arbor, Mich.: University Microfilms International, 1996. Order No. 963,1644. DAI 57-05A, p. 1890.

Leabo, Karl, ed. *Martha Graham.* New York: Theatre Arts Books, 1961.

Leatherman, LeRoy. *Martha Graham: Portrait of the Lady as an Artist.* New York: Knopf, 1966.

Lepczyk, Billie. "Martha Graham's Movement Invention Viewed through Laban Analysis." In *Dance: Current Selected Research*, Volume 1, pp. 45–64. Edited by Lynnette Y. Overby and James H. Humphrey. New York: AMS Press, 1989.

Lloyd, Margaret. "Martha Graham." In her *The Borzoi Book of Modern Dance*, pp. 35–76. New York: Knopf, 1949.

"Martha Graham (1894–1991)." *Ballet Review* 19, no. 3 (Fall 1991): 18–31. Reminiscences by Marian Seldes, May O'Donnell, Stuart Modes, and Francis Mason.

Martin, John. "Martha Graham." Chapter 9 in his *America Dancing: The Background and Personalities of the Modern Dance*, pp. 187–205. New York: Dodge Publishing, 1936.

Maynard, Olga. "Martha Graham." In her *American Modern Dancers: The Pioneers*, pp. 105–125. Boston & Toronto: Little, Brown and Company, 1965.

Mazo, Joseph H. "Martha Graham: Casta Diva." Chapter 6 in his *Prime Movers: The Makers of Modern Dance in America*, pp. 153–196. New York: William Morrow, 1977.

McDonagh, Don. "A Chat with Martha Graham." *Ballet Review* 2, no. 4 (1968): 18–28.

——. *Martha Graham: A Biography.* New York: Praeger, 1973.

McGehee, Helen. *To Be a Dancer.* Lynchburg, Va: Editions Heraclita, 1990.

——. "Working for Martha Graham." *Dance Research* 3, no. 2 (Autumn 1985): 56–64.

Moore, Lillian. "Martha Graham." In her *Artists of the Dance*, pp. 298–303. New York: Thomas Y. Crowell, 1938; reprint Brooklyn, N.Y.: Dance Horizons, 1969.

Morgan, Barbara. *Martha Graham: Sixteen Dances in Photographs.* New York: Duell, Sloan & Pearce, 1941; 1st rev. ed. Dobbs Ferry,

N.Y.: Morgan & Morgan, c. 1980. This edition includes a "Complete chronological list of dances composed by Martha Graham from April 1926 to December 1980."

Muir, Jane. "Martha Graham." In her *Famous Dancers*, pp. 89–97. Biographies for Young People. New York: Dodd, Mead & Company, 1956.

Nimri, Keram. "A Study of the Selective Theatrical Environment Exploring the Internal Symbols Between Graham's Choreography and Noguchi's Set-Sculptures (1946–1947 Productions)." Unpublished dissertation, Ohio University, 1995. Ann Arbor, Mich.: University Microfilms International, 1995. Order No. 953,4174. (DAI source not given.)

Noguchi, Isamu. "Noguchi: Collaborating with Graham." In *Isamu Noguchi: Essays and Conversations*, pp. 80–89. Edited by Diane Apostolos-Cappadona and Bruce Altshuler. New York: Abrams, in association with The Isamu Noguchi Foundation, 1994.

Or, Eileen. "Body and Mind: The Yoga Roots of Martha Graham's 'Contraction' and 'Release.'" In *Proceedings of the Conference "Border Crossings: Dance and Boundaries in Society, Politics, Gender, Education and Technology*, pp. 203–213. Ryerson Polytechnic University, Toronto, Ontario, Canada, May 10–14, 1995.

Oswald, Genevieve. "Myth and Legend in Martha Graham's *Night Journey*." *Dance Research Annual XIV* (1983): 42–49.

——. "A Vision of Paradise: Myth and Symbol in *The Embattled Garden*." *Choreography and Dance* 2, pt. 3 (1992): 27–37.

Palmer, Winthrop. "Martha Graham: American Electra." Chapter 4 in his *Theatrical Dancing in America: The Development of the Ballet from 1900*, pp. 43–57. New York: Bernard Ackerman, 1945.

Polcari, Stephen. "Martha Graham and Abstract Expressionism." *Smithsonian Studies in American Art* 4, no. 1 (Winter 1990): 3–27.

Propper, Herbert. "Space/Symbol: The Spatial Concepts in Selected Dances of Martha Graham." Unpublished dissertation, University of Michigan, 1977. Ann Arbor, Mich.: University Microfilms International, 1977. Order No. 772,6338. DAI 38-06A, p. 3147.

Purcell, J.M. "Notes on *Dark Meadow*: In Print, On Tour." *Ballet Review* 5, no. 2 (1975–1976): 97–100.

Robertson, Marta Elaine. "'A Gift to Be Simple': The Collaboration of Aaron Copland and Martha Graham in the Genesis of 'Appalachian Spring.'" Unpublished dissertation, University of Michigan, 1992. Ann Arbor, Mich.: University Microfilms International, 1993. Order No. 930,3812. DAI 53-10A, p. 3406.

Rogosin, Elinor. "Conversation with Martha Graham." In her *The Dance Makers: Conversations with American Choreographers*, pp. 25–40. New York: Walker & Company, 1980.

Sears, David. "Graham Masterworks in Revival." *Ballet Review* 10, no. 2 (Summer 1982): 25–34.

——. "Martha Graham: The Golden Thread." *Ballet Review* 14, no. 3 (Fall 1986): 44–64.

Shelton, Suzanne. "Jungian Roots of Martha Graham's Dance Imagery." In *Society of Dance History Scholars Proceedings*, pp. 119–132. Sixth Annual Conference, The Ohio State University, 11–13 February 1983.

Sherman, Jane. "Martha and Doris in Denishawn: A Closer Look." *Dance Chronicle* 17, no. 2 (1994): 179–193.

Snyder, Diana. "The Most Important Lesson for Our Theater." *Ballet Review* 10, no. 4 (Winter 1983): 7–20.

——. "Theater as a Verb: The Theater Art of Martha Graham 1923–1958." Unpublished dissertation, University of Illinois at Urbana-Champaign, 1980. Ann Arbor, Mich.: University Microfilms International, 1981. Order No. 810,8668. DAI 41-11A, p. 4545.

Soares, Janet Mansfield. *Louis Horst: Musician in a Dancer's World*. Durham, N.C. & London: Duke University Press, 1992.

Sorell, Walter. "Two Rebels, Two Giants: Isadora and Martha." In his *The Dance Has Many Faces*, pp. 170–181. Cleveland & New York: World Publishing, 1951.

Stewart, Louis C. "Music Composed for Martha Graham: A Discussion of Musical and Choreographic Collaborations." Unpublished dissertation, Peabody Institute of the Johns Hopkins University, 1991. Ann Arbor, Mich.: University Microfilms International, 1991. Order No. 912,5560. DAI 52-04A, p. 1127.

Stodelle, Ernestine. *Deep Song: The Dance Story of Martha Graham*. New York: Schirmer Books; London: Collier Macmillan Publishers, 1984.

——. "Graham: 'I Am A Dancer.'" *Ballet Review* 12, no. 3 (Fall 1984): 59–71. An extract from *Deep Song: The Dance Story of Martha Graham*. New York: Schirmer Books; London: Collier Macmillan, 1984.

Terry, Walter. *Frontiers of Dance: The Life of Martha Graham*. Women of America. New York: Thomas Y. Crowell Company, 1975.

——. "Martha Graham." Chapter 8 in his *The Dance in America*, pp. 83–99. rev. ed. New York: Harper & Row, 1971; reprint New York: Da Capo Press, 1981.

Tracy, Robert. *Goddess: Martha Graham's Dancers Remember*. New York: Limelight Editions, 1997.

——. "Noguchi: Collaborating with Graham." *Ballet Review* 13, no. 4 (Winter 1986): 9–17.

Trowbridge, Charlotte. *Dance Drawings of Martha Graham*. New York: Dance Observer, 1945.

Choreography and Dance
1999, Vol. 5, Part 2, p. 87
Photocopying permitted by license only

Afterword: A Poem

I know I am too close to Martha's works.

Those of us (dancers) who sweated
blood to be able to perform
the works naturally feel possessive of them.
That is the nature of paying for something.

Martha knew this and she resented it because she
could no longer possess them as a dancer.
"I resent having to tell you anything about the
work because I had to discover it myself," Martha
once chided.

But the works are not ours and never will
be, except for the finite time allotted
us during performance, and of course, then
they are ours like our skin is ours.

And when I am gone there will be no difference
The wind will sound the same
Not even a whisper will be heard above
                    the silent concentrated faces of those
                    others working and wanting for
their place on the stage.

                                   Donlin Foreman[2]

---

[2] Donlin Foreman, *Out of Martha's House*, page 52.

Choreography and Dance
1999, Vol. 5, Part 2, pp. 89–90
Photocopying permitted by license only

Notes on Contributors

Nolini Barretto danced *Chhau*, a classical Indian technique, before coming to study at the Martha Graham School of Contemporary Dance in 1983. She has worked at the Martha Graham School for the last ten years, and has been Administrative Director since 1994. She completed a Masters degree in Arts Administration from Teachers' College, Columbia University, where she was awarded the Louis V. Gerstner Award for academic achievement. Nolini Barretto has been a consultant for the New York Foundation for the Arts and the National Shakespeare Conservatory. She and her husband live in Stamford, Connecticut. They have enjoyed themselves as restaurant critics in New York for the past three years.

Donlin Foreman was associated with the Martha Graham Dance Company for eighteen years. He was coached and directed by Martha Graham in every major male role in the repertory. He has been invited to perform at the White House, and received the President's award for Outstanding Achievement in the Performing Arts from the University of Montevallo. His international career includes performances with the Feld Ballets, NY; La Scala Ballet, Milan; the International Dance Festival, Prague; and Jacques d'Amboise's National Dance Institute, NY; where he originated numerous roles. He is featured in the WNET/Dance in America videotapes: *Conversations with Martha Graham, Clytemnestra, Trailblazers of American Modern Dance*, and *Martha Graham Dance Company in Japan and Paris*. Foreman is Associate Professor of Dance at Barnard College in New York. His first volume of poetic writings, *Out of Martha's House*, was published in 1992.

Leslie Getz is the founder/editor *of Attitudes & Arabesques*. Her two-part translation of "The Diaries of Antoine Bournonville from 1792" appeared in *Ballet Review*. She has contributed a number of annual book lists and specialized bibliographies for conference proceedings of the Dance Critics Association. Her book *Dancers and Choreographers: A Selected*

Bibliography was published by Asphodel Press/Moyer Bell in 1995. Leslie Getz lives in New York City.

Alice Helpern is currently Director of the Merce Cunningham Studio in New York. She taught dance at Hunter High School, Vassar College, New York University, and the Martha Graham School. Trained professionally in ballet and modern dance, she holds a Ph.D. in dance from New York University. Her monograph, *The Technique of Martha Graham*, was published by the Morgan Press in 1994. She also writes criticism for *Ballet Review*, and served as a site visit consultant for the Dance Panel of the National Endowment for the Arts.

Helen McGehee, principal dancer with the Martha Graham Dance Company for more than twenty-five years, now lives in Lynchburg, Virginia, where she is professor emeritus at Randolph-Macon Woman's College, and teaches and lectures on dance. McGehee performed several principal roles originated by Graham including Medea in *Cave of the Heart*, the Bride in *Appalachian Spring*, and the Woman (Ariadne) in *Errand into the Maze*. She created the role of Electra in *Clytemnestra* and participated in the creation of many Graham ballets during her tenure in the company. A choreographer in her own right, she presented her work in New York and Paris for many years in the 1950s and 1960s. She is the author of *To Be A Dancer*, published in 1989.

Mark Wheeler, head of the Department of Dance at the University of Georgia, was introduced to the technique and theater aesthetic of Martha Graham while a dance student at Indiana University in the early 1970s, eventually seeing Graham and her company in a performance and lecture-demonstration there. He received further Graham-based training from Denise Jefferson and Mari Kajiwara at the Alvin Ailey American Dance Center in New York, and from Ahuva Anbari at the Ohio State University, where he earned the Ph.D. Wheeler has presented and published other studies of appropriation of the Orient by modern dance. He choreographs regularly at the University of Georgia.

Choreography and Dance
1999, Vol. 5, Part 2, pp. 91–93
Photocopying permitted by license only

Index[1]

---

[1] This index does not include the text of Leslie Getz, "Martha Graham: A Selected Bibliography," pp. 79–85.

CHOREOGRAPHY AND DANCE
AN INTERNATIONAL JOURNAL

Notes for contributors

Submission of a paper will be taken to imply that it represents original work not previously published, that it is not being considered for publication elsewhere and that, if accepted for publication, it will not be published elsewhere in the same form, in any language, without the consent of editor and publisher. It is a condition of acceptance by the editor of a typescript for publication that the publisher automatically acquires the copyright of the typescript throughout the world. It will also be assumed that the author has obtained all necessary permissions to include in the paper items such as quotations, musical examples, figures, tables etc. Permissions should be paid for prior to submission.

Typescripts. Papers should be submitted in triplicate to the Editors, *Choreography and Dance*, c/o Harwood Academic Publishers, at:

5th Floor, Reading Bridge House	PO Box 32160	3-14-9, Okubo
Reading Bridge Approach	Newark	Shinjuku-ku
Reading RG1 8PP	NJ 07102	Tokyo 169-0072
UK or	USA or	Japan

Papers should be typed or word processed with double spacing on one side of good quality ISO A4 (212×297 mm) paper with a 3 cm left-hand margin. Papers are accepted only in English.

Abstracts and Keywords. Each paper requires an abstract of 100–150 words summarizing the significant coverage and findings, presented on a separate sheet of paper. Abstracts should be followed by up to six key words or phrases which, between them, should indicate the subject matter of the paper. These will be used for indexing and data retrieval purposes.

Figures. All figures (photographs, schema, charts, diagrams and graphs) should be numbered with consecutive arabic numerals, have descriptive captions and be mentioned in the text. Figures should be kept separate from the text but an approximate position for each should be indicated in the margin of the typescript. It is the author's responsibility to obtain permission for any reproduction from other sources.

Preparation: Line drawings must be of a high enough standard for direct reproduction; photocopies are not acceptable. They should be prepared in black (india) ink on white art paper, card or tracing paper, with all the lettering and symbols included. Computer-generated graphics of a similar high quality are also acceptable, as are good sharp photoprints ("glossies"). Computer print-outs must be completely legible. Photographs intended for halftone reproduction must be good glossy original prints of maximum contrast. Redrawing or retouching of unusable figures will be charged to authors.

Size: Figures should be planned so that they reduce to 12 cm column width. The preferred width of line drawings is 24 cm, with capital lettering 4 mm high, for reduction by one-half. Photographs for halftone reproduction should be approximately twice the desired finished size.

Captions: A list of figure captions, with the relevant figure numbers, should be typed on a separate sheet of paper and included with the typescript.

Musical examples: Musical examples should be designated as "Figure 1" etc., and the recommendations above for preparation and sizing should be followed. Examples must be well prepared and of a high standard for reproduction, as they will not be redrawn or retouched by the printer.

In the case of large scores, musical examples will have to be reduced in size and so some clarity will be lost. This should be borne in mind especially with orchestral scores.

Notes are indicated by superior arabic numerals without parentheses. The text of the notes should be collected at the end of the paper.

References are indicated in the text by the name and date system either "Recent work (Smith & Jones, 1987, Robinson, 1985, 1987)…" or "Recently Smith & Jones (1987)…" If a publication has more than three authors, list all names on the first occurrence; on subsequent occurrences use the first author's name plus "*et al.*" Use an ampersand rather than "and" between the last two authors. If there is more than one publication by the same author(s) in the same year, distinguish by adding a, b, c etc. to both the text citation and the list of references (e.g. "Smith, 1986a"). References should be collected and typed in alphabetical order after the Notes and Acknowledgements sections (if these exist). Examples:

Benedetti, J. (1988) *Stanislavski*, London: Methuen.
Granville-Barker, H. (1934) Shakespeare's dramatic art. In *A Companion to Shakespeare Studies*, edited by H. Granville-Barker and G.B. Harrison, p. 84. Cambridge: Cambridge University Press.
Johnston, D. (1970) Policy in theatre. *Hibernia*, **16**, 16.

Proofs. Authors will receive page proofs (including figures) by air mail for correction and these must be returned as instructed within 48 hours of receipt. Please ensure that a full postal address is given on the first page of the typescript so that proofs are not delayed in the post. Authors' alterations, other than those of a typographical nature, in excess of 10% of the original composition cost, will be charged to authors.

Page Charges. There are no page charges to individuals or institutions.

INSTRUCTIONS for AUTHORS

ARTICLE SUBMISSION ON DISK

The Publisher welcomes submissions on disk. The instructions that follow are intended for use by authors whose articles have been accepted for publication and are in final form. Your adherence to these guidelines will facilitate the processing of your disk by the typesetter. These instructions do not replace the journal Notes for Contributors; all information in Notes for Contributors remains in effect.

When typing your article, do not include design or formatting information. Type all text flush left, unjustified and without hyphenation. Do not use indents, tabs or multi-spacing. If an indent is required, please note it by a line space; also mark the position of the indent on the hard copy manuscript. Indicate the beginning of a new paragraph by typing a line space. Leave one space at the end of a sentence, after a comma or other punctuation mark, and before an opening parenthesis. Be sure not to confuse lower case letter "l" with numeral "1", or capital letter "O" with numeral "0". Distinguish opening quotes from close quotes. Do not use automatic page numbering or running heads.

Tables and displayed equations may have to be rekeyed by the typesetter from your hard copy manuscript. Refer to the journal Notes for Contributors for style for Greek characters, variables, vectors, etc.

Articles prepared on most word processors are acceptable. If you have imported equations and/or scientific symbols into your article from another program, please provide details of the program used and the procedures you followed. If you have used macros that you have created, please include them as well.

You may supply illustrations that are available in an electronic format on a separate disk. Please clearly indicate on the disk the file format and/or program used to produce them, and supply a high-quality hard copy of each illustration as well.

Submit your disk when you submit your final hard copy manuscript. The disk file and hard copy must match exactly.

If you are submitting more than one disk, please number each disk. Please mark each disk with the journal title, author name, abbreviated article title and file names.

Be sure to retain a back-up copy of each disk submitted. Pack your disk carefully to avoid damage in shipping, and submit it with your hard copy manuscript and complete Disk Specifications form (see reverse) to the person designated in the journal Notes for Contributors.

GORDON AND BREACH PUBLISHERS • **HARWOOD ACADEMIC PUBLISHERS**

Disk Specifications

Journal name _____

_____

Date _____ **Paper Reference Number** _____

Paper title _____

_____

_____

Corresponding author _____

Address _____

_____

_____

_____ **Postcode** _____

Telephone _____

Fax _____

E-mail _____

Disks Enclosed (file names and descriptions of contents)

Text

Disk 1 _____

Disk 2 _____

Disk 3 _____

PLEASE RETAIN A BACK-UP COPY OF ALL DISK FILES SUBMITTED.

GORDON AND BREACH PUBLISHERS • **HARWOOD ACADEMIC PUBLISHERS**

Figures

Disk 1 _____

Disk 2 _____

Disk 3 _____

Computer make and model _____

_____

Size/format of floppy disks

☐ 3.5"   ☐ 5.25"

☐ Single sided   ☐ Double sided

☐ Single density   ☐ Double density   ☐ High density

Operating system _____

Version _____

Word processor program _____

Version _____

Imported maths/science program _____

Version _____

Graphics program _____

Version _____

Files have been saved in the following format

Text: _____

Figures: _____

Maths: _____

PLEASE RETAIN A BACK-UP COPY OF ALL DISK FILES SUBMITTED.

GORDON AND BREACH PUBLISHERS   •   HARWOOD ACADEMIC PUBLISHERS